ELVIRA'S FAITH

Elvira and her son Saul in Sanctuary

ELVIRA'S FAITH
and
BARACK'S CHALLENGE

The Grassroots Struggle for the Rights of Undocumented Families

The Story of Familia Latina Unida/Sin Fronteras

REV. WALTER L. COLEMAN

2ND EDITION

WITH WRITING & COMMENTARY BY
ELVIRA ARELLANO, REV. EMMA LOZANO,
CONGRESSMAN LUIS V. GUTIERREZ,
DR. JOSÉ LÓPEZ, & DR. JOHN WOMACK

WRIGHTWOOD PRESS

Wrightwood Press
www.wrightwoodpress.org

Edited by Rick Spaulding and Maurice York
Book design by Maurice York

Cover art: detail from "Nuestra Señora de la Guadalibertad, Patrona de los Migrantes"

NON-PROFITS, LIBRARIES, EDUCATIONAL INSTITUTIONS,
WORKSHOP SPONSORS, STUDY GROUPS, ETC.
Special discounts and bulk purchases are available.
Please email sales@wrightwoodpress.org for more information.

August 2017
ISBN 978-0-9801190-5-3

WE DEDICATE THIS ACCOUNT OF FAITH AND STRUGGLE
TO THE FAMILIES,
WHO BY THEIR COURAGE AND WITNESS
HAVE FOUND TRUTH IN THE FACE OF POWER,
LOVE IN THE FACE OF HATE,
AND RESURRECTION IN THE FACE OF BETRAYAL ...

AND TO THE NEXT GENERATION WHO ARE TAKING
THEIR PLACE IN THE STRUGGLE

❧ CONTENTS

PART THREE:
THE RESURRECTION SPIRIT OF THE GRASSROOTS

REFLECTIONS ON THE MOVEMENT

APPENDICES

LIST OF PHOTOGRAPHS - *following Part Two*

❧ SUMMARY TIMELINE

The Civil Rights Movement and the Latino Movement for Justice

1954	"Brown v. Board of Education" Supreme Court decision	MAY
1955	Montgomery bus boycott	DECEMBER
1960	Lunch counter sit-ins begin in Greensboro, NC	FEBRUARY
1963	March on Washington – Martin Luther King, Jr. delivers "I Have a Dream" speech	AUGUST
1965	Voting Rights Act signed	AUGUST
1969	Fred Hampton assassinated in Chicago	DECEMBER
1972	Edward Hanrahan defeated for Cook County States Attorney	
1975	Jose Cha-Cha Jiminez loses race for Chicago's 46th Ward	
1983	Harold Washington elected mayor of Chicago	APRIL
	Rudy Lozano assassinated	JUNE
1986	Luis Gutierrez wins alderman race, Chicago's 26th Ward	MARCH
	Immigration "amnesty bill" (IRCA) signed by President Reagan	NOVEMBER
1987	Harold Washington re-elected	APRIL
	Harold Washington dies in office	NOVEMBER
1988	Emma Lozano begins community organizing in Deadville and founds Pueblo Sin Fronteras	WINTER
1992	Luis Gutierrez elected to the US Congress	NOVEMBER
1994	NAFTA goes into effect	JANUARY
1995	Million Man March in Washington, D.C.	OCTOBER
1996	Adalberto United Methodist Church founded	MAY
	Immigration reform bill (IIRAIRA)—"the broken law"— signed by President Clinton	SEPTEMBER
	Coordinadora 1996 in Washington, D.C.	FALL
1997	Barack Obama seated as Illinois Senator for District 13	JANUARY
	Meeting of Rev. Coleman and Congressman Gutierrez	APRIL

2000	Elvira Arellano arrives in Chicago	JUNE
	"Human chain" protest of 15,000 divides Ashland Avenue	OCTOBER
	Million Family March in Washington, D.C.	OCTOBER
2001	Senator Dick Durbin first introduces the DREAM Act	AUGUST
2002	Elvira Arellano arrested in raid at O'Hare Airport	DECEMBER
2003	Familia Latina Unida forms, with Elvira as its first president	FALL
2004	Rep. Gutierrez introduces the SOLVE Act in Congress	MAY
2005	First mega march in Back of the Yards, Chicago	JULY
2006	Second mega march in Downtown Chicago	MARCH
	May Day work boycott and national marches	MAY
	Chicago march for executive moratorium on deportations	JUNE
	Elvira takes sanctuary in Adalberto United Methodist Church	AUGUST
2007	Elvira leaves sanctuary; arrested in California and deported	AUGUST
2008	Rep. Gutierrez endorses Sen. Obama's campaign for President	
2009	Familias Unidas tour of churches in 30 cities	FEB - JUNE
	Lincoln United Methodist Church replanted in Pilsen	JULY
2012	DACA executive order issued by President Obama	AUGUST
	President Obama re-elected	NOVEMBER
2013	Emma Lozano organizes the Children's Campaign	MARCH - APRIL
	Gang of Eight (Senate) and group of eight (House) negotiate comprehensive immigration reform bill	MARCH - JUNE
	Immigration reform bill passes Senate, no vote in House	JUNE
2014	Elvira paroled and returns to the United States	MARCH
	President Obama's executive orders on immigration	NOVEMBER
2015	Emma installed as pastor of Lincoln United Methodist Church	AUGUST
2016	Supreme Court non-decision	JUNE

CHICAGO

Map of Principal Locations

1 - O'Hare Airport

2 - Midway Airport

3 - Humboldt Park
   Home of ✠ Adalberto United Methodist Church
   Part of congressional district of Luis Gutierrez

4 - Pilsen
   Home of ✠ Lincoln United Methodist
   Church (and St. Pious Church)

5 - Hyde Park
   Home of Harold Washington,
   Carol Moseley Braun, and Barack Obama
   Location of Rainbow/PUSH headquarters
   (Bordered by Washington Park to the west,
   the Midway and Jackson Park to the south)

6 - Back of the Yards
   Location of § Swap-o-Rama
   Endpoint of Grand March in 2005 (same route taken
   again on July 4, 2013)

7 - Union Park
   Start of Mega-march in 2006 (and first march of the
   Children's Campaign in 2013)

8 - Downtown
   Location of ✸ Federal Building on State and Jackson and
   ICE Headquarters on West Congress Parkway and Clark

 Preface
to the 2nd Edition

E lvira Arellano's sanctuary took place in a Chicago church founded by Emma Lozano. Her sanctuary united two Latina mothers, one born a few miles north of the border, the other some miles to the south. It redefined the immigration issue as an issue of family unity—and, more deeply, as an issue of the forced migration of Latinos by the policies of the north. The movement for the rights of the undocumented argued that the United States had a responsibility to respect the human rights of the families that were formed in the north and the children who were born there. The movement unified the different faith traditions of Latinos in the United States as never before. This grassroots movement would inspire the largest marches of Latinos—with and without papers—in the nation's history and would go on to win the support of the nation's first African American President, despite the gridlock caused by an obstructionist Congress. The Democratic Party would champion the cause of the undocumented and their families, winning the popular vote but losing the 2016 election due to the peculiar race-driven electoral structure of the United States political system.

As I write this introduction to the second edition of Elvira's Faith, Donald Trump has been the President of the United States for some thirty days. The new President was swept into office on a wave of racism and hatred and has unleashed immigration enforcement agents to seek out and deport every single one of the estimated eleven million undocumented persons residing in this country. With the stroke of his pen, almost all of the gains and protections won for families seeking to stay together during the years of struggle recounted in this book have been eliminated. The President has pledged to add ten thousand more agents to his "deportation force," along with new judges and new detention facilities—and a multi-trillion dollar wall on the border. The fear that once gripped the nation after the

2001 attack on September 11th has now been transformed into the hatred of immigrants through a purely political act of scapegoating. The hopes of millions of people seem to have been dashed on the rocks of that ugliest of human emotions.

In the pages of this second edition, however, I believe the reader will find the irrepressible spirit of resurrection that time and time again turns defeat into victory. For this reason we offer the story of Familia Latina Unida—not as a lost struggle, but as the revelation of a force that is irreversible in history, precisely because of this Spirit of Resurrection. Elvira's story—with its continual moments of miracle and resurrection—is unique, but it is also one of millions. The intersection of these families from the south meeting the historic Civil Rights movement in the United States exposed the basic denial of human rights in the north. Just as criminalization took the place of Jim Crow laws to suppress people of color, so too immigration laws have criminalized millions of the undocumented. The emerging unity of Latinos with and without papers gradually won the hearts of the African American community. Through the sympathy this unity engendered, families like Elvira's emerged from isolation and rallied the support of the majority of the nation, even as the white supremacist "states rights" political structure propelled a racist minority to power.

The sanctuary movement begun by Reverend Lozano and Elvira Arellano has spread not only to other churches, but to universities and other institutions, and even to whole cities and counties, in defiance of President Trump's attempt at mass deportation. The revelation of this human rights struggle cannot be hidden by the deceptive democracy in the United States, which has long been the disguise it adopted to dominate a long-suffering continent. This struggle will transform North America and give birth to an internal force in the north capable of bringing the victory of the Spirit of the Americas to the countries of the southern continent as well. In this context, the election of Donald Trump is only a temporary dam in the path of the river of freedom. Like all dams, it only serves to gather the power of the river for its next surge forward.

> But let justice roll on like a river,
> righteousness like a never-failing stream!
> —Amos 5:24

Rev. Walter L. Coleman

PART ONE
ELVIRA'S FAITH

 1

Elvira's Family

The Lord is my light and my
Salvation; whom shall I fear?
The Lord is the stronghold of my life;
Of whom shall I be afraid?
—Psalm 27:1

My full name is Elvira Arellano Olayo. I was born on the 20th of January 1975, in the municipio of Maravatío in the state of Michoacán, Mexico. I am the daughter of Gregorio Arellano Garcia and Maria Francisca Olaya Albino. I am the youngest of five children: three women and two men. My grandfather, Nemorio Arellano Cabrera, was a bracero in 1959. We lived with him in his house in the village of San Miguel Curahuango, which belongs to Maravatío. My father was the youngest of his siblings, and my mother took charge of looking after my grandfather as if he were one child more, preparing his food and getting him to a doctor when he got sick. Thanks to my grandfather, my mother and father never lacked for anything to eat because my grandfather was an ejidatario.

My grandfather worked the land, planting corn and chiles. My grandfather also made chairs. During the week he cut the wood, prepared the pieces, wove the seats of the chairs and had them painted. My mother learned how to paint different colored flowers for the chairs, but sometimes my grandfather had another person do the larger flowers. He sold the chairs on Sundays, and my six-year-old brother liked to go with my grandfather because he bought him animal-shaped cookies, which he shared with us. In my house there was never a lack of bread

3

because my grandfather always got up early to go to mass at six o'clock in the morning, and then went to get bread for our breakfast. My grandfather was our closest paternal figure since my father was always away working in some other Mexican state, selling chairs so that we would lack for nothing.

My mother liked to raise chickens, turkeys, pigs and cattle. The cows calved, and my mother then could milk them and sell the milk, generally leaving two liters of milk for us children. If someone needed more milk, my mother did not hesitate to sell it to them, leaving us with only one liter. We made rice with milk and added water so that there would be enough for all of us.

My childhood was very beautiful, in spite of the fact that when I was one and a half years old, my mother had an accident and nearly died. She slipped on a banana peel that caused an internal hemorrhage that she ignored. A few days later she went to the doctor, and they had to give her an emergency operation, removing her ovaries and uterus to save her life. She clung to life because she never stopped thinking of us, her children, who were still very small. My nine-year-old sister took care of me at night. At her young age, my sister also had to bathe me in the pool, a spring where water comes out. She told me that sometimes, because of the soap, I used to slip out of her hands, crying and trembling with fear. She always bathed me while asking God not to let me drown. Every time she remembers this event, she hugs me and asks me to forgive her for all the water I swallowed while she was bathing me.

In the mornings my oldest sister had to go to school, and she would leave me with an aunt who took care of me and my three-year-old sister. My eldest sister told me that my aunt used to have one of her daughters make soup for us. My cousin used to make soup with so much broth that my aunt would scold her because it turned out to be more water than soup. My cousin used to tell her that she did that so that there would be enough for everybody. Whenever someone invites me to eat and tells me they have put more water in the soup so there will be enough for all, I think of that time in my life. In spite of her tender age, my sister cared for us with a lot of love and a sense of responsibility. We, her little brothers and sisters, were her life. My sister told me that I used to call her "Mama." When my mother came back from her operation, I looked at her as if she were a stranger and didn't want to go to her. I think it was hard for my mother since, due to her operation, she could not take care of me. When I cried, it was my sister who took care of me.

My little brother, who was only six, used to shuck corn (maize) and take it to the neighbors to sell. Sometimes the neighbors told him that they couldn't buy the corn because he may have gathered it without permission or stolen it. He used to ask them to please buy it, because he needed the money to buy bread for his brothers and sisters. My other brother, who was seven, had learned how to weave chonguitos, little chairs for children. When he returned from school, he wove chonguitos to earn a little money. While he was weaving, he used to sing a song of Pedrito Fernandez, which went: "Now it's been a year that my father has been over on the other side."

My father did not go to the United States but rather to the U.S.-Mexican border region. My father was in Mexicali, Baja California North, as he was a seller of chairs. My grandfather called him, and he got the news of what had happened to my mother. The news affected him a great deal, but, thank God, the person with whom he worked told him not to worry—he would loan him a little money. My father set out to return home, but in that time the journey was one of many days on the road. The roads were not as they are now, and it took my father much longer than expected. He had to work more when he got back to Mexicali because he had to pay off the debt, but the cost was worth it.

My mother managed to survive, and now they are together and happy. After one of his trips to Mexicali, my father brought us many American pennies when he came home. Somebody had bought a chair from him, and he ended up with these pennies as change. Some of the pennies, formed in the shape of a cross, now decorate the floor in the entryway to the house where Saulito and I now live.

2

The Secret of Rudy Lozano

If my people, who are called by my name, will humble themselves and pray and seek my face and turn from their wicked ways, then will I hear from heaven and will forgive their sin and will heal their land.
—2 Chronicles 7:14

C hicago was home to the family of Guadalupe Lozano, a Mexican steelworker who had made his way up from Mexico through the Southwestern United States to Hammond, Indiana. He and his family became one of the first families in Pilsen, a neighborhood that was to become Chicago's first historic Mexican community.

Guadalupe's son, Rodolfo "Rudy" Lozano, became a student activist and a union organizer. Rudy later led the fight for the first amnesty bill for undocumented immigrants. He grew into manhood in a city dominated by one of the last Democratic machines. The city was politically apportioned into wards, voting precincts that were tightly controlled and directed by ward bosses who marshaled the voting power of the ward towards the interests of the city's Democratic office holders. Mayor Richard J. Daley, the storied long-time mayor and figurehead of Chicago politics, was credited with turning out the vote that elected John F. Kennedy as President in 1960. He reputedly held back the Westside ward totals until it was known exactly how many votes were needed to win, and then delivered the appropriate number. Chicago was known as the town where you voted early—and often—and where cemetery precincts competed for turnout with high-rise public housing.

Many Chicago wards were shaped and re-shaped by tides of ethnic communities that ebbed and flowed throughout the city. The Mexican community neighborhood of Pilsen was located on the South Side of the city. In the '60s, Pilsen was a rapidly growing Mexican community, receiving new migrants every day in addition to the new children born into its hard-working families. Elsewhere in the city, a Puerto Rican community from "La

Clark" on the Near North Side and "La Madison" on the West Side was driven north by urban renewal to Lincoln Park, and was finally pushed west to Humboldt Park. This near West Side neighborhood would become the political center of the Puerto Rican community in the nation. Southern white migrants filled the Uptown community on the far north side, and the powerful Irish and Polish communities dominated the northwest and southwest side. Chicago's downtown was a center of finance and trade—the Italian Mafia and city hall politics.

Yet the driving political conflict in Chicago was between the white, downtown Democratic power structure and the vast wasteland of African American communities on the Southside and Westside of the city. Chicago's West Side became the temporary home of Dr. Martin Luther King, Jr. when he made his first visit north in the summer of 1966 to challenge segregated housing, leading marches through the rock-throwers of nearby Cicero. The Westside also gave birth to the largest and most active chapter of the Black Panther Party. Something about the dynamics of Chicago caused the young Panther leaders, Fred Hampton and Bobby Rush, to reach out to the Latino and poor white communities, who joined together to form what became known as the "Rainbow Coalition"—an organization that aspired to supersede the entrenched power structures and artificial divisions created by the ward structure.

The powerful Mayor Daley seemed to recognize the political opposition that was growing in this new Rainbow Coalition, perhaps recognizing in it some suggestion of his own rise to power from a Southside Irish street gang. He commented at a press conference that he "could crush the rainbow anytime he wanted." The ominous sentiment bore fruit when Fred Hampton was killed in a police raid on December 4th, 1969. State's Attorney Edward Hanrahan, the man positioned to succeed Daley as mayor, had authorized the raid. In response to the assassination, and under Bobby Rush's leadership, the Rainbow Coalition mounted a four-year campaign to expose the treachery that led to this unjustified home invasion in the dark of night. This campaign led in 1972 to the first mobilization of the African-American and Latino communities against Chicago's Democratic machine in a citywide election. The Rainbow Coalition that Daley had failed to crush defeated State's Attorney Hanrahan. After the election, the People's Law Office took on the case of the Hampton family against the Chicago Police Department, the Cook County State's Attorney and the Federal Bureau of

Investigation. Their victory in 1983 made Chicago the site of the nation's only court-documented state assassination.†

During the decade between 1972 and 1982, when the wheels of justice seemed to turn so slowly, the grassroots coalition grew, neighborhood by neighborhood. These years also saw the early incubation of the housing boom that would break the world's economy some thirty-five years later. The city's strategy was called "gentrification." Formulated as "The Chicago 21 Plan—the Plan for Chicago in the 21st Century," the idea was to replace low-income Black and Latino communities with condominium islands that would attract the white middle class back into the city. The city began urban renewal in the first of a series of concentric circles around the downtown area. As each circle was successfully gentrified, the next ring would become desirable for speculators and developers. Real estate became the driving force of Chicago's economy.

As the African American community continued to organize and assert itself politically, the "Coalition Against the Chicago 21 Plan" formed from the seeds of Fred Hampton's Rainbow Coalition. Housing, as well as employment, health care and education, became issues linked to city hall's determination to "whiten the inner city" and starve out the African American, Latino, and poor white communities by neglect—and by police intimidation.

The Puerto Rican movement grew out of the fight against urban renewal and police brutality led by the Young Lords in 1968. It combined with the traditions of the Puerto Rican independence movement, and breathed new life into that anti-colonial movement. Chicago began to feel like a collection of peoples who had been displaced from their homelands in Africa, in the South, in Puerto Rico and in Appalachia. Now they were again being displaced to make way for white gentrification. Brought to the city to work in industry, they were no longer needed by the global economy in this new center of finance and trade, and they were to be disposed of. The recurrence of a campaign of displacement brought back bitter memories of the separation of families, forced sterilizations, and the destruction of neighborhoods beset by drugs, violence and broken families.

I remember meeting with Rudy Lozano in Pilsen, along with Jose Cha-Cha Jimenez, leader of the Young Lords, in 1970. Rudy later organized

---

† For the complete account of this trial, see Jeffrey Haas, *The Assassination of Fred Hampton: How the FBI and the Chicago Police Murdered a Black Panther,* Chicago Review Press, 2011.

CASA in Chicago as part of a national organization of young Mexicans led, in California, by Jose Pepe Jaques Medina. Later, Lozano would bring the Mexican community into the Coalition Against the Chicago 21 Plan, urging the coalition to include the rights of the undocumented in its demands on city hall. Rudy brought the same demand for rights for undocumented immigrants to the International Ladies Garment Workers Union (ILGWU), where he worked as an organizer, and to the community's demand for a new high school.

From 1972 to 1982 the grassroots movement of the Rainbow Coalition grew increasingly involved in the attempt to wrest political power from the Democratic machine. In the special election that followed Richard J. Daley's death in 1976, Congressman Harold Washington relied on these same grassroots organizations to make his first run for mayor. Washington was unsuccessful in his bid. Three years later, however, Jane Byrne defeated Michael Bilandic on the strength of the African American and Latino vote. She quickly turned the city government back into the hands of Daley loyalists, the machine politicians and developers who wanted to implement the Chicago 21 Plan. Byrne's controversial few years in office set the stage for the historic battle in 1983 between Jane Byrne, Richard M. Daley (the son of the former mayor), and Congressman Harold Washington to become Chicago's next mayor. Chicago had not seen a truly open election for mayor in over thirty years, since Richard Daley had entered office and erected the city's political machine to maintain the power and endurance of his administration. This pivotal election confirmed the effectiveness of the grassroots movement's dramatic use of the tools of community mobilization and voter registration—tools that would prove deeply successful for Barack Obama twenty-five years later. Washington challenged the community to register 50,000 new voters if they wanted him to run. Relying on the old Coalition Against the Chicago 21 Plan, we formed People Organized for Welfare and Employment Rights (POWER), and fought for the right to register people outside of welfare and unemployment offices. We registered 43,000 new voters in five weeks. Voter registration fever swept the city. By November, 250,000 new voters had gone on the rolls, mostly from the African American and Latino communities.

Congressman Washington ran at a time when Reagan's "trickledown economics" (his Vice-President had called it "voodoo economics") was the watchword of the nation. Harold Washington and the grassroots movement traveled upstream, against the trickledown economics of Reagan and the "trickle out" gentrification policy of Jane Byrne. He saw that the movement of redemption brought by the prophets of the sixties—Dr. King and Malcolm—was now threatened by the Reagan-led movement of national arrogance and the idolatry of greed. Chicago was a base from which to restore the balance. Rudy Lozano joined with Alderman Danny K. Davis to form the Black/Latino Coalition for the Election of Harold Washington. A new generation of Puerto Rican leadership, forged in the struggle against gentrification and the struggle for Puerto Rican independence, carried Washington's banner on the North Side. The African American community defied and surprised its own established leadership, turning out in record numbers to elect Harold Washington.

Washington fought the old machine for three years until he finally won control of city council in special elections held in seven wards. The role of Latinos in the coalition became especially important in what were called "council wars." Luis Gutierrez provided the decisive vote in city council with his election in the 26th ward. Gradually, Washington created a broader coalition that brought in many young whites and the begrudging participation of the white ethnic northwest side and southwest side communities. For the first time in decades, the city saw the creation of more affordable housing than upper class homes. In 1986, Washington negotiated "the dream ticket" with the Polish community, which slated Carol Mosley Braun to run for U.S. Senator against the incumbent, Alan Dixon. Against the odds, Braun prevailed, becoming the first African American to hold an Illinois seat in the U.S. Senate, and the first African American female Senator in the nation. Barack Obama later held this seat, and from it he launched his historic Presidential bid.

Rudy Lozano was assassinated in his home in front of his children shortly after Washington's election, in June of 1983. Lozano had been Washington's choice to become Chicago's first Latino deputy mayor. He would not see the fruits of the Black-Latino coalition that he had helped forge in Chicago. Nor would he see the amnesty bill passed in 1986, during the Reagan administration, that legalized millions of Mexicanos, thousands of whom he had worked with. After Rudy Lozano's murder, his sister, Emma, spent four years in an unsuccessful effort to find his killers and the conspirators behind his assassination. Then she turned to fulfilling his legacy. She also began to unfold the secret that Rodolfo Lozano held in his heart. Gentrification, the effort to whiten the inner city of Chicago, could be defeated, not by taking city hall, but by the sweat, blood and tears of Mexican families.

Streaming up from Mexico—filling low-paid jobs, saving while they sent money home, raising large families—they filled up the former ethnic neighborhoods of the Southwest side, the Northwest side, and half of the Chicago suburbs. Years after Mayor Harold Washington's death, Chicago was not a city of the white middle class; it was a Black and Brown town, ready to introduce the United States to its first African American President and to the national movement for legalization of undocumented immigrants.

🔥 3

Elvira's Journey North

Now the Lord said to Abram, "Go from your country and your kindred and your father's house to the land that I will show you. And I will make of you a great nation, and I will bless you, and make your name great, so that you will be a blessing."

—Genesis 12:1-2

O
n August 15, 1991, I graduated with a business secretarial diploma. It was not really a course I liked because I wanted to study to become a beautician, though I never said so to my mother. It was really my mother's idea for me to study to be a secretary. She looked for a school, and in the end she told me I should register there. I was not a very disciplined student, but I graduated and started to look for a work opportunity.

At first I worked in a bakery counting the bread at a wage of $10 for seven days of work. A few months later, I started to look for another opportunity and found office work at the Miranda Brothers store. I tried to make myself useful by tending to the customers, and a few months later my boss thanked me for being so helpful and supportive. I became a person they trusted a lot, and I was glad I was able to do my work well. In May 1996, there was a very difficult situation in Mexico because of the devaluation of the Mexican peso and NAFTA. I had worked for three years in the grocery store as a secretary. I got to know the economic situation of my employers, in a time when many businesses went bankrupt and many business owners were in debt to the point of losing their property.

At that time I was earning about 365 pesos, which was $36 for a six-day workweek. I did not have many economic needs since I did not have many responsibilities, but in those years the doctors found that my mother had diabetes. My father looked even worse with his own illness. He was going to specialist doctors to find out what he had because it was becoming visible in his spine, and he was having trouble walking. I decided to look for a better work opportunity in my own country.

I went to live in Reynosa, Tamaulipas, because the wife of a deceased cousin was living there. The wife, Maria, gave me a hand, letting me live in her house and only asking me to help a little with the food. She did this in appreciation of the many things that my mother had done for her when she lived in Michoacán. My mother had helped her wash her children's clothes when they were small, and she was also thankful that I had helped her a lot, taking care of her little children. When I arrived at Reynosa, I had illusions about working as a secretary, but such work was very difficult to find as one needed to have a border crossing card to get into the United States, and also to know English and how to use computers. I didn't have those qualifications. I had no choice but to work in a factory where they made stereos for Japanese automobiles, the midnight to 7 a.m. shift, earning about $20 per week. It was not an easy situation at all.

My friends who lived in the United States began to encourage me to go there to find an opportunity for my family and myself. One evening I received a call from my cousin, Lupita, who was living in the United States. She called to ask me if I still had plans of going to the United States, and I told her "yes." In less than two days I was ready to travel to Mexicali, Baja California North, to try to cross the border. I traveled alone, full of illusions, making plans about the great help I was going to be able to give my parents.

A relative sent me $200 to finance my trip to Mexicali. I arrived and stayed at a hotel in the middle of the city. It was a Friday. I went out to buy a little food. I bought a rotisserie chicken, tortillas, and chiles in vinegar, which became my supper that night. The next day, Saturday, an old friend of the family arrived to check up on me. He arrived with a giant hamburger, fries and a large soda with a lot of ice. He had bought this food in the United States before crossing into Mexico. After we ate, my friend took me to the house of the person who was going to take me over to the United States. I recall that this man had a son who looked to me like a drug addict. He frightened me, because he looked so strange, and he spied on me behind the door. Right then I did not care how I would get over; I only did not want to be in that house in danger of something happening to me.

My only option was to cross at the line, the best chance without risking my life. I had to cross with a document from another person. I made the attempt, but they arrested me, and I was processed to be deported. At that time in 1997 I did not know the United States laws. While I was under arrest, I remembered my mother above all. She had never wanted any of her children to go far away from her. She always said we were "poor but happy." They freed me at 10 p.m. I met a couple that had made the same attempt. They invited me to sleep in the house where they were staying. The following day, Sunday, we were at the line monitoring it to see when we could try to cross, but that day the situation was impossible because the "Migra" were on alert.

The next day, Monday, I tried to cross at the turnstile, which is the place where people enter Mexico. Fortunately, I was able to cross the border. My friend was there, and we went to Salinas, California. There I stayed for eight days waiting for the chance to go by airplane from San Jose, California, to Seattle, Washington.

My relatives came to get me at the airport. I started a new life in the state of Washington. At first it was very difficult, but the thought of helping my parents made me persevere. I started to work, taking care of children and working in a laundry. At the end of 1997, I met Saulito's father. The relationship was not what I had hoped, and I decided to face my responsibility as a single mother.

Ever since I had been very young, I had always wanted to have a child. However, even when talking with Saulito's father, I told him I would only have one. For me, Saulito was a planned and wished for child. He was neither an accident nor a mistake, because he came to bring joy and meaning to my life. I have never been ashamed, nor will I ever be ashamed, of being a single mother, because Saulito loves me more than anyone in this world.

When I was two months pregnant, I dreamed one night of the street in my hometown. Suddenly I saw a "migra" who was chasing me. I began to tremble and became so frightened that it seemed that my baby was jumping around in my womb. I woke up so afraid that the only thing I could do was try to calm down and touch my belly so that the baby would calm down too. In that moment I never imagined that we would experience my arrest by the Migra together.

In Yakima, Washington, I learned to drive a car and managed to buy one of my own for $600. What really motivated me to learn to drive was that Saulito was very sickly, and I never liked being a burden to anybody. I have always liked being independent, and so I learned to drive. In 2000 I decided to travel to Chicago because there I had friends and relatives from my hometown.

4

New Life Comes to "Deadville"

A voice cries out: In the wilderness prepare the way of the Lord, make straight in the desert a highway for our God. Every valley shall be lifted up, and every mountain and hill be made low; the uneven ground shall become level, and the rough places a plain. Then the Glory of the Lord shall be revealed, and all people shall see it together, for the mouth of the Lord has spoken.

—Isaiah 40:3

In 1987 Emma Lozano turned away from her faithful quest to find those behind the assassination of her brother, Rudy. She ran for alderman of the 32nd ward on Chicago's North Side to help Mayor Washington's re-election campaign. After his re-election and her defeat, she became part of the Parent Community Council, the group set up by Washington to develop school reform in Chicago. Significantly, the council designed a system of Local School Councils to guide reforms that for the first time permitted undocumented immigrants to vote in elections and serve on local school councils.

After Washington's death in office in December of 1987, Lozano set about organizing her local community. We had just married and were starting a new family. Together we were looking for something new, something stronger than the political movement we had just been through. Without being fully conscious of it, we were searching for a movement of faith and family, a movement that could not be compromised by the arrogance and corruption of politics.

Emma Lozano picked a seemingly strange corner of the Chicago North Side's 32nd ward to make her stand. The mix of Polish, Southern whites, Mexican Americans and Puerto Ricans called it "Deadville." A poor community stuck next to the expressway, it yet had a very powerful man in charge. Congressman Dan Rostenkowski was the chairman of the House Ways and Means Committee and the fourth or fifth most powerful Democratic politician in Washington. The sixteen square blocks of Deadville were in fact the remains of one of Chicago's oldest Polish communities.

Rostenkowski's house and home office sat next to the expressway and across the street from St. Stanislaus Catholic Church. Pulaski Park was nearby, and the elementary school was called Kosciusko. By means of the Kennedy Expressway, Deadville was only five minutes from downtown Chicago and the Loop. We learned later that Congressman Rostenkowski and his developer friends had allowed the neighborhood to decline and the streets to be divided among three different gangs. In the meantime, they began to buy up property in preparation for a dramatic and lucrative gentrification.

Emma saw something else stirring into life in this forsaken tract of aging houses. She looked at the children pouring out of the overcrowded school and at the parents waiting to pick them up and walk them home. A host of migrants from Mexico had been flowing into the neighborhood for two decades. They married U.S. citizens and had U.S. citizen children, but they remained without legal status. They worked hard, paid taxes, saved and bought buildings to live in, and organized businesses to serve their growing community. They accomplished all this, and still managed to send money back to Mexico to their families living there. Except in the mornings and afternoons around the school, however, the streets did not reveal the new life that had come to Deadville.

With our children going to Kosciusko Elementary School, Emma began to organize against the severe overcrowding. One thousand two hundred students, mostly Mexican, were squeezed into the hallways and closets of a school built for five hundred students. The principal and most of the teachers spoke only English and rarely spoke with the parents who came to drop off and pick up their children. It was one of the lowest performing schools in the city. When the first Local School Council elections were held across the city, Lozano fielded a slate of candidates. She won with 700 votes, the highest local school vote total in the entire city. What really had happened at Kosciusko, as well as in other schools around the city, is that the invisible families came out of the shadows, voting and running for office for the first time.

From her position on the Local School Council, Lozano organized the *Asamblea*. The Assembly met every four months, was open to all who lived in the neighborhood, and became an alternative government for neighborhood issues. For the first time, the majority of residents had a vote. Their first priority was their children's education. From the *Asamblea* they launched a five-year fight that won the construction of a brand new school building and sparked a citywide movement against overcrowded schools. The struggle against overcrowding merged with the citywide and national struggle for bilingual education that was under attack everywhere. Lozano's organization, Pueblo Sin Fronteras, also formed a partnership with Latino media, which was beginning to grow by leaps and bounds in the burgeoning Latino community.

Who were the families that came out of the shadows? Mostly it was the mothers, who came out to take an active role in the movement for better education during the day and then hurried back home to shop and cook dinner before their husbands returned from their low-paying factory jobs. Somehow these women summoned the courage to go with their baby strollers to the fifth floor of City Hall, to confront lines of police, to mobilize and march and have press conferences, to go on hunger strikes, and to stand up to thugs organized by racists in Congressmen Rostenkowski's ward organization—thugs paid for by developers who were alarmed that Mexicans stood in the way of gentrification. These women also had the courage to stand up to other Mexicans, born in this country, who sided with the old order in Deadville and called them "wetbacks." Gradually the mothers overcame the self-hatred that crippled these Mexican Americans, won their respect, and, with the victory of the new school and the newfound dignity it brought for all Latinos, consolidated a new Latino unity.

Sin Fronteras organized the classes that were required for legalization under the amnesty bill of 1986, passed during the Reagan years. The classes became schools that taught survival skills and how to engage in the struggle of organizing a neighborhood. Over three thousand people successfully passed through them to get their papers. Among these was an individual who would become part of the leadership of Sin Fronteras. Jacobita Alonso came across the Mexican-United States border in the trunk of a car. She married a man who was verbally abusive and tried to keep her out of the movement. Somehow, she managed in this situation to raise her beautiful children and to take a leading role organizing her people. Her example provided the inspiration for the slogan of the new movement: "Raise your family, organize your community."

There was another division in the community that the "invisible people" had to overcome. The neighborhood was divided into turfs claimed by three different gangs. Many of these members were the sons of undocumented immigrants; among them were Hector Torres and Adalberto "Junior" Villasenor. When the women set up tents and embarked on a twenty-five day hunger strike in protest against the demolition of a block of housing, the 32nd ward organization mobilized thugs to drive them out. The women's tents were pitched in vacant lots near the housing. The thugs broke into their evening prayer circle, and one of the younger ones attacked Jacobita Alonso.

Hector Gomez, then only fifteen years of age, came to Jacobita's tent after the attack to offer his support. Jacobita was understandably skeptical. Hector returned to the leaders of the three gangs, demanding that they act to "defend our mothers." As for the individual who had assaulted Jacobita, a circle was set up for Hector to fight him, one-on-one. Hector won. Later Hector Gomez returned to the tent, where he kissed Jacobita's hand. "We are here," he said. "Don't be afraid." Jacobita embraced him, an embrace that brought together generations separated by the culture of the street in which the youth had been forced to grow up. When confronted by sixty young warriors from the gangs the following day, the thugs turned and ran.

A few weeks later, the *Asamblea* challenged the ward organization's control of Pulaski Park. At a public meeting, held only in English, some of the women demanded translation. The ward bosses refused and wanted to continue the meeting, but "Junior" walked to the front, took the microphone and said, "Either this meeting will be translated, or this meeting will be over." Faced with the organized support of the youth of the community, the ward bosses had no choice but to carry on the meeting with a translation into Spanish.

For Emma, the criminalization of young Latinos, dropped into the life of the street and rejected by the schools and police, was just another form of the criminalization of undocumented immigrants. Lozano and Sin Fronteras worked with these young gang members, established programs for them, and often mediated gang disputes. Some left the gangs and joined Sin Fronteras. Some of them had their young lives cut short. Adalberto "Junior" Villasenor was tragically murdered in a drive-by shooting on one fateful Cinco de Mayo.

Jacobita Alonso was, like most mothers of the families, a very faithful Catholic. The neighborhood church, however, was tightly controlled by Congressmen Rostenkowski and, under his direction, attempted to retain its old Polish identity. On some Sundays, hundreds of Mexicans, many undocumented, would crowd into the basement for mass while a few elderly whites occupied the elaborate sanctuary above them. The priest opposed the efforts of the Mexican Catholics to organize their own community and provide a better education for their children; he condemned the families for their activism, calling it a sin to oppose the government. He even suggested that Satan controlled the *Asamblea*. The Mexican congregants were active in their church and depended on their faith—but they wanted a church that would support their efforts.

Confronting the priest for his statements against them, Jacobita reminded him that the Mexicans filled his collection plates every Sunday. She was told, "The church's money did not come from them" and that, for all he cared, "they could go and become Pentecostals." The mothers, the *comadres*, called a press conference to denounce the racism in the church. They then decided to form their own church. They reached out to a pastor who had joined them on the picket lines and led prayers for them, Franklin Guerrero. To their surprise, Guerrero was not a Catholic, as they had assumed, but a Methodist. No matter. They studied the social principles of the Methodist church, agreed with them, and petitioned the Methodists to become a church. The church was named "Adalberto," after the young leader who had had the courage to stand forward to protect the community, and who had paid the ultimate price. The little church brought together Latinos who would have otherwise been divided by their faith institutions.

The establishment of this little church had a great importance for the families. It was not an easy task. The families faced immense pressure from the Catholic Church. The Methodist tradition mirrored many of the Catholic traditions that allowed for child baptisms, first communions, confirmations, and *quinceañeras*, which were important to them. It also allowed them to seek guidance from the scriptures, unfiltered by church doctrine. It encouraged a direct relationship to God, unfiltered by the priest in the confessional. Finally it allowed for a more lively church service with stronger preaching and free flowing prayer and testimony without prohibiting them from saying the Rosary together. We began reading scripture together to find support for the struggle in which they found themselves. Most religious leaders had applied the Old Testament command to welcome the stranger as the appropriate way to address the situation of the undocumented. We found a greater similarity to the story of Abraham, his children, and the Israelites themselves. The families identified with the people of God who were forced to go to Egypt to survive. They found themselves in the stories of Abraham, Isaac, Jacob, Joseph and Moses. They were not strangers; they were the people God had chosen to make himself known in the world, in the United States. When God told Jacob to take his family to Egypt where he would make them a great people, as many as the stars in the sky, they felt God had his hand on them, heard their cries, and gave them a destiny.

They persevered in their effort to practice their faith in the midst of the struggle. In the Gospels and in the letter from James, they found out that Jesus had taken the side of the oppressed against the hypocrisy of the temple and the cold oppression of the Roman Empire. As the struggle for legalization surfaced and grew, they more and more saw themselves as subjects, not objects—the people God chose, not foreigners whom the people of their new nation were called to accept with tolerance. The Virgin of Guadalupe, seen in the words of the twelfth chapter of Revelations, was their mother, the woman chased by the *Migra* across the desert. And that Virgin of their traditions was still with them, guiding them through dangerous times. The miracle of her appearance to Juan Diego, a poor man, in 1531 would serve to unite not only the pueblo of Mexico, but also the people of the Americas in their search for justice.

Our church became a connecting point, drawing Evangelicals and Protestants as well as Catholics. We honored the Virgin of Guadalupe in the Mexican Catholic traditions, prayed like Evangelicals, and read the Bible in social context like Methodists. As we sought to support the faith of a people in struggle, the church became a bridge between the religious denominations that doctrine and institutional competition had carved into the Latino community. A few years later, some of the congregation would form a procession, on December 12th, and carry their own Virgin of Guadalupe into another Catholic church, friendlier, that welcomed them. Gradually, our new little church began to work closely with dozens of Catholic churches in Chicago and around the nation.

Their determination to maintain their own traditions, especially their expression of faith in the Virgin of Guadalupe, made for hard times in the Methodist church. They would eventually overcome this opposition, but this expression of their faith, combined with their activism, made it difficult for the Methodists to find a pastor to work with them. Undaunted, the families decided to send me to a Methodist seminary, and I then became their pastor. I was an unlikely and unworthy choice, but yet an affirmation of the families' faith, that God works through the most unlikely of people to intervene in the affairs of men.

The faith and courage of the families that came together in this little church enabled Lozano and Sin Fronteras to nurture a new Latino unity that recognized the value of every member of the community. New life rose up within Deadville, overcoming the divisions that had been imposed upon it from without. Together they were Mexicans, with and without papers, Puerto Ricans, Salvadorans, Guatemalans, Catholics, Protestants, and Evangelicals. In this corner of Chicago, a new unity bound together people who were called to work hard, stay together as families, raise their children, and sustain the struggle for justice and the rights of the undocumented immigrants in their midst. Time would show that seeds were being planted in this very humble place in Deadville, seeds that would blossom into a powerful unity of many faiths and a grassroots movement for legalization of undocumented immigrants.

🌿 5

Elvira in Chicago

I cry out to God most high, to God, who fulfills His purpose for me.
—Psalm 27:1

I arrived in Chicago, Illinois, on June 5th, 2000. My cousins picked me up at the airport, and I stayed with them in their apartment in the "Back of the Yards" neighborhood for one day. On the second day, Kika came for me. I ended up living in Aurora, Illinois, with the sister of Saulito's baptismal godmother.

It was very hard for me to find work. I realized for the first time that one needs a social security number and work permit. At first my comadre's sister took care of Saulito for me, as he was only one and a half years old. We were living in a basement that had only one door and one window, which measured 16 inches by 6 inches. I found temporary work in a plastics factory. It was not very far from where I was living. My comadre's sister would come home from work, and then her brother and I would go off together to our jobs. When we returned, she would leave again. I felt this was a big help because she took care of Saulito in the day, while I gave him his bottle and changed him at night. My Saulito was a good baby and did not cause any headaches. One day they called Kika to work an hour earlier than usual. When I arrived, I found that nobody was there, and my baby was alone. I looked at him sleeping so innocently. I felt great pain to see my baby alone, so I embraced him and cried, imagining in that moment what disaster might have happened.

This event occurred a few days before the Fourth of July in 2000. Right away I called Jose, the older brother of my comadre, and asked him to take me to my cousins in Chicago, since one of them did not work and could help me take care of Saulito. It was very hard to find work. Finally I found a job in a supermarket, where I was given a complicated set of shifts, sometimes in the night and sometimes in the day.

I inquired at a day care center about leaving Saulito with them, and they told me I would have to give them $50 to hold a place. I gave them the money and then asked at the supermarket where I worked if I could have a morning shift, because I had enrolled my child in a day care center. My immediate supervisor told me that he would have to talk to the owner about it. The next day he gave me the reply, which was that they couldn't give me the shift. They considered me a good employee, but if I didn't want the evening shift, I should look for another job. I thanked them and told them that I would only work the remaining days of that week. I deeply appreciated that, because of this job, I had food and a home for my son and myself.

It was very difficult to find another job, so I began to sell Jafra products to people I knew, and to work for a temporary worker agency, where I was paid on a daily basis. If I worked on Saturdays, I was paid by the day, so as not to accumulate overtime. Some days I was called, others not. It was a hard month, the hardest in my life.

Another of my cousins had lost his job. He didn't have a car, but I did. He told me he had found an announcement in the newspaper in which they were asking for people to work in the airport, cleaning airplanes. I had never driven on the expressway, and I didn't know the city very well, but we set out for the airport. We went over to the World Services Company, where they interviewed us right away. They didn't take my cousin for the job, but they did take me. The wages were $6.50 per hour.

On the day I had an appointment to get my work ID, I got lost on the way to the airport. When I finally got off the expressway and asked where the airport was, they said it was only a few blocks away, but I was about to reach Midway Airport—not O'Hare. Instead of taking the I-90-94 expressway north, I had gotten onto the I-55, which was had taken me southward. Finally I gave up and came back to my home, disgusted, and told my cousins I had gotten lost. The next day, my cousin told me to follow him, got on the expressway, and showed me where to get onto the I-90-94. He got off at the next exit, while I continued on to find O'Hare Airport.

From there I remembered how to get to the airport and find the offices of my future employer. Everything seemed normal. It was a dreamy time because I had only been on an airplane in 1997, when I traveled from San Jose, California, to Seattle, Washington; and then again in 2000 from Seattle to Chicago, Illinois. When I was a child, occasionally I saw an airplane going through the sky above my village. Since my father used to leave my village by plane to go to another city to work, I remember that I used to yell to the airplane and say to the other children, "There goes my daddy in that airplane!" And I yelled to him, "Goodbye, daddy, we'll wait for you here. Come back soon!"

When I got on the first airplane to clean it, my heart gave a jump, because never in my life had I imagined that I would be in an airplane. Working at O'Hare Airport was the most beautiful time in my life. If I were born again, I would work there again, because it was in that job that I met my best friends— friends who had come from Guatemala, Honduras, El Salvador, Puerto Rico, and, of course, Mexico. In the worst moments of my life, they were there for me, and cared for both my son and me. There I met my comadre, Kirym, from Guatemala, who would later ask me to be the godmother for the confirmation of her children Edgarito and Anayansi. We became very close, working, and caring for our children. They witnessed how I had to support Saulito and the great demands that were placed on me as a single mother. When at last they were confirmed in the church and had received the Holy Ghost, they asked for God to change our lives, and for me not to be deported.

6

A Partnership with Luis Gutierrez

Thus says the Lord, the God of Israel, Let My people go, that they may hold a feast to Me in the wilderness. But Pharaoh said, Who is the Lord, that I should heed his voice. And let Israel go? I do not know the Lord, and moreover I will not let Israel go.

—Exodus 5:1-2

The struggles over the issue of immigration in the United States have gone on since the time of the Civil War. Before that, the issue was the forced migration created by the slave trade, and the attempt of the Slave Power to expand slavery by annexing Texas and other territories through the Mexican War. A system of insuring cheap labor has been a part of the U.S. economy since the captains of industry—also known as the Robber Barons—built their railroads, ships, factories, and refineries. As the need for cheap labor grew, the United States government not only allowed immigrants in, but also recruited and encouraged them to come. Whenever the economic cycle suffered a down turn and unemployment began to rise, the Congress and the President tossed these immigrants by the wayside. Between 1870 and 1930, over 30 million immigrants came to this land. In the 1930's, U.S.-born Latinos were deported to Mexico along with the undocumented; years later, when World War II began, they received draft board letters calling them back.

A growing "free trade" movement during the Reagan, Bush and Clinton years—the 1980s and the 1990s—accelerated the U.S. economy at the expense of Mexico, Central America, and the Caribbean. President Reagan's "amnesty" bill of 1986 was recognition of the need for cheap labor; this need continued throughout the prosperous times of the Clinton administration. The North American Free Trade Association (NAFTA), passed in 1994, resulted in the U.S.-forced devaluation of the peso and a virtual takeover of Mexico's financial system, as well as the dumping of U.S. corn, beans and rice into Mexico and the destruction of millions of agricultural jobs. Just as these two economic manipulations forced Elvira Arellano from her home in Michoacán, so did they force millions of others to make the dangerous trip to the north, where American employers welcomed them.

The first modern attack on undocumented immigrants came from the right wing of the political spectrum. In 1994, Governor Pete Wilson's campaign for Proposition 187 in California, while it backfired, exposed the development of a white supremacist movement intent on driving brown-skinned people from the United States. This anti-immigrant movement even coined a new label: "illegal aliens." This wave of protectionism preyed upon the fear of an emerging reality, a truly multicultural and multiracial United States. The white Evangelical right helped to inculcate this fear into their parishioners. Ironically, the commitment of these pastors to the renewal and protection of the deteriorating nuclear family did not extend to families of color. The white supremacists found allies in the Republican Party, and formed a strange alliance with the party's corporate interests. Party leaders feared that "red states" were becoming brown, and would join with "blue states" that had turned black. Significantly, the fast growing Latino Evangelical movement grew increasingly uncomfortable with its white sponsors. Latino congregations would come to find that 15% of its pastors and 40% of its congregations were undocumented immigrants.

By 1996, there was a formidable anti-immigrant caucus in the Republican-controlled U.S. Congress. President Clinton agreed to the passage of a harsh immigration law in order to get concessions on his other priorities. Under the Clinton and Bush administrations, which both worked to meet the need of business for cheap labor, the 1996 immigration law was not strictly enforced. Continuing Congressional pressure on the President, however, increased the number of raids, and deportations gradually increased. The dissemination of fear and hatred directed at undocumented immigrants, and the Latino community in general, became a common tool of the Republican Party for mobilizing its base. In spite of this hostile environment, hard economic times in Mexico, Central America, and Caribbean islands like Haiti, and an economic boom in the United States, drove estimates of the number of undocumented laborers to over 12 million.

In response to the 1996 strict immigration law, California activists joined with unions seeking the growing Latino vote and called for a mass mobilization in Washington, D.C. At the center of this call was long-time activist, Jose "Pepe" Jaques Medina. He had been one of the early leaders of CASA and a close friend of Rudy Lozano, who had named his second born after Pepe Jaques. I met this profound organizer in the 1970s when he was traveling around the country, defying an order of deportation. I had supported his case then, and fully supported his new call for the *Coordinadora 96* to descend on the nation's capital. Sin Fronteras sent busloads of people to Washington, D.C. There was, however, little follow-up to the *Coordinadora 96*, and the coalition in California broke down due to infighting. Activists who, like Rudy Lozano, had worked for the cause of undocumented immigrants in unions were having success. Unions, which traditionally had viewed undocumented immigrants as the enemy, were now becoming increasingly interested in political influence and looked longingly at the Latino vote. The new service unions, led by the Service Employees International Union (SEIU), plunged into fruitful organizing campaigns among Latinos, both with and without papers. A conference of the rank-and-file activists in 1997, led by Farm Labor Organizing Committee (FLOC) President Baldemar Velasquez, inspired a young Jesuit priest to take the issue of undocumented immigrants to the Guadalupan societies in New York. These first conversations gave birth to the Coalition for Dignity and Amnesty.

One afternoon, a member of the new coalition came to our church in Chicago. He invited us to send a busload of people to a demonstration in Washington, D.C. Lozano joined the coalition and arranged a bus for the families to travel in. At the coalition's next meeting, a proposal was made for groups in each state to get their Congressmen to introduce a new amnesty bill in the House of Representatives. Sadly, only Sin Fronteras was able to deliver.

Illinois's only Latino Congressman was Luis Gutierrez, an old Chicago ally from the Harold Washington years. Gutierrez had split from the Washington coalition after the mayor's death in office and supported Richard M. Daley to become Washington's successor. He made this move in return for Democratic support to draw a Latino majority Congressional district in the redistricting that would be done following the 1990 census. Gutierrez later ran in this new district and won. Gutierrez had begun to participate in the immigration fight even as an alderman in the city council. In his new position, he found himself representing the heart of the Chicago Mexican community, as well as his own Puerto Rican stronghold. He walked a tight rope between his support from the Mayor and his ties to the Puerto Rican independence movement. Gutierrez even opposed the NAFTA bill in 1993, which Daley's brother, Bill, had narrowly managed to maneuver through Congress, but was still able to keep Daley's support in successive elections.

In response to the request by the Coalition for Dignity and Amnesty, Sin Fronteras gathered thousands of postcards urging Gutierrez to introduce a new comprehensive legalization bill: *Amnistia para Todos!* Lozano and about two hundred Sin Fronteras members surprised Gutierrez at a local park district meeting. After Emma and her *comadres* presented Gutierrez with the postcards, I wandered out of the field house to the edge of the park. Soon Gutierrez followed. We sat down on a park bench. In truth, it was the first time we had talked since Harold Washington's death in 1987, when he made his decision to endorse Daley's candidate over the candidate of the Harold Washington coalition—the coalition that had opened the way for him to become an alderman.

I can't say I was ever bitter over Luis's actions, or even angry with him during the decade that had passed. We had made a decision never to criticize him publicly for his action, although many in the remnants of the Washington coalition did so. In truth, most of the other Latino and African American aldermen followed suit and joined forces with Mayor Daley after he was elected in 1989. At least Luis had gotten something substantial for his community: the first Latino majority Congressional district in Illinois and the first Latino Congressman. He had negotiated with great boldness to win Daley's endorsement. It was the same boldness that had brought him to stand before a rally of 12,000 after Washington's death and call for a march on city hall, where the Daley forces were retaking the city in the middle of the night. Yet his arrangement with Daley, however bold, was part of the mayor's strategy to divide the Black-Latino coalition that had overthrown the most powerful Democratic machine in the nation.

On reflection, the formation of the original Black-Latino coalition in the 1960s and again in the early 1980s had been unbalanced. Latinos had come in as junior partners, and there was little understanding in the African American community of the tragic history of colonization that had shaped the Latino community. The Civil Rights movement had, over time, been rewritten as a movement for integration and assimilation, burying the reality that there are more people of African descent south of the border than to the north of it. Restoring the Black-Latino coalition on a more balanced foundation would require developing leadership in the Latino community commensurate with what Dr. King, Harold Washington, and so many others had achieved for the Black community.

The collapse of the Washington coalition did not leave the newly elected Mayor Daley free of a now-awakened African American vote, or the threat of a new Black-Latino coalition. Daley would have to concentrate his efforts for the next ten years to win substantial support in the African American and Latino communities. His determined effort to divide the Black-Latino coalition would become emblematic of the new dynamic. The Irish leadership in City Hall continually made concessions to city alderman and other elected leaders in the Black community and tried to establish a Black leadership who would work with them.

As we sat there in the park, I felt in Luis Gutierrez a longing for the spirit of the people's coalition that had begun his political career. Given the situation in Congress in 1997, however, Gutierrez was naturally reluctant. "I'll be a laughing stock!" he said. Fortunately, I did not have to do all of the work. Looking to build Latino unity, Lozano, months previously, had taken a group of Mexicans to support a Puerto Rican demonstration of supporters who sought a statue of Pedro Albizu Campos—the notable leader of the Puerto Rican independence movement—in Humboldt Park. Surprised, the Puerto Ricans welcomed the hundred or so Mexicans waving Mexican flags and shouting Puerto Rican slogans. It was the beginning of what was to become an historic Mexican-Puerto Rican coalition. This remarkable demonstration of common cause helped persuade Luis to introduce the legalization-for-all immigration bill in the Congress—a bill that, Lozano knew, would help to mobilize the people.

Lozano continued to build support in Chicago and around the nation. In October of 1997, the Coalition for Amnesty and Dignity called for national demonstrations around the country in support of Gutierrez's bill. This call began a long struggle with the Democratic leadership. Immigrant rights organizations, community-based-organizations, and unions, who were attached to the Democratic leadership, arranged for a competing demonstration on September 15th that seemed to pre-empt the coalition's march. Ignoring the call for amnesty for all 12 million people, these better-funded organizations—with deeper ties to Washington insiders and Washington money—were forwarding the more limited demands and reforms that would later form the heart of the DREAM Act. Senator Durbin and these organizations were intent on blunting the influence of the amnesty movement. As became clear in the ensuing years, the Democratic leadership wanted the Latino vote, but they did not want to alienate the white vote, which the Republican Party was working to mobilize against undocumented immigrants.

Gutierrez joined with Sin Fronteras to support the amnesty demonstration. Thanks to intense organizing efforts, the October march was double the size of the earlier Party-sponsored mobilization—and cost a fraction of the money. "We didn't have buses," said Lozano, "so we made feeder marches from the north side and south side and walked 12,000 people the five miles to the Federal Building." Despite evident successes such as this, the Coalition for Dignity and Amnesty began to fall apart, infiltrated by ideologues more interested in proving that capitalism didn't work than in winning legalization for 12 million people and their families. This collapse, when coupled with the political maneuvering of the Democratic Party, confirmed the belief within Sin Fronteras that the voice of the undocumented not only needed to be heard, but needed to lead the national movement.

In the midst of this coalition building, Sin Fronteras responded to an emergency call from the Zapatistas. The Zapatistas had arisen from the rain-soaked mountains of Mexico's southern-most state of Chiapas on the day NAFTA went into effect in 1994, when they descended on the capital and executed a brief military occupation. Later retreating to the mountains, they became a dramatic voice for the indigenous peoples of Mexico and Guatemala and established a powerful resistance to U.S. domination of Mexico and Latin America. Zapatismo was not a traditional movement of the left. The Zapatistas, motivated by their mix of indigenous Mayan beliefs and Christian spirituality, sought to "govern from below," by the witness of those without a face or voice. The movement called on those at the margins to take dramatic action to form new coalitions of people who did not seek to dominate, but to serve and inspire and cajole. The first principle of the Zapatistas—"don't coerce, persuade"—called for a new style of work.

In June of 1998, the Zapatistas asked us to organize a high level delegation to come to Chiapas during the World Cup soccer games. They believed the army would move against them while the Mexican media were distracted by the draw of international "football." We convinced Congressman Gutierrez, Congressman Rush, Jesus Chuy Garcia, and two Methodist pastors to make the trip with us. This U.S. contingent made a number of statements condemning government actions against the Zapatistas. Congressman Rush, in particular, drew President Zedillo into verbal combat with him in Mexico's leading newspaper. Rush refused to back down, and Zedillo actually organized a helicopter visit to a town in Chiapas, where he anticipated the

Congressman would be. Guided by the Zapatistas, we changed our plans and went to a different village. The mission the Zapatistas had asked us to take on had been successful: to surround them with the safety of publicity during the World Cup. Our trip had a second, unintended outcome that would prove significant in the upcoming struggle involving families facing separation by deportation. The journey had forged the first collaboration between Sin Fronteras, Congressman Gutierrez, and Congressman Rush.

After our trip to Chiapas, we attended several *encuentros* of the Continental Front of Community Organizations (CFCO). At these meetings, grassroots organizations from across the Americas came together to help create a movement of and for the people—the poor, the marginalized, the dispossessed, and the voiceless. Organizations that were funded by governments or the United Nations—NGOs—were allowed to attend, but not to vote. Among the grassroots organizations were Christian communities that had sprung from liberation theology, but continued to grow when the theoreticians and the Catholic Church abandoned them. There were women from Costa Rico who were resisting the exploitation of U.S. corporate-controlled banana plantations; Mexicans who were seizing abandoned land at the margins of cities and building communities to help migrants survive; Haitians who were suffering at the hands of Dominicans, and Dominicans who were suffering at the hands of Puerto Ricans; and many others caught in the trickle-down system of exploitation and economic displacement, that was creating a mighty river of people flowing away from destitution in the south, towards the stability and promise of the north. These groups bore witness to the millions of people on both American continents who suffered from an intricate system of domination on an international scale, headquartered in the United States, which seemed to exist for the sole purpose of satisfying the lifestyle of an unimaginably opulent society on the other side of the Rio Grande border.

As the 2000 Congressional elections began, Gutierrez became known for two issues: supporting legalization for undocumented immigrants, and getting the U.S. Navy out of Vieques. The struggle to get the Navy out of Vieques had aroused the Puerto Rican community. Gutierrez's successful negotiation, several years earlier, to release the Puerto Rican opposition taken as political prisoners as a result of the independence movement, garnered him more support. To dramatize the plight of the undocumented, Sin Fronteras proposed a "human chain" to cut Chicago in half and shut down traffic for twelve minutes—a symbolic gesture in support of the twelve

million people who lived in the shadows of society. Fifteen thousand people stretched along Ashland Avenue from the South Side to the North Side
and, after stopping traffic for 12 minutes, made their way to a rally at Union
Park.

The leadership of the Democratic Party decided to run the law partner of Senator Durbin's son against Gutierrez in an effort to keep the Latino
community under control. Gutierrez's well-financed opponent created a
campaign issue out of the incumbent's advocacy efforts, saying that the
Congressman was too wrapped up in the issues of legalization and Vieques,
and was ignoring the bread-and-butter issues of the district. Gutierrez never
backed down. On the day of the Human Chain, he was returning from
Vieques, where he had been arrested as one of many taking part in nonviolent sit-ins; he traveled directly to join the protesters at the rally. The
national press followed him from the airport and reported what they saw at
Union Park. For three days, the front pages of Chicago newspapers bore
articles and pictures showing thousands of Mexicans shouting, "Navy out of
Vieques!" and thousands of Puerto Ricans shouting, *"Amnistia!"* Overnight,
legalization had become more than an immigrant issue—it had become a
Latino issue. Gutierrez demolished his primary opponent. Significantly, as
an outcome of the swirl of events in this regional election, the Congressional Hispanic Caucus began to take the immigration issue seriously for
the first time.

"We were building coalitions now, looking for a way to pass the bill,"
recalled Lozano, "and continuing to mobilize our community month in and
month out." Meetings with Congressman Bobby Rush and Congressman
Danny Davis, African Americans and old allies, showed promise, as did
meetings with Rev. Jesse Jackson. The first national African American leader
to come out publicly for legalization of undocumented immigrants, however,
was Minister Louis Farrakhan.

While the media had worked diligently to marginalize the minister, his
influence in the Black community was undeniable. Farrakhan decided to follow up his Million Man March in 1995 with a "Million Family March" five
years later. The minister formulated a national program of action. Lozano,
learning of the plan for the march, organized a group of twenty-five Latino
leaders to meet with the minister at his home in order to convince him to
link the cause of Latino families to the themes of the march. One of the participants looked at the minister and said, "Minister, twelve million people
are not an *issue*; they are twelve million children of God." The cause res-

onated with the minister; he granted Lozano and several Latino leaders from Chicago speaking roles at the huge mobilization on the Washington Mall in October of 2000.

Farrakhan's support for legalization of undocumented immigrants neutralized the fear of African American congressmen, that they would be attacked by the nationalists for supporting Latinos who, some said, were taking away jobs from African Americans. In a short time, the entire Congressional Black Caucus came to the support of comprehensive immigration reform. The minister's eloquent statements struck a powerful note, giving a prophetic vision of the inevitable majority that would one day emerge from the unity of African Americans and Latinos.

At this time, Sin Fronteras was reaching out to organizations and unions that had opposed comprehensive legalization in favor of more limited demands acceptable to dominant corporate and political interests in the United States. Gradually, these organizations began to shift their support to the comprehensive approach of Gutierrez, responding to pressure from their own members. The SEIU supported Gutierrez, as did the largest coalition of multi-ethnic community-based organizations, the Illinois Coalition for Immigrants and Refugee Rights (ICIRR). The leadership of these organizations and unions in Chicago moved similar groups across the nation to action. Sin Fronteras put past differences aside, reaching out to work in common cause with all of these unions and advocate organizations, yet retaining our freedom to move independently when the struggle required it. These advocacy organizations were sincere in their support of undocumented immigrants, yet they also had other interests that tended to tug against what, for us, was our core purpose. The problem we faced was endemic to the cause. The Civil Rights movement had Dr. King, SCLC, and John Lewis at its forefront. The union movement had Samuel Gompers, the AFL, and Walter Reuther. The movement for the rights of undocumented immigrants—which would become one of the largest social movements in the history of the United States—was, by contrast, the only movement in which those most affected did not lead it and did not speak for it. It became the task of Sin Fronteras to allow the voices of the undocumented to be heard.

Accepting this task did not mean that Sin Fronteras could act exclusively or independently. We maintained our relationships with left–wing activists in the Mexican community, Mexican businesses, and the Latino media, and strengthened our bond with Latino elected officials. Lozano was confident in the integrity of her early insight: that the fate of undocumented immigrants depended upon a unified Latino community.

The hard-fought battle in pursuit of this truth, begun with Lozano's election to a local school council, culminated in November of 2000 with the election of Cynthia Soto, the first Mexican representative to the Illinois House on the North Side. This hard-fought election—the same election in which Gutierrez defeated Durbin's candidate challenger—put Sin Fronteras on the political map. Through Gutierrez's leadership, opponents in that race became allies, revealing to Lozano a new way of working with Latino elected officials. After the election, Sin Fronteras took the position that it would back any incumbent who supported the legalization of undocumented immigrants. A series of resolutions in support of legalization in the Chicago City Council, the Cook County Board of Commissioners, and the Illinois state legislature soon followed. Eventually, both the mayor of Chicago and the governor of Illinois would become close allies in the battle for legalization.

🔥 7

Sin Fronteras

Teach me your way, LORD; lead me in a straight path because of my oppressors. Do not turn me over to the desire of my foes, for false witnesses rise up against me, spouting malicious accusations.
—Psalm 27:11-12

From a forgotten corner in Chicago, a little organization of mostly undocumented women, with no money and no professional organizers, had brought together a new coalition that launched the ten-year struggle for a new immigration law. The coalition, which consolidated behind Gutierrez's bill, spread across the nation. The lesson we learned was one that Rudy had taught: "Change is not made by extraordinary people, but by ordinary people who do extraordinary things."

Sin Fronteras became a center of advocacy for individuals and families who became entwined in the impossible complexities of a broken system. Among the many immigration cases that poured into our office was the case of the Bolivar family. Señora Bolivar was a strong, resourceful woman from Bolivia who had made her way to the United States illegally, had struggled to survive in a variety of jobs, and had become an activist. She was traveling with her three children, all U.S. citizens, in an overcrowded car to New York for a conference of *jornaleros*. The car was stopped by the highway patrol in Pennsylvania. The officer asked for identification from everyone in the car; when she could not provide proof of citizenship or legal residency, she was arrested and turned over to the immigration authorities.

Chris Bergin, the attorney for Sin Fronteras, took her case. Sin Fronteras raised money with the intention of sending Bergin with the Bolivar family to Pennsylvania for a series of court dates. When Señora Bolivar's final date came up, there was only enough money to send her and her attorney, but not enough to pay for the children to take the long bus trip. While the family was in the church for final prayers before the Señora departed, the children began crying, fearing that they would not see their mother again. Jacobita Alonso and associate pastor Beti Guevara were moved to go out on the street in order to raise the money so that the children could go. The generosity of the Division Street community poured forth, and the money was raised. The family felt that their prayers had been answered. Señora Bolivar and her children, together with their attorney, departed for Pennsylvania.

After the judge heard the case, Bergin took his seat in the courtroom with a sense that they had lost, and that the judge would rule against them. Then a strange thing happened. The judge noticed the children and asked them to step forward. He asked them to speak, and they explained that they were U.S. citizens. They told the judge about their life, their dreams, and their love for their hard-working mother. Incredibly, the judge ruled in her favor, awarding her a permanent residency card, saying, "These are wonderful children, and they deserve to be able to stay here with their mother."

Other cases came to Sin Fronteras as a result of the byzantine complexity of the immigration laws, unclear instructions from federal agencies, and the misinterpretation of these by corporations and local businesses who where frightened of coming under scrutiny. Comprehensive immigration reform legislation aimed to end the system of undocumented labor and replace it with a legal, understandable way to insure that foreign workers were operating within the recognized system of laws that governed society. Enforcement of such a new system, however, could only realistically go into place if the millions of immigrants working outside the law were given legal status. Efforts to introduce enforcement measures without legalization were manifestly unjust to millions of workers and inflicted cruel and inhumane punishment on their families.

One such enforcement measure pursued by the Bush administration, and later by the Obama administration, was called the "no-match letter." Literally hundreds of thousands of letters were sent to employers asserting that the social security numbers they had submitted for their employees on the I-9 form did not match the names in the social security records. The employers received instructions to straighten out the inconsistency or terminate the employee. As the fight against this enforcement measure unfolded, the social security records were revealed to contain hundreds of thousands of errors: misspelled names, unrecorded name changes as a result of a change in marital status, transposed numbers, and more. No-match letters were sent out accusing thousands of U.S. citizens of being "illegals." Lawsuits were filed to stop the use of no-match letters and to halt legislation that would establish a mandatory E-verify system for all U.S.

employers. The Obama administration even increased the number of no-match letters, added address criteria to the match, and compelled all employers with federal contracts to use a computerized system to verify the social security numbers of its employees. When questions arose about the use of this kind of verification system, Familia Latina Unida took the position that some kind of verification system could be put into place, if, and only if, it were accompanied by a pathway to legalize currently undocumented workers. This position reflected our determination to end the system of undocumented labor, while recognizing the dignity of the millions of workers that participated in this economy.

The struggle to defend immigrant workers and to protect their families from the injustice of no-match letters began when workers from hotels, factories and department stores who had received no-match letters came to Familia Latina Unida. Roberto Lopez, legal coordinator for Familia Latina Unida, developed a strategy for each case. In one instance in 2003, over one hundred Target workers at various stores in the Chicagoland area were given no-match letters. Lopez brought them together, formed an emergency organization with store coordinators, and began holding weekly meetings. As with similar cases in the Civil Rights Movement, success required developing of a plan involving legal research, political strategy, and non-violent direct action. Our legal team discovered that the Social Security Administration had no power to enforce the letters. We adopted a strategy of advocating that the no-match letters were meant only for record keeping, rather than as a basis for firing or dismissal. Through Congressman Gutierrez's office, we found an IRS representative who would agree not to penalize the company. Yet we still needed to get Target executives to come to the table. We decided to have a hundred people go into a Target store at the same time and fill their shopping carts with items from throughout the store. They would then line up at the checkout registers. When their turn came to pay, they would loudly announce, "We cannot shop at Target because Target is unfair to Latinos and is firing Latino workers." This was repeated at dozens of stores. Target workers reported that hours of overtime were spent in the evening trying to put the items back in their respective places.

The executives, eventually, did come to the negotiating table. Billy Ocasio, alderman for the 26th ward, sent Target executives a letter informing them that he could no longer support the construction of a Target store in his ward, if they continued to use the no-match letters to fire Latino workers. Congressman Gutierrez convened a meeting with Target executives, representatives from the Social Security Administration, and the Internal Revenue Service. Familia Latina Unida and Target workers attended. All the Target workers regained their jobs.

We recognized that this success was only temporary. The victory, however, brought the issue out into public view. A large part of our difficulty in achieving justice arose because the issues around immigration, like the twelve million immigrants themselves, were invisible. Actions such as the one involving Target workers built a base of leaders and families that were willing to fight. They were part of a movement. As in other struggles, the workers found their dignity restored and stopped viewing themselves as "illegals." They had rights.

Sin Fronteras developed its ability to organize people and to marshal the Spanish-language media. The Congressman showed his own creative leadership and, along with the Sin Fronteras attorneys, proved willing to explore legal strategies in a political context, and established a powerful defense against deportations. These organizations and groups, in various combinations, would be put to work in hundreds of cases over the next decade.

The Bolivar case was emblematic of the many stories and struggles that began to flow through our little organization. Sin Fronteras was undergoing a spiritual transformation. Adalberto United Methodist, as the church that housed the movement, became the center for this transformation. We developed a theology of the seasons that joined the rhythms of our political and spiritual development. In December, during Advent, we prepared. At the center of the season of Preparation Time was the celebration of the Virgin of Guadalupe. For our congregation, she represented a messenger sent by God to an oppressed and conquered people to let them know that God loves them, and that he has a special place and destiny for them in His Providence. From January through March, we lived the Gospel and gathered the people in outreach. Leading up to Easter, we organized and marched on the centers of power. In the seven weeks after Easter, we celebrated the resurrection among the faithful. After these four seasons, following the life and journey of Jesus, we began again: springing back into action during the seven weeks of Pentecost; consolidating the organization of the people through the seven weeks of Kingdom time; leading national mobilizations during the seven weeks of Harvest Time; and finally, during the seven weeks of Assembly Time, pulling together those who had come through the Harvest with us. The new movement of faith joined together the descendants of Juan Diego, who had heard the Virgin of Guadalupe tell him that God was with the oppressed, and the Evangelicals, who sought to reclaim their faith from the powerful and live according to Scripture.

We began to attract more and more families threatened with separation by the broken immigration laws. We fought their cases in court when we could, in the streets when necessary, and worked to keep their families together by any means necessary. Always we prayed and praised God together. The Scripture, which said, "What God has joined together, no man should separate," seemed more worthy of obedience than the 1996 immigration act. Millions of people fighting to keep their families together found themselves victimized in a nation where the divorce rate rose every year, and where many marriages lasted no longer than two years. The divisions in the community created by arguments over religious dogmas, encouraged by institutional denominations, seemed only minor obstacles. We maintained our identity through our bond with the Virgin of Guadalupe, but prayed and sang like Pentecostals, and studied Scripture like Methodists. There was a great hopefulness for the passage of a new immigration law, but there was a greater hope that we were becoming a people of God, a people whom God would never abandon.

As Sin Fronteras carried on its work, Elvira's story continued. She tells the next step in her journey...

As a result of the terrorist attacks of September 11, 2001, the federal government began to carry out raids in airports all over the country in the name of national security. On December 10, 2002, eight federal officers arrived at my home to ask me if I had weapons or a permit to carry weapons, as if I were a terrorist, and my answer was "No." They asked me if I had some relative with whom I could leave my son, because I had to go with them, and when I told them that I didn't, they threatened to give my son to the state. I told them that my son must go with me, that I myself paid for his care while I was working, and that the government had not been supporting my child. They agreed to let him stay with the person who had been caring for him and arrested me. It was about 8 p.m.

I appeared before a federal judge; the charges were that I had used a false social security number to work in a federal facility. They allowed me to go free under the signed promise that I would obey all the judge's orders. Firstly, I had to not leave the country or change my state of residence, because if I did those things I would face more charges. The judge assigned a lawyer to defend me.

The following day I went to the Mexican consulate to ask for help, and they replied that if the authorities were going to deport me, I would have to go. I left all my information, and the communications media began to call me to ask for interviews. I told them I could not talk to them, because I had to go to the immigration office and to see my lawyer.

The Spanish-language media, Channel 66 (Univision) and Channel 44 (Telemundo) in Chicago, told me that if I would speak up and tell what was happening, someone would be able to help me, as well as those others who were also under arrest. In the detention center I met two parents who were suffering and worrying about their family. They were just parents who wanted the best for their family, so I decided to make my first declarations to the Spanish-language press. When I went to see my lawyer, she asked me not to say anything to the press. I thought, well, now I've done it, but if they are going to put me in jail, let them do it and enjoy themselves. I am not going to allow myself to be humiliated, as if I were a terrorist, when my only crime was to have worked to ease my parents' hunger and to give my son a better life.

My arrest happened on a Tuesday; on Wednesday, I got a call from the director of a coalition of organizations. He invited me to testify about the raid, and also to see how they might help me, since his was an organization that defends immigrants' rights. That is when I met my pastor from the Adalberto United Methodist Church, Reverend Walter Coleman, and my new comadre, Señora Emma Lozano. With them I would begin my struggle not to be sent to jail, or deported.

🔥 8

The Virgin of Guadalupe

lvira explained to me, "If it was just me, just about me, then I would have gone back to Mexico. Why would I stay in a country that treated me so badly? But my son, he is a U.S. citizen. They cannot throw him away like he is garbage. I will stay and fight for him." Had the American Dream enticed Elvira to come to the United States? Perhaps thoughts of a life with things she could never have in Mexico had passed through her mind. Yet clearly her conscious motive was her commitment to the gift of the son whom she felt God had given her.

She had discovered, while working at O'Hare Airport, bringing the workers together to stand up for their rights, that she was an organizer. Now, step by step, she would move from defending her own right to stay with her son in this country, to standing up for all those other parents in a similar situation. She was called to speak at meetings large and small. In most places she found people who also had immigration cases, and they sought her out for advice. She learned quickly what could be done, and whom they could turn to for help, depending on their situation.

I remember her speaking at a meeting at the Casa Atzlan Community Center. Her speech was concise and clear. She did not speak like a victim, and, as a result, could speak for all those who were. Gradually she and Emma Lozano became closer, drawn together in their common cause. Many organizations wanted to claim Elvira. Some wanted to use her in support of their own agenda, but did nothing to defend her. In Emma Lozano she found someone who was committed to winning her case, who was devoted to her as a friend. For her part, Emma felt Elvira belonged to the whole movement, not to any one organization.

These two women, one born a few miles north of the border, the other born miles south of the border, became inseparable "struggle sisters," drawing strength and faith from each other. Elvira chose Adalberto UMC as her church in Chicago: "It seemed like an honest church, and the message was usually about fighting for justice for the undocumented." Elvira was a Catholic, but she chose a Methodist church that honored the Virgin of

Guadalupe and respected her Mexican Catholic traditions. Elvira joined in the annual journey through the seasons of faith and the stages of resistance. Each year began with preparation, proceeded through the seasons of witness and outreach, and culminated with a march on Washington, D.C., in support of legalization.

The terrorist attack in 2001 had dramatically changed the political situation in Congress. In response, we sought to broaden our alliances. One year, we worked in concert with SEIU to collect thousands of postcards that were then delivered by delegations to the Capitol. The next year, in 2003, the Hotel Workers Union took the lead and called for a "Freedom Ride" from cities throughout the nation to the Statue of Liberty in New York City. The buses set out across the country in June, many of them carrying undocumented workers and their families. Each of the buses would stop in seven or eight cities for rallies on their way to New York City. The union leadership, often from the building trades, would welcome the buses, demonstrating the across-the-board support of the Labor movement for legalization.

Decades previously, young organizers like Rudy Lozano had forced the unions to offer a path to membership to undocumented workers. By leading membership drives in the communities—drives that were frequently viewed with hostility by the union leaders—Rudy and his compatriots helped to steadily increase the number of undocumented workers in the union ranks, especially among the service unions. By the late 1990s, organized labor officially came out for legalization, though only a few unions put actual resources behind the drive for an amnesty bill. This history made the public support of the unions for the Freedom Rides even more significant. For Emma, they were a culmination of the work begun by her brother.

For Elvira, and for the church she had joined, the Freedom Ride was a spiritual journey. The Sin Fronteras/Adalberto bus was filled with families and their children. While the buses sponsored by various unions and the advocate groups were filled with American flags, our church bus was filled with Mexican flags and statues of the Virgin of Guadalupe. Adalberto families testified in each city, gradually building support and unity based on their moving witness. Elvira's testimony became ever stronger and stronger.

When the Chicago buses finally reached the park overlooking the Statue of Liberty, the rally had already begun. Elvira and Emma got off the bus, gathered the people and began to march, not to the rally, but to the edge of the water, carrying the statue of the Virgin of Guadalupe and singing. As the people saw her with the Virgin, about half the crowd came from the rally to join her. When they reached the shore, she stood holding the Virgin high above her head in a challenge to the Statue of Liberty across the water. The deeper meaning of this gesture cannot be surmised at this point in Elvira's journey. The rest of her story has the task, as it were, of unveiling its mystery.

While Lozano and Arellano worked hard to build unity on this Freedom Ride, clear differences were emerging amongst the various factions. Among the undocumented immigrants themselves, the gesture towards joining with and unifying the entire Latino community was fostering a movement of transformation and faith whose strength lay in the power of the fast-growing Latino vote. The leadership of the Labor movement, the Democratic Party, and the advocate groups, on the other hand, were trying to shape the cause towards the goal of immigrant assimilation. Nothing less than a broad coalition could have the political and social influence necessary to pass legislation in Congress. Until such time as these disparate groups, with their various issues and agendas, could unite with the grassroots movement, the larger Latino community would only see the legalization effort as one of survival and self-determination against the very real dangers of racism and oppression. Only a grassroots movement based on Latino unity and self-determination could provide a real defense for the twelve million undocumented immigrants and their families.

The political culture of the United States places a high value on freedom and liberty. For a privileged segment of society, the concept of liberty had become twisted to grant a license for individuals to grow rich at the expense of others, and to serve their own selfish interests without regard for the consequences to others. The Civil Rights struggle of the 1960s fundamentally challenged the misunderstanding of liberty that had settled into the norms of white society. The Freedom Movement insisted that the goal of freedom required justice for all. The movement for the rights of the undocumented posed the same question in a new context: Does justice for all include undocumented immigrants and their U.S. citizen children, people who were forced from their native lands by economic policies of free trade and military intervention and who were given employment in the United States at cheap wages? The progress that the grassroots movement had made from the time of the assassination of Fred Hampton to the election of Harold Washington fourteen years later was based on the Black-Latino coalition and the practical insight its leaders had gained into the master plan of the machine politics they opposed, the Chicago 21 Plan and its developers and financiers. Further progress required an equally thorough insight into what might be called the World 21 Plan: how not thousands, but millions are being exploited and then cast aside. An equally long preparation would be necessary for a grassroots movement that honestly sought to raise a new generation of leaders and to ensure that the Spirit of Truth might be heard.

✿ 9
Familia Latina Unida

What God has joined together let no man pull asunder…
—Mark 10:9

As for me and my family, we will serve the Lord…
—Joshua 24:15

Through Emma Lozano and Sin Fronteras, Congressman Gutierrez was easily persuaded to take on Elvira's case. In September of 2003, the Congressman introduced a private bill for her in Congress, a bill that would confer legal permanent resident status on her if passed and signed by the President. Gutierrez, fresh from having trounced Senator Durbin's chosen candidate, moved quickly to get Durbin to introduce the same private bill for Elvira in the Senate. The introduction of the two bills, even though it was unlikely they would ever be passed through either the House or Senate, stayed the order of deportation against Elvira and allowed her finally to get a work permit. They allowed her to stay, work, and raise her son for four years after her arrest.

Lozano was able to provide a small salary for Elvira at Sin Fronteras with the assistance of the Chicago Alliance of African, Asian, European and Latino Immigrants of Illinois and its supportive executive director, Dale Assis. She was given the task of organizing mixed-status families—families with U.S. citizen children, or families with a U.S. citizen parent and an undocumented spouse. The Sin Fronteras legal program brought in several of these families every month; Elvira began to meet with them and bring them together to support each other with their cases. Out of the legal program, we created a new organization, specifically focused on the needs of families impacted by the immigration system: Familia Latina Unida. Julie Contreras became its first secretary. Elvira became its first president.

Undocumented immigrants faced countless raids, both on the job and in their homes. Whenever a raid would take place, Familia Latina Unida would get a call, and we would have another dozen immigration cases to fight. While the official system viewed the targets of these raids as groups of workers without papers—without "authorization to work"—what we saw were families with citizens, members of our churches, with U.S. citizen children in our schools. Our purpose in fighting each of these cases developed into the ideal of bringing the human reality of this faceless enforcement to the fore and making it visible. We were determined to confront the lie—the "cover story" used by Immigration and Customs Enforcement agents—that they were focusing on criminals. ICE agents would use this narrative to obtain a warrant for someone who had failed to show up in court. They would go to that person's house and, not finding them home, proceed up and down the block checking papers, making arrests of people who had no criminal involvement. Though they succeeded in terrorizing the neighborhoods, the overall effectiveness of ICE was questionable. Even as the deportation numbers grew, people were still arriving every day from Mexico.

Against this background of harassment and indignity, Emma Lozano called a meeting of all the Latino elected officials in Illinois. It was held in Humboldt Park in a room above the La Bruquena Restaurant. At that meeting, Lozano outlined a ten-point legislative plan to make Illinois an "immigrant freedom zone." Lozano extracted promises from the participants for action at the city, county, state and federal levels of government. Piece by piece, these legislative bills were passed. Chicago's status as a "sanctuary city" extended beyond the city's borders as Cook County became a "sanctuary county" in which local police were prohibited from sharing information with federal immigration agents. Undocumented students were allowed in-state tuition. The children of undocumented parents were given access to state-supported health care.

The promise to grant driver's licenses to undocumented workers was one that went unfulfilled. This fight involved the Illinois state legislature and a coalition of over one hundred not-for-profit advocacy organizations under the umbrella of ICIRR. The competition amongst the organizations was always percolating just under the surface. We noted that when they lobbied a legislator, they usually had other items on their agenda. Even so, each one expressed to us privately, that if *they* had been in control of the operation, they would have made stronger commitments. Despite such deal-making behavior, we found that some of the organizers were truly committed individuals, especially Madeline Talbot, who brought a passion and toughness to the struggle that won over the hearts of the families.

Working alongside these organizers in the state capital, we noticed another difference in our approaches: the advocacy groups concentrated on winning over Republicans, while Familia Latina Unida felt that pressure should be put on the Democrats, with whom we had political leverage. Willing to trade off other issues to win our greater goal, we hoped to get Democratic lawmakers to make our issue a priority. The advocacy groups had other interests to protect, including their own financial stability, and did not want to endanger their relationship with the Democratic allies who helped them with funding. This difference would become one of the key issues in the national struggle that was to come.

In search of support for the driver's license legislation, we sought out individual legislators to speak with. This was the first time Familia Latina Unida came into contact with then-Senator Barack Obama. He was not easy to find, but our little delegation eventually caught up with him in one of the hallways of the legislature on Good Friday—Elvira and Saulito, Emma, and Alexandro Dominguez, who had been falsely accused of rape, deported, and then returned to establish his innocence through DNA evidence. The Senator not only committed his vote for the driver's license legislation—he promised Elvira he would help her stay in this country with her son. Obama's support became part of the unanimous commitment of both the Latino and Black caucuses in the state legislature. The Senator put his arm around Elvira, and had his picture taken with the group.

Familia Latina Unida brought together a meeting in Springfield of the state immigrant services coalition, ICIRR, with Congressman Gutierrez. Previously, the coalition had followed Senator Durbin and had had an uneasy relationship with Gutierrez. The coalition sought the Congressman's support for state funding of a citizenship program. Our intention was to bring the coalition into alignment with Gutierrez's position of legalization of all undocumented immigrants, and away from Durbin's. Durbin, though he supported Elvira's cause and was frequently an ally, did not want to burden the Democratic Party itself with the risky position of legalization for all. Gutierrez did, in fact, support what came to be a multimillion-dollar fund for the coalition and convinced the governor to give it his support. A meeting was scheduled to finalize the agreement with the coalition, the governor, and Latino legislators. When we raised the question of driver's licenses at that meeting, we were informed that both could not be done. Behind our backs, driver's licenses for undocumented immigrants had been traded for funding for the advocate groups. It was a painful lesson.

The narrow defeat of the driver's license legislation did not discourage the families. They marched to a different drummer. What they remembered was a thousand Latinos marching down the circular stairs in the state rotunda and singing, "There is no God greater than our God." Confidence and faith in the movement was building. Governor Rod Blagojevich, who took office in 2004, continued to move forward with the consolidation of Illinois as perhaps the most immigrant-friendly state in the U.S. Although Blagojevich later would be imprisoned for a variety of scandals, he owed his election to the support of Congressman Gutierrez. Gutierrez's 4th Congressional was the only Chicago district that Blagojevich carried in the Democratic primary. Gutierrez became his principal advisor on immigration issues, and immigrant rights became a hallmark of his administration.

Familia Latina Unida continued to take up the cause of individuals and families who stumbled over the peculiar contradictions and cruelties of the immigration system. The irony of the cases against most of these original families is that they had gotten into trouble when they had applied for legalization of an undocumented spouse through section 245(i), a program that was first created in 1994 and ultimately discontinued by Congress in 2001. Under the 245(i) program, a U.S. citizen or a legal permanent resident could apply for citizenship for a spouse or relative, or, if the citizen was over eighteen years old, for a parent. The undocumented person did not have to leave the country while the application was pending. However, the time to process the application could last as long as several years. During that time, with registered name and contact information on file, the applicant was not given legal working papers and had no protection against being picked up and deported. This program, with its tumultuous history of argument, cancellation, and renewal, is one of the stranger parts of immigration law. The catch in the 245(i) program was, that if the applicant had been deported and then returned to the U.S., they were no longer eligible for protection under the program and would be deported again. The 1996 immigration reform act, passed by a Republican Congress and Democratic President two years after 245(i), established a mechanism for "expedited deportations." If a person had been stopped trying to cross the border, they were fingerprinted and turned back. They did not know that, technically, they had been "deported"—and therefore lost any protection under 245(i) in the future. In fact, Elvira herself was a victim of this process of expedited deportation.

In 2004, the 245(i) program was no longer accepting applications, but Maria Benitez had applied for protection under the program many years previously. When Maria was called in for her final interview in the 245(i) process, the family planned a celebration and went in together. Maria and her husband, Rodolfo, had three U.S. citizen children, and she was four months pregnant. At immigration headquarters they were escorted into an interview room. They were laughing, anticipating the relief of finally getting her papers, and the ensuing celebration. Three men came in, asked the pregnant Maria to stand, handcuffed her hands behind her back, and placed restraints on her ankles. In front of an enraged husband and crying children, she was taken away for immediate deportation.

The Benitez family contacted Sin Fronteras lawyer Chris Bergin, who immediately contacted Lozano and Arellano. They, in turn, got Congressman Gutierrez to come downtown to immigration headquarters. Gutierrez brought Senator Durbin with him, and the following day they held a press conference. We wrote letters to the White House and organized a rally in her defense; Senator Durbin and Governor Blagojevich both protested her deportation. Nothing seemed to work. Maria was ultimately deported to Mexico, just three days before Mother's Day. During this time the President of Mexico was visiting Chicago. Familia Latina Unida organized a meeting in the Mexican community of Pilsen for the President, and the community chose Elvira to speak as their representative and address him. Characteristically, Elvira did not plead her own case, instead pleading the case of Maria Benitez. The Mexican President, Vicente Fox, and his wife, Marta, were moved by the presentation. In the following weeks, Marta contacted Laura Bush. At last, through a humanitarian visa, Maria returned to Chicago in September, to her husband and family—in time for the successful delivery of her child. The Benitez family has continued their fight for her legalization every year, using various tactics, and they remain together in Chicago to this day.

Cases like that of the Benitez family came to Familia Latina Unida every month, and we fought for each one. It was not hard to be passionate about these cases. At that time, an estimated four million U.S. citizen children had at least one undocumented parent. In most cases, the children stayed in the United States after one of their parents was deported. They often remained separated for years from their father or mother. The passion of the family members in each case was expressed with tears or, worse, by stoic expressions of silence and anger. Familia Latina Unida was able to take up the fight for justice in so many cases because the Sin Fronteras Legal Program also came to the aid of its families. Congressman Gutierrez and his dedicated staff, led by District Director Salvador Cerna, were also of great help. As a result of these combined efforts, Spanish-language media focused more and more attention on the issue of the separation of families.

In the church, we spent time with the children, helping them to understand what was happening to their parents. We reassured them that they were loved and would be cared for, that we would work to bring back their father or mother by any means necessary. The families that, together, formed the first organization of Familia Latina Unida were by no means criminals. They were hardworking people who loved their families, brought joy to their children and spouses, and put all of their strength into ensuring the survival of their families. Why was the government destroying their lives and their livelihood, a government that had been happy to accept their taxes? Some of the families had taken out loans from mortgage companies and bought houses at high interest rates. They were valued where they worked, and were good parents to their children.

At last in May of 2004—the same month that Maria Benitez was deported—we saw a breakthrough. Gutierrez successfully introduced the first comprehensive immigration reform bill into Congress—known as the SOLVE Act—with Senator Kennedy introducing the companion bill in the Senate. Gutierrez had done his work, but the many Latino advocacy organizations had not completed theirs. A coalition was in the making, though not yet fully formed. The fledgling alliance lacked a common vision and strategy. The families that made up Sin Fronteras, however, were clear. They believed that victory would require the full participation of many forces, and our organization worked hard to connect these various forces to Gutierrez's effort in the Congress. We believed that victory would be the outcome of a movement of faith and family, a movement in which Latinos would create a new spiritual and political unity to challenge the racism and greed embedded within the business and politics of the nation.

While a large and politically complex coalition was coming together to pursue a national legislative solution, the grassroots resistance to escalating deportations, and its concomitant separation of families, mobilized a clearer, more unified "human rights movement. " The legislative coalition was filled with contradictions and betrayals by seeming allies. It failed to break through the partisan paralysis in the Congress. The resistance movement to the deportations and separation of families, in contrast, was consistent, and grew stronger through local victories like the one at Target. This movement, however, needed a clearly defined objective, one that would provide real relief from the growing assault on the Latino family.

Despite its determination and energy, the grassroots movement that began in Deadville still lacked the power to shape the immigration issue effectively. Other groups, well meaning, but with other agendas and other constituencies, continued to define undocumented immigrants as foreigners who had illegally crossed the border to get a piece of the American dream. By forwarding this definition, they denied undocumented immigrants the support of the whole Latino community, of which they were truly a part: by the sacrament of marriage, by the bond of love with their children, and by the history of their faith and their struggle against colonialism and racism in the Americas.

In June of 2005, with legislation stalemated in Washington, D.C., the families of Familia Latina Unida were determined to take their cases directly to the White House. Three busloads of families with U.S. citizen children made their way to Washington, D.C., to file petitions for pardons with the President of the United States. They became a major story for the Latino media members who accompanied them on the trip. Long bus trips with children are not easy. This trip to the nation's capital, the first of many, was filled with hope. We watched movies, sang songs, practiced and invented new *limos* (chants). And during the long hours in the darkness, here and there, families traded stories, and prayed. The idea that a group of parents and children could come together, make their way to the capital of the most powerful nation in the world, and have their stories be heard began to grow in them. Losing this fight would mean, for most of them, losing everything they had worked for. They told each other how they had crossed the border—some in trunks of cars, some in trucks driven by bandits, some on foot across the desert. Most knew of someone who had died in the crossing. The different experiences merged as they shared them, uniting them in a common bond.

Yet this strong sense of community mixed with a discordant isolation and solitude. Most of the families were waiting for a date, the day on which they would have to face the final decision of the government for deportation. As we had maneuvered and delayed, dates would be postponed, keeping those at risk within the community. Still, as the inevitable final date approached, each family realized that they would be called to step up alone. Some would arrive at their final dates to find that they had become a focus of the national struggle. There was Providence working among the families, a Providence that would cause their witness to bring about a turning point in the national struggle. Yet they were ordinary families who, above all, participated in the joy of raising children. They shed tears, followed by laughter, followed by more tears and then more laughter.

When the families at last reached the halls of the Capitol, they went to both Democratic and Republican members of Congress, walking down the halls, going into office after office. Some meetings were very positive, and we believed minds were swayed as they saw the love that bound together the families that the law was separating. Yet the effort to obtain pardons was rejected. The families turned at last to Congressman Bobby Rush. Rush's willingness to take up the struggle for these Illinois families revealed the central quality that would make Chicago the heart of the grassroots movement for justice and for the rights of undocumented immigrants. A one-time member of Student Nonviolent Coordinating Committee (SNCC) and leader of the Black Panther Party, now a member of Congress and the man who had delivered Barack Obama his only election defeat, Rush was also a man of faith, a pastor who had founded his own church on Chicago's South Side. We at Sin Fronteras had seen his faith and courage first hand in Chiapas on the mission to help the Zapatistas; naturally, Familia Latina Unida would turn to Rush once the pardon effort ran aground. Rush talked with and listened to each of the families. His concrete human connection with these families helped to win the support of the Congressional Black Caucus, which included another Congressman who had been involved in the Harold Washington movement: Michigan's John Conyers, chairman of the House Judiciary Committee, through which reform legislation would have to pass. The visit to Congressman Rush resulted in a private bill that he would introduce into Congress, seeking protection for 38 individuals, including Maria Benitez.

Successful in the House, we were stymied in the Senate. Elvira had, the previous year, confronted Senator Durbin about his failure to support comprehensive immigration reform in favor of his new, narrower bill for the "DREAM students." Durbin had then refused to renew his private bill on her behalf. Unable to seek out Durbin's assistance, we went to the junior member from Illinois, Senator Barack Obama. In Obama, we had hope. The last time we had met him in the halls of a government building had been in Springfield, Illinois, where he had promised to help Elvira. When he had finally taken the U.S. Senate seat that had been created by Harold Washington for an African American—elected just the previous November—he did so under the Senator Durbin's sponsorship. Obama, however, had persisted in developing closer relationships with the African American Church and the bastion of African American leadership in Chicago. His religious orientation in the Black church reshaped his political approach, distinguishing him from traditional leadership, and broadened his appeal to Evangelicals—especially Latino Evangelicals—who had formerly supported Republicans for religious reasons. His U.S. Senate staff included young African American professionals who had emerged from the political struggle in Chicago, and who had close ties with the veteran organizations of that struggle. His advisors, however, came from a circle of powerful Democratic Party leaders. When we inquired at his office, Senator Obama declined a meeting and turned down the families' request to introduce Rush's bill in the Senate. A staff person told us that he could not jump over the senior Senator.

Returning to Chicago, disappointed at the national level, the families yet continued their struggle. Sin Fronteras sponsored resolutions supporting them in the Chicago City Council, the Cook County Board, and the Illinois State legislature. Dozens of families testified in the hearings that followed, telling their heartrending stories of families threatened with separation. These hearings finally gave a human face to undocumented immigrants, and their stories appeared in the mainstream press. In addition to resolutions supporting their cases, all three levels of Illinois government debated and passed resolutions in support of comprehensive immigration reform, as well as resolutions demanding an immediate moratorium on deportations that separated families. Months of careful organizing and courageous witnesses began to turn public opinion. As public opinion changed, some families began to win their cases; others had their deportations delayed indefinitely. Family unity began to define the immigration issue—at least, in Illinois. The attempts to develop protections from federal immigration law did not spread to other states beyond the municipal limits of fellow sanctuary cities such as New York City, Madison, and San Francisco. In contrast to the successes in Illinois, the right wing of the Republican Party developed its own strategy to pass repressive laws and policies at the state level, culminating in the ultra-repressive Arizona legislation in 2010. It was not until 2011 that the national movement began to dig in and fight the immigration battle at the state level. Sadly, it was too late in states like Arizona and Georgia.

It took courage for the families to testify. Many had never spoken in public. They were forced sometimes to speak in English. They were required to tell their most personal stories in front of powerful men, with bright lights and cameras flashing in their faces. Often, both parents and children interrupted their testimony with tears, and just as often, grown men and women—veteran members of the city council or state legislature or the United States Congress—responded with involuntary tears of their own. It took courage, because there were opponents who spoke out in hatred against them, calling them criminals and much worse. When such opponents talked about these parents and called their children "anchor babies," they insinuated that the parents had had children for no better reason than an excuse to stay in the United States. For a people brought up in a culture that makes one especially sensitive to shame, these attacks were the hardest to endure. It was Elvira who, by her example and her frank and honest talks with the families, helped them to gain the courage they needed.

While these families were testifying at hearings, making the long, hard trips to Washington, D.C., and journeying to the state capital in Springfield, they were still fighting their own individual cases. The Familia Latina Unida attorney, Chris Bergin, had never practiced any other kind of law, and he became an expert. His commitment and creativity won the respect of the judges in immigration court. In the midst of a profession where hundreds of attorneys were ripping off undocumented clients for money, Bergin won delay after delay, and in some cases legalization for the families.

Yet we did not always win, and we made mistakes. The father of one large family was arrested at his home—in front of his children—at 5:00 a.m. He had worked at the same company for twelve years and had become a trusted supervisor. We advised him, out on bond and fighting his case, that he could speak with a reporter from the Chicago Tribune. Unfortunately, the reporter used the name of the man's employer in the story. The next day he was fired, leaving the family destitute. After his deportation, his oldest daughter, separated from her father and watching her life fall apart before her eyes, attempted suicide. When a person made a commitment to go public and to fight for justice, we owed them the same level of commitment in return. Familia Latina Unida never turned its back on any of those who stood up to make the case for all the families and for all of the four million U.S. citizen children. If a father or a mother was deported, as in the above tragic example, we felt a weighty responsibility to help the family out in the meantime, and a responsibility to help the father or mother to return.

A large number of people continued coming into the country without papers, even with increased border enforcement making the crossing much more dangerous. When those who are deported return, they know that they face prison if they are caught, and they know they can never achieve legal status. They come to be with the ones they love, and to support and help raise their children. When someone returns, the whole family comes to church. During common prayer they often stand up and thank God that they are back together. The whole church applauds and embraces them. Hunted criminals outside the church, they are honored here, on Holy Ground, for affirming that what God has joined together, no man should separate.

✿ 10

The Grand Marches

"The witness of the families was the spark;
The locutores were the wind that turned it into a prairie fire."
—Emma Lozano

Every year since 1997, Familia Latina Unida had worked to mobilize marches in Illinois in support of Gutierrez's legislative efforts. Our marches were large, in Chicago terms, usually between 10,000 and 15,000 people. As Latino media became increasingly attracted to Elvira's story and the stories of the families she was organizing, a new dynamic came into play. Not only the news reporters but also the *locutores* (Latino radio hosts) began to get involved. *Locutores* throughout the country were becoming more and more active, broadcasting, for instance, warnings of roadblocks and rumors of raids by Immigration and Customs Enforcement (ICE) agents. The competition among the *locutores* in Chicago, however, was particularly intense. The best-known *locutor* was Rafael Pulido "Pistolero", who dominated the morning show on Univision radio. His competition came from "El Chocolate" on a competing station. While Lozano focused on Pistolero and phoned into his shows three or four times a week, Arellano was similarly working with El Chocolate.

A group styling themselves the "Minutemen" had formed in Arizona in August of 2004, claiming to be patriots. Members of this right-wing paramilitary group patrolled the Mexican-United States border, claiming they were doing the job the federal government was failing to do by looking for "illegals" to turn over to the border patrol. A woman named Rosanna Pulido (no relation to Rafael Pulido) became the spokesperson of the Minutemen in the Midwest. A former lobbyist for the National Rifle Association, she was media-savvy enough to get picked up by major news stations. She threw slanderous statements at the undocumented community; the fact that she was a Latina only angered the community more.

Father Marco Cardenas, a Catholic priest and a frequent guest on Pistolero's radio show, called up the DJ one evening in the spring of 2005 and suggested that they take on the slanderous statements of the Minutemen and Rosanna Pulido. The next morning began with Pistolero calling out the Minutemen on his show and Father Marco joining in to give courage to the people through the Holy Scriptures. Pistolero began to gather a group that included Lozano, Father Marco Cardenas and an immigration lawyer named Rosalba Pena. Several times a week on his show, they discussed legislation, talked about immigration cases, and answered questions from callers. On one of these shows, Father Marco brought up the idea of a mass march for immigration reform. Pistolero seized on it and set the date for July of 2005.

El Chocolate responded by calling for his own march on a separate date. Elvira then held a press conference demanding that the two *locutores* work together. "We must have unity in our community," she said. As a result of her call for joint coordination, we scrapped the existing plans and scheduled a new march to take place in July at the Back of the Yards, an area on Chicago's South Side behind the former stockyards. Both DJs promoted the march every day for a month. Pistolero had strong contacts with his advertisers, from whom he enlisted contributions and support for the march. Familia Latina Unida handled the logistics. Pistolero showed a genius for mobilization and an intimate understanding of his listeners and his community. He had an innate sense for just when and how to push his audience, step-by-step, until they were ready to march.[†]

At this time, Familia Latina Unida took the well-publicized bus trip to Washington, D.C., to tell the stories of the families and their U.S. citizen children, and to meet with Bobby Rush and other members of Congress. The Spanish-language press followed the trip, and they also publicized the march when the buses returned to Chicago to begin the march. By 2005, Spanish-language television and radio, led by Univision, had become one of the most powerful media forces in the United States. Its audience was the fastest growing ethnic population in the nation; its financial base was a Latino-owned business community that depended exclusively on the Spanish-speaking market. The result of this combination of grassroots organizing, media publicity, and financial support was the largest march for immigration reform in any city to that date. Over 100,000 people marched and held a rally to hear a series of speakers. Congressman Gutierrez returned to Chicago to be with the people. His speech brought the crowd to a fever pitch. The Grand Marches had begun.

---

† Appendix A contains a first-person account from Father Marco and Emma Lozano about the origins of this march and how it was organized.

The popular success of the Grand March, called in cooperation with the *locutores*, convinced the new Latino media giants to put the full power of their stations behind the movement for legalization. In Chicago, we had seen this phenomenon with the African American media. During the Harold Washington election, WVON and other black-owned radio stations had become the main organizing focus for the voter registration movement that signed up over 250,000 new voters and propelled Washington into office. Yet despite this support in the business community, Latino political and organizational leaders were distrustful of the *locutores*. Before the march, they had ridiculed Pistolero mercilessly, predicting its failure. After its success, they begged for time on the radio—though they continued to exclude him from the spotlight.

Rafael Pulido, on the other hand, showed both extraordinary skill and extraordinary commitment. He was perhaps the top-rated Spanish-language personality at the time. Himself having emerged from the shadows of society, he began his campaign to bring the community out of the shadows. He had witnessed the murder of his father in the dangerous waters of Mexican politics. Overcoming his fears, he sacrificed a very lucrative career in service to a cause that genuinely moved his heart.

The radio, with its free-talking *locutores* and its river of anonymous callers, was irrepressible. The reach of this popular and democratic vehicle greatly exceeded the organizational capacity of the grassroots movement and would play a significant role, not only in mobilizing on a massive scale, but in directing the powerful voice of the Latino community towards the government. In time, the President's administration would try to restrain the corporate leadership that supported the media markets, but with limited success. Latino media depended on its listeners, and so did the business advertisers. The listeners wanted legalization!

The extraordinary success of the July march led Father Marco to suggest a second march. Pistolero's genius had placed the first march in the heart of the South Side Mexican community, home turf, where people felt safe. Working this time with El Chocolate, Familia Latina Unida decided to mobilize the next march in downtown Chicago. In September, fifteen thousand Latinos marched from Union Park to the plaza of the State of Illinois Building. Latino radio and its *locutores* were developing their skills and their courage. The grand march of July had been much larger, but the bold move to go downtown represented an escalation for an invisible community whose numbers were as yet unknown to the general population.

In November, Emma and I arranged a meeting with Pistolero and Congressman Gutierrez. We wanted to get the main mobilizer together with the main legislator so that they could move strategically. The two joked for a while at the Hollywood Grill on Chicago's North Side and then turned to serious business. Pistolero felt we should move on Washington, D.C., and mobilize a *planton*. Gutierrez countered, formulating a very important goal: "We need to mobilize in each city, where we are strong, and where, with little money, we can turn out really large numbers. Our objective will not be just another march on Washington. This time, we will show the nation the strength, unity and numbers of the Latino community, with or without papers."

Pistolero began to work his network of *locutores* around the nation. Familia Latina Unida began to reach out to its own national contacts. Then in December, the movement experienced a blow: Congressman Sensenbrenner introduced the most repressive anti-immigrant legislation in the history of the country—the Border Protection, Anti-terrorism and Illegal Immigration Control Act. Along with a litany of harsh employment and deportation provisions that would criminalize immigration infractions, the bill sought to mandate the construction of seven hundred miles of double-layered border fencing. Passed by the House in the waning days of 2005, right before the Christmas break. It scarcely made the news. As the infamous bill made its way to the Senate, immigrant groups around the nation began to call for resistance. Lozano traveled to Denver, Colorado, for a meeting with grassroots leaders, mostly from California. At the meeting, Lozano called for mass marches in March in every city, citing our experience in Chicago and the success of the network of *locutores* that Pistolero had been developing. Those present agreed with the strategy and set the date for March 10th.

Having returned to their cities, the organizers each began to move the date back as they encountered the difficulty of managing the necessary logistics. Concerned that the delays could derail momentum, Lozano and Arellano decided to go ahead on March 10th. The driving force behind this mobilization continued to be Pistolero. His involvement brought in Univision and Telemundo television. Arellano and Lozano organized press conferences, the families told their stories, and the nightly news put them at the top of the news hour. The Spanish-language news began to publicize the date, time, and starting point for the march every night. The witness of the families was the spark, and Latino media was the wind that turned it into a prairie fire.

Lozano and Arellano then made a mistake. In their generosity and sincerity, they opened up responsibility for the logistics of the march to the Mexican groups in the city. Soon the established advocacy groups joined in what became an endless series of meetings. Fruitless arguments over small details became the natural result of a battle of small egos. A loose structure formed by the advocacy groups, the Marzo Dies Coalition, attempted to take control of a mobilization they had had no part in forming, and no ability to promote. The coalition's leaders attacked Pistolero as too crude and unsophisticated to lead the mobilization.

In spite of this tempest in a teapot, Lozano and Arellano continued to work with Pistolero to carry out a careful week-by-week plan. They applied for permits and pulled in speakers, including Mayor Daley and, of course, Congressman Gutierrez. At one meeting, the Coalition decided they didn't want any elected officials to speak. At that point, Arellano and Lozano walked out of the meeting. Firmly in control of the logistics for the demonstration, they claimed the first part of the program and gave the back-end to the coalition's lengthy list of little-known speakers.

Eight hundred thousand people gathered in Union Park and walked the route from Union Park to the Federal Building. The city was unprepared for the scale of the demonstration, but the mayor was a speaker. As a result, the police did not divert the march to a "safe area." It filled the downtown streets for blocks around the Federal Building. Speeches by Arellano, Lozano, Mayor Daley and Congressman Gutierrez gave the enormous crowd the feeling that they had finally come out of the shadows and were leading their own struggle. They had become what Pepe Jaques later called "the Mass Leader."

Later that March, inspired by the massive turn out in Chicago, Los Angeles held a march for over a million people. The ideal of Gutierrez for grassroots action on a national scale, articulated in a restaurant in Chicago one afternoon five months earlier, came to fruition. Hundreds of thousands marched in cities all around the nation, revealing that the Pueblo was everywhere, from Raleigh, North Carolina, to Seattle, Washington, to Providence, Rhode Island.

The subsequent large-scale coordinated marches on May 1st were strongly backed by the unions and the established advocacy groups that supported comprehensive immigration reform. Overwhelming numbers of undocumented workers boycotted their jobs for the day to join the marches. Just before the May Day marches, a massive raid had taken place in Pilsen at the IFCO Company, which made pallets for Target stores. Roberto Lopez and Elvira quickly organized the workers who were slated for deportation and began to mount a legal defense. Following the May 1st mobilization, Arellano began a hunger strike in a small *placita* in Pilsen, at Blue Island and 18th Street. Flor Cristomo and other IFCO workers joined her. The hunger strike, which continued for twenty-five days, drew daily media attention and thousands of proponents. The hunger strikers slept under makeshift tents, held prayer meetings, sang songs, and spoke with a steady stream of supporters. Their demand was for an immediate moratorium on all deportations and consequent separation of families. With the legislative defeat in Congress and the Democratic leadership's decision to demobilize the movement, Elvira and Emma were also praying for signs of a resurrection.

Something happened during this hunger strike that still remains in my mind to this day. About fifty people were gathered around the hunger strikers. Elvira was doing an interview in a little tent. As I stood at the edge of the *placita*, I saw an old Polish man in a plain, faded suit pulling a suitcase on wheels behind him. He walked up to me and said in a heavily accented voice, "The Church should teach the people history." I nodded my agreement. Pointing to the hunger strikers he said, "Now I prefer these people. They are closer to God." He made his way to Elvira, and they engaged in a conversation in Spanish for about ten minutes. He then began to walk across the street towards the library. I looked away for a minute, and when I looked back, he had disappeared. One of the men came up to me and whispered, "Don't you know who that was?" I did, or it seemed that I did. The old gentleman looked exactly like the recently deceased Pope. Was it the leader of the Church, returning to bring a message that God was with us, even if his Church was reluctant? Certainly we received the message. It was one of many that helped renew us for the struggle ahead.

That June, Sensenbrenner's bill was defeated in the Senate, and the McCain-Kennedy comprehensive immigration reform bill passed in its stead. Sadly, the Republican-controlled House refused to even consider the Senate's version of the legislation. Instead, House Republicans organized a series of hearings around the country in an attempt to build a movement against immigration reform. These Republicans would soon force McCain, Kennedy's co-sponsor of the Senate bill, to abandon support for reform as he prepared his bid for the Presidency. The attack on undocumented immigrants became

a main political plank in the Republican Party platform. The Democrats likewise withdrew their support, deciding that immigration was a third rail of
politics. As Rahm Emmanuel, a Chicago Congressman who would become
Barack Obama's chief-of-staff, would later express it, immigration reform
would have to wait until the second term of a Democratic President.

After the March 10th mobilization in Chicago, Familia Latina Unida
withdrew from the Marzo Dies Coalition as the Democratic leadership gradually assumed control of it, then dissolved it completely when the House set
aside reform legislation later in the spring. The Democrats, who had bought
their way into control of the marches, now wanted the movement to disassemble. Presuming that they already had the Latino vote secured, they tried
to make the immigration issue go away so that Republicans would not be
able to use it to mobilize their own base.

From the faith of the families to the marches of a grassroots movement,
the hopes of undocumented immigrants across the nation had been raised.
The illusion of an easy victory, however, was dispelled by leaders of the advocacy groups, who, having fought for control, now retreated at the request of
the Democratic leadership. An even greater challenge now emerged. With
all attempts at legislation having failed in Congress, President Bush
announced an immigration enforcement crackdown.

After the retreat of the Democrats and in the face of the growing
Republican opposition, Arellano and Lozano called for another grand
march. The motivating demand of the march would be a moratorium, an
executive action that the President could take to stay all deportations until
legislation could finally be passed. The idea of moratoriums had become
popular in Illinois when Governor Ryan declared a controversial moratorium on the death penalty. In that case, new DNA evidence had revealed so
many men to be falsely convicted that the Governor had said, "The law is
broken; the system is broken. We will declare a moratorium until the
legislature can fix the law."

We had one such case of false conviction that was very close to us.
Alexandro Dominguez had been arrested for rape when he was seventeen
years old. He was convicted, served years in prison, and then was deported.
Sure of his innocence, he re-entered the country illegally and fought to get
DNA testing that would exonerate him. Familia Latina Unida took on his
case and won. Alexandro became a leading member of Familia Latina Unida,
organizing the families in Waukegan, IL. He also kept us involved in the
struggle for the wrongfully convicted and the demand for a moratorium on
the death penalty.

The parallels seemed obvious to us. The immigration system was broken. There should be a moratorium on deportations and the separation of families until Congress could finally agree on how to fix it. When we first raised the demand publicly, we were simply trying to keep families together by any means necessary. The concept of a moratorium started to gain traction. We began to argue that our situation was similar to that of Abraham Lincoln, who had faced a paralyzed Congress and a divided country. The Emancipation Proclamation was, in fact, an executive action. With it, Lincoln had signaled the turning point in the Civil War by declaring all slaves in Confederate territory to be free, thus re-defining the war as one for the liberation of an entire people. We became convinced that the road to a legislative solution ran through the White House and an executive order by the President.

With only token support from the coalition groups, the resulting march in June of 2006, from Union Park to downtown Chicago gathered over 80,000 people. The program of speakers again featured Mayor Daley and, of course, Congressman Luis Gutierrez, calling for the moratorium. United Farmworker legend Delores Huerta had traveled to Chicago to join the march. During the program, she turned to us and said, "This march is different. The May 1st marches became parades. This is a march of determination. This is a movement."

Congressman Gutierrez took the demand for the moratorium to Washington, D.C., where, as Chair of the Immigration Task Force, he convinced the Congressional Hispanic Caucus to send a letter to President Bush demanding the moratorium. Emma and I were asked to come to the Capitol Building to meet with Caucus members and explain our demand for executive action, its legality, and its precedents during the Bush and Reagan administrations. The Caucus adopted the position favoring a moratorium on deportations until the system was fixed—its official position throughout the Bush and Obama Presidencies.

The IFCO workers, caught up in the raid by immigration agents and scheduled for deportation, had been the focus of the hunger strike and the moratorium march. Now, in the fall of 2006, their court date was approaching. Congressman Gutierrez, hopeful for a resolution, took three Chicago-area Congressmen with him to ICE headquarters to meet with the local regional director. Once before he had confronted the regional director after ICE had arrested dozens of mothers at a factory on Mother's Day. That meeting had resulted in a change in policy allowing the mothers to be released on their own recognizance. Even so, that was before the ter-ror attacks in 2001, and the sea change in the country's attitude toward immigrants.

While several hundred supporters picketed outside of ICE headquar-ters, Gutierrez and the three Congressmen found themselves confronting an arrogant and insulting regional director, who essentially suggested that they were ignorant of the law and told them to mind their own business. Insulted, Gutierrez left the office. Protests and pickets leading up to the IFCO court date continued. On the day that the workers came before the judge, hundreds of people crowded the courtroom, both inside and outside. The immigration judge postponed the case for over a year, saying, "Let's give the Congress a chance to change the law. Why should I deport these people when in a few months the law may provide for them to stay?" Prayers had been answered!

Yet by August, there remained little action on immigration reform or on the moratorium. While ICE had honored Gutierrez's private bill on Elvira's behalf from 2004, and its renewal under Bobby Rush's private bill in 2005, they now told us that they would not renew her stay. She would be deported in August of 2006. Elvira had a decision to make. She had devoted four years of her life to organizing on behalf of the families of the undocu-mented, and had played a key role in developing of one of the largest grassroots movements in this nation's history. Through all of this she had remained a caring and loving mother to Saulito, who was now doing well in school. He told his mother, "I want to stay and continue the fight." She began to look at her options.

🔥 11
Sanctuary

Judge for yourself whether it is right in God's sight to obey you rather than God. For we cannot help speaking about what we have seen and heard.

—Acts 4:19-20

I n our church, we discussed the concept of taking sanctuary. Sanctuary was one of the many ways we had found of preventing deportation, as we looked everywhere to defend what were now several hundred families whose cases we had taken on. There had been a well-known sanctuary movement in the 1980s. In that movement, churches had given sanctuary to refugees who had fled without visas from the repressive governments in El Salvador and Nicaragua. Since the U.S. government supported these murderous dictatorships, the refugees had little hope of gaining refuge legally in the United States. For the most part, that sanctuary movement operated like an underground railroad, keeping the refugees safe and moving them from place to place. In spite of the dangers, some of the priests and pastors who had offered their churches for sanctuary had done so publicly. Some of them had even gone to jail. I traveled to New Mexico and Arizona to meet with some of these old faithful veterans.

The situation of our families was different from those who sought refuge in the '80s. They were already public figures. If they were going to hide, it would be better to just get false papers, move to another city, and disappear. Some of them took that option. Elvira, already the most well known undocumented leader in the country, was not going to be able to hide—quietly, unseen, unknown—in one of our churches. Indeed, our purpose was different than those brave pastors and religious leaders, who were part of a non-violent movement of civil disobedience against U.S. policy in Central America. The purpose of Familia Latina Unida, from the beginning, had been to put a human face on the immigration issue, to redefine it as an issue of family unity and opposition to family separation. We sought to empower undocumented immigrants to speak for themselves, and to enable their families to give a clear, powerful, public witness. Sanctuary, for Elvira, would be an act of civil disobedience; the church would simply be her willing accomplice.

I told Elvira that the church would offer her sanctuary. She talked it over with Saulito. She prayed. And she decided. We composed a letter to ICE in which Elvira declared her purpose: "I am in the church. Don't use me as an excuse to break into people's homes and check their papers. I am not hiding. This is an act of civil disobedience for which I am willing to take the consequences." We then called a press conference for August 15, 2006, at Adalberto United Methodist Church, 2716 W. Division St., Chicago, Illinois. We invited some of the church members, so that a supportive group would be present. Elvira carefully prepared her statement, and we reviewed it with our attorney. I made a last minute call to my Bishop, Bishop Hee Soo Jung, to let him know what was going to happen. He was very supportive, and offered his blessings. We had the letter hand-delivered to ICE, and we put out a press release.

On the appointed day, Elvira was ready for the high-pressure press conference. She explained her reasons for going into sanctuary, not to avoid the law, but to protest its injustice. "My son is a U.S. citizen," she declared. "He has the right to grow up in this country, but he cannot stay here alone. I am asking only to stay here and raise my son." She spoke in Spanish, with Emma translating in English: "No matter if I have to go to jail for twenty years. I am going to fight for my rights, my son's rights, and the rights of my people." As she spoke these words, Saulito looked up at her and began to cry. Her voice broke, but she held her head high, and she said in English, "I am not a criminal. I am not a terrorist. I am a mom." †

Elvira held the floor for questions for another fifteen minutes and then retired to the back of the church for a series of one-on-one interviews. The media trucks didn't move after the press conference. Only then did we realize that Elvira would become a national voice, an international voice, for undocumented immigrants and for the mixed-status family. Over the next three months, Elvira's sanctuary appeared in the media over 20,000 times. The networks and major cable stations parked their TV tower trucks in front of the church for almost two months. They were there, watching, twenty-four hours a day—afraid that if they left, they would miss the dramatic imagery of federal agents breaking into the church.

---

† The full text of Elvira's statement can be found in Appendix B.

We had not anticipated the response of the press, much less that of the people. During the first six months in sanctuary, over seven thousand people came and signed in to visit and pray with Elvira. Many were threatened with deportation themselves. Some were already separated from a loved one in their family. They came both to support and to pray for Elvira, and to ask Elvira to pray for them. Elvira, who for so many years had organized Familia Latina Unida to create outer strength for the families, now turned to nurture their inner strength. She and Jacobita Alonso led a rosary every afternoon at five o'clock.

The first Sunday in sanctuary brought a packed church. The August weather was hot, and we had no air conditioning. No one moved, and a crowd of people listened to the service while standing outside the open church door on the sidewalk. Elvira read Scripture, as she would do every Sunday during her year in sanctuary, and delivered her own message.

The Northern Illinois Conference of the United Methodist Church was well represented at the service. Key ministers from a dozen Christian denominations, priests from the Catholic Church, and important Muslim and Jewish leaders also attended. When I rose to deliver the sermon, I felt that it was an opportunity to explore the deeper meaning of Elvira's action. One theological basis for her decision to remain in sanctuary can be found in the Acts of the Apostles. When there is a contradiction between man's law and God's law, Christians—and people of faith generally—are called to bear witness to the fact that they must act in accord with God's law: "But Peter and John replied, 'Judge for yourself whether it is right in God's sight to obey you rather than God. For we cannot help speaking about what we have heard and seen.'" (Acts 4: 19) When the media and others asked us if we were not afraid that ICE agents would break into the church and put us in jail (as they had threatened to do publicly), we responded, "We fear God more than we fear Homeland Security."

The little storefront church became the equivalent of the White House pressroom for the immigration movement. Every victim of a raid, of a traffic stop, of a minor infraction that led to deportation brought their case to the church, and we held a press conference with them. We responded to each new development in the progress of immigration reform legislation. The media, for a change, reported *our* position on the issue of immigration. Elvira broke the ice that had kept the people's side of the immigration story from being heard. Her message was simple and well thought-out. She repeated it over and over, determined to get through the sensationalism of the media and speak directly to the people.

While Elvira and Emma handled the constant stream of Spanish-language interviews, I did the English-language cable programs, sitting with some of the worst racists I have ever encountered. I learned that in dealing with such hateful personalities, the best approach is to speak directly to the listeners, and ignore the questions and comments of the host. The best known of the cable TV commentators who used the anti-immigrant cause to build a following worked for CNN. He made many unsubstantiated attacks on undocumented immigrants, such as saying that they were responsible for bringing leprosy into the United States. Lou Dobbs was in total control of his show. He was rude and insulting and made most of his guests feel like fools. Following the May Day marches, Lozano had been asked to participate in one of his shows. Knowing what to expect, Lozano had prepared herself and had given a fifteen-minute monologue. Dobbs finally ended the segment by saying, essentially, "I give up." Sanctuary gave us a platform to launch national campaigns quickly because of the daily media coverage. Lozano and Arellano called for a boycott of the principal cable company that ran the Lou Dobbs show. Representatives of the cable station came to meet with us at the church after thousands of people had discontinued their service. A few years later, a boycott aimed at Lou Dobbs actually drove him off the air.

Congressman Gutierrez came quickly to visit with Elvira after her announcement, accompanied by press coverage in both the Spanish- and English-language media. Governor Blagojevich and Mayor Daley issued public letters of support within days of her taking sanctuary. The Chicago City Council, the Cook County Board, and the Illinois State legislature passed resolutions supporting her action and demanding her legalization. Three years of hard and consistent organizing—of testifying, protesting peacefully, passing resolutions, and gaining letters of support—paved the way for Chicago and the state of Illinois to stand with a young woman, fighting against the full weight of the federal government, its laws, and its myriads of armed agents—simply to stay with her son.

Why didn't the *Migra* just come in and arrest her? Perhaps a researcher will someday uncover the reason. They came close. Seven nights into sanctuary, they brought fire trucks and immigration vans and parked both in front and in the back of the church. Pistolero was parked in the back of the church with the Univision truck and a group of men. Toribio Barrera was part of the security team. Toribio was fighting his own case against deportation. He had become a hero in Joliet, Illinois, when he singlehandedly saved some thirty children from a burning school bus. The fire department gave him an award and trained him as a volunteer firefighter. He would finally win his case after a five-year struggle, during which delegations of firemen would show up at each court date in full gear to support him. That night, Toribio spotted the fire trucks and, using his newly gained expertise, told Emma, "These trucks are not here for a fire. The ladders are set up wrong." They were planning an assault directed at the second floor of the church, where Elvira and Saulito slept. Emma mobilized dozens of the people who were praying in the church to go to the front and to the back of the building and to begin singing "Dios Mas Grande." In about an hour the fire trucks and the *Migra* left.

Community support for Elvira took many different forms. The Puerto Rican Cultural Center, using the Puerto Rican flag, posted a changing color guard twenty-four hours a day for months. The stream of supporters coming through the church sometimes went late into the night. People gathered on the sidewalk in front of the church, singing, praying and sometimes just chillin', depending on who they were. Supporting Elvira, street gang members could be found on the rooftops of many buildings, calling to report any suspicious vehicle. The little church that provided sanctuary for Elvira had many friends in many places. The church had hosted an Alcoholics Anonymous group that brought in hundreds of ex-cons, some still active in the various competing street gangs. The church had always been open to small businesses, organizations, and families in the community. It had initiated health campaigns with parents at elementary schools, youth programs for high school students, and a program for prisoners returning to the community. All became united in their defense of Elvira. Everything we had done as a church now seemed to have been a preparation to make this sanctuary work.

For whatever reason—the presence of the media trucks, the strong political support from official sources, the faith of the visitors, the fear of a violent neighborhood reaction, the tradition of honoring the sanctity of the church, Elvira's strong appeal in the Latino community, or perhaps through their combination—ICE agents did not come for Elvira. Her sanctuary became a vehicle to spread the truth—that the immigration issue was about families staying together—throughout the Latino community and out into the nation.

The opposition—especially the right wing anti-immigrant groups—was furious, outraged that Elvira could apparently stand off the entire United States government. They began a campaign to discredit her on the internet, on radio talk shows, and on cable television. Several times they tried to bring their campaign to the door of the church. A group calling themselves "Mothers against Illegal Immigration" held a press conference, denouncing Elvira, and denouncing the government for not going into the church to arrest her. The media gave them big play. They were vicious. They accused Elvira of child abuse and of subjecting her son to a false imprisonment. They branded her an immoral woman who had had a child out of wedlock and who had kept Saulito from his father. Strangely, their criticism echoed similar criticism we had received from liberal immigrant rights advocacy groups. For them, Elvira was not the right symbol for the movement.

Our response was simple: we did not choose Elvira; God did. And we reminded the activists that God had once chosen another single mother, to bring about the birth of Jesus. In truth, Elvira's integrity, her faith, and her sincerity were so strong–her actions so honest, and so motivated by love for her son and for her people—that no amount of sniping could silence her voice. Still, the criticisms stung her. Sometimes she doubted that she had made the right decision, that she was doing the right thing for her son. Saul's maturity, even at his young age, proved to her that she was on the right track. "He is my little man," she said. He was strong, and growing in courage every day.

Opposition groups seized on this deep love of a mother for her son and twisted it into a portrayal of ugly self-interest. Claiming that Elvira had given birth to Saul simply to stay in the United States, and that she was now using him as a tool to stay on U.S. soil, became a common line of attack. In August of 2006, four loud-mouthed women from Mothers Against Illegal Immigration showed up in front of the church, having publicized their intentions to hold a fourteen-hour vigil to shine a light on Saul's "child abuse" at the hands of Elvira. They found about two hundred people in a prayer circle, alternately singing and praying, preventing the hateful women from getting inside. Their publicly stated purpose was to come to Chicago to report Elvira to DCFS, simultaneously notify the police and ICE of the purported child abuse, and have Saul removed to protective custody. Yet on their arrival at the church, the women showed their true colors. They were not there to protect Saulito. Unashamedly, they screamed in hate that the future of this country belonged to their children, not to the Latino children of the illegals. They represented a force, a real current in the nation, that was engaged in a battle to keep the United States a white majority nation. The media coverage of this little confrontation with four hysterical women was intense for several days. The battle for the hearts and minds of the people of the United States was going on before our eyes. We were beginning to win this battle as the opposition exposed its own hate and racism.

Another battle to build support for Elvira, which unfolded at the same time, was more complicated. Several months before Elvira went into sanctuary, our church had been invited to participate in a commemoration of Rosa Parks at the South Side church where Congressman Bobby Rush served as pastor. Our choir sang as part of the ceremony. When Congressman Rush spoke, he compared Elvira to Rosa Parks and called the struggle for legalization of the undocumented the Civil Rights struggle of the present day. When Elvira spoke, she said that she admired Rosa Parks and saw her as a role model to be emulated. Mary Mitchell, a Sun-Times columnist who had studied the life of Rosa Parks in great detail, also spoke at the ceremony.

Just a week before the incident with the four women at the church, Mitchell wrote a page two column in the Chicago Sun-Times entitled, "Blacks Know Rosa Parks and You, Arellano, Are No Rosa Parks." It was both a vicious personal attack on Elvira and an attack on the struggle of the undocumented. The article accused Elvira and the entire grassroots movement of trying to ride on the backs of the African American struggle for justice. The column hit a nerve in the black community. Competition for jobs, as well as tension over the control of neighborhoods and community institutions, was always just below the surface. Republicans, trying to win support in the Black voting bloc, encouraged and even disseminated this message of competition with Latinos, exploiting the notion that Latinos were riding on the backs of the Civil Rights movement. Minister Louis Farrakhan's strong support for the Latino movement for legalization, and his clear analysis of the basis for unity kept some voices—and importantly, some Black radio personalities—from following the Republican line and attacking Elvira Arellano. Congressman Rush's support, along with increasingly strong statements from members of the Congressional Black Caucus, also helped to maintain the unity of African Americans and Latinos.

The second stage of this battle to divide the Black and Latino coalition came from the Minutemen. A Minuteman front organization put out a press release saying they were coming to capture Elvira and turn her over to the government. They attempted to recruit a particular black minister and his church to join them. That minister had a relationship with one of the larger street organizations that dominated the area where his church was located. We called a joint press conference with Familia Latina Unida, several African American activists, and the public affairs spokesperson for that particular street organization. The press conference condemned the police frame-ups of black men and called for indictment of a police captain who was well known for torturing suspects into confessions. The minister got the message; the busloads of his parishioners that he had promised never materialized. The presence of a lone African American in strange clothes and dreadlocks, just arrived from California, accompanied by a square-looking white man in a suit giving him directions, revealed the truth about the source of the effort to divide the Black and Latino community.

A third attack that threatened such division was the claim that the undocumented were doing the jobs that no one else wanted to do. It was an insult to thousands of black men and women who were unemployed and wanted to find work. The complexity of the economic system involving undocumented labor would gradually emerge a few years later. The economists would conclude that undocumented immigrants were a major force in the economic recovery and actually created jobs in the economy. Their complex analysis, however, was difficult to communicate through the mass media. The Obama administration even prepared to take it as a public position, but then retreated. Not until 2011 would a U.S. Senator hold hearings to bring out the empirical evidence that showed the economic contribution of undocumented immigrants as a force for job creation.

During the year that Elvira lived in sanctuary, a new coalition of African American religious leaders emerged as the central voice for the clergy in the Black community. Pastor Marshall Hatch, Bishop Trotter, Reverend Albert Tyson, and Reverend Jeannette Wilson headed it. The coalition welcomed me into their meetings, and I worked closely with them. They asked me to speak at one of their meetings about the undocumented, the issue of family unity, and the theological and political issues that were involved in this struggle. I was unaware of the meetings that they had had after Mitchell's article appeared and after the episode of the Minutemen's African American visit to our church. I was called by Jeannette Wilson and told that a delegation of ministers wanted to visit Elvira, to pray with her, and to hold a press conference.

More important than the media attention that accompanied the visit was its spiritual force. Those prayers stayed with all of us, including Elvira. She had been shaken by Mary Mitchell's column. Elvira admired, even held in awe, the struggle of African Americans for justice. She truly looked at Rosa Parks as someone to be admired and emulated. The personal attack confused her. The magnificent and moving prayers of forty leading African American clergy in Chicago healed her self-doubts and let us know that the movement for Justice and Dignity was a continuum in which Latinos and Elvira were now taking their place. When the pastors broke out spontaneously in song, singing, "We are Standing on Holy Ground," we felt we were close to God, with the breastplate of righteousness protecting us. By 2008 the healing would be complete. Congressman John Lewis, a legend of the Civil Rights movement of the sixties, would speak in Atlanta to a meeting of several thousand and anoint Elvira as the Rosa Parks of the Civil Rights movement of today.

While Elvira was a leader of Familia Latina Unida and Sin Fronteras, Lozano was convinced that Elvira belonged to the movement as a whole. Even when Latino organizations disagreed with her position in support of Gutierrez's bill in Congress, their leadership continued to support Elvira's actions. The entire national leadership of the Labor Council for Latin American Advancement (LACLA) came to spend time with her and held a press conference in her support, as did leaders from Mexican American Legal Defense and Educational Fund (MALDEF) and the League of United Latin American Citizens (LULAC) and almost every other major Latino civil rights organization. Led by SEIU's Tom Balanof, representatives of seven labor unions with significant Latino membership came to the church and made their support known at a major press conference. In the battle for the hearts and minds of the American people, Elvira's sanctuary was, for a time, a national platform for various forces to make their best case for legalization. The message of the grassroots movement had become the demand to protect the unity and love of families. Elvira and Saul were its human face.

The truth of her action and of our decision to provide sanctuary, however, goes deeper: "The question is not whether we will win this battle, but what kind of people we will be when we win." Providing sanctuary to Elvira should not be viewed simply as a matter of Christians welcoming a stranger in need. Rather, sanctuary should be seen as a sign of support for her devotion to the movement that she embodied, as a sacrifice required by the magnitude of the transformation that the movement hoped to achieve. Her vision of a people who cannot be separated by borders, who can unite with all other peoples in this country, and who can change this nation into a fountain of justice for the world, is the dream of which Dr. King also spoke. It can only become a reality when we become new men and women, or, as Gandhi said, when we become the change we are looking for.

At the heart of this vision is the reality of two women: Elvira Arellano and Emma Lozano. One was born just north of the border, the other south of the border. Their unity could overcome the theft of Texas and New Mexico and Arizona and California from Mexico by military force. Their unity could overcome the European colonization of Mexican culture and give birth to a renewal of their faith. Their unity could fulfill the high purpose of the appearance of the Virgin of Guadalupe to Juan Diego in 1531.

To fulfill this prophetic role, we had begun in Deadville with the strategy: "Raise your family; organize your community." That is what Elvira was doing in sanctuary: performing an effective act of resistance by raising her son in the country in which he had a right and a destiny to be raised. Because of Elvira, our strategy had changed to "Unity in the Latino Community," and now its connection to the Civil Rights movement had become clear. In truth, the Spirit of Peace and Brotherhood has been active in world history for over a century. Working to free the least and most downtrodden of God's people— the Untouchables of the Indian caste system; African-Americans and South Africans suffering under Jim Crow and apartheid; and, in the present day, the "illegal aliens" in the United States—this spirit has renewed its activity, now under the name of the Lady of Guadalupe.

The response of the Methodists to the controversy that surrounded one of its small Latino churches was spirited. The Methodist bishops continued in their support, especially Bishop Jung of the Northern Illinois Conference. Bishop Carcaño, who led the Methodist National Commission on immigration, made two visits to pray with Elvira. Methodist pastors from throughout the nation called and sent messages, and many came to visit us.

There was also Methodist opposition. A few congregations objected to our defiance of the law and our harboring a fugitive. Strangely, the opposition came together around the issue of the presence of the Virgin of Guadalupe in our sanctuary. We survived, and the General Conference affirmed our sanctuary effort. My Bishop, Bishop Hee Soo Jung, was a constant source of encouragement and strength to me. Once when I was a little discouraged by the response of the church, he admonished me: "Pastor, look at the dialogue you have begun in the church, in all the churches!"

There is a long tradition of priests standing with the Latino and immigrant population of their churches. St. Pius Church in Pilsen, pastored by Father Chuck Dahm, had been a beacon of both hope and comfort for Mexican immigrants for decades. A group called the Priests for Justice for Immigrants became active there and took part in the marches and in pushing for comprehensive immigration reform. Perhaps the most influential pastor in the community-at-large was Father Marco Cardenas. Father Marco had joined the media in calling for the first Latino grand march (described in Chapter 10), and he was part of the group that began the discussion about opening Catholic churches as sanctuaries.

The Catholic priests gathered and presented a letter to the Cardinal, recommending that they begin opening their churches as sanctuaries. The Cardinal referred the letter to the lawyers for the archdiocese, declining to even meet with them. The answer was an unequivocal "No." The priests reluctantly retreated. While they had failed in their effort to declare sanctuaries, the incident raised the debate over the leadership and role of the church in the struggle for legalization. The church as a whole took a stronger stand, and the priests continued to find ways in which they could advance the struggle. Several of the priests came regularly to pray with us, and stood with us at various public events.

On the other hand, priests like Father Marco—who had publicly stood with the undocumented and had given them scriptural and prayer support when they spoke out—faced inevitable bureaucratic torture behind the closed doors of the Catholic hierarchy. Publicly in support of comprehensive immigration reform, the Catholic Church was, in actuality, most deeply concerned with maintaining the wealth and political influence that came by means of its white congregants and their hefty contributions. Those who actually practiced what the church preached were isolated and punished, and some were driven from the life of service they had lead for decades. At critical times in the struggle, the support of the Catholic Church evaporated.

When we received a phone call about an effort to start the New Sanctuary Movement among the churches, we were excited and ready to share our experiences. We made the trip to Washington, D.C., where we sat in a meeting for about four hours as lawyers and professional organizers made reports and handed out mountains of paper with instructions about how to establish sanctuary—what to do and what not to do so that the church would be protected. When we finally were given a chance to present our own experiences, we found only a few true believers ready to go into action. While several churches did actually take people into sanctuary over the next few years, the New Sanctuary Movement in most places became another not-for-profit vehicle to get funding for its so-called organizers. It never really exerted much of a force. In a few places in the country, committed pastors continued to bear witness under the name of sanctuary, but the extraordinary witness of the undocumented themselves was rarely duplicated.

The Latino Evangelicals were a different and refreshing story. The poorest of the three major national associations of Latino Evangelicals—the National Coalition of Latino Clergy and Christian Leaders, or CONLAMIC—was also the first to take a strong position. They came to Washington, D.C., time and time again to lobby their Congressmen and Senators, and held prayer meetings in the Capitol. The sound of Spanish prayers—*el clamor*—with one hundred to two hundred pastors raising their voices together in complementing praise, would ring out in the hallways and into the offices of the congressmen. They would stop and listen as the powerful faith of the Evangelicals shook the humdrum whispers of Congress. The social involvement of Latino Evangelicals went many years back to the formation of A.M.E.N. and to a few prophetic pastors, such as Rev. Pedro Windsor, who were close allies of Familia Latina Unida.

Rev. Miguel Rivera, a fearless and faith-driven pastor who tirelessly built the association across the nation, led CONLAMIC. While some of the churches were old, large, and established, the majority were new and grew up from the grassroots. A dedicated pastor would begin with house meetings, gradually raise the money for a building, and through perseverance, find himself blessed with a congregation of five hundred to two thousand people in a few years. Many of the members of these congregations were undocumented immigrants, yet it was the congregants themselves who owned these churches, so there were no bishops or bureaucracies or lawyers to tell them what they could or could not do. We found strong support for Elvira's sanctuary among the Evangelicals, and soon found that they were taking people into sanctuary—quietly, without fanfare, as a matter of their faith.

The support of the Evangelicals was not confined to Latinos. An Indian pastor came to visit Elvira and two weeks later brought a well-known Evangelical preacher who had become famous because he had brought the cause of the undocumented to House Republican leader Denny Hastert. A former supporter of Hastert and the Republicans, this Evangelist was now stepping away from the party. He was being punished for his move. His funding had dried up, and he had lost the airplane he used to fly around the country.

Martin Luther King III arranged for us to accompany the Evangelist and himself to Washington, D.C., with a busload of the families. We held a press conference in front of the House of Representatives, from which we marched to the White House, led by Saulito.

The Republicans had courted the Latino Evangelicals, focusing on their opposition to both abortion and gay marriage, and on their support of prayer in the schools. This trip to Washington showed the cracks that were forming in that attempted alliance. Led first by CONLAMIC and then by the more mainline Latino Evangelical associations, this growing force in the Latino community not only shifted its support away from the Republicans, but moved many white Evangelicals to do so as well. The faith and the numbers of the undocumented in these Evangelical and Pentecostal congregations created an undeniable momentum that shook the Evangelical establishment. For them, as for Elvira, the issue was the fight for family unity and against the injustice of racism.

The work we had done earlier around the "immigrant freedom zone" in Illinois gave us a certain security. Chicago and Cook County had become sanctuaries, meaning that local law enforcement was prohibited from making attempts to identify undocumented persons in order to turn them over to ICE agents for deportation. Resolutions creating these policies in Chicago and Cook County referenced Elvira's sanctuary and articulated support for her action of civil disobedience.

Across the nation, however, the right wing of the Republican Party was moving aggressively to enlist local law enforcement and vigilante forces in efforts to purge undocumented immigrants from local communities. Conservative Republicans in the state houses began to pass severe and repressive legislation. Despite the sanctuary laws on the books, Illinois was not immune from such attacks. One instance occurred in nearby Waukegan, Illinois.

Familia Latina Unida had first become involved in Waukegan through the case of Alexandro Dominguez. Through Alexandro we came to know other families fighting deportations, some of whom joined us on the trips to Washington, D.C., and Springfield, Illinois, to testify. One of these was the family of little Charlie Martinez. Charlie was hospitalized with terminal cancer and was fighting for his life. His mother stayed with him in the hospital twenty-four hours a day. His father worked every day to support his family, and every night made the long drive to the hospital in Milwaukee to be with his son. Martinez—as all the undocumented did—drove with one eye on the rearview mirror, knowing that a traffic stop could mean deportation and separation from his wife and son. When we heard that Charlie needed a bone marrow transplant, we opened up the church to screen potential donors, under the leadership of Julia Contreras. Charlie's father came forward publicly, appearing with me on a Fox TV show to send out his plea for a bone marrow donor for his son. When asked if he was afraid that his public appearance would get him arrested and deported, Martinez said with determination that his only concern was for the life of his son: Could they not understand this? We found a donor for Charlie, but sadly the treatment was not successful, and Charlie died. The Martinez family stayed in the struggle with us. One year later, they were blessed with the birth of another son.

Alexandro and the Martinez family faced a very racist local government in Waukegan. Waukegan police routinely set up roadblocks to stop cars and ask for driver's licenses. If an undocumented driver did not have a license, their car was impounded, and they were charged five or six hundred dollars to retrieve it. Waukegan's budget swelled with millions of dollars from this extortion of undocumented immigrants. It was not a surprise, therefore, when the Waukegan City Council moved to adopt the 287(g) Program, a government program that utilized local police to identify undocumented persons and turn them over to federal authorities for deportation. This was the program that later empowered Arizona's infamous Sheriff Arpaio to mount an assault on the Latino community in Tucson.

Familia Latina Unida was invited to help local organizations in the fight against Waukegan's participation in the 287(g) Program. Familia Latina Unida had a long relationship with the principal Catholic church in Waukegan. A Mexican priest, who was a member of Familia Latina Unida, had been assigned to this church and had developed an impressive "liberation theology" grassroots movement there. Then, quietly, he had been reassigned and sent back to Mexico. The presiding priest who replaced him took a moderate position in the crisis in Waukegan over the 287(g) Program. He sponsored a reconciliation meeting with the mayor and offered to support the 287(g) Program, as long as guarantees could be made that would protect people from racial profiling. Emma Lozano and her allies from LACLA in Waukegan broke up the meeting. Afterwards, they set up headquarters in a Baptist Latino church and organized a boycott. Stores that would sign a letter to the mayor opposing the 287(g) Program were given a sign telling people to support their business. Those stores that lacked a sign were boycotted. The boycott went on for months; it won the support of three-fourths of the businesses and the great majority of the Latino community. Although the city council did not withdraw their application to become a 287(g) town, the controversy scared off the federal government from participating. In the years to come, boycotts would become a crucial tactic in the struggle against those forces that wanted towns and states to take over the role of immigration enforcement.

As the weeks in sanctuary turned into months, the media focus on whether ICE would come into the church to arrest Elvira turned into a fascination with the life that she and her son led in sanctuary. Reporters and photographers spent days and nights in the second floor apartment above the church, following her around, taking pictures, as she went about her life. CNN's Soledad O'Brien and her camera crew spent two days with Elvira. Another crew came to photograph her when she was selected as one of Time Magazine's "20 Most Important People of the Year." Geraldo Rivera turned the church into a TV studio in a moving piece he did for Fox News. They were all sympathetic to Elvira, and they were putting a new face on the immigration issue. It was clear to the flocking media that she was just an ordinary, but extremely dedicated, mother, helping Saulito with his school work, getting him ready for school, talking about his problems in school, and having fun with him. The closeness of this mother-son relationship gave the lie to those who tried to discredit her motives. First and foremost, Elvira had taken her stand because of her son.

The media coverage lasted much longer than we had expected, but eventually it began to die down. After the grand marches, the failure to pass the comprehensive immigration bill had demoralized much of the movement around the country. We discussed with Saul what role he wanted to play. He was quite fierce: "I want to fight for my mother!" Saul wrote a letter to President Bush and practiced reading it aloud in English. We called a press conference to release the letter, but Saul announced that he was going to D.C. to deliver the letter personally.

This trip was the first of many that he would take with Emma Lozano to talk about his mother's case and the issue of family separation. In Washington, D.C., Saul and Emma met with Congressman Gutierrez, who escorted them to the White House gate, where a guard took the letter. The President himself never responded, though the White House sent a form letter back to the church. The media, however, told the story to the nation—the story of a little boy who wanted to stay in his country but who also wanted and needed his mother to stay with him. Emma and Saul then made a long trip

to Miami to appear on Univision's major show, *Sabado Gigante*. They began
to travel to different cities to campaign for Elvira's freedom.

Finally, they took their speaking tour to Mexico City. There they met
Pepe Jaques Medina, who had returned to Mexico and had been elected to
represent the Mexican Diaspora in the United States as a *Diputado* in the
Mexican lower House. It was only natural that Medina would bring Elvira's
case before the Mexican nation. He arranged for Saul to address both
Houses of the Mexican Congress. Resolutions were passed calling on President Bush to give Elvira the right to stay in the United States with Saul. As
the Mexican and international media surrounded Saul with hundreds of
cameras and reporters, Saul recited his message clearly: "Stop the deportations and separation of families. Let my mother stay with me in the United
States."

Having given a longer than usual press conference, Saul, age 6, walked
away, only to be surrounded again by reporters. "That's enough," he said.
"You missed it. It's over!" Like his mother, Saul had no desire to talk to the
press or to be famous. He just wanted to get on with his life with his mother.
Later in the year, Medina would bring a multi-party delegation of *Diputados*
from Mexico to support Elvira and stand beside her in the church.

Elvira only gave permission for Saul to travel if his trips did not interfere
with his schooling and his homework. She was determined that she would
give him the life and education he had a right to, even though they were in
sanctuary with the world watching. Her greatest concern was the stress the
situation was putting on him. She went to great lengths to make his life as
normal and as safe as possible. Every morning, church members took him
to school and the staff brought him inside, avoiding members of the press
and potential enemies alike. Elvira and Emma had been asked to help a
group of parents at this school two years before, when the school had experienced the largest drop in test scores in the city. A long battle resulted in the
choice of a new principal and a whole new group of teachers. With Elvira's
help, the school had rebounded. The new staff was eager to take care of
Saulito, to support him and protect him.

A security detail from our organization gave him round-the-clock protection, but tried to stay out of his life except when he wanted to play games
with them. The fear that federal agents would break in with guns was real in
Saul's mind. He had seen men with guns come to arrest his mother in front
of him. The threats of right wing militia to come and liberate Elvira and turn
her over to ICE were known to Saul, but he never wavered in his determi-

nation to stay with his mother and continue to fight. Saul was not alone. He won the hearts of millions of people because of his courage, but also because an increasing number of Latinos had known someone like him—a little boy or girl whose mother or father was taken away by men with guns.

Immigration was a central issue in the November 2006 mid-term elections. The Democrats campaigned in the Latino community in support of comprehensive immigration reform. Republicans used Elvira as a symbol to campaign against. Elvira urged Latinos to register and then to come out and vote. On election night, a crowd gathered at the church. Spanish-language television recorded Elvira's celebration as the results came in. The Democrats gained control of the House of Representatives.

An analysis of the election showed that the electorate had rejected many of the most strident anti-immigrant Congressmen. We felt that a human face had finally been put on the immigration issue, the face of honest hard-working families with U.S. citizen children and of a mother who loved her son. It seemed that the electorate had determined they did not want to see millions of people rounded up like animals and deported in front of the tears of their children. There were sobering signs, however. The Democratic Party leadership was less than enthusiastic about passing immigration reform. Rahm Emanuel, whose district adjoined that of Congressman Gutierrez, was chair of the Democratic Congressional Campaign Committee. He had fielded a slate of candidates who were more conservative and too often ducked the immigration issue entirely. In the months to come, Gutierrez and Emanuel would battle in public and in private meetings both in Washington, D.C., and in their home districts in Chicago. Still, that night, all we saw was victory—a long and hard-fought victory!

Gutierrez worked tirelessly in Congress to develop a bi-partisan bill that would bring legalization for the maximum number of the undocumented. President Bush and his advisor, Karl Rove, had also seen the results of the mid-term election. Gutierrez reported to us that he had been invited to the White House to meet with Rove. The Latino Evangelicals remained active in the Republican Party, but they were threatening to leave the party, which would result in the loss of a substantial share of the Latino vote that Bush had won in his run for the Presidency in 2004. The shift of the Latino Evangelicals was also having a decided influence on the ranks of the white Evangelicals, a key element of the Republican Party's base. The family unity argument that Elvira and Emma had worked so hard to project in the media was now appealing to the family values constituency of the religious right.

As the Christmas season approached, there was a spirit of hope in our church, and hundreds of people came through every week to pray. Sadly, many of these were people who had already felt the pain of deportation in their families. Our original core of families still lived day by day. Elvira and I initiated a thirty-day fast that coincided with Ramadan. For several evenings the church was filled with brothers and sisters from the Muslim community, including some of their most important leaders. As Ramadan went on, people from other Christian faiths joined in the evening prayers and in the ensuing discussions. After Ramadan, we celebrated the novena for the Virgin of Guadalupe. Again the church was filled every night with prayers and song.

Gutierrez was working tirelessly, negotiating with the House, with the Bush administration, and with Senator Ted Kennedy in the Senate, who, in turn, was negotiating with Senator McCain. The result in the House of Representatives was a bill that came to be called the STRIVE Act. It followed what had become the general formula for comprehensive immigration reform: strong border enforcement, verification of legal status by employers, and employer sanctions for those businesses that did not follow the law. In return, undocumented workers and their families would be able to register, get a work permit, and begin a long process to become citizens. They would have to learn English, pay taxes, and go through an extensive background check. After five years they would become legal permanent residents. After five additional years they could become citizens. Restrictions might result from the background check. Those workers who had previous deportations, who had returned illegally, or who had criminal convictions would not be able to become citizens. Essentially, the STRIVE Act was similar to the bill that had passed the Senate in 2005 only to be ignored by the Republican-controlled House.

The opposition forces that geared up to fight the bill reflected, as much as anything, the emergence of what would later be called the Tea Party. They were challenging the established Republican leadership represented by Senator McCain and President Bush. As had happened before, the eleven million undocumented immigrants and their families, with their U.S. citizen children, simply became pawns in a political battle. Republican leaders were concerned with garnering the Latino vote, as were the Democrats. No one seemed to care about the inherent injustice in the system of undocumented labor that had developed to such enormous proportions in both the United States and Europe. Instead, hate stirred to a fever pitch in the Republican base, while the Democrats seemed ambivalent. On the one hand, Senator

Kennedy was intensely serious about passing the compromise, while on the other, Congressman Rahm Emanuel was focused on holding together the center-of-the-road coalition that had won back the House and was now his power base.

The immigration rights movement itself was deeply divided. The District of Columbia coalitions were committed to supporting the bill. They had received significant funds for their operations, and their continued funding depended on delivering legislation no matter what was in it. Some of their local affiliates, however, opposed the bill. The Latino-led coalitions, represented most prominently by the Congreso Latino, were adamantly opposed to the bill. Partly this represented their competition with the beltway-based coalitions for funding, and partly it represented their ideological position. They attacked Gutierrez ruthlessly as though he had authored the bill, rather than having struggled to negotiate the best compromise possible. The more left-leaning members of the Latino coalitions opposed the bill because it focused on violations of immigration law and ignored the issues of labor and trade that, they rightly felt, were at the root of this unjust economic system. They opposed the strict enforcement provisions, which they feared would establish a virtual police state in the Latino community.

The long struggle to bring organized labor to the table in support of legalization also ran into difficulties. The trade unions, especially those in construction, feared the influx of Latino workers since they had virtually excluded Latinos and African Americans from their tightly controlled unions. The service unions persisted in trying to get legal status for their members, but their increasing preoccupation with obtaining power inside the Democratic Party put them at the beck-and-call of the Democratic leadership.

The Catholic Church welcomed excuses to criticize the bill. It gave them the freedom to focus on other priorities, especially the issues of abortion and gay marriage. The Latino Evangelicals remained firm in supporting the bill, as did President George Bush.

Gutierrez acted as the point man in negotiating the bill. I recall him correcting himself one time in conversation and saying, "I guess it's *our* bill; we have to stand behind it." The bill was a long way from the two bills he had introduced almost a decade ago. Those had provided a path to legalization based on work, and did not contain the onerous enforcement provisions. He argued that the STRIVE Act was the best bill he could achieve given the political make-up of the House, the Senate, and the White House. In the end, his fundamental concern was to legalize as many people as possible. He correctly predicted that the enforcement provisions would be made into law even if the bill did not pass, because political support for them existed in both the Republican and Democratic parties. At least if the compromise passed, millions would be legalized. Emma and Elvira believed the choice was clear. There were really only two alternatives: the road to comprehensive immigration reform, or the road to deportation.

Elvira studied the bill carefully and talked with people holding different positions. Philosophically, she stood with those who viewed the immigration issue as a problem of labor and trade. She recalled that her original position had been, "I did not come to the United States for the American Dream; I came because of what the American nightmare did to my *pueblo*." The memories of her own journey and its causes were still fresh in her mind. She had seen her father's land turn unproductive because of NAFTA. She had seen the company she had worked for dissolve in the banking take-over during the Mexican fiscal crisis. She had worked in the dangerous *maquiladoras* and faced the reality that she could not eke out a living—much less provide support for her family. Elvira also recalled her struggle to find work and survive without papers in the United States. And then there was Saulito, and all the Saulitos of all the families that had been formed in this country. The struggle that had begun to secure her right to stay with Saulito in a country in which he had a legal right, but she did not, had become a struggle for millions of people in her same situation. Yet her own situation was more difficult now because Elvira, convicted of using a false identity and of re-entry after deportation, would not have been able to legally become a citizen under the bill.

Elvira discussed, and she prayed. She then made her decision. She called a press conference and came out strongly in support of Gutierrez and the STRIVE Act. "No matter that it does not include me. It is the best we can get for the most people at this time." She also warned the community that the enforcement provisions in this bill would be put into effect anyway, even if no one received a path to legalization. Elvira emerged as a leader, rising above her own personal situation.

In the end, the Democrats were responsible for the failure of the bill to pass the Senate. President Bush made a dramatic national address outlining why he supported comprehensive immigration reform. If the bill had passed, even with strong Democratic support, the Republican Party would have gotten credit in the Latino community. The Democratic leadership wanted to avoid this situation. They quietly let organized labor and the Catholic Church off the hook. They played up the opposition from the left, even though such groups represented insignificant numbers in the Latino community. They began to suggest that smaller alternatives, such as the DREAM Act and AgJOBS bill (which provided legalization for farmworkers only), could be passed without all the enforcement provisions, although they knew this was politically impossible.

The withdrawal of support from the Catholic bishops and significant sectors of the AFL-CIO caused the bill to fail in the Senate. After its failure brought about massive disappointment in the base, the Democrats regrouped for one more attempt, but that also was doomed. To be fair, Ted Kennedy and Harry Reid gave it their all to pass the bill. Rahm Emmanuel, and those forces aligned with him who felt it was better politically for the Democrats if the bill failed, made sure President Bush's initiative went down.

The failure of the STRIVE Act signaled an increase in deportations. President Bush played to his base in preparation for the next election. Senator McCain, getting ready for his own Presidential bid and the looming conservative primary battles, dropped his support for his own bill. Comprehensive immigration reform was dead in the water. All that was left was the road to deportation.

For Elvira, in sanctuary, the situation was dire and personal. The families facing deportation came to pray with her—their hopes dashed, their families in tears. After five long years of struggle, the last year of which she had spent in the cauldron of sanctuary, Elvira needed to make a decision. She was clear-headed in her analysis and, as always, relied on her own experience of being an undocumented person with a U.S. citizen son. What did she really want? What did the undocumented really want? With all the politics swirling around this issue, no one was asking this question. The undocumented remained politically invisible.

Elvira formulated her position carefully, reflecting on the thoughts and feelings she had had when she first was arrested and first decided to struggle against her deportation: "If it was up to me, I would go back to my own country. This nation has done nothing but abuse me and disrespect me. On the other hand, Saul is a U.S. citizen and has the right to live, go to school, work here, and be treated as an equal. He has never known another country. But he cannot stay here alone because he is too little. He needs his mother. Therefore I will fight to stay here until he is twenty-one years old. Then if this nation still wants me to leave, I will go back to my *pueblo*, and Saul can make up his own mind about what he wants to do."

We formulated her position and discussed it with Gutierrez. We were basically saying, "Give undocumented immigrants with U.S. citizen children temporary papers that will allow them to stay, even with no road to citizenship attached." We raised the money to take two busloads of families to Washington, D.C., once again. Our objective was to deliver this new position to Speaker Nancy Pelosi. Elvira made her statement to the press, and the Latino media accompanied the families on the journey to the nation's capital.

Inside the Capitol, the families trudged through the hallways of the House and Senate, stopping in to speak to a Congressman or a Senator, one after another, and to make their position known. Congressmen had to look into the eyes of the children and listen to the appeals of mothers. Speaker Pelosi gave us hope, saying, "I think the members will go for this proposal." Followed by a large group of reporters and cameramen, the delegation made a point of giving notice to all three branches of government. After meetings in the Congressional offices, the group went to the Supreme Court building. There they joined another group of families from Miami, Florida.

The reason for these two groups coming together needs some explanation. When Elvira first entered sanctuary, lawyers came to the church and asked permission to file a lawsuit on Saul's behalf, asserting that it was his right as a U.S. citizen child not to be deprived of his mother. While the suit was denied, it brought forth important new arguments. We decided not to pursue an appeal, but instead joined with the Miami group to file a class-action suit on behalf of all U.S. citizen children with undocumented parents. The lawsuit provided a good organizing tool to recruit families from states all over the nation to take part in the struggle. The suit made its way up through the judicial system. While we were in Washington, D.C., the Supreme Court was in the process of deciding whether to consider the case.

After the Congress and the Supreme Court, the combined group of families, with several hundred children, marched long blocks to the White House while the sun began to set. As before, when Congressman Gutierrez had escorted Saulito to the White House with his letter to the President, the delegation received only a cold denial of entry from the armed guard at the southwest gate.

By mid-summer of 2007, it became clear that the Democratic leadership had had its fill of the immigration issue. The Party could wrap the failure of comprehensive immigration reform around the necks of the Republicans in the next election, while moderate Democrats in difficult districts could actually oppose reform in order to win their elections. It was decision time, as the first anniversary of sanctuary approached. Elvira and I went on another fast to seek direction.

🔥 12

Leaving Sanctuary

Therefore have I set my face like flint, and I know I will not be put to shame. He who vindicates me is near. Who then will bring charges against me? Let us face each other! Who is my accuser? Let him confront me! It is the sovereign Lord who helps me...

—Isaiah 50:8

E lvira announced at a press conference that we would begin a hunger strike on August 1st. Its purpose was to determine the future direction she would take, as the anniversary of her resistance in sanctuary approached. For a year, Elvira had been the principal spokesperson for the national movement, and the little church had become a weekly media forum for groups and cases of injustice. She recognized that this focus could not continue, given the fickle nature of media sensations in the United States. "We have been here for a year and nothing has happened. We need to make a move."

Her alternatives were few. She could simply disappear, a choice she could have made the year before. Eleven million people lived successfully with false papers and names, working and raising their children in the shadows. Elvira had decided against this before, and she decided against it again. The Mexican consul had come to the church and offered to negotiate her voluntary deportation to Mexico, thus avoiding the threat of imprisonment made by Homeland Security. Elvira listened carefully to their proposal. At a time when the movement was facing terrible discouragement, when we needed a gesture of advance, this possibility seemed more like a retreat.

We were besieged by media trying to find out what her decision would be, as well as strange individuals we took to be spies for Homeland Security. Ten days into the fast she made her decision. She would leave sanctuary and find a way to travel to Washington, D.C., to face arrest in front of the U.S. Congress. She would attempt to use her plight to revitalize the movement as the next election cycle approached.

I called up Jacqueline Jackson, the celebrated wife of Rev. Jesse Jackson, and asked her to go to lunch with me. Jackie had joined Congressman

Gutierrez in the non-violent direct action in Vieques, Puerto Rico, and had led dozens of national campaigns. While she kept a home and an office at Operation PUSH in Chicago, Jackie's activities were centered in Washington, D.C. I reviewed the events of the last year with her, and we spent time talking about the issue of family unity. Jackie agreed to help. We set a press conference for August fifteenth, the first anniversary of sanctuary. Jackie spent hours with Elvira, guiding her with the experience of a movement veteran and the wisdom and love of a mother through the statement the younger woman would make. The bond Elvira felt with this great woman gave her confidence. Flanked by Jacqueline Jackson and about one hundred religious and community leaders, Elvira gave a statement in both English and Spanish.†

We held the press conference at five o'clock in the afternoon. Elvira did three hours of interviews, and then we dismissed the media from the church. After prayers, about two hundred people filled the church and the apartments upstairs, cooking, eating, praying, singing, and talking. Outside in the darkness of the backyard, about seventy-five Aztec dancers began their circle to the pounding of drums. Sometime in the evening Elvira slipped out to join the dancers, exhausted herself, and laid aside her fears until the first light of dawn crept upon the city.

Jacqueline offered to help organize a delegation to accompany Elvira to Washington, D.C., for the September twelfth confrontation, but problems arose. Our sources told us that ICE agents were waiting to grab Elvira as soon as she stepped out of the church to send her to prison. We felt confident that we had convinced the world, and ICE, that Elvira would stay in the church until shortly before September twelfth, when she would try to make the trip to Congress. That gave us some time and some cover.

We made the decision to slip out of sanctuary and travel secretly to Los Angeles, which had the largest concentration of Mexicans in the United States. Our plan had been to appear in Los Angeles and then again slip away, making similar appearances at churches in northern California, Texas, New York and Maryland before going to the mobilization in Washington, D.C., on September twelfth. The problem we faced was avoiding ICE agents on the planned journey.

We equipped two vans and parked them about twenty blocks away from the church. Elvira finished her disguise for the trip, and we were ready

---

† The full text of Elvira's announcement can be found in Appendix C.

to leave the church during rush hour. I went upstairs to bring her out and found Saulito crying. He was afraid for his mother. For one year he had seen her behind a blockade, surrounded by media and under threat of ICE agents and occasional hostile demonstrators. Yet the church itself had been safe for all that time. Their life together had gone well. Now he feared she would be arrested and taken away from him. Saulito had traveled to a dozen cities and to Mexico to represent his mother and their struggle. "Let me go. I will fight for us," he had said. Elvira and her son spent some time in private discussion and then emerged, both ready for the trip.

We had had several discussions about how to handle the media on the trip. A Chicago Tribune photographer had grown very close to Elvira and had stayed in the church with her on and off for months taking photographs. The photographs had appeared in a special edition of the Sunday Tribune magazine section, which had included a powerful and comprehensive article by Don Terry. In addition, a reporter from *Hoy*—the Spanish-language daily published by the Chicago Tribune—had also been a consistent visitor to the church, and we felt she could be trusted with our plans. Both the reporter and the photographer wanted to accompany us on the trip. Unfortunately, the photographer sought permission from his editor to make the journey. As a result, the Tribune bosses made a decision to publish an article saying that Elvira was leaving sanctuary to go to California. We quickly told the Tribune and *Hoy* reporters that our plans had changed and that we instead were going to wait and go directly to Washington, D.C., as planned. Then we left for California.

To avoid detection, we took a roundabout route that brought us into the mountains of Colorado. We stopped by the roadside and checked in on our throwaway phones. (Our regular cell phones had been disconnected.) We were told from home that the Chicago Tribune had put out another story on the internet saying that Elvira had left sanctuary and was traveling by car to California. Our present location was in the district of Congressman Tom Tancredo, one of the most virulent anti-immigrant politicians in Congress. His district was also home to large groups of militia, some of whom had sworn to take Elvira by force. We considered redirecting our course, or even turning back. We prayed together by the side of the road, and Elvira decided we should continue on as planned. I could feel the tension as we drove on in silence.

About an hour later we were listening to a compact disc by Rosalba Peña as the road took us higher and higher up into the mountains of

Colorado, until we drove just above the clouds. The sun turned orange and then red in the sky and began to sink into the blue-green majesty of the mountains. The van in which I rode with Elvira and Saul became filled with Peña's song.

> When I see these mountains,
> When I see these trees,
> I want to sing
> Oh lord,
> You are marvelous
> Yes lord,
> You are marvelous
> When I look at all the land,
> When I see your people, my God, I want to cry,
> Oh my lord
> Where is your love? Yes my lord,
> Where is your love?

A last penetrating flash of the red sun burst miraculously in answer, and behind it a rainbow appeared. Suddenly I heard a cry come from Elvira's breast, as if all fear had left her, as though God had answered the singer's question in her heart and she was without fear, confident that she was in God's hands. We travelled on through the long night and into the next day until we reached Los Angeles.

Emma flew ahead of us to meet with Father Richard at the Catholic church known as "La Placita," Our Lady Queen of Angels Church. Emma asked Father Richard for sanctuary in his church for Elvira and told him she would arrive in a few hours. It so happened that this thoroughly dedicated priest had been left alone and in charge of the church. No one else needed to be consulted. Marta Solar Sanchez—the genius and experienced wife of Jose Pepe Jaques, "the Father of the immigration movement"—joined Emma. Together, Marta and Emma had brought Saulito before the Mexican Congress when Elvira was in sanctuary, and they had prepared the resolution of support, which the Congress had passed. They made arrangements for our arrival and for a change of cars once we delivered Elvira to her California sanctuary.

Word of Elvira's arrival spread quickly. Several thousand marched for legalization and came to a rally at which Emma spoke. She invited people to come to the church to hear Elvira. The next day, Elvira held a press conference, at which she reaffirmed her call for an end to the separation of families and repeated her intention to travel to Washington, D.C.: "If they are going to tear me from the arms of my U.S. citizen son, let them do it in front of the men and women in Congress who have so failed our U.S. citizen children."

Our plan had been to have Elvira appear and speak during the morning mass and then to have her disappear into the crowd when the mass ended. We would go from there to a subsequent appearance at a large church in Sacramento on Monday evening. After the press conference on Saturday, however, representatives of the New Sanctuary Coalition asked to meet with us. They requested that Elvira make appearances at three other sanctuary churches in Los Angeles. Although this was a serious deviation from our plan, Elvira, moved by the men and women who had taken sanctuary in those churches, agreed to help.

Our experience with the New Sanctuary movement had not been particularly positive. We believed they had used sanctuary as a fundraising tool in an effort to bring support to their churches, and had given only token support to the undocumented. Moreover, those people in sanctuary were hidden, while church leaders and coalition staff spoke for them. Even so, the testimony of the families—who were following Elvira's example in taking sanctuary—and the sincerity of the priests and clergy, combined with the wonderful faith of the crowds at each of the churches where Elvira spoke, moved all of us. In song and prayer and Scripture, in each of the churches, we experienced a people who stood firmly united, saying, "Yes, My Lord!"

We returned safely to Father Richard's church for an afternoon press conference on August nineteenth. Unfortunately, in its effort to mobilize people, the coalition had released Elvira's route to the media, and thereby to ICE agents. Strange-looking individuals appeared in the church plaza; one demanded entrance into the living quarters, provoking a quarrel. We quickly attempted to get Elvira and Saulito out of the church in a different car, hoping to take her to where the vans were waiting. About ten minutes away from the church, we noticed a white van following us. Within minutes, seven other vans converged on our car, and we found ourselves surrounded by twenty or thirty ICE agents wielding automatic weapons.

The ICE agents demanded that Elvira get out of the car. Saulito began to cry and threw his arms around her. One of the agents grabbed Elvira's arm to pull her out, but she put her hand in his face and told him, "Wait. I am going to talk to my son." Startled by her calm authority, the ICE agent stepped back. Elvira talked quietly to Saulito who, for the second time, was seeing armed men take his mother from him. She reassured him and asked him to be brave, then collected her things and stepped out of the car. She was handcuffed and taken to one of the white vans. We heard one of the ICE agents exclaim jubilantly, "We got her!" When the van drove off, the rest of the agents walked backwards still pointing their weapons at us, got into their vehicles and sped away. This was, of course, a high profile arrest. Yet the coldness of the ICE agents—leaving a child behind with no provisions—is to this day repeated over and over again.

We regrouped at the church and spent the next forty-eight hours contacting the press, lawyers, and elected officials; then we gathered in prayer before the detention center, in an effort to protect and comfort Elvira. Sleepless for long hours, I don't remember many details from those days of waiting. Later, viewing the television coverage, I saw myself separated from the crowd, on my knees, praying. Suddenly I remembered that moment, praying by a fence, with my back to the cold, concrete detention center. I saw the rainbow again in a waking vision, and in the rainbow, an angel carrying Elvira. The angel spoke to me quietly, inside my mind: "She is in Mexico, Pastor. All of Mexico is now her sanctuary." We need not have worried. She was, in fact, not in that detention center, but on the road to the border and freedom. In a tribute to the support Elvira had garnered, Homeland Security made the decision not to charge her, as they had consistently threatened to do. Instead, they acted on a previous order of deportation, and within forty hours escorted her across the border, where she was received by Mexican government officials and given a hero's welcome by the community.

Several days later we re-established contact with Elvira in Tijuana. We brought Saulito across the border, where he was emotionally reunited with his mother for a few hours. Elvira was already actively engaged in a hectic schedule of meetings with organizers and media. She and Saulito decided that he should continue on with Emma and finish the trip through the cities where we had set up rallies before arriving in Washington, D.C., on September 12th. She received criticism for not keeping Saulito with her, but Saul was a little man, and determined to continue the struggle. It was decided that we would return Saulito to Elvira after she was settled back in her hometown in Michoacán.

I recall that when we were driving back across the border there were about twenty or so lines of cars, each with fifty or sixty cars slowly going through the crossing. The border between Mexico and the United States is one of the busiest borders in the world. The deep connections between these two countries, both economic and familial, cannot be severed by a misguided and bigoted desire to rid the United States of brown-skinned people. I had my clerical collar on and rode in a van full of people. The border guard did not even ask for my identification, much less those of others in the van. It occurred to me that we could have brought Elvira directly back into the United States at that time.

Saulito's fear and emotional distress at the second loss of his mother to the U.S. government turned into anger and determination. He was ready to travel and to speak his piece wherever there were people ready to hear. He was much in demand, but we had little money for travel. Waiting at an airport, ready to start our trip, I received a call from Martin Sheen, the actor, who made a second contribution to our cause—enough for us to proceed with the full plan. We never did find out how he got my cell phone number or who put him in touch with us.

Before completing the journey to Washington, D.C., Saulito, Emma, and I traveled to eighteen cities in twenty-three days. In each city there were press conferences, meetings with local activists, radio and TV interviews, and a rally or a large meeting, usually in a church. The national network of activists who had responded to Elvira's call was made up, first and foremost, of families who faced the same situation as she—the threat of the separation of their families. They, in turn, took her cause, their cause, to their churches and communities. The response to little Saulito was emotional and overwhelming. In their eyes, he was their own son, a little David who faced Goliath. He was the living embodiment of the issue Elvira had brought to the consciousness of the nation: a U.S. citizen son who had lived all of his life in this country, now facing deportation with his mother, or a life spent separated from the most important person in his life.

In Saulito's mind, he was still campaigning for his mother to be able to stay with him in the United States. During the trip we got reports of efforts in Mexico to have Elvira appointed as a diplomat to the U.S. by the Mexican President, which would have given her the right to return. Elvira did, in fact, go to meet with Felipe Calderón, who had succeeded Vicente Fox. Eventually, Saulito saw and talked with hundreds of children like himself. As his mother had done, Saul began to fight not just for himself, but for all of the people in his situation.

In New York City, over forty Latino elected officials turned out for the press conference that we held in the city council chambers. In most of the cities—from Providence, Rhode Island to Houston, Texas, from Detroit, Michigan to Sacramento, California—it was the churches that opened their doors to us. Elvira's sanctuary and arrest had challenged and opened the hearts of the community of the faithful. The issue of the undocumented was not only a political and economic issue: it was a moral issue, a challenge to people of faith concerning their commitment to their belief in family values.

With the plan to travel to Washington, D.C., Elvira had intended to put the cause of the families directly and visibly before the Congress, which had cast it aside. On September 12th, families and activists from thirty states gathered in the House office building. Congressman Gutierrez and several members of the Congressional Hispanic Caucus listened to their testimonies and engaged in a frank and honest discussion. The caucus had supported the most recent comprehensive immigration reform bill, in the form of the STRIVE Act, only to be criticized and battered by Latino leaders who considered it too strict on enforcement. The failure of the bill had unleashed a demoralizing wave of deportations. Caucus members now asked for the trust of the community to return to the battle—and they received it.

Elvira had left sanctuary, risking twenty years in prison, to try to make the journey to Washington, D.C. She had hoped to rekindle the grassroots movement for legalization of the undocumented, and to force at least some members of the Congress to represent their cause. In the years to come, the Congressional Hispanic Caucus, sometimes led and sometimes prodded by Representative Luis Gutierrez, would keep the battle alive against the separation of families. Neither the Republican Party nor the Democratic leadership would be able to marginalize twelve million immigrants; rather, they would find strength and power in their unity with the fastest growing ethnic population in the United States: the Latino community. Elvira did accomplish that part of her mission. More importantly, Elvira affirmed the humanity of the immigrant families, which formed here in this land of immigrant families. They need not be ashamed. They need not be silent.

The Statue of Liberty is known to the nation as a symbol of freedom and, in many ways, a monument to immigrants—a beacon and an invitation to them. She was sited to face the ships that had to pass by her as they entered New York harbor. The famous words engraved on the pedestal of the Statue—which housed the American Museum of Immigration in the '70s and '80s—remain true to this day.

> *Give me your tired, your poor,*
> *Your huddled masses yearning to breathe free,*
> *The wretched refuse of your teeming shore.*
> *Send these, the homeless, tempest-tost to me.*

The Statue of Liberty represents a Greek goddess, Libertas, who was seen as the embodiment and personification of America—as the spirit of America—for well over a century. She was known by many names, but was most frequently called Columbia. This name—with the Latin root *columba*, or dove—was the one that the country's Founding generation used; indeed, the nascent plan for a capital for the country sealed the name of the nation's spirit to that of her greatest general and first president: Washington, in the District of Columbia. The planners and architects of the Capitol—beginning with Thomas Jefferson—envisioned this great building as her home, referring to it as the Temple of Liberty. Until Congress named "The Star-Spangled Banner" the official national anthem in 1931, America's national hymn was "Hail, Columbia!"

Poetry, paintings, sculpture, and music in honor of Columbia were commonplace throughout the early history of the United States. These works of art reveal a long tradition of Columbia herself as an immigrant to America. A cotton handkerchief from 1784 shows Washington leading Independence by the hand to introduce her to America, who sits beneath a palm tree in the form of an Indian princess. A fresco painted in one of the House chambers by Constantin Brumidi in 1856 shows Columbia and the Indian Princess standing together in honor over a shield depicting Washington. The great bronze statue placed atop the Capitol dome in 1863 shows Columbia—here called "Freedom"—wearing the feathered headdress of the Princess. In 1871, the poet Walt Whitman wrote a poem called "The Song of the Exposition"—later used to help commemorate America's centennial on July 4, 1876—in which he described a parallel to the many migrations of people who have arrived in this land, but taking place in a realm of spiritual beings. He envisioned Columbia, the spirit of America, greeting Calliope, the Greek muse of epic poetry, as an immigrant to these shores who had arrived at last after a path that took her through many nations over long eras of time. So today should she greet the Virgin of Guadalupe, the Indian princess, as Elvira's gesture in the year of the "freedom rides" suggests. Marta Sanchez Soler's brilliant work of art helps to unwrap this mystery further, hinting at what the Founding Fathers of this great nation knew to be true:

that Columbia, the name of the territory where our capital resides and the name that we hailed in our original national anthem, is two-fold. She is a spirit of Liberty and Freedom and a spirit of Peace and Brotherhood, a Greek goddess and an Indian princess, and the two are one.[†]

[†] See the last two pages of the photographs section, immediately following Part Two, for images of Columbia and Marta Sanchez Soler's sculpture.

13
Elvira in Mexico

R odolfo Lozano had advocated for an organization on both sides of the border, "Sin Fronteras." Rudy had been a member of CASA and his fellow members, Pepe Jaques Medina, and his life partner, Marta Sanchez Solar, built support for Elvira in Mexico while she was in sanctuary. When Elvira was deported from the United States and banned from returning for twenty years, they made a place for her in the movement in Mexico. Her deportation not only failed to stop the grassroots movement that she had so inspired, it gave it new life. The movement of Familia Latina Unida even spread into Mexico and Latin America.

Representing Familia Latina Unida, Elvira led demonstration after demonstration in Mexico in solidarity with the movement in the United States. Her weekly column appeared in New York's largest Spanish-language daily and was circulated over the internet to thousands of activists and grass-roots leaders. Familia Latina Unida existed in the new spirit of the people. It was a source of spiritual renewal in the face of a culture of materialism and individualism that was destroying so many families. Her son, Saulito, stayed with us in Chicago every summer and led the two children's marches on the White House. He was still able to draw wide media attention for his clearly spoken message, even in the American media. Elvira, working with Pepe Jaques Medina and Marta Sanchez Solar, organized meetings to bring Mexican activists in the immigration struggle in the United States to Mexico. She helped them to join with Mexican organizations and legislators to force the Mexican government to put pressure on the U.S. government. When I saw Elvira in Mexico, strangely, she repeated the words I had heard the angel say: "Welcome to my country, Pastor. All of Mexico is my sanctuary."

Elvira joined with Pepe Jaques and Marta to launch a massive, effective grassroots movement to defend the rights of migrants from Central America as they moved north to the United States border, enduring an unbelievable number of murders, rapes, and robberies at the hands of both the cartels and the Mexican government. The multi-national exploitation of Latin America forced millions of men and women to leave their homes to find work elsewhere. This exploitation is perhaps the most important challenge of our time. The issue of the millions of undocumented immigrants in the U.S. will never be resolved until the root cause of such displacement is addressed, and a change in the present U.S. policy towards Latin America is adopted.

Elvira and Pepe Jaques have said that the issue of the undocumented is part of an international struggle, which exists in Europe as well as in the United States. The truth about how Euro-American capitalism depends for its profitability on the exploitation and oppression of millions of people, who are marginalized as migrants, must be acknowledged. All talk about movements of democracy is moot, while this basic economic injustice remains hidden. Elvira said at the very beginning of her resistance in 2002, "I did not come to the United States for the American Dream, but because of what the American nightmare did to my country." The grassroots movement in Mexico can help the United States confront the truth about the immigration issue.

After her deportation to Mexico, Elvira made a decision to return to her family home in Maravatío. Many urged her to find a base in Mexico City where the action is. But with her brother, she restored the little house in Maravatío in which she had been raised, which is next to the houses of her parents and her sister. Saulito would come to know the generations of his family. Elvira, like many of the undocumented in the United States, had been separated from her father for over a decade. Their reunion brought relief from a longstanding pain. Each morning she would be awakened by the roosters crowing and the chorus of barking dogs wandering through the dirt streets of her neighborhood. Elvira would continue to take responsibility for her aging parents, a responsibility that had impelled her to undertake the long journey north in the first place. Trips to Europe and throughout Latin America to tell her story would continue. The struggle to help Central American migrants would take her on dangerous caravans to Chiapas, throughout Mexico, and often back to the seat of the national government in Mexico City. But she would return always to her family. Elvira's decision to make her home in Maravatío not only allowed Saulito to get to know his family, it provided for his security. When she traveled to Europe and throughout Latin America to tell her story, she was assured that he was surrounded by those who would protect, love and guide him.

Saulito, however, remained determined to participate in the movement that was etched on his heart. On several occasions, Saulito stowed away on the buses Elvira had arranged for protestors to travel from Maravatío to

Mexico City. Like tens of thousands of other young people, he would never forget the sight of armed men taking away his mother. Many of these thousands will someday return to the United States with these memories, and with full legal rights as citizens.

Even in the security of her family, however, there was the threat of danger. In 2010, Elvira faced several threats of Saul being kidnapped in attempts to extort money. Mexico had become a dangerous and violent place. What Elvira could see clearly was that the violence had its roots in United States policy. What she could also see clearly was that the migrants, traveling back from the United States, as well as the migrants traveling up from Central America and through Mexico on their way to the United States, suffered the most from this explosion of violence. Elvira bravely helped to organize caravans, to protect the migrants, and to expose the plight that they faced. More than once, she found herself surrounded by men with guns and barraged by death threats. Even as she pressured the Mexican government to demand protection for the undocumented in the United States, Elvira worked to expose the root of this violence.

PART TWO
BARACK'S CHALLENGE

❦ 14

Preparing for
President Obama

O ur first Sunday back in the Adalberto United Methodist Church after Elvira was arrested was emotional. Our theme that Sunday was resurrection. The twelve-member team that had brought Elvira to California spent time telling the church about the journey: the miracle in the mountains that gave us confidence; the powerful meetings in Los Angeles; and the military-style capture that tore Elvira from Saulito's arms. Several of the young men on the trip felt they had let Elvira down. In truth, there had been some tactical mistakes and some confusion in the flurry of activity in Los Angeles. We had known—and we knew that Elvira had known—that her effort to confront her accusers would end in deportation. Still, it hurt. Elvira's immediate immersion in the movement in Mexico lifted our spirits. She was defiant, and plunged immediately into the plight of the migrants on the border. Her rise in Mexico was a kind of resurrection. She was a heroine—celebrated in the Mexican Congress, entertained by the President, and constantly in the Mexican media. Elvira continued to inspire us. We emerged from the church that Sunday ready to continue the struggle.

New momentum came quickly. With Elvira deported, Flor Crisostomo stepped forward to help to lead the next phase of the struggle. Flor had emerged as a leader in the fight to stave off the deportation of the IFCO workers, and she had worked closely with Elvira from the time of the hunger strike in Pilsen. The fight for the IFCO workers had played a significant role in building the grassroots movement by inspiring the demand for a morato-rium on deportations. As Elvira's time of decision had approached, so had Flor's. Facing a final order of deportation, Flor had decided to follow Elvira into sanctuary.

We decided our next step should be to protest the actions of Con-gressman Rahm Emanuel. Congressman Emanuel's public statement that "we will not deal with immigration reform until the second term of a Dem-ocratic President" revealed his true intentions. He had clearly engineered the scuttling of comprehensive immigration reform by the Democratic lead-ership. Flor led a sit-in outside, and sometimes inside, Representative Emanuel's Congressional office that lasted three weeks. We were putting the Democrats on notice.

We began to mount a campaign to focus attention on the economic realities that lay behind the massive migration of Mexicans into the United States. Flor kicked off the campaign with a press conference on a cold day in front of the Board of Trade in Chicago. To date, the role of the North Amer-ican Free Trade Agreement (NAFTA) in the destabilization of the Mexican economy has never really surfaced in the Congressional debates. The imple-mentation of NAFTA in 1994 was a crucial element in creating the system of undocumented labor. The historical effects of this legislation were essential for understanding that the families faced with separation were not respon-sible for their plight. Chicago's Bill Daley—Mayor Richard Daley's brother and Obama's future chief-of-staff—had led the fight to pass NAFTA in Con-gress. Chicago labor unions had fought hard against it, along with Congressman Gutierrez and three African American Congressman. This political battle was an example of how the division within the Democratic Party has deep and far-reaching consequences for the neighborhoods of Chicago.

NAFTA resulted in two economic events that drove millions of Mexi-cans north, where a flush American economy was eager to hire them. First, U.S. banks called in the Mexican debt and forced a devaluation of the Mex-ican currency, which put millions out of work and made life increasingly difficult. Elvira lost her job as one of the first victims of this financial collapse. The terms of NAFTA forbid the Mexican government from interfering with U.S. banks and financial institutions that were active in Mexico; as a result, American banks virtually took over the Mexican financial system.

The second economic disaster resulted from the fact that NAFTA elim-inated tariffs on corn, rice, and other agricultural products sold by U.S.

agribusiness in Mexico. These multi-national giants dumped corn and rice into Mexico at prices that were less than the cost of production. Mexican small farmers could not compete, and as many as six million people were put out of work. Elvira 's grandfather gave up his efforts to produce corn on the small plot of collectively owned land he had been farming and took to selling odds-and-ends at a small store in Marot Via. Some—again like Elvira—had made their way to the *maquiladoras* zones on the border. American factories moved across the border into this zone to capture cheap labor. They paid less than a living wage and subjected the women to incredible dangers. Many of these women disappeared or were found dead.

Flor had experienced similar hardships and had left her children with her mother in Mexico. Emma and I and Elvira went to visit Flor's children while she was in sanctuary. We saw with our own eyes the devastation NAFTA had left in its wake. In the past, farmers had taken their crops to the highway and sold them to buyers. As part of the massive economic reconstruction of the agricultural trade in Mexico, a new highway had been built which by-passed Flor's town. The results were visible. Over two-thirds of the houses were vacant. Weeds covered the fields, where for generations the *pueblo* had planted and harvested corn for survival and for sale. Those who remained lived off of checks sent back home by family members gone north to the United States to work.

When Flor entered sanctuary, our hope was that we could bring public attention to the economic realities that had driven her to the north. In fact, her story got extensive coverage, but mostly in the Spanish-language media. The English-language media that had been captivated by Elvira quickly turned away from Flor. Her children were already in Mexico. The harsh reality that parents such as Flor faced did not move the English-speaking media. Flor could not even travel back to see her children, for fear that she would not be able to return to work in the United States and thus lose her means to send the money that her mother and children survived on. Flor stayed in sanctuary at Adalberto United Methodist Church and told her story to hundreds of groups and journalists who came with an open mind, trying to understand the immigration issue. Finally, she disappeared into the sea of undocumented migrant workers, still active in the struggle.

In all of this, we learned a hard lesson about United States history. The argument we had made for the right of U.S. citizen children to have their parents with them—the argument for family unity—had been effective in winning broad support. On the other hand, the dominant media was not

willing to point the finger at U.S. economic policies—and NAFTA in particular—as the real villain in the immigration crisis. The fact that U.S.
policies drove Flor and Elvira from their communities to the north, where
their cheap labor was welcomed, should have shown that those who shoul-
dered the blame for creating the scourge of undocumented labor were really
its victims. The media—and, sadly, white America—were not willing to
accept the fact that the great prosperity of the United States had come from
the suffering of Latin America. For this nation to pass a just economic
reform, its people must understand how NAFTA and other free trade deals
have helped create the system of undocumented labor.

For the most part, Familia Latina Unida just did its work. We followed
the cases of the families where they led us—no matter where they led us—
with a commitment to keep these families together by any means necessary.
That same determination had led to the introduction of several immigrant
legalization bills in Congress; to the use of private bills to delay individual
deportations; to the marches against Congressman Sensenbrenner's bill and
the marches for comprehensive immigration reform; to the demand for the
moratorium; and, finally, to sanctuary. At each stage of the struggle, Lozano
and Arellano had reached out to build coalitions. Sometimes, as during the
big marches, the coalitions had turned against them as selfish egotistical
desires and the competition for funding became dominant.

At the same time, Latino civil rights organizations and national coalitions of immigrant rights service organizations had been doing their thing,
or, as they called it, "building capacity." As far as we could tell, this meant
garnering grants from foundations both big and small. What they lacked was
any popular national leadership. The ever-growing millions of Latino citizens
and legal permanent residents—as much as the millions of undocumented
immigrants—lacked leadership they could look up to and trust. Elvira Arellano was the only nationally known undocumented leader, and she had been
deported. Congressman Luis Gutierrez had grown into his leadership role
through consistent advocacy for the undocumented, but he was an elected
official, and lacked a national organization.

After the eighteen-city tour with Saulito and the September 12th meeting in Washington, D.C., Lozano convened a series of conference calls with
grassroots leaders around the country. She organized a conference in Washington between this rag-tag national coalition, calling themselves the
National Alliance of Latino Leaders, and the members of the Congressional
Hispanic Caucus. The meeting was an attempt to repair frayed relationships,

since many caucus members—including Luis Gutierrez—had been under attack by local organizations.

Lozano reasoned that the Congressional Hispanic Caucus was the only real instrument of power that the families had to negotiate for them. She wanted to begin to build pressure inside the Democratic Party, especially if there were to be a new Democratic administration. Overall the meeting was successful, and restored relationships. Members of the Caucus were convinced that the community would support them if they renewed their effort to pass a bill legalizing the undocumented. The meeting was helpful to Gutierrez, who served as chairman of the immigration task force of the caucus. The caucus members no longer feared being castigated by organizations if they passed a compromise bill, or being attacked by the community if they were unable to pass anything. One member of the caucus pleaded with the alliance, "Please trust us, and we will commit ourselves to work for you." One dissenting voice came from an activist in Phoenix, Arizona. Salvador Reza asked that the caucus focus on the terrible repressive movement growing in support of Sheriff Arpaio. The caucus was reluctant to focus on a local situation and decided to continue with their efforts to pass new federal legislation. As we would all soon learn, the repression in Arizona would not go away.

A second effort to bring together leadership and an organization for the undocumented came from Mexico. It was the initiative of Jose Pepe Jaques Medina, who served as a *Diputado* representing those Mexican citizens who lived in the United States. Medina skillfully brought together representatives of all the parties to host the convening of a *Parliamiento de los migrantes* in the chamber of deputies in Mexico City. Pepe Jaques began the parliament of over one thousand Mexican leaders with an address to the assembly by Elvira. She seemed to be stronger and more confident than we had ever seen her. She was back in her own country, and had the support of at least some elements of the government, as well as that of the Mexican people. She condemned the government of the United States for its treatment of migrants and condemned the Mexican government for its failure to defend and protect Mexicans in the United States. She ended her speech by announcing that she was starting another hunger strike. A representative of the ruling party—a National Action Party (PAN) member—rose to criticize her and was booed out of the chamber.

Three days of hotly debated resolutions and organizational proposals followed. Members of the PAN and the Institutional Revolutionary Party

(PRI) from the United States focused on demands on the Mexican government to provide more financial assistance to their parties. A structure was established and meetings were to be called over the next several years. Resolutions were passed. Yet no real leadership organization emerged that could overcome the political divisions in Mexico.

While Familia Latina Unida worked to re-enliven the movement, the nation's eyes turned toward the 2008 Presidential election and the emerging contest between Hillary Clinton and Barack Obama to become the Democratic Party's nominee. The Clintons had established strong ties with Latino leadership during Bill Clinton's two terms in office. Thus most of the nation's Latino elected officials lined up behind Clinton. Senator Clinton, in turn, took a strong position in favor of comprehensive immigration reform. While both the Chicago political establishment and its principal African American opposition leaders were behind Obama, a Clinton connection in Chicago did exist. Alderman Danny Solis, who represented the Pilsen community in the 25th ward, Chicago's oldest Mexican community, was organizing for Hillary. Solis's sister was Clinton's campaign manager. In an effort to build Latino unity in the immigration struggle, Lozano had renewed her relationship with Alderman Solis, based on his early history with her brother, Rudy. Solis was sincerely committed to legalization and had been helpful in getting Mayor Daley to take one of the strongest pro-immigrant positions of any big city mayor during the Bush administration. Solis asked Lozano to become part of an Illinois committee to support Hillary Clinton. After a discussion with Elvira, Emma agreed.

As a Senator, Barack Obama had been a reluctant supporter of comprehensive immigration reform. The Senator's chief-of-staff, who had been part of Harold Washington's administration, had called me at one point to set up lines of communication with the Latino community. I set up a meeting with a small group of leaders, but he failed to show. The relationship between the Senator and the Latino community grew worse when he supported a bill that poured millions of dollars into building a wall along the border without any concessions for the undocumented already in the country. Facing outrage from the Latino community and the Spanish-language media, Senator Obama had turned to Gutierrez for help. A meeting with some seventy-five Latino leaders was then called at the Instituto Progresso Latino center, where Senator Obama asked Gutierrez to sit next to him and guide him through the meeting. Faced with open hostility, the Senator had apologized for his vote and suggested that he was only trying to forge relationships with the Republicans so that together they could pass comprehensive immigration reform. The Congressman had argued that the community should give him a chance, and the meeting had ended with a cool truce. Gutierrez went on to become the first Latino Congressman to endorse Barack Obama for President.

When the debates started during the Democratic primaries, Senators Clinton and Obama began to vie for the Latino vote. Hillary began by bringing out her campaign manager, Patti Solis Doyle, the first Latina to lead a Presidential campaign. Obama countered by pointing to his endorsement by Congressman Gutierrez. Clinton became stronger and stronger in the debates. She committed herself to a moratorium on deportations that separated families, until Congress could pass comprehensive immigration reform. Obama came back with a similar, but more vaguely worded, commitment. Each debate showed an increasingly pro-Latino Clinton, and an Obama trying to keep up, attempting to match her commitment to legalizing immigrants. Clinton went even further and committed to a renegotiation of NAFTA, citing the devastating effect the free trade agreement had had on Mexican farmers as well as on American industrial workers. Obama again followed suit in a desperate attempt to improve his dismal showing among Latinos in the primaries. Clinton was sweeping the "Raza."

Clinton recruited veteran United Farmworker leader Delores Huerta. Huerta had stood side-by-side with Cesar Chavez for three decades. She also had marched with us for the moratorium in Chicago, and had come to support Elvira publicly while she was in sanctuary. The fiery Mexican union organizer began to challenge Senator Obama for his failure to support Elvira and stop her deportation. The primaries in California, Nevada, and New Mexico—states where the Latino vote was critical—reflected the impact of her criticism. The Obama campaign reached out to Gutierrez and Lozano over and over again to come to his defense. What could they say? He had refused to introduce a private bill on her behalf.

By the time of the traditional candidate appearances at the national Latino gatherings of LULAC, MALDEF, and the National Council of La Raza in the summer of 2008, Senator Obama had become an outspoken advocate of immigration reform. At the candidate forum for the National Council of La Raza, he made his strongest statement and his strongest commitment. He said he would pass immigration reform within the first 100 days of his administration and became eloquent in his defense of the undocumented: "When communities are terrorized by ICE immigration raids, when nursing mothers are torn from their babies, when children come home from school to find their parents missing, when people are detained without access to legal counsel, when all that is happening, the system just isn't working and we have to change it." †

In early June, when candidate Obama locked down sufficient delegates to win the nomination, Familia Latina Unida prepared to hold him accountable to his commitment to pass immigration reform in his first 100 days. We formed a committee and began to recruit families and encourage our allies across the nation to do the same. We needed to find a way for the youth to take the lead in the struggle with the Democratic Party, since older leaders and established organizations would be reluctant to do so.

We formed "Latina," a group of young women. Their first action was to go to Pennsylvania in solidarity with Crystal Dillman, the wife of Luis Ramirez, who was murdered by racists in a random act of violence. A small town in Pennsylvania had passed a controversial law against undocumented immigrants, attempting literally to drive them out of town. The passage of the local law reflected a growing right wing racial movement in that region of the state, and it gathered a lot of media attention. In the nearby town of Shenandoah, Luis Ramirez was simply walking in the park with his wife when a group of young racists, offended by his relationship with a white woman, attacked him and beat him to death. Given the climate created by the recent passage of the anti-immigrant law in the next town, the hate killing gathered national publicity.

The young women of Latina were moved by the courage of Luis's wife, Crystal. In her statement she stood up to the racists who had killed her husband and who were running her town. She was almost completely isolated in her own community as she pressed for justice. Latina members raised the money to travel to Pennsylvania on a bus. They adopted a striking uniform, with berets and sharp shirts. Once in town, they marched to the courthouse in a military formation and stood guard outside. Crystal, who seemed not to have a friend in the entire town, came out and broke into tears of gratitude at seeing their support.

The role of the youth, the next generation, is always one of the most critical aspects of any grassroots movement. In the struggle for legalization, the role of the youth would also turn out to be one of the most hotly debated. The establishment attempted to turn undocumented young

---

† Senator Barack Obama, Speech at NCLR. July 15, 2008.

people against their parents and even against other Latino young people with papers, including those U.S. citizens who had undocumented parents. Latina was an effort to attract young people to a more principled position and to open the door to a more militant resistance. The generation of the Brown Berets, CASA, and the Chicano youth movement had faded into the past. Latino empowerment had made winning elections and establishing not-for-profit institutions and businesses possible. But who would raise the really important questions for the next generation?

Most of these young Latinos would have few of the possibilities open to Anglos. Would they choose to try to assimilate into a society that denied them their humanity? Would they try to make their own way in unity and collaboration with their brothers and sisters of Latin America? When Latina said, "No human being is illegal," they were stating their belief in a different kind of social order, a different future for themselves and their generation. When they quoted Malcolm X and said, "By any means necessary," they were putting backbone into the movement for the legalization of undocumented immigrants.

In July of 2008, six weeks before the Democratic National Convention, Emma Lozano, José López, and I met with Congressman Gutierrez at his apartment on the Northwest Side of Chicago. We came with a proposal to mount a movement for immigration reform at the convention. In his characteristic style, Luis responded by telling stories about his experiences with the Obama campaign over the last six months. One might expect that the campaign would have leaned heavily on this popular Congressman, but, in fact, they had kept him at arm's length. The Obama team, led by David Axelrod and Rahm Emanuel, knew Gutierrez well. They clearly needed Gutierrez's support, but just as clearly did not want to owe him. Gutierrez told us that Obama cited his support during the debates, and rolled him out in minor campaign roles, but left him sitting in a hotel room during major rallies.

Then the Congressman turned suddenly to our proposal: "Who can we get for this campaign?" We mentioned names of leaders close to us. "We need to go bigger. Let's get the whole team together." Chicago is a tough town with a history of personal battles, but Gutierrez continued to have the power to convene. Within two weeks, we were in the Little Village community with a room full of Latino elected officials and community leaders, preparing for the convention. At that meeting in August, sixty Latino organizations formed the Ya Basta Coalition. Our demand was for an immediate moratorium on all deportations until Congress passed comprehensive immigration reform and the President signed it.

The Ya Basta Coalition showed the seriousness of its demand for a moratorium by sending a statement asking for support to every delegate going to the convention. Ya Basta next organized a march and press conference in front of the Homeland Security office on West Congress Parkway. Latina, in full uniform, provided security for the march. About twenty of the delegates attended and committed to including immigration reform in the Democratic platform and making it an issue at the Democratic Convention. Gutierrez tried every way he could to raise the issue at the convention. The convention, however, became a well-orchestrated stage show whose purpose was to launch Barack Obama's bid for the Presidency. The Obama campaign was in total control and the immigration issue was reduced to a whisper.

While the convention was going on, Emma and I traveled to Mexico City to be with Elvira and Pepe Jaques Medina, who had organized a conference to call attention to hate crimes against migrants. We brought Crystal Dillman from Pennsylvania to testify at the press conference, and we brought her son to be with his grandparents. Latina raised a thousand dollars to give to Crystal to help her survive. We presented her with the check, and Pepe Jaques arranged a series of meetings in support of her effort to prosecute those who had murdered her husband, Luis.

While in Mexico City, Emma and I watched Barack Obama's acceptance speech with Elvira in the apartment of Jose Pepe Jaques Medina. A few *companeros* gathered around; Saulito played on the floor, glancing at the TV screen as candidate Obama spoke. All he said was, "It is not acceptable in the United States of America to separate a child from his mother."

The choice in the election clarified, however, as candidate Obama's Republican opponent, Senator McCain, completely renounced his support for reform, stating that he recognized the error of his ways and that he would now vote against his own legislation. On Election Day in November, Latinos turned out to vote in record numbers, giving President Obama victories in Florida, New Mexico, Nevada and Colorado, states that he could not have won without the Latino vote.

Right after the Democratic Convention, the Obama campaign had produced a list of priorities for his first one hundred days. Immigration reform had been number four. By December, it didn't even appear on the list.

🌿 15

Retracing Elvira and Saul's Journey

P
resident Obama won a landslide victory, giving the Democratic Party a supermajority in both the House and the Senate. Immigrant hysteria had failed to take root in the electorate. The national polls showed strong support for some form of legalization, especially if an immigration bill could avoid separating families with undocumented parents and U.S. citizen children. In this political environment, mounting a legislative campaign in the first one hundred days appeared to be an easy task. A D.C.-based coalition, with affiliates in cities across the country, formed to carry the ball across the goal line. The coalition was inundated with funding offers from various liberal foundations. The expressed objective was to build the broadest coalition possible for comprehensive immigration reform, in cooperation with the new Obama administration.

I was asked to attend one of the early meetings of the new national coalition. Around the table in a luxurious building in Washington, D.C., sat about sixty people. They represented immigrant rights coalitions, labor unions, D.C. policy analysts, advocates, business leaders, and consultants from the Obama Administration. The principal national Latino organization represented at the table was the National Council of La Raza, whose executive director would soon be appointed as a White House staffer to handle Latino affairs. Beside me sat a Chicago lobbyist who had been hired as a consultant by the White House to advise on community coalitions. This group was much different from the one Lozano and Elvira had pulled together. Many members came from well-funded organizations that provided immigrant services, but had hired expensive, professional organizers of the Alinski tradition. What we referred to as the "organizer industrial complex" was thus well represented around the table. Others were policy specialists who worked for liberal think tanks in Washington, D.C.

I listened for a while, as they laid out a strategy, complete with charts and statistics, aimed at mobilizing support for comprehensive immigration reform. Then I asked a simple question: "Where is the bill, and who is going to present it?" There was no answer; rather, a flurry of insider speculation by those who seemed to be in the know. I suggested what seemed to be commonly understood in Chicago and other cities, that comprehensive immigration reform had been dropped from President Obama's list of priorities for his first one hundred days. I saw nods of agreement from the organizers there from different cities, but was interrupted by the White House consultant, who said, "I know from personal conversations that the President is absolutely committed to passing comprehensive immigration reform in the first one hundred days." In truth, I didn't know how far to go, how strong to be. At least this group was committed to passing legislation that would give our families relief. I was also in a part-time staff position for Congressman Gutierrez, and did not want to be interpreted as speaking for him. I suggested that we mobilize on the day of the inauguration, either in D.C. itself, or regionally. The coalition decided to urge groups around the nation to engage in ten days of action leading up the inauguration.

Familia Latina Unida continued to press the Ya Basta campaign leading up to the inauguration. There were days of prayer, marches, and press conferences. On the day of the inauguration, we began a demonstration in Chicago in front of the Homeland Security offices and marched to the Federal Building, then to the Chicago Temple downtown for a prayer service. Similar actions were taken around the country. Elvira and Pepe Jaques organized press conferences in front of the United States embassies in Mexico City, El Salvador, Honduras, and Guatemala. Our demands were simple: "stop the deportations until you pass immigration reform, and pass immigration reform in the first one hundred days!"

On the day of the Inauguration, the hope in the Latino community drained visibly from faces all across the nation. It was as if they had been invited to a banquet and then were left waiting outside in the cold while others walked in, well dressed, well fed, and full of laughter. President Obama's Inaugural Address put the nail in the coffin containing their expectations. "One line, one line, in a one hour and thirty minute speech," screamed Gutierrez. "One line, one line," said Latino media. "One line, one line," bewailed Latino leaders, who had not been approached with jobs or contracts. Even the District of Columbia coalition shook their heads, but the White House consultant again promised he had secret knowledge that President Obama was absolutely committed to comprehensive immigration reform in the first one hundred days—or, at least, the first six months.

Calling on the coalition that Gutierrez had convened going into the Democratic Convention, we organized a meeting at a Northwest Side Catholic church. We intended to continue building pressure on the Obama administration; we invited a broad group of organizations and the Spanish-language media. Familia Latina Unida mobilized the families to attend the meeting, and a number of families from the church itself also came. Talking with the priest before the meeting, I found out that seven members of his congregation had been deported in the last forty-five days—all with families, and all with U.S. citizen children. "How can this be stopped?" he asked me.

One of the families we brought to the meeting was that of Diego and Francisca Lino. They were one of the families who, based on Diego's United States citizenship, had applied in good faith to legalize Francisca's status through the 245(i) program. Like others before them, they were called in for their final interview only to be informed that Francisca was slated for deportation. She had been deported once before and had returned without authorization to rejoin her husband and her three U.S. citizen children. Strangely, the government had approved visas for her two children by a previous marriage, and they were on their way to legalization with Diego as their adopted father. Diego was now facing the prospect of supporting and raising five children without their mother. Francisca's deportation was set to occur in a few weeks. I stepped outside to speak with Congressman Gutierrez before he came in. I explained the facts of the case, and we talked about alternatives we could pursue to protect Francisca.

The meeting proceeded with speeches from various organizations, generally calling for mobilization to support comprehensive immigration reform. Emma and the Lino family were seated in the front row—all seven of them, well dressed for the event. The Congressman motioned for me to come up and speak to him on the stage. "Tell me again about this family," he said. "Tell me how much time we have to stop her deportation." I did so. Then the Congressman got up to speak. He looked at the Lino family, then called them to come up on the stage with him. He embraced Francisca emotionally and, with his arm around her, said the magic words, "Before they take this mother away from her family, they will have to take me to jail!" I cannot honestly say that we had planned for the Lino family's tragic situation to go out on national Spanish-language media, but go out it did.

Gutierrez decided to fight the deportations immediately without waiting on the Obama administration to propose legislation. He initiated a campaign that used the witness of families facing deportation to move the nation. The Familia Unidas campaign was born that day! The Lino family became the symbol of what was continuing to happen to families across the nation while President Obama delayed on his promise to stop the separation of children from their mothers.

Following President Obama's election, a great controversy had arisen in Illinois over choosing his replacement in the U.S. Senate now that he had been elevated to the Presidency. Illinois Governor Rod Blagojevich had the power to appoint that replacement. In the weeks that followed, accusations swirled that the governor was attempting to sell the appointment to the highest bidder. The accusations led to an FBI investigation.

In an apparent effort to sidestep the investigation, Blagojevich decided to appoint Roland Burris, a popular African American politician who had twice won statewide office. Senator Durbin publicly opposed the appointment and was soon joined by President Obama. The opposition of the Democratic leadership to the appointment of an African American politician of documented public credibility, however, greatly angered the African American community. Congressman Bobby Rush mobilized hundreds of African American clergy to support Burris and held a series of public rallies. Blagojevich held firm to his appointment, though the investigation into his attempts to sell the seat before he appointed Burris would lead to his impeachment and, ultimately, his conviction and imprisonment.

We had learned during the struggle against Elvira's deportation that U.S. senators had the power to stay deportations by introducing a private bill in the Senate, a power that members of the U.S. House of Representatives lacked. After he was confirmed in his seat, I went to see Senator Burris in the Senate office building. I asked him to help us with our campaign to keep families with U.S. citizen children together, and gave him the list of families for which Congressman Rush had introduced a private bill in the House. I explained that Rush's bill in the House of Representatives could not stop deportations without complicated legislative action, which was not likely in the near future. On the other hand, a U.S. senator's introduction of a private bill created an immediate stay on deportation.

Burris is a good man with a long history in Illinois politics. Generally, in his career, he had the support of the predominantly white Illinois state Democratic leadership. He had proven ability to get votes statewide, and his career in office had been scandal-free. He was angered by Durbin's opposition to his appointment to the Senate seat, the seat which Mayor Harold

Washington had helped secure for Carol Moseley Braun—Illinois's first African American senator—and which Barack Obama had just held. Durbin seemed to be trying to fill the seat with a white politician whom he could control. Burris was clearly moved by the cause of family unity. That March he introduced the first of several private bills for our families, and Francisca Lino received an immediate stay on her deportation.

Congressman Gutierrez convinced the Congressional Hispanic Caucus to request a meeting with the White House. At his urging, the caucus specified that the only item on the agenda would be immigration reform. Gutierrez also pushed to have the official position of the caucus—a call for a moratorium on deportations until Congress passed reform—to be part of the meeting. There followed a sad and disrespectful train of delays and postponements.

Returning to Chicago, Representative Gutierrez began to organize. A meeting was arranged at St. Pius Church in Pilsen. We decided on a simple agenda: open with prayer; have three United States citizens testify on behalf of family members facing deportation; and then ask the Congressman to respond to their testimonies. The meeting would close with a request for family members of those facing deportation to come forward and fill out petitions to the President, documenting their cases.

The St. Pius meeting went well. We saw Luis Gutierrez with tears in his eyes as Francisca Lino and others gave their testimony, and especially when the children spoke. When Luis spoke, he invited others to come forward and fill out petitions for their loved ones, family members, and even school friends. Several hundred people walked up to the altar and then down to the church basement, where volunteers took down the details of their case and provided letters to the President that they could sign. We had invited several Evangelical and Protestant pastors to attend the meeting. They politely sat in the front row. They were not introduced, invited to pray, or asked to stand with the priest before the assembly. We decided to work with Gutierrez to have the next meeting at an Evangelical church in Humboldt Park.

St. Pius was a wonderful church with an historic involvement in the struggle for justice for immigrants, but we were aware of the reluctance of the Catholic hierarchy to take a strong position. We had been working for several years with Rev. Miguel Rivera and the National Coalition of Latino Clergy and Christian Leaders (CONLAMIC), a national association of grassroots Latino Evangelical churches. We had prayed with them in the hallways of the Capitol Building. We knew that they had been giving sanctuary quietly to the undocumented in many of their churches. Along with other Evangelicals, they had tended to vote Republican, especially owing to the Republican positions on abortion and gay marriage. On the other hand, their churches were filled with undocumented immigrants who voted overwhelmingly for Barack Obama when McCain abandoned them. Latino Evangelicals were clearly the fastest growing faith group in the Latino community. They were independent, and many owned their own church facilities, along with a network of radio stations. No hierarchy could tell them what to do. Moreover, hundreds of Catholics were leaving the Catholic faith every day and joining the Latino Evangelical movement. The Catholic hierarchy had unleashed a charismatic movement, which failed to stop the fall in their membership; they were clearly worried. We felt that Evangelical participation in this new family unity campaign would not only help us, but would force the Catholic Church to respond competitively, something many of the priests were anxious to do out of genuine commitment.

Through the efforts of Dr. José López, we held the next meeting in Humboldt Park at Rebano Companerismo, one of the older Latino Evangelical churches, which had a mixed Puerto Rican and Mexican congregation. There are three major Latino Evangelical associations in the United States. The leading pastors of two of these associations preach in churches almost next to each other. They are both on Division Street in Humboldt Park, and five blocks west of Adalberto UMC, where Elvira had been in sanctuary. Rev. Miguel Rivera from CONLAMIC joined our meeting and united all three associations in an historic event. Catholic priests and Methodist pastors joined a group of about forty pastors, and an enthusiastic faith-filled crowd of over a thousand. The preaching was strong, and the testimonies of the families were powerful. Puerto Ricans from Humboldt Park who supported the undocumented proved a secret ingredient to the day: a Puerto Rican man gave witness for his wife, who had been deported. He brought down the house.

Congressman Gutierrez also spoke. His words were inspired. He gave a speech that he would come to repeat and give nationally. The Congressman recalled his own marriage, the months of preparation, the classes and the vows before God. He recounted the joy and assurance he felt knowing that his wife and children would there be each night when he returned home. And then the Congressman asked people to feel the pain and anxiety of husbands and wives and children who did not know if their family would be there when they came home. The families who were being torn apart then gave their testimony, demonstrating that pain. This speech became the touchstone of the Familias Unidas movement in the Latino community—a spiritually based, grassroots movement, not a liberal vs. conservative debate about "immigrants" and "assimilation." The shift in message we had fought for was now made manifest: from "welcome the stranger" to "what God has joined together, let no man break asunder." Pastor Freddy Santiago breathed in the Holy Spirit before he exclaimed, "We are not Evangelicals or Catholics or Methodists today: today we are throwing religion out the window. Today we are the body of Christ!" Through song, prayer, the preached Word, and heartfelt testimony, divisions between citizen and resident and undocumented immigrant—between Catholic, Protestant and Evangelical—had been left behind in a rush of unity and spiritual power.

We then formed the Familias Unidas steering committee, which included the representatives of Priests for Justice, the three national Evangelical associations, the United Methodist Church, Familia Latina Unida, and the Puerto Rican Cultural Center. The Chicago representatives of the national immigration coalitions were also invited to join so that their groups in other cities could support the faith-based campaign. After the meeting at Rebano, we met in Evangelical, Catholic, and Methodist churches in thirty cities between February and June of 2009. Lozano and I would go to each city, meet with the pastors and local organizations, interview and prepare the testimonies, and provide logistics for the Congressman to come in. In fact, we were retracing the trip we had made with Saulito after Elvira was deported, the trip that Elvira was prevented from finishing! I thought to myself, Gutierrez will finish what Elvira started. The first meeting in the national tour was held in Providence, Rhode Island, where one of the original organizers of the Coalition for Dignity and Amnesty had pulled together Catholics, Methodists and Evangelicals into a coalition that seemed to draw from the entire city. While new leadership continued to emerge throughout the tour, older veterans reactivated their bases to bring together broader coalitions. Rev. Pedro Windsor in Chicago led us to Rev. Ray Rivera, director of the Latino Pastoral Action Center in New York. Windsor and Rivera were early pioneers in the effort to merge the Latino Evangelical movement and the movement for Latino empowerment and social justice. Rivera possessed the talent of uniting competing factions in New York City from across the faith spectrum, as well as a broad coalition of local, state, and Congressional officials—including the iconic Congressman, Charlie Rangel. Increasingly, members of the Congressional Hispanic Caucus, the Black

Caucus, and other Congressmen and Senators began to show up at the meetings. They were visibly moved by the testimonies and by streams of families coming forward to file their petitions as if responding to an altar call.

In San Francisco, we held the meeting in a Catholic church in the Mission District. Speaker of the House Nancy Pelosi, herself a Catholic, sat by Congressman Gutierrez and listened to three groups of U.S. citizen teenage girls, who told what the loss of their mother and father meant to them. Emma and I watched as tears smeared her makeup. When she got up to speak, she said clearly, "This separation of families must not be allowed to happen in the United States of America." Speaker Pelosi committed not only to moving immigration reform along in Congress, but also to asking the President to stop the deportations until legislation was complete.

Chicago again brought together powerful forces. The Cardinal of the Chicago Archdioceses had recently taken over as president of the National Council of Catholic Bishops in the United States. Working with the Chicago priests, we planned a meeting over which Cardinal George would preside. The priests worked hard to prepare for the event, but twenty-four hours before it was to begin, the Cardinal informed the priests that Representative Gutierrez must not be allowed to speak at the event because of his pro-choice vote on an abortion bill. When the priests threatened to have the meeting without the Cardinal, he responded that he would not allow Catholic churches to be used for Familias Unidas events in Chicago, or anywhere else in the nation. Hearing the Cardinal's position, Gutierrez quickly called him and arranged a meeting. "I am a faithful and obedient Catholic," he told Cardinal George. "I will do as you ask. If you want me not to attend the meeting, then I will not attend." The Cardinal agreed to have Gutierrez sit in the front row of the church, but not to speak. When Gutierrez walked into the church, he received a standing ovation for almost ten minutes, while the Cardinal looked on.

To his credit, the Cardinal made his strongest statement in favor of comprehensive immigration reform to date. He placed the issue of family separation in the context of Catholic doctrine. Major media throughout the nation carried his statement. After the Cardinal finished his talk, Pastor Freddy Santiago, from Rebano, delivered an Evangelical lesson from the Bible—in a Catholic church.

Local media and national Spanish-language media carried every meeting. Gradually, the Familias Unidas campaign broke into the national American media and onto the cable stations. The White House felt the pressure, but continued to delay the meeting requested by the Congressional Hispanic Caucus—the meeting in which the only agenda item would be immigration.

The first hundred days dragged on. While there was no action on immigration reform, the Obama administration seemed intent on revising deportation practices. In May of 2008, ICE, under the Bush administration, had carried out one of the last great workplace raids. ICE agents had undertaken a massive raid on workers in a poultry processing plant in Postville, Iowa, where they arrested hundreds of workers, leaving husbands, wives, and children alone and without support. Religious groups and labor unions had rallied to the cause, and Congressman Gutierrez had made the long drive from Chicago to bring the crisis of the families into public view. The company's exploitation of the workers and the plight of the families had played out before the nation. Now, in early 2009, the Obama administration began making a shift away from the enforcement methods of the Bush administration. Homeland Security would, henceforth, pursue employers directly, and place more emphasis on apprehending undocumented immigrants through cooperation with local law enforcement, rather than by direct raids. As part of this shift, the Obama administration unveiled new "partnership" agreements under a section of the Immigration Act called 287(g), which allowed ICE to train local law enforcement to check papers of suspects, and authorized local officers to detain undocumented immigrants in order to turn them over to ICE for deportation. The provisions of 287(g) had evolved into a pilot program, created in the latter months of the Bush administration, called Secure Communities. Under the Obama administration, Secure Communities rapidly expanded to hundreds—and eventually thousands—of localities across the country.

Though the Obama rules stated that Secure Communities was meant to focus on "criminal aliens," federal cooperation with local law enforcement—and the modernized biometric tools and databases it created—was a virtual endorsement of racial profiling for politically ambitious sheriffs and police chiefs. The worst of these characters emerged in Arizona, Sheriff Joe Arpaio. One long-time activist, Salvador Reza, had warned of the danger he represented at a meeting of the National Alliance of Latino Leaders two years previously. Sheriff Arpaio quickly became a national symbol of the right wing, anti-immigrant, anti-Latino bigot. He made racial profiling a matter of policy and declared that he would arrest every undocumented person in Arizona. Ironically, though the published goals of Secure Communities tried to shift the focus of deportation efforts away from minor offences and towards criminal behavior, the Obama administration's policy of authorizing local officers to cooperate in immigration enforcement enabled Sheriff Arpaio to carry out a campaign of hate and terror. The overt racism of Sheriff Arpaio would finally force a congressional demand for a civil rights investigation by the Justice Department.

Despite such outrageous behavior, the grassroots movement in Arizona received little support until a year later, when the state legislature followed Arpaio's campaign with a law that criminalized the undocumented and made it mandatory for local law enforcement to demand papers—and to arrest those without them. It became the most repressive immigration law in the country. The Obama Justice Department filed suit to try and strike down the state law, though the profiling and the mandate to check papers withstood the challenge. The attempt to push immigration policy down to the state level would ultimately lead the Obama administration to oppose the very laws for which it had opened the way.

The first one hundred days passed without action on comprehensive immigration reform. The National Immigration Forum held a national convention, using their substantial resources to bring organizations from throughout the country to Washington, D.C. A few of us from Familia Latina Unida attended, and our worst fears were confirmed. The organizer industrial complex was clearly not prepared for a battle with the leadership of the Democratic Party.

When the White House finally set a date for a meeting with the Congressional Hispanic Caucus in mid-June, we convinced some of the advocacy organizations to hold a vigil. We brought families from Chicago, and other groups came with families as well. We hoped to put as much pressure on the White House as possible by surrounding the meeting with the presence of real families fighting to stay together. The White House responded by postponing the meeting again. We carried on with the vigil, with the prayers, and with the testimonies of the families.

The meeting with the Congressional Hispanic Caucus was rescheduled for ten days later. President Obama met the caucus in the Oval Office and promised again to pass comprehensive immigration reform. He appointed a working group and put Homeland Security Secretary Janet Napolitano in charge of the initiative. She was expected to meet with both Senate and House leadership to develop legislation. The President assured the Congressional leaders that legislation would be in front of the Congress by the fall.

Gutierrez came back to the United Methodist chapel a few blocks from the Capitol where families holding a daylong vigil were waiting for him, surrounded by TV cameras and reporters. The Congressman gave an optimistic report of the meeting, informing everyone about the working group that had been set up and the proposed target of legislation in the fall. The Congressman then asked me to come outside and meet with him in the car. I did so, and he proceeded to tell me about a private meeting with the President that occurred afterward. In effect, President Obama told Gutierrez to stand down, to back off. I told Luis that I thought Barack meant that he had no intention of moving immigration reform in the fall, or ever, if he could avoid it.

While Gutierrez and the grassroots movement for immigrant legalization were more vocal in their criticism than other groups, we were not alone. Rev. Jesse Jackson and others were already calling for a jobs bill and an infrastructure program that would generate jobs in the cities. Many more were critical of the bailout of the large banks and investment companies, while home foreclosures were not addressed. Our Chicago sources in the White House were bringing us a very clear, if disturbing, message. There would be no New Deal approach to unemployment, such as Roosevelt had taken. The private sector would be rescued with the hope that its recovery would provide jobs. Sadly, the President and his team were looking at deportations of undocumented immigrants as a part of his jobs program, since deportation opened up low-paying jobs for unemployed American citizens. While still professing his support for comprehensive immigration reform, President Obama actually opposed it, and would likely intensify deportations and the torturous separation of families.

16
Spiritual Renewal

While we were fully engaged in the Familias Unidas campaign, the Northern Illinois Conference of the United Methodist Church honored us with the calling and opportunity to replant a church in the neighborhood of Pilsen. We were given what is called a two-point charge: we still had responsibility for Adalberto United Methodist Church, where Elvira had been in sanctuary; in addition, we were given the responsibility for a new church, Lincoln United Methodist Church.

While Adalberto was located in a predominantly Puerto Rican community, and lent itself well to our efforts to build Latino unity on behalf of the undocumented, Lincoln United Methodist was a beautiful building located in Chicago's oldest Mexican community and, for decades, a center of organizing for immigrant rights. Emma and I had been living in Pilsen for several years. Before Elvira had gone into sanctuary, she and Saulito had lived next door. Together, Elvira and Emma had organized a controversial and hard-fought community campaign to help turn around the troubled elementary school that Saulito attended. He continued to attend Cooper Elementary School while Elvira was in sanctuary, and the new school leadership provided real protection for him. Just before I received the appointment to replant Lincoln United Methodist Church, we lost our home to a mortgage-refinancing scheme that more than doubled our monthly payments. Fortuitously, the church came with a parsonage, a new home that also would also serve as an office for Familia Latina Unida.

The appointment to replant a church, although a challenge, was a blessing and showed that the Methodists supported our ministry. We were very grateful, but the controversy over the Dark Virgin had preceded us in our new church. It had left a bitter taste, even though both our Bishop and the national church had reaffirmed our position on the right of the faithful to worship within the context of their own traditions. A previous pastor had allowed a small statue of the Virgin to stand in the garden outside the church. Following their effort to get us thrown out of the Methodist Conference over the issue of the Virgin of Guadalupe at Adalberto Church, a group of Latino Methodist pastors came in the middle of the night to destroy the statue at Lincoln Church with sledgehammers. When we came to the church, which had dwindled to a few people, we re-established the statue of the Virgin of Guadalupe in the garden. A wonderful family took on the commission to plant and care for a beautiful rose garden around the Lady of Guadalupe. While living in this country for twenty years without citizenship papers and with five U.S. citizen children, they still remembered that their prayers to the Virgin had saved them from drowning in the crossing.

We believed that the passionate theological differences over the Lady of Guadalupe were the result of two different conquests of the people of the south. The Spanish Catholics had fought the Virgin for two hundred years, as they tried to complete the conquest of the Aztecs and the Mayan peoples. Protestants and then Evangelicals picked up the fight after the Catholics conceded and led the way for the United States to gain domination over the Mexican economy. We would neither give up our belief in the Virgin of Guadalupe, nor our determination to unify the Latino faithful.

The church grew quickly, and by July of 2009 the Sunday service had a full house, and the voices of families, young people, and children filled the church and the basement of the parsonage seven days a week. Most importantly, building up a new congregation from scratch allowed us to define and characterize our ministry more clearly. While we focused on the struggle of each family to stay together, our most important ministry was to help them with their faith. In building the Lincoln Church congregation in Pilsen, we reinforced our fundamental determination: There is no question that we will win the fight for legalization and family unity, because that battle is already won in heaven. The question is, what kind of people we will be when we win. Will we become the change we are looking for, a people who will fulfill the destiny God has chosen for us?

At the heart of our ministry was the commitment to live in God's time and Scriptural holiness. We strengthened our faith together through eight seasons, led by Scripture. We believed, and were confirmed in our belief, that each year we were called to prepare ourselves for God to intervene in our lives as he planted a seed that through the year would grow to a harvest each fall. No matter what had happened the year before, we started over again, as individuals, as families and as a community of the faithful who served God and the people of God. And every year we found our faith deepened.

Besides new families, something else happened in Pilsen that would prove important to the struggle in the coming year. The church attracted new young leaders from the community—some who were undocumented, some who came from undocumented families, and some who had been deported and returned. These young people had grown up in the gang neighborhoods of Pilsen, but they loved and honored and took responsibility for their families. Many had married very young and had small children. In their hearts, they all understood the grassroots movement, but had never had the opportunity to participate in it.

It is hard to ignore the irony of two young men in the community who had grown up together, one born here, one brought here as a baby. Both made their way through the life offered to young people in Pilsen, which included the street life as well as sub-standard schools. Both were arrested for street crimes as juveniles. Both married and had children to whom they were devoted. Yet one would emerge from these early years, develop a skill and get a good job, while the other would be deported and separated from his wife and children.

One summer evening we were showing a film about Elvira and Familia Latina Unida. A young woman came out of the church to talk to me while I was sitting on the front porch of the parsonage. " I am ready to devote my life to this struggle. Put me to work," she said. Miriam Perez had married and had children while she was still undocumented. She fought her case in the immigration courts and received a limited deportation of one year. For that year she returned to Mexico, and her family stretched out between Mexico and Chicago. When she came back, she put herself through college on a basketball scholarship and earned a degree in Health Education. When she came to talk to me, she was playing semi-pro ball and had been offered a lucrative contract to play pro ball in Spain. She turned down the contract offer to work in the new church and to organize a remarkable youth organization, La FuerZa Juventud, which was destined to play a significant role in the struggle of the next two years.

After President Obama's election Latino media was under great pressure to exclude criticism of him and the Democrats. Sometimes the grassroots movement received strong coverage from Spanish radio and TV, and sometimes the movement was shut out. At a time when we needed our own media, the new church became home to two young filmmakers, Sergio Perez and Giovanny Gomez, who lived in Pilsen. They produced a stream of YouTube videos and one full-length film. Their work allowed us to spread the word of the grassroots movement that was developing in Chicago across the nation.

At a difficult time in the struggle, the Spirit of Peace and Brotherhood replenished our forces and fortified our spirit, and we felt blessed. Yet every Sunday, more and more families facing deportation beseeched help and succor in morning prayers, often joined by the pleas and tears of children afraid of losing one of their parents. So much had happened at our first church, Adalberto, which continued to move forward. And now, inconceivably, a new church with new families, new friends, new children, was born and rose up in our ministry. What keeps a movement alive is its renewal. Each new chapter in the unfolding history of God's people introduces these new stories and demands our heart's full attention.

🔥 17

Grassroots Leaders

Holding a march on May 1st had become a tradition in Chicago, and around the nation, although the numbers dwindled each year. The coalitions of the left that had been invigorated by the marches in 2006 didn't seem to grasp that those mobilizations had little to do with their leadership. Their preparation for the marches involved endless meetings with little work being done. Familia Latina Unida began the year determined to keep the pressure on the Obama administration. In order to keep the coalitions focused, Lozano approached Rev. Jesse Jackson and Operation PUSH to get their participation. Committee meetings were held at the headquarters of People United to Save Humanity.

Lozano also went to her base of local Latino elected officials and asked them to mobilize. The position of the march was, "No Legalization, No Re-election," a slogan that gradually began to take root around the country. Familia Latina Unida groups in Houston and Providence took the same position in their marches. The demand was aimed at the passage of comprehensive immigration reform, but it was accompanied by a strong demand for a moratorium on deportations until the law was passed.

On May 1, 2009, Rev. Jesse Jackson addressed a crowd of several thousand people gathered at the Daley Center. He made his most critical statement to date of the Obama administration for its failure to stop the separation of families. After he spoke, he stood watching the crowd. Jackson had chosen to march with the people in an effort to understand what they were feeling. He turned to me and said, "These people will never forgive Obama!"

In an effort to rekindle the debate in Congress, Gutierrez introduced yet another version of the comprehensive immigration reform bill. While the bill included both enforcement and legalization provisions from past bills, he did not include most of the provisions written by previous Republican co-sponsors, nor did he make any effort to get new Republican sponsors. This bill was aimed at getting the Democratic Party to begin committee hearings and at unifying the immigration movement.

We began a series of meetings with the District of Columbia coalition, Reform Immigration for America (RIFA). In fact, we reached agreement with the immigrant rights coalitions. Broad recognition of the President's true position was now unavoidable, although reports of favorable discussions with the White House continued to circulate. Moreover, the coalition agreed to begin a campaign to pressure the Democrats in the House to begin hearings on Gutierrez's bill. A kick-off mobilization was planned for October 13, 2009.

Familia Latina Unida raised money on the street corners and sent four buses to join the Chicago delegation. We brought many of the families who had testified during the Familias Unidas tour. The mobilization had two parts: a kind of Familias Unidas meeting in a church near the White House, and a demonstration at the White House. Familia Latina Unida coordinated the church meeting by bringing together groups and families from around the county, many of who had participated in the national tour earlier that year. CASA Maryland coordinated the demonstration in front of the White House, drawing on their substantial District of Columbia and Maryland base. It was the first time we would coordinate with CASA Maryland; we were finding them to be a true ally, willing to confront the Democratic leadership.

This willingness to confront the President and the Democratic leadership was not consistent throughout the D.C. immigrant rights organizations. Tensions arose between groups based in different cities and the policy groups in the capital. A meeting took place between representatives of the coalition and White House staff every two weeks. I could not help but compare the coalitions' relationship with the White House and relations with the White House during the Civil Rights movement, especially during the March on Washington. Communications with the Kennedy White House had been strained. Civil Rights leaders had not shared their strategy with the President, whom they were pressuring to support the Civil Rights bill. Most of the Civil Rights groups never met with the White House, and those who did had been viewed with suspicion.

We began to re-evaluate our approach to the national coalitions. Certainly, we needed to continue to work with them. They had a formidable and well-funded national network that had been developed to lobby for the passage of a comprehensive immigration bill. There were some wonderful and very intelligent and effective leaders in the coalition. Some groups, like CASA Maryland, were not only dependable allies, but had strong Latino leadership close to the undocumented community.

On the other hand, the November mobilization and the Familias Unidas tour in 2009 had put us back into contact with the grassroots movement and interfaith leadership around the country. We recalled times when groups like ours had been excluded from national coalition meetings. The first meeting in the Familias Unidas campaign had taken place in Providence, Rhode Island. Even the media wondered why we had picked Providence, but there was a reason. Juan Garcia from Providence was a Guatemalan organizer whom we had met in the 1990s, and had been part of the old Coalition for Dignity and Amnesty. He was indeed a capable organizer, but I doubt he was ever paid as such. He had office space in a small Catholic church, one of the poorest congregations in Providence. He was tireless. He had his own radio show on the Spanish-language station in Providence and seemed to know everybody.

I remember coming to Providence to set up logistics for Congressman Gutierrez to travel to the meeting. Garcia picked me up, driving a Univision truck with a cameraman sitting beside him. We stopped on the way in from the airport to do an interview promoting the meeting. We went from restaurant to restaurant to talk to the *pueblo*. Through his persistence, sincerity, and commitment, Juan had formed close relations with immigrant rights agencies, churches, the media, and elected officials. He had a long list of families who would testify. They were his people. Somehow, Juan, with the loyal support of his brother, managed to bring in enough money to support his wife and children. In terms of his ability to mobilize the community and to influence key people in the power structure, Juan and his committee of mostly undocumented families were as strong as any of the immigrant rights organizations in any city we had visited. Juan, however, was never invited to the White House, or even to the national coalition meetings.

There were many committed people like Juan. They were scattered around the country, working day by day, year in and year out: Maria Jimenez in Houston; Lorena Melgarajo in San Francisco; Jose Sandoval in San Jose, California; and so many others. These people were accountable to the undocumented communities, and they had close relationships with grassroots movements in their home countries. We began to turn to them for direction.

Almost immediately after the mobilization in Washington, D.C., in October 2009, the coalition led by RIFA (Reform Immigration FOR America) changed its position. Instead of building a national campaign around Gutierrez's bill in the House, the coalition changed the focus of its energy and resources to the Senate. The White House directed this shift. Senator Schumer announced that he was preparing to introduce a bill in the Senate, but our sources suggested that the White House had already convinced Schumer three times to hold off on introducing his bill. Also accommodating the White House, Speaker Pelosi took the position that the House would wait on the Senate. This decision allowed Speaker Pelosi and the House leadership to postpone any action on immigration reform until the Senate produced a bill. We organized meetings in New York and California to move Gutierrez's bill, but the House leadership refused to even hold hearings. The Senate did not act, and the Obama administration actually intensified the number of deportations. A report surfaced that President Obama would have deported nearly 400,000 people in his first year, a definite increase from the Bush years.

We made a move to begin discussions with the only other national coalition, the National Congreso Latino. The Congreso included NDLON, the National Day Laborers Organizing Network, which had been active in Arizona. It also included many of the California leaders with whom Lozano had had contact in 2005 at the time of the first grand march for immigration reform. The Congreso's opposition to the comprehensive immigration compromise bills during the Bush administration had forced us to work with RIFA in order to build support for what were the only practical hopes for legalization. Gutierrez's unity bill, which eliminated objectionable enforcement amendments that had been included by the Republicans, made it possible to go back to the Congreso. We had high hopes that the Congreso would provide an effective counterweight to RIFA and its unwillingness to confront the White House and the Democratic Party leadership.

Familia Latina Unida arranged for Gutierrez to speak at the National Congreso meeting in Albuquerque, New Mexico. As always, Gutierrez's speech moved some 700 delegates, causing them rise to their feet again and again. The Congreso overwhelmingly approved a resolution supporting Gutierrez's bill. More importantly, the Congreso decided to concentrate its pressure on the House of Representatives, providing a counterbalance to the White House's hold on the Senate. It was our hope that the Congreso would put enough pressure on the national coalition in the District of Columbia to have them come back to their October position.

❦ 18

The Coalitions Concede

We had a bill in Congress and a movement that was, based on their public statements, unified behind it. The movement was much broader than it had been before. The Familias Unidas initiative had swung the Latino Evangelical churches into action, and they, in turn, had begun to bring some support from the mainstream Evangelicals, cutting into the Republican's social conservative base. On the other hand, we had lost the ability to mobilize the millions of people we had brought to the streets in 2005 and 2006. There was no clear target. The Republicans were still attacking us, but the Democrats were our real problem. They continued to say they supported our cause, and they continued to do nothing.

White House intimidation was an on-going problem. We could not always see the dealmakers, but we could see the results. RIFA's October shift in strategy, after having stood up at a press conference to support Gutierrez's House bill, was a prominent example. RIFA was still sitting on an enormous amount of funding. They decided to organize a March on Washington on March 21, 2010, at the site where King had given his famous "I Have a Dream" speech. The conditions were similar. Then as now, the ten-year struggle of a grassroots movement had persisted long enough to have a favorable Democratic President and Congress, but President Kennedy had been reluctant to let the Civil Rights legislation go to Congress. The March on Washington had really been aimed at forcing Kennedy to get off the fence and support the Civil Rights bill.

As the day approached, the timing seemed even better. The Congress had been held over for final consideration of the Affordable Care Act. The original legislation had been compromised so much that progressive Democrats were threatening not to vote for it. Moreover, President Obama alienated the Latino community by saying publicly that the bill "does not, and will not, cover 'illegals.'" The community recalled his campaign promises, when he had referred to the families of the undocumented. Now the undocumented were "the illegals." There was considerable pressure on the Latino members of Congress to vote against the bill.

The Center for Community Change organized a press conference at the Press Club in Washington, D.C., demanding a meeting with the White House. In an effort to put forth a stronger voice than that of the District of Columbia-based advocates, they asked Emma Lozano to speak. Emma spoke about the cruelty of the separation of families and then said the magic words that would be repeated around the country: No Legalization, No Re-election. All these factors gave the coalition maximum pressure to get the President to move on immigration reform.

The day before the march—and the vote on Health Care Reform—the President scheduled a meeting with the advocates in charge of the march, to be followed by a meeting with the Congressional Hispanic Caucus. As always, White House staff, along with the leadership of the national coalitions, worked out a list of those to be invited. The final list of advocates included representatives from national coalitions, some religious leaders, and some labor leaders. Most of the attendees pledged their allegiance to the President and expressed confidence that he would work to pass comprehensive immigration reform after he had won the long legislative battle for health insurance reform—legislation that, to top it off, excluded undocumented immigrants from being able to even pay their way into the system. The President was invited to give a taped message to be played at the march.

After the advocates conceded, the members of the Congressional Hispanic Caucus agreed to support the health insurance reform bill, but received no corresponding commitment for immigration reform. Gutierrez was left virtually alone in his opposition. One congressman admitted, "We threw Gutierrez under the bus."

The moment was lost. Familia Latina Unida managed to sneak in a few speakers to address the crowd, which included tens of thousands of the undocumented who had been bused to D.C. for the march. The organizers put a lid on criticism, and played the taped message from the President.

After the March on Washington, the unity behind comprehensive immigration reform quickly deteriorated. The National Congreso Latino leadership took the opportunity to declare that RIFA's strategy was a failure. They broke from their commitment to support the Gutierrez bill in the House and, instead, unveiled a "down payment" strategy aimed at the U.S. Senate. This strategy sought to push through Durbin's more limited DREAM Act and legislation for agricultural workers, supported by both the United Farmworkers Union and the Growers. The unveiling of their new strategy also put them back into competition with RIFA for money from big-time funders.

Familia Latina Unida and Gutierrez argued that the down payment legislation would be accompanied by amendments that would make it intolerable for the rest of the undocumented. Gutierrez also argued that it was wrong to negotiate with ourselves, reducing our demands before we even got to the table. After all, the President was still publicly committed to legalizing all undocumented immigrants.

This public commitment would soon disappear quietly as the strategy of the Democratic leadership became clear. The Democrats, led by Durbin and the White House, sought to make a legislative issue of the DREAM Act—the least offensive to anti-immigrant, anti-Latino voters—and drop the demand for legalization of other undocumented immigrants. Overnight, organizations of Dreamers, most of whom were actually too old to benefit from the proposed legislation, sprang up around the country. Funding for DREAM Act organizing fell like manna from heaven. Small groups of the Dreamers visited the offices of Senators and members of Congress and received great publicity. The White House met with several of the groups and told them that all that stood between passing the DREAM Act were Gutierrez and the Congressional Hispanic Caucus. The Dreamers then directed their protests at the Caucus members who were still holding out for legalization for all undocumented immigrants.

The main argument of the Dreamers—echoed by Senator Durbin and other members of the Democratic leadership—was, that while their parents were guilty of illegal entry, these young people were innocent. In effect, they should not be punished for the sins of their parents. In Chicago, parents of young students who had been recruited by the Dreamers came to us in tears. "They have turned our children against us," they said in disbelief. We agreed with Gutierrez that the DREAM Act down payment strategy was a ploy to derail comprehensive immigration reform. Gutierrez predicted accurately that the Democratic leadership would not commit themselves even to pass the DREAM Act, but would blame its failure to pass on the Republicans in an effort to win back the betrayed Latino vote.

For Familia Latina Unida, the down payment strategy not only undermined the need of millions of people for legalization, it distorted the entire immigration issue. The Dreamers not only denounced their parents, but they also pledged allegiance to the United States and the American Dream. The basic injustice of the American Nightmare that had driven so many millions of people to leave their homes and their countries was artfully concealed. Overnight, some of the Dreamers became super patriots, volunteering to join the army and fight in Iraq and Afghanistan. Some knew better, but were swept along by the illusion of a possible victory. The DREAM Act served as a tool by which the grassroots movement we had been trying to build, a movement of faith and of truth, could be attacked. Another greater truth also needed to be acknowledged: the truth of family. Elvira and Flor and millions of other immigrants came north to help their families. They believed in the family, and willingly sacrificed themselves for the ideal that they held in their hearts. The rampant individualism and selfish materialism that is inherent in present day society may be a leading cause of the downfall of so many American families, but it is not an explanation for the mass migration of twelve million people to this land.

Senator Melendez and Congressman Gutierrez met with President Obama in August 2010 and received a promise that he would support a bill in the Senate to be put forth by Melendez. The President favored bringing up the bill in the lame duck session after the fall Congressional elections, when Senators would not feel vulnerable to anti-immigrant, anti-Latino attacks.

The November election was a rout for the Republicans and a disaster for the Democrats, especially in the House of Representatives. The Republicans achieved an overwhelming majority. The disassembling of the President's election coalition; the favoritism of the bailout of the bank and insurance companies; the cruelty and suffering caused by mortgage foreclosures; and high unemployment, cost the Democrats dearly. Still, they had majorities in the lame duck session that followed the election. In spite of promises made to the Congreso, Democratic senators had put off consideration of the DREAM Act and the AgJOBS bill until after the midterm election. And then, as we expected, they did nothing. The President's promise to Senator Melendez to support consideration of his comprehensive immigration reform bill also did not materialize.

Congressman Gutierrez then shifted his position and almost single-handedly forced a vote on the DREAM Act in the House. Uninvited, he broke into a Democratic leadership meeting to get it on the agenda. Even minutes before the bill came up for a vote, members of the leadership were trying to stop it. It passed overwhelmingly in the House, but failed in the Senate for the lack of five Democratic votes.

Gutierrez's effort on behalf of the DREAM Act was sincere. It served to unmask the cynical strategy of the Democratic leadership. More importantly, it helped to rebuild unity with the students who had fallen for the ploy of the DREAM Act. We had always supported efforts to provide legalization for those who came to this country as children. We recognized that, politically speaking, theirs was a more winnable case than that of their parents. Our position was, simply, that you do not negotiate with yourself or you will end up with nothing.

The "down payment strategy" divided the movement, and it produced nothing. At a meeting with Gutierrez in December, the President told members of the Caucus that "no immigration legislation is going to be able to be passed in the next two years given the Republican majority in Congress. We will try to stop bad things and wait till my re-election." Most of the advocate coalitions gave up on changing federal policy and redirected their efforts to local and state struggles. Their funders did likewise. Meanwhile, the Department of Homeland Security sustained deportations at a record 400,000 per year.

Familia Latina Unida's position remained constant: we support legalization for all through comprehensive immigration reform and a moratorium on deportations until it is passed. We were preparing for the next phase of the struggle, convinced that the grassroots movement must lead from below.

19

Campaign for American Children and Families

T he new congregation at Lincoln United Methodist Church gathered a committed group of young people. In the spring of 2010, our
daughters—Tanya and Joline Lozano—organized a walkout from
three high schools. The walkout drew about four hundred young people,
who then gathered for a rally for legalization. The group included undocumented students, United States-born sons and daughters of undocumented
parents, and their Latino classmates. The young people demonstrated a new
way of mobilizing. They combined music, poetry, and passionate speeches,
yet their position was clear: they were for legalization *para todos*, and
opposed separating off the DREAM Act.

By summer their numbers had grown. The young people organized a
camp for the peewees. They conducted a health outreach screening program.
Its aim was to test undocumented families for signs of treatable diseases and
to provide treatment for them in order to make up for the exclusion of
undocumented immigrants in the Affordable Care Act.

The youth also raised money to pay for three buses for a Children's
March on Washington. They were going against the grain since, by the summer of 2010, almost all the advocacy organizations in both coalitions had
dropped the demand for comprehensive immigration reform and opted to
support the DREAM Act. In Washington, D.C., we held a press conference
in front of the Congress; then some forty of the young people and children
accompanied Representative Gutierrez to a meeting with House Speaker
Pelosi. The Speaker again listened to the stories of the struggle to keep families together, and promised to unite the effort for legalization to the passage
of the DREAM Act.

After the meeting with Speaker Pelosi, the whole group, joined by
young people from CASA Maryland, marched in the hot sun to the White
House. As on other occasions, no one from the White House came down to

meet them, but they did get good press coverage. The high spirits of the families, the children, and especially the young people were hard to explain. It didn't matter that almost all of the other groups had bought into the idea of the down payment strategy. What mattered was their conviction. What mattered was that they were fighting for themselves, their families, their community and their people.

The Republican take-over of the House of Representatives in November made it clear to us that legislation would not be passed to stop the deportations any time soon. Instead, we decided to return to our earlier demand for a moratorium. We would call on President Obama to issue an executive order to stop the deportations. Led by the young people, who now called themselves La FuerZa Juventud, seventy-five to a hundred people gathered at the Immigration and Customs Enforcement office at Congress Parkway and Clark Street in Chicago. They would march for about thirty minutes in the cold weather, and five or six people would then sit down to block the doors and wait for the inevitable arrest. They resumed their demonstration the following week, and continued to demonstrate week after week thereafter. Some of the young people were arrested nine or ten times. One cold Monday, a father joined his two sons in being arrested. That unity between the generations confirmed the faith in our hearts that we were on the right path. We found ourselves, however, alone in these acts of civil disobedience, and in the demand on President Obama. We asked organizations in other cities to take similar actions, but few did so.

We then recruited the Latino aldermen to join us. Led by Pilsen Alderman Danny Solis and Humboldt Park Alderman Roberto Maldonado, as many as eight of the Latino City Council members joined in the march and the act of civil disobedience and were arrested. Finally, they held a press conference at City Hall to demand that the President use his executive authority to stop the deportations. The City Council members were much stronger in their criticism of President Obama for his failure to live up to his campaign promise than the advocate groups. The City Council members, after all, owed their positions to Latino voters, not to liberal foundations.

When Mayor Richard M. Daley announced that he would not seek another term, the beginning of the campaign to replace him heightened the militancy of the Latino elected officials. Rahm Emanuel resigned as Obama's Chief of Staff to run for mayor. He started his campaign with a twelve million dollar war chest, and the endorsements of Mayor Daley and the President of the United States. While there was token opposition in the African American community, Emanuel's advantages in fundraising and Obama's endorsement made it difficult to mount strong opposition. Gutierrez himself considered running. In the end, he felt his first obligation was to continue the struggle on the immigration issue. While the Latino community was disappointed, his decision helped to revitalize the grassroots movement when it was at a low point.

Familia Latina Unida formulated an idea for a new campaign and took it to Gutierrez, who refined and improved it as he always did. Over five million young people and children under the age of eighteen are either undocumented themselves or have parents who are undocumented. We argued that these children and young people had the right to a family, a right that President Obama had supported in his campaign and a right that the polls showed was supported by the great majority of U.S. citizens. Our new campaign attempted to join support for the Dreamers with support for the families under one banner in an effort to reunify a divided movement. We arranged two large rallies, one in Los Angeles with CHIRLA and one in New York City with Road To New York. The rallies were massive and enthusiastic, and they revitalized those in the movement who had been fighting for family unity. There was still some criticism from DREAM Act groups who wanted Gutierrez to push for a stand-alone DREAM Act bill.

We took on the case of Hector Nunez, a young soldier who returned from Afghanistan, where he had carried out the dangerous task of clearing IEDs from the roads being used for troop transport. He returned home only to find that his wife, whom he had helped to apply for legalization, was being prevented from re-entering the country with his young son. We held a press conference with Army Specialist Nunez across the street from the ICE office as part of our weekly civil disobedience protest. Gutierrez brought Nunez's case to national attention. What was this country doing by deporting the wife of a soldier who was putting his life on the line in Afghanistan?

After the failure of the Democrats in the Senate to pass the DREAM Act in December of 2010, Congressman Gutierrez was ready to begin the Campaign for American Children and Families. We convened a version of the original Familias Unidas coalition with advocate groups and religious leaders representing Catholics, Evangelicals, and Protestants, and a plan to sweep through thirty cities beginning in January of 2011. This campaign proved more difficult to organize, given the reluctance of many to confront President Obama directly and the strain it put on our resources right from the beginning. Gutierrez recruited several members of Congress to stand with him in Washington, D.C., along with representatives of the advocate groups in an effort to kick off the national campaign. We got a desperate call from his office that none of the groups were producing families or young people to testify as witnesses for the new Campaign for American Children and Families. We loaded up two vans with families and children and young people and drove fourteen straight hours through the night, walking into the press conference just as it began.

That was a sign of the difficulties we would face, and our attempts to set up meetings in different cities confirmed it. Although we had received agreements from both national coalitions and from the religious leadership, no one would set up dates for meetings in February, March, or April. We went back to our Familia Latina Unida network of grassroots leaders and pastors. The first meeting was held in Providence, Rhode Island, followed by meetings in Boston, Houston, Austin and Dallas. After the established immigrant rights organization in Boston declined to organize an event, Centro Presente put together a strong meeting; in Houston, Pastor Melendez responded; in Dallas, we turned to Pastor Lynn Godsey; in Austin, an ad hoc group of activists. We were not alone!

The meeting in Providence was encouraging. Our friend Juan had kept together the coalition we had formed two years ago during the first Familias Unidas tour. A permanent group of Evangelicals, Catholics, and Methodists had stayed together, had taken over an old elementary school building, and had organized a school for social action for their church members. The auditorium was filled, and the overflow crowd of 1,500 people stretched out into the street and listened to the testimony of the families and the young people facing deportation and separation.

Gutierrez made the case that President Obama could issue an executive order to stop the deportations. He relied on a memo that had been generated by ICE in response to a request from the White House when the Congressional Hispanic Caucus had demanded to know what powers the President had to stop the deportations. The Morton Memo outlined a series of alternatives, including administratively closing cases and offering parole. Gutierrez made his argument in city after city. He would read Obama's campaign promise and then read from the Morton memo: "Mr. President, you have the discretion to stop the deportation of these young Dreamers and the parents of the four million U.S. citizen children." Coming after testimonies of young people, children, and spouses of those facing deportation, Gutierrez's argument became clearer and more penetrating. Gradually, the campaign gained momentum, adding the local American press to Spanish-language television and radio. As the campaign grew, advocate groups and religious leaders in different cities began offering to set up rallies. It was not until Gutierrez came back to Chicago, though, that the campaign got the full attention of the White House.

We organized an event at Lincoln United Methodist Church where we had full control of the agenda. In addition to three moving testimonies, La FuerZa Juventud—with over one hundred and fifty young people and children—performed to stirring music. The program began with ten-year-old Rosalba Valdez singing her original Mexican *corrito*: "Obama, Obama, don't take away my father." Tears flowed throughout the church. At the conclusion of the program, the young people came back down through the aisles and joined hands with the families: "They are your soldiers. They will fight for you. They will never abandon you."

We had recruited a friendly Associated Press reporter and had given her special access to the families and to Congressman Gutierrez. For the first time, the Congressman's message, strengthened by the support he felt that day, was aimed directly at the President: "If Obama does not use his authority to stop the separation of families, then I will not be able to support him in the next election, as much as I would like to." The AP article ran in over 500 newspapers across the country, and the White House got the message. As the campaign continued in city after city, the President's poll numbers dropped nearly twenty points in the Latino community. Commentators began to speculate on what the lack of Latino turnout would mean for his ability to carry certain key states necessary for his re-election.

Gutierrez's message to the President was powerful, eloquent, and diplomatic. La FuerZa Juventud and Familia Latina Unida were less subtle. They began the Lockbox Campaign and constructed a mock ballot box. It was about ten feet tall and had Obama's picture on it. The young people began taking it with them, registering people to vote, asking them to fill out a ballot for Obama, but to put it into the lockbox. If Obama did not use his executive authority to stop deportations, then they would not take it out and cast it on Election Day. The voter registration effort was aimed particularly at young Latinos, and the half-million young Latino citizens who turn eighteen every year.

La FuerZa followed up its Lockbox Campaign with a walkout from thirteen high schools and a rally downtown outside of City Hall. The spirited rally occasionally moved to block the street, but was set upon by police.

The youth showed great discipline in their response and thus sent a message to President Obama, as well as to his representative on the fifth floor, Mayor Emanuel. His re-election effort would face a militant youth resistance.

Gutierrez persuaded the Congressional Hispanic Caucus to send a letter to the President requesting him to use his executive power to stop the deportations of young DREAM Act students and the parents of U.S. citizen children. The caucus requested a meeting with the President to get a response to their letter. President Obama had told the Congressional Hispanic Caucus, in December 2010, that no legislation had a chance to pass the Republican-controlled Congress. Facing a reactivated movement he thought had been put to sleep, President Obama now called for a new legislative initiative for immigration reform. He flatly stated that he did not have the authority to stop deportations, despite his own Department of Homeland Security's internal memorandum. He then delayed meeting with the caucus, and instead told delegations of Latino celebrities, "I do not have the authority to stop these deportations. Tell Gutierrez to stop saying I do." Univision's leading news commentator reversed his earlier position and confronted Congressman Gutierrez on Sunday morning television saying, "Why do you persist in this demand on the President when he has already clearly stated he cannot do it?"

Under pressure, Gutierrez refused to back down. When the President finally met with the caucus, Gutierrez emerged from the meeting saying, "The issue of whether the President has the authority to use prosecutorial discretion has been settled. He has it. The issue is now whether he will use it." President Obama did admit to the congressmen that he had the power, but argued that it would be politically harmful to his re-election effort for him to use it. For Familia Latina Unida, political arguments are of no consequence. We are an organization of families facing imminent separation and young people facing deportation. The President has the power to stop these things, and we cannot quit until he uses it.

After the failure of the DREAM Act, almost all of the advocacy organizations adopted the position that the struggle at the federal level was over. They decided to focus on local and state immigration issues. In some instances, such as in Arizona, the struggle for survival against an overtly racist power structure might remind one of the Civil Rights movement, with Sheriff Arpaio playing the role of Bull Connor. To defeat these local law enforcement attacks on the immigrant community, the advocate groups targeted the 287(g) program run by Homeland Security, which empowered local officials to screen those arrested even for traffic offenses, to check for their papers, and to turn over undocumented persons to ICE for deportation. The National Day Labor Organizing Network led the effort in the courts and in the communities.

Other advocacy organizations focused on building support for state legislation to assist immigrants, and on opposing blatantly anti-immigrant legislation. This strategy had the advantage of avoiding confrontation with the Democratic leadership as well as justifying their requests for funding. Its weakness was that it did not stop the deportations, which were estimated to be approaching the one million-person mark since President Obama took office.

We worked hard to merge the national Campaign for American Children and Families with local and state campaigns. We were mainly successful because Gutierrez always drew bigger crowds than any of the organizations could draw on their own, and because he brought massive media attention. We often felt that the organizations and pastors were willing to call rallies, but had no faith that we could win. It was easy to get discouraged. At one point Gutierrez told Emma, "This movement is me, you, and your husband. That's it."

CASA Maryland agreed to work with us to organize a second Children's March on the White House.[†] Our idea was to bring the lockbox and have two thousand people walk by and place their Obama ballots into it. We put the word out, set the date for July 26, 2011, and began to mobilize. At the same time, Congressman Gutierrez was attempting to organize a cross-section of congressmen to join him in getting arrested in front of the White House. He recruited Congressman John Lewis, the Civil Rights legend; Congressman Honda, an Asian American representative from California; and Congressman Raúl Grijalva, an Arizona progressive. Together, the four of them signed a letter to the President saying that they planned to get arrested in front of the White House if he did not agree to use his executive powers to stop the deportations. During the resulting dialog with the White House, Gutierrez was told, if you bring the lockbox from Chicago, you will lose your chance to get a favorable response from the President. Gutierrez asked us to leave the lockbox behind, and we agreed.

The day before the march, the annual convention of the Council of La Raza had invited the President to speak. If he had allies anywhere in the

---

† The campaign proposal as we first formulated it can be found in Appendix D.

Latino community, he thought, it was here. He had handpicked their president to be a key White House aide. La Raza was also one of the three national gatherings before which he had made his campaign promise to pass an immigration reform bill in the first hundred days. When his speech turned to immigration reform, he was prepared to recite his standard position that he could not do it alone, that only the Congress could stop the deportations by passing legislation, and that the Republicans were in the way: "I know some people want me to stop the deportations on my own, but I can' t...." A chant erupted throughout the crowded auditorium, "Yes you can! Yes you can!" It went on for about ten minutes, and the President was visibly shaken. The Campaign for American Children and Families, led by a determined Congressman Gutierrez, had won the argument in the Latino community. The community believed the President *did* have the power.

The next day, as we gathered before the White House, it was reported that deportations had actually reached the one million mark. The rally began with speeches, testimony, and performances by La FuerZa Juventud. Gutierrez appeared alone. The other three Congressmen were no-shows. One called to apologize that he had been summoned to the White House for a special meeting. Undaunted, we followed Gutierrez to the steps of the White House, where he and a group of leaders locked arms and waited to be arrested. Later, we found that the President had responded to Gutierrez with a personal letter that morning. The letter basically told Gutierrez that the President was denying the request and would not implement the alternatives listed in the internal Morton memorandum.

As always, we returned to Chicago in good spirits. The struggle was long, but we were doing what we felt God had asked us to do, what our conscience demanded. New leaders were emerging, a whole generation of new leaders. We would win, no matter how long it took. In a movement of faith, one does not count the numbers or the media coverage. Back in Chicago we planned to disrupt a Homeland Security hearing meant to whitewash the Secure Communities program. Before the meeting began, La FuerZa stretched a human chain across a busy downtown street and sat down, stopping traffic for nearly thirty minutes before police broke up the action and arrested several people. During the meeting, after about fifteen minutes of testimony, the crowd of about one thousand walked out and held another round of civil disobedience outside.

Other actions targeting the Secure Communities program were going on around the country. The pressure on President Obama was building. The next day we heard the news. The Obama administration announced a new policy utilizing prosecutorial discretion to avoid deporting young people who had been brought to this country before they were eighteen, as well as barring deportation of the parents or spouses of United States citizens.

🔥 20

Secure Communities

While we were focusing on the President's executive authority in order to stop the deportations, other immigrant rights organizations continued to oppose the administration's implementation of the Secure Communities program. Arguing that they were only going after those undocumented immigrants with criminal convictions, Homeland Security established a cooperative program with county jails to turn over those who were arrested and lacked papers to Homeland Security for deportation. According to the agreement, county officials would run the identity of those arrested through a federal database. If a person were undocumented, they would inform ICE, who would place a hold on the person for 48 hours so that he or she could be picked up. Statistics proved that the majority of those turned over by local authorities were guilty, at worst, of traffic violations. Homeland Security used the program to pump up their deportation numbers while hiding behind the smoke screen of the criminal justice system.

We felt that the best defense against Secure Communities and the 287(g) program was to win our demand that the President use prosecutorial discretion to close the cases of those with no serious criminal records. The Secure Communities program was a clear encouragement for local law enforcement to racially profile Latinos on minor traffic violations in an effort to purge Latinos from their districts. The National Day Labor Organizing Network (NDLON) waged a vigorous attack on the program, led by their outstanding young attorney, Chris Newman. It was unlikely to be successful given the political consensus in this nation, which sought the deportation of undocumented persons with criminal records, but it was a good fight, especially at the local level, and brought more pressure on the Obama administration.

In Chicago, our close friend Father Jose Landaverde led the fight. Landaverde's mission was located only a few blocks from the Cook County Jail. Families of those arrested came each day to ask for his help. I don't think he ever turned down anyone. In his efforts to free those who were arrested, Landaverde obtained a very good working knowledge of the system. The key to the system, he found, was the administrative hold that ICE placed on the prisoners. The established immigrant rights organizations had met with the Cook County Sheriff's office numerous times in the preceding months without result. We felt they weren't asking the right questions. Landaverde's Virgin of Guadalupe Mission and Lincoln United Methodist Church held a pray-in in front of the jail. We demanded a meeting with the sheriff at Landaverde's mission. The Salvadoran Father wanted to put the sheriff and his subordinates in the middle of the families of those they were turning over to ICE.

When the meeting date was set, we contacted a friendly National Public Radio reporter to cover and record the meeting. "Where does it say in the law that the county jail is required to respect the administrative hold received from ICE?" we asked. The sheriff's people said they were required to respect the hold because it came from the federal government. We asked again, "Where is the law that says you have to do that?" The NPR reporter went with the story and repeatedly questioned the sheriff over a three-week period.

At Landaverde's urging, newly elected Cook County Commissioner Jesus Garcia began developing a Non-cooperation ordinance. Garcia was the leader of the 22nd Ward Independent Political Organization—the group founded by Emma's brother, Rudy. In New York City, Council-woman Melissa Mark-Viverito was developing a similar ordinance at the urging of Make the Road New York, but it had been partly compromised in negotiations with Mayor Bloomberg. Garcia relied on an attorney from the old Mayor Washington administration and drafted a much tougher ordinance. Cook County became the first local district in the nation to refuse to cooperate with ICE. It turned out that administrative holds did not have the force of law.

This victory was temporary. Homeland Security announced that Secure Communities would be implemented nationally in 2013. We had found a loophole that allowed Cook County to temporarily opt out of the program. Ultimately, immigration law and enforcement is a federal matter, and must be addressed at the federal level. The same argument that we had used against the Arizona law—namely, that immigration is only subject to federal authority—would be used against our Cook County ordinance.

The Secure Communities program and the 287(g) programs enabled racists like Sheriff Arpaio in Arizona to establish dragnets in the Latino community, looking for the undocumented. The Obama administration claimed that these programs focused only on the criminal element, not hard-working, law-abiding families. Even with Cook County's non-cooperation law in place, ICE agents walked the streets of Mexican neighborhoods checking papers and destroying lives and families. The reality is that the failure to pass comprehensive immigration reform had left us with a well-funded federal bureaucracy that targeted all undocumented immigrants. Gutierrez and Arellano had both explained to the immigrant rights organizations that if the compromise bills did not pass, the enforcement provisions that they opposed would go into effect anyway. And they did. With no legislation possible, our only defense was to push President Obama to bring the policy of Prosecutorial Discretion into effect.

🌱 21

Southern Roots

F
amilia Latina Unida had had some success in its effort to build unity with the African American community. We had petitioned Minister Farrakhan to take his historic position in favor of legalizing the undocumented before a million African Americans at the Washington National Mall when he spoke at the Million Family March in 2000. We worked with Congressman Bobby Rush, who introduced—and re-introduced—a private bill on behalf of forty families of undocumented immigrants. Congressman Rush also spoke out publicly on the issue. Senator Roland Burris added his support by introducing private bills and voicing support for the right of these families to stay together. Rev. Jesse Jackson walked with us on our marches and added immigration reform to his speeches around the nation, focusing particularly on the persecution of undocumented Haitian refugees and the economic injustice that caused their journey to the United States. Gutierrez had joined rallies in Atlanta with Congressman John Lewis, and in Detroit with Congressman John Conyers, and had worked hard to develop unity with the Congressional Black Caucus.

Now that we had won the concession from President Obama to use his executive authority on behalf of immigrant families, we hoped to unite more strongly with the African American community. When we had envisioned the Campaign for American Children and Families in prayer and in discussion a year before, we had written in our notes: We should finish the campaign in the South, in unity with the historic roots of the Civil Rights movement.

Congressman Gutierrez held a press conference in Chicago to clarify the meaning of President Obama's new position. He announced a meeting at Juarez High School to further explain the new policy and to give assistance to those who would qualify for prosecutorial discretion. What was clear was that Homeland Security had a new policy and no idea of how to implement it—and, apparently, not much will to implement it either. We used the first 100 cases to test the new system; the Congressman took them through the regional office himself. At the same time, he arranged for top officials from ICE to brief the Congressional Hispanic Caucus members and their staffs on the details of the new policy.

In effect, immigrants who had been brought to the United States before they were eighteen, or who had significant family or community ties and no criminal record, were eligible for prosecutorial discretion. Their cases would be closed, leaving them with no legal status, but ineligible to be deported. Many would become eligible for a work permit. It was not a program you could apply for; rather it was a protection available to anyone who was now in the process of being deported or who would be arrested in the future. In reality, if the policy were carried out fully and completely, seven million undocumented persons would be protected from deportation. It was—or it could be with continued community pressure—the moratorium we had long fought for. It met the demand Elvira had made shortly before she went into sanctuary.

Pressure mounted on Homeland Security to implement the policy, which would trigger a review of 300,000 pending cases. A memo was sent to all ICE officials and immigration court judges calling on them to implement the policy immediately. Community pressure would be important, but advancing the struggle case by case could potentially create a class of seven million people who could not be deported. The argument to legalize them would become much more powerful if we could first protect the whole class from deportation.

We began winning cases in Chicago, first through Congressman Gutierrez's office and then directly through our volunteer legal program at the church. The first real tests, however, would come in Alabama and South Carolina. Not only would the new policy receive its severest test in the South, but our vision of Black Latino unity depended on renewing the grassroots movement at its source. When we had laid out the campaign at the beginning of the year, we had seen its conclusion would be in the Deep South. Many attempts had been made to separate the Latino struggle for the human rights of immigrants from the African American Civil Rights movement. We remembered bitterly the media attacks on Elvira and the newspaper column, "…You, Arellano, are no Rosa Parks!" In Atlanta in 2010, we had had a foretaste of what could happen in the South during a Familias Unidas meeting. John Lewis had joined us then, declaring, "This is the Civil Rights struggle of this era." We had, however, no real understanding of the dynamic events that would now take us to Alabama and South Carolina.

Following the example of the right wing movement in Arizona, the Republican-dominated legislature in Alabama passed the nation's most repressive anti-immigrant law. It required that local police check for the papers of everyone they come in contact with, and criminalized those who could not show papers. It also invalidated all contracts with undocumented immigrants, including contracts for gas, water, and electricity. Lastly, it required parents of all children enrolled in public schools to show proof that they were legal residents or citizens. When the law went into effect, there was a mass exodus of Latinos from the state. In some schools, over half the children stopped attending. Local police in some areas began stopping as many Latinos as they could on the highways and streets and turning them over to ICE for deportation.

I proposed that Gutierrez go to Alabama, and he responded enthusiastically. The Congressman decided to demand that the Department of Homeland Security implement its new policy of prosecutorial discretion and immediately release eligible people when they were turned over by local law enforcement. He argued publically that it was a contradiction for the Justice Department to challenge the Alabama law (as they were), while Homeland Security cooperated with the same law by deporting people turned over to them by local law enforcement. We hoped to take the wind out of the right wing's sails. They needed to know that if they arrested an undocumented person, the likelihood was that that person would walk away from ICE and back to their family. Gutierrez reminded the people of Alabama, that Alabama can pass as many laws as it wants to, but Alabama cannot deport you.

On October 22, 2011, as the sun rose over Alabama, Congressman Gutierrez landed in Montgomery. On the same day, memorial services were being held for Rev. Fred Shuttlesworth, legendary co-founder of the Southern Christian Leadership Conference. While the Civil Rights movement had fundamentally changed the entire nation, Alabama was now reverting to its former practices. This time its hatred was directed at Latino immigrants. A thick fog of fear rose from the green hills of the state where, nearly half a century ago, the bombing of a church killed four little girls and woke up the nation to the violence of the racism that scarred the land of the free.

Gutierrez had to travel to Eufaula to attend the NAACP state convention. He found strong allies for the new Civil Rights struggle. The convention was filled with veterans of the Civil Rights movement, and they possessed a direct and personal understanding of the urgency of the immigration issue. The same men who had persecuted Black people in the sixties, lynched young men, raped women, and bombed churches were now attacking Latinos. The African Americans in Alabama, and those whites who chose to cross the color line and stand with them, could sense the racism in the events swirling around them. They were willing to fight such injustice as they had fought it before.

Driving north on his way from Birmingham to the convention, Gutierrez passed by fields that lay empty for lack of the migrant labor that the new law had driven from the state. He also saw the for-profit prisons, run by businesses that had attempted to hire out their own convicts to harvest the crops for 35 cents a day. When he returned to Montgomery, he heard the reports of school children, afraid to go to school; of calls to families, threatening to cut off their water if they could not prove they were legally in this country; and of long lines of people waiting to prove their citizenship, so that they could renew their license plates. His first stop was the radio station, La Jefa, which served as the main source of reliable information for the Latino community. Once on the air, Representative Gutierrez called for Latinos in Montgomery to turn out for a rally that afternoon.

The rally took place at the biggest stadium in Montgomery. The question was whether the Latino people could rise above the fear that had settled over Alabama. Gutierrez had come to see for himself and to show the *pueblo* that they were not alone. The *pueblo* responded to his call. For two hours the families streamed in through the doors of the stadium until they were over three thousand strong, filling every seat. The rally was a success—an important first step and something to build on.

As the sun set and darkness fell over Alabama, the Congressman made his way north to Albertsville. While Montgomery worked to uphold its legacy—the bus boycott that had inaugurated the Civil Rights movement in 1955—the Albertsville mayor and police chief were eager to use the new immigration law to attack the thousands of Latinos that had come to the city to work in the chicken processing plants. No media were invited to the meeting in the church, which was already packed with brave families who refused to be treated as less than human beings. When Gutierrez arrived, heartfelt applause rose to greet him. The Congressman's message was: We will support you from all over the nation if you will stand and fight.

Two days later, back in Washington, Gutierrez followed up a letter to Secretary Napolitano by meeting with ICE chief John Morton. He then received promises from members of the Congressional Hispanic Caucus to join him in Alabama. When Napolitano testified before a Congressional committee, she stated that Homeland Security would not cooperate with Alabama's new law. Gutierrez issued a statement saying, "I appreciate the Secretary's remarks and look forward to action that backs up her words. I have made it clear to Secretary Napolitano that I am monitoring the situation in Alabama closely, and want to make sure that the policies of the federal government with regard to targeting deportation of serious criminals takes precedence over the scatter-shot approach of the state law."

The Congressman and I shared a room that evening in Alabama. We used the time to recall some history. Here in Alabama, where so much history had been made, it was almost mandatory to review the Civil Rights struggle. Gutierrez—a Puerto Rican who grew up in the Midwest—had not been part of it, but he had been inspired by it. We reflected that while that struggle had confronted outright racists—such as the sheriffs in Alabama—it had also taken on a very popular Democratic President, John F. Kennedy. In fact, the March on Washington had begun as a march on Kennedy, because—like Barack Obama—he had held back from passing federal legislation, fearing that he would lose more votes from Southern whites than he would gain from African Americans.

One of the architects of the Civil Rights movement, James Foreman, had once explained to me their fundamental strategy: We are going to make the federal government live up to the promises of Reconstruction and undo the Hayes Compromise. That is, the Civil Rights movement aimed to make the federal government enforce the Constitution against the States Rights racists. The task of the Latino movement for legalization of immigrants was not easy. Like Kennedy, Barack Obama was a vote counter, perhaps even more so, and the undocumented could not vote even if they were legalized. On the other hand, the Latino vote as a whole grew by leaps and bounds every year.

I think Gutierrez took courage from the African American leaders who had been willing to challenge the Democratic Party, even its so-called liberal wing. We reflected that our protests had had little effect on Republicans, while the Democrats had taken the threat of the denial of the Latino vote quite seriously. The real danger to the progress of the movement for social justice resides with Democrats, who think that they can take the Black and Latino communities for granted by assuming that they have nowhere else to go. Later, Gutierrez was to incorporate a line into his speeches: "Do you think Rosa Parks consulted the DNC before she sat down in that bus? Do you think she worried about its effect on the next election? No, she sat down because it was right."

On November 21st, Gutierrez returned to Montgomery. He did not come alone. With him were ten congressmen from throughout the nation, who had come to hold a hearing in the Montgomery City Council Chambers. In the hearing, city officials and religious leaders listened to Latinos who had been profiled and arrested. Their testimony lasted for four hours.

Gutierrez and the other congressmen then traveled to a crowded Sixteenth Street Baptist Church. Outside, a crowd of several thousand gathered to hear the speeches being made inside, to pray, to chant and to sing. They lit candles as the darkness fell. Gutierrez entered and walked to the pulpit—where Dr. King had spoken so often—to a crowd that included local legends of the Civil Rights movement shoulder to shoulder with Latinos who had made up their mind to take up the struggle for justice. The movement had reached a decisive moment in history, a moment in which two world historic communities joined together, determined to walk down one road together.

The courts began to strike down first one and then another provision of the Alabama law. A statewide grassroots movement to repeal the law began to grow. Politicians began to retreat. The fear that had driven so many from the state had been countered, and thousands made the decision to stay and fight.

The grassroots leaders on which Familia Latina Unida depended were different in every state. What united them was their level of commitment. None of them made organizing a career; rather, it became part of their lives. They were bold, independent, and loved their people. In South Carolina—which followed Alabama in passing a very repressive anti-immigrant law—Diana Salazar stepped forward. Diana had helped Emma Lozano organize one of the first Familias Unidas events and had been with us in Mexico City for the first meeting of the Assembly called by Jose Jaques Medina to bring the Mexicans in the grassroots movement together. South Carolina's law mandated that local law enforcement stop and demand proof of legal status from suspicious people. As with the Alabama law, its basic goal was to criminalize the undocumented. It was scheduled to go into effect on January 1, 2012.

Lozano worked with Salazar to mobilize people for a rally at which Gutierrez would speak. He would explain the new prosecutorial discretion defense. Again, the plan was to take the wind out of the sails of the state law and keep people from running away in fear. Salazar's network included leaders from five Catholic churches. They did not have the active support of the priests, but they had strong bases. Latino businesses throughout Charleston also pitched in to support the mobilization. The only Spanish-language radio station in Charleston had closed, but the channel lived on by rebroadcasting an AM program from Chicago. The lead morning DJ for that program was our friend, Pistolero, who had gone through some difficult times and had left Univision radio. A group of small businessmen in the Mexican community had joined together to put programs on the air, and had recruited Pistolero to make a comeback. Always popular, he had quickly built a following. Salazar arranged for public service announcements, and Pistolero promoted the event. In only ten days, people not only heard about the rally, but they came from throughout the state.

As always, the meeting would focus on some key cases, especially from the town of Ridgeton, where racial profiling was in full force, with Latinos already being picked up and being held for ICE in anticipation of the law going into effect. The crowd packed the local Longshoreman's hall, a predominantly Black local that strongly supported resistance to the new law. The event drew over a thousand people and involved a broad band of pastors and local elected officials. Gutierrez explained the new prosecutorial discretion guidelines. When he committed to return in order to support the people who had testified about their deportations, he brought down the house.

Three weeks later, Gutierrez returned with Gabino Sanchez, a father of two U.S. citizen children who was facing deportation, and accompanied him during his appointment with ICE. Lozano and Salazar brought two other young men's cases, and he committed to fighting for them as well. Both had been arrested while driving. They were charged with driving without a license and then turned over to ICE, which set bond at ten thousand dollars. Anticipating Gutierrez's visit, Homeland Security brought in the Regional ICE coordinator from Atlanta for the meeting. The young man in custody was immediately released without bond. The coordinator made a commitment to review all three cases according to the new discretionary guidelines. A week later, one received a letter stating that his case had been administratively closed.

A defense committee was formed in Charleston, volunteers trained—and the cases continued to roll in. Under Salazar's leadership, the hard work of preparing people's records so that they could receive prosecutorial discretion went on every day. The grassroots movement continued to grow. People now had confidence that they could defend themselves. Legal action against the law struck down some of the worst of the racial profiling provisions, and a coalition to repeal the law was formed.

We came away from South Carolina convinced that the defense the Obama administration had provided could protect millions of people. It was up to us to mobilize the community to ensure their protection. One of the cases we left unresolved was the case of Gabino Sanchez, whose struggle would soon become an important part of the history of the movement.

🌿 22

First Victories

Prosecutorial Discretion and DACA

Our work in Chicago, South Carolina, and Alabama convinced us that the new policy of prosecutorial discretion could be made to work. Two conditions, however, had to be met: the community must be informed, and the Department of Homeland Security must be held accountable. We had a strong political card to play in the effort to hold Homeland Security accountable. Every six months, they were required to make a detailed report on deportations. The report for the first six months in 2011 showed that 46,000 parents of U.S. citizens had been deported. If the report for the first six months in 2012 did not show a great improvement, then no argument could be made that would move the Latino community to turn out and vote for President Obama—no matter how reactionary, no matter how hostile his Republican opponent.

Familia Latina Unida developed a detailed proposal to meet the first condition, which required the development of Discretion Defense Commissions in twenty cities. The advocacy groups in both national coalitions accepted the proposal. It was enthusiastically embraced by Familia Latina Unida's own national network.

The continued pressure began to pay off. The Obama administration announced a new rule, which allowed U.S. citizens to apply for a hardship waiver to legalize spouses and other family members without leaving the country. Up until then, couples with families had had to leave the country and travel to Juarez, Mexico, to apply for the waiver. Gutierrez had pointed out that this stipulation was bizarre, since the State Department had cited Juarez as too dangerous for civilians to travel to. Once in Juarez, after waiting for months for a decision on their waiver application, most families were told not only that their waiver was denied, but that the undocumented family member was barred for ten year from re-entering the country. Several families in our churches had gone through this devastating ordeal, among

155

them Army Specialist Nunez and his wife. The Obama administration hailed the new rule as a strong support for family unity.

Yet Homeland Security began to pull back from its commitment to the new prosecutorial discretion policy. Some district offices were not implementing the policy at all. A new memorandum came out further limiting the number of people whose cases would be closed. Moreover, the government began backing off on its commitment to offer work permits to those whose cases were closed. Some of the national advocacy groups issued scathing reports on Homeland Security's failures in implementing the policy. Gutierrez got Hispanic caucus members to complain, and Secretary Napolitano was raked over the coals by Democratic members in committee meetings in both the House and the Senate.

Meanwhile, the Republicans were accusing President Obama of backdoor amnesty and threatening to pass legislation limiting his discretionary powers. The White House cited the strong Republican opposition in an effort to silence criticism. In a similar effort to respond to criticism, Secretary Napolitano announced a pilot review of all existing cases to determine which ones could be closed using the new discretionary guidelines. The review spread slowly to other cities, but the percentage of cases closed rarely went above 7%. The low numbers of closed cases only intensified the cynicism in the Latino community and the Latino media towards the Obama administration.

On the other hand, we were continuing to win cases in Chicago—both those taken up by our church, and by Congressman Gutierrez's office. We needed more pressure at the local level around the country. Our strategy of organizing defense committees only took hold in half a dozen cities. In most cases, the immigrant rights coalitions were not willing to fight individual cases, or were not closely enough in touch with the community to know about those who were arrested. Immigration lawyers were reluctant to apply for prosecutorial discretion, preferring to take in thousands of dollars for cases that they knew had no chance of winning.

A strange turn of events in 2012 helped us to find a path forward. Gutierrez had intervened with ICE in South Carolina to get Gabino Sanchez released on his own recognizance. From his District of Columbia office, Gutierrez's able staff appealed to ICE to close his case, using the criteria for prosecutorial discretion. Certainly Gabino seemed to fit all the criteria. He had been bought to this country at the age of fourteen. He had married and was supporting his two U.S. citizen children. He was a homeowner and paying his mortgage, and he had no criminal record. Homeland Security, however, decided to deny the request for prosecutorial discretion and informed the Congressman's office that Gabino Sanchez would have a deportation hearing in February. Gabino had, over nine years, acquired seven tickets for driving without a license. ICE argued that such a record showed disrespect for the laws of the United States.

Gabino's courage and willingness to fight his case in public provided us with what we needed to bring pressure on the Obama administration. Gabino's latest traffic stop ended in his arrest because of the government's 287(g) program, which invited local law enforcement to cooperate with ICE in scooping up people without papers. The recent South Carolina law, taking the 287(g) agreement to an extreme, mandated local law enforcement to ask for papers and turn those without them over to ICE for deportation. In his six previous stops, Gabino had been given a ticket for driving without a license, had paid his fine, and had then been released. In most of his stops, no other tickets aside from driving without a license were issued—not for speeding, not for running a stop sign. Gabino had simply been racially profiled, stopped, and given a ticket for driving without a license. To support his family and U.S. citizen children, he had to work. To get to his job, he had to drive to work. The very things that qualified him for prosecutorial discretion made him vulnerable to racial profiling by South Carolina local police.

If Homeland Security was sincere in implementing the new policy, then Gabino Sanchez should have his case closed. Moreover, his case would be heard in Charlotte, North Carolina, the site of the upcoming Democratic National Convention. We began to formulate a campaign around Gabino Sanchez's case. At Gabino's hearing, we would put South Carolina's unjust law and ICE's responsibility for implementing its new policy on trial. If the case were not properly closed, a demonstration at the convention would remind Latino voters of the President's ultimate responsibility.

The location of the hearing was ideal. Most importantly, Gabino, his wife Laura, and his two beautiful children, were the right family to bring this issue to the nation's attention. They were two wonderful parents, and the joy their children showed spoke to the strong bonds of love they shared. Why would the government want to destroy this family and the lives of two United States citizen children? Both Gabino and his wife were willing to stand up for themselves and for all the other families. We knew that the media and the people would see, like Elvira, that they were genuine.

Representative Gutierrez made a commitment to be with Gabino when he went to court. Our strategy depended on a strong mobilization at the courthouse to make credible our threat to demonstrate at the Democratic Convention. Gutierrez had gone to North Carolina with the first Familias Unidas tour. He was not confident that our small, agency-based coalition would bring a significant turnout. We had a strong organization of our own in South Carolina, but it was too long of a trip to bring large numbers north to Charlotte. We needed some new forces.

Frustrated by the slowness of most immigrant rights coalitions to organize defense committees as they had promised, we turned to the Evangelical pastors who had hosted Gutierrez on his two national tours. I contacted Pastor Lynn Godsey in Dallas. I found him equally frustrated with the national Evangelical organizations, "immobilized by the politics" of Washington, D.C. Godsey weighs a good four hundred pounds, but he moves around the state like a lean young man, filled with the Holy Spirit, and committed to defending undocumented believers in churches all over Texas. The pastor had organized a meeting of over one hundred pastors, and I had presented the model we developed at our own church for defending people by use of prosecutorial discretion. Godsey had not only established a defense committee in Dallas that forced recognition from ICE, but he had traveled throughout the state of Texas—even to Oklahoma and California—training pastors and establishing defense committees. Godsey had contacts with pastors in Charlotte, as well as with a nationally known Evangelist, Pastor Adrian Amado, who was planning a major crusade in Charlotte later in the spring.

I went to Charlotte with a small team of Familia Latina Unida organizers a few days before Gutierrez was to arrive for Gabino Sanchez's court date. We met with the immigrant rights coalition and then with many of the pastors whom Godsey had contacted on our behalf. We also talked with the Catholic priests and their church leaders. Susan Collins, who worked in Gutierrez's office, had arranged for an excellent lawyer to represent Gabino Sanchez. When Gutierrez arrived, several hundred people joined him and Gabino in front of the Charlotte courthouse. The hearing produced a continuance until May 15th. After the press conference at the courthouse, which was covered nationally, Gutierrez and I met with about sixty of the pastors. After a good discussion, Gutierrez agreed to come back to Charlotte to attend Pastor Amado's crusade in April and help to organize for the May 15th hearing.

I didn't know if we would have been able to mobilize adequately at the Democratic Convention, but we were developing a credible threat under the watchful eyes of the White House. A Familia Latina Unida member, Sergio Perez, produced a moving video called "Gracias Gabino," and a FuerZa Juventud leader, Geovany Gomez, composed a moving song by the same name. The video and the song went on YouTube and all over the internet.

Gutierrez returned, as promised, for the April crusade with Pastor Amado. He addressed several thousand of the faithful and characterized the May 15th mobilization as a spiritual pilgrimage for the salvation of the Latino family. Evangelist Amado followed Gutierrez with a powerful, moving twenty minutes of prayer and a spiritual call to mobilize for Gabino Sanchez, who stood with humility, dignity and determination before the crowd with his beautiful wife and two children.

In April, Pepe Jaques and Elvira called on Emma and myself to come to Mexico. I think the constant contact with Elvira and the struggle in Mexico kept the truth of the immigration issue before us every day. Pepe Jaques, now retired as a *Diputado* after the expiration of his term, organized a forum in support of a law that would protect migrants coming from Central America who were traveling through Mexico. A long campaign, led in part by Elvira, had gotten the legislature to pass a law protecting migrants from the brutal extortion, murder, and rape that they faced at the hands of the cartels and sometimes at the hands of corrupt government officials. The President, however, failed to implement the protections. The forum was to be held in the Mexican Senate, under their sponsorship. Pepe provided for Emma and myself to attend the conference, and he asked me to speak.

The issues were clear. Under pressure from the Obama administration, President Calderón refused to protect the migrants, using the shocking violence as a way to slow the migration from Central America to the United States. Mexicans can pass easily into Guatemala just by showing their passport. Those coming from Guatemala, Honduras, and El Salvador, however, have to apply for a visa to enter Mexico at its southern border. The application process is slow and expensive, forcing migrants on their way to the United States illegally—to enter Mexico riding on top of fast-moving and dangerous trains. Traveling this way, they are vulnerable to cartel bandits and government police looking to rob them. Rape and violence against women are rampant. Massacres of large groups of migrants stirred public outrage, but President Calderón's subservience to the United States kept him from enforcing even the moderate protections of the law.

Elvira had raised the issue of Mexico's treatment of migrants within weeks of her return to Mexico. She had joined with others to organize caravans to ensure their safety, sometimes being confronted by armed gangs. Many of the migrants were young parents like her, trying to return to their families in the United States after they had been deported, or after they had returned home to care for a sick parent, or to attend a funeral of a loved one. She worked with some courageous priests, such as Father Solalinde, who ran refugee centers for the migrants and spoke out boldly against both the government and the cartels.

This trip was the tenth time we had traveled to Mexico to support Elvira's work. Each time we found her a stronger and more effective leader. We spoke together on one of the panels. The movement in Mexico was engaged in a struggle that was the mirror image of the struggle in the United States. We were trying to get the President to use his executive power to defy a law that Congress had passed. They were trying to get the President to implement a law that had already been passed. At the root of the violence and exploitation in both countries stood the United States. The Obama administration had not only pressured President Calderón to refuse protection to the migrants in order to slow migration, he had continued to press for free trade agreements in Central America, which, like NAFTA, were causing massive unemployment and driving more people to go north to survive.

The trip made clear the reason why we had to tell the whole story behind the immigration issue. It also brought home to us the reality of the violence in Mexico. The reason for the growth of the cartels was the twenty million people in the United States who buy drugs illegally. They make up the bulk of the market. The guns also came from the United States, both the guns of the cartels and of the Mexican army. A violent but ineffective war with the cartels had resulted in sixty thousand people being killed in Mexico. We knew from our own experience about the thousands of young people in the United States who had been killed in gang wars. Massive unemployment—the direct result of United States trade policies—made young men easy recruits for the cartels and the street organizations in the United States, and initiated them into the dehumanizing business of death.

We came away understanding that the chickens would come home to roost—that the violence and the dehumanization would ultimately return to its source with a vengeance. This challenge, too, had to become an integral part of our work in the United States. But for now, we had to put our energies into the campaign and the confrontation in North Carolina.

A week before the May 15th hearing, we sent Sergio Perez and Geovany Gomez to Charlotte to prepare the mobilization. We raised enough money to pay for gas for the trip from Chicago, but after that they would be on their own. The two young organizers did an amazing job, connecting with the Evangelical pastors and the Catholic priests and reaching out to the community at large through the radio stations. On the radio, Geovany would tell Gabino's story, sing the song he had written, and call for people to come out on May 15th. When I finally joined them at one of the stations, I found that even the DJ's were crying and calling for the people to join in the demonstration. We had also asked a young Asian woman from the immigrant rights coalition—whose mother Gutierrez had saved from deportation—to go to Charlotte and work with the immigrant rights coalition there. Our organizing team tried to work with every group and help them come together.

Gutierrez arrived in Charlotte on a hot North Carolina day. Diana Salazar drove Gabino and his family up from South Carolina. The pastors' part in the march to the courthouse was the most impressive event, and they made up the largest presence in the crowd, but everyone was there. Inside, the government lawyers ducked the issue of prosecutorial discretion. In accordance with the new policy, the court granted Gabino Sanchez a hearing in one year to get a permanent resident card. A few weeks later, Gabino got his work permit and his driver's license. It was a victory for Gabino and his family, and a face-saver for Homeland Security.

On the same day, May 15th, we organized protests and press conferences in Los Angeles, Chicago, and New York. In Washington, D.C., in solidarity with Gabino Sanchez, CASA Maryland took our demand to implement the discretionary guidelines directly to the White House. We quietly continued to circulate a plan to demonstrate at the Democratic Convention if President Obama did not act. We believed that the White House received our message. All that remained was to hold the District of Columbia forces in line.

Senator Rubio, the rising Latino hope of the Republican Party, formulated a watered-down version of the DREAM Act to try to entice Latinos to support his party. The White House pressured Congressman Gutierrez to attack his effort. Instead, Gutierrez publicly announced that he would be glad to work with Rubio on anything that would stop the deportations. Of course, Rubio's bill went nowhere, but it did pressure President Obama to try and hold onto the Latino vote. Republicans began talking about how the President had broken his promise to the Latino community to pass immigration reform in his first 100 days. At the same time, shamelessly, they were blasting him for his policy of prosecutorial discretion.

A meeting of the House Democratic Caucus with Secretary Napolitano was arranged, ostensibly to build up support for approval of the Homeland Security budget in Congress. Instead, Gutierrez and the Secretary had harsh words over her deportation policy. Gutierrez cheerfully reminded the Caucus members how many of their districts he had visited with the message of "Family Unity." Others joined Gutierrez in criticizing her policy, and the Secretary never even got to discuss her budget. This confrontation with Secretary Napolitano, although not public, showed the fruits of the Familias Unidas tours. When Gutierrez mentioned his stops in the districts of those in the room, Minority Leader Pelosi spoke up saying, "And you were in my district too." Congresswoman Zoe Lofgren had once been the point person in the House when Democrats wanted to stall immigration reform. I remembered the Family Unity meetings in San Jose, organized by Jose Sandoval, and the consistent pressure he had brought against her. Now, Zoe Lofgren was one of Secretary Napolitano's most vocal critics. The heartfelt testimonies of the families at Familias Unidas rallies in cities across the nation had moved the mountain of political opportunism, even if only a little.

Later that week I went to Washington, D.C., to join the Congressman in a meeting with the leaders of the advocacy organizations. They had been invited to the White House to discuss passing immigration reform in 2013, a move meant to distance them from the resistance we had reignited in North Carolina. Gutierrez hoped to avoid the spectacle of concessions by the official leaders. He explained the District of Columbia strategy to them. He let the White House know that a letter would be circulated among the Democratic Caucus members to call for Secretary Napolitano's resignation if the prosecutorial discretion policy were not fully implemented by June 29th. He told the leaders about the confrontation with Secretary Napolitano. Somehow, he ignited hope amongst them that something could be accomplished. Informed of their meeting with Gutierrez, Secretary Napolitano withdrew her invitation to meet with the advocacy groups the following Monday. Instead of meeting with her, the advocacy groups held a press conference demanding that Secretary Napolitano fully implement the policy of prosecutorial discretion. Gutierrez smelled victory. He told me that, even if the Hispanic Caucus as a whole backed down, he had ten Congressmen who would sign and circulate a letter calling for Napolitano's resignation.

More than once this grassroots movement for justice and the rights of undocumented immigrants had won the battle for the hearts and minds of the public, only to lose the battle in the corridors of power in Washington. This dynamic repeated itself with the country's religious establishment. Catholic and Protestant leaders had withdrawn their support for comprehensive immigration reform at a crucial time in 2007. The Family Unity movement had focused much of its attention on the fast-growing Latino Evangelical churches. Since both Catholics and Protestants were steadily losing members to the Evangelicals, we felt that an Evangelical challenge might move the entire religious establishment. Moreover, the Latino Evangelicals were increasingly independent and committed to Scripture, rather than to political or financial considerations. The powerful Latino Evangelical demand to stop separating families surged steadily throughout the entire Evangelical movement, including the white Evangelical organizations that had formerly been staunch allies of the Republican Party.

As Gutierrez skillfully forced the deportation issue with Democrats in Congress and with the national advocacy organizations, the District of Columbia Evangelical leaders held a remarkable press conference. They called for immigration reform in order to stop the separation of families. Most significantly, leaders of Focus on the Family joined this broad group. Focus on the Family represented the extreme right wing of the Evangelicals, and their newly announced position reversed the one they had taken in earlier statements. We were pleased to see Pastor Gabriel Salguero, who had helped organize one of the first Familias Unidas events in New York, serve as a spokesperson at this historic press conference.

For once, the forces in the District of Columbia held. Yet in victory, the self-imposed limitations of the self-appointed leaders of the grassroots movement were all too apparent. One of the representatives of the advocates said that he had been asked, in a meeting with the White House, if the advocates would accept legislative relief for the Dreamers as enough. Who were these people, given authority only by virtue of their funding, to determine what millions of people would accept? The Democratic leadership, and especially Senator Dick Durbin, had been successful in lowering the bar of immigration reform by choosing the leaders with whom they would negotiate. We had won the only victory available to us. Millions would benefit. As I boarded the plane back to Chicago, I left the District of Columbia with the clear insight that the movement must be restructured, and that the faith of the people must serve as its base, if the victory the people deserved was to be won.

The campaign to push prosecutorial discretion had succeeded. We started getting unrequested closings of cases and stays of deportation from ICE, first a trickle, and then steady stream. Finally, the President announced an executive order offering an application for a two-year deferment of deportation and a work permit to undocumented youths under the age of thirty who had come here before they were sixteen, and who were in or had completed high school, and who had no criminal record. The order would allow over a million people to come out of the shadows, get driver's licenses and live and work legally in this country. President Obama's speech announcing the policy suggested that it was a temporary fulfillment of the DREAM Act, but in fact the policy was much more. It offered protection to a much broader group than Durbin's DREAM Act. While Durbin's Act had been aimed at college students, the new policy gave protection to many more people—people such as Gabino Sanchez.

Together with the first executive order for prosecutorial discretion and the rule change for the legalization of undocumented spouses of U.S. citizens, Present Obama had come to the defense of over half of the undocumented in this country. In effect, he ordered a moratorium on their arrest and deportation. Still, President Obama's order did not include the parents of United States citizen children. The President seemed to want to energize the youth vote in preparation for his 2012 re-election campaign. Regardless, the grassroots movement recognized progress, and millions of people understood that the only way to victory was through persistent struggle.

President Obama's new policies, in line with the goals of the campaign for American Families and Children, dramatically accelerated his enthusiastic support in the Latino community. In addition, they totally isolated candidate Romney from those voters. Barack Obama was now sweeping the Latino vote in percentages that almost equaled his support in the African American community. The Latino vote would prove decisive in certain swing states in the upcoming Presidential race. Moreover, the polls showed that over 70% of U.S voters supported his decisions to issue executive orders.

We still had to maintain pressure and expand our ability to defend people using the new policies, but we now felt the real possibility of victory. The moratorium was at least partially in place. The families and the young people were safe. Even if Romney defeated President Obama, he would have difficulty turning back these policies, because we had won the hearts of the majority of the people. Moreover, Gutierrez and his allies would have a much stronger bargaining position in Congress. The extreme, right-wing Republicans were no longer getting the deportations they wanted, and public opinion was against them.

On August 15, 2012, in our church, I watched Emma fill out the request for deferred status for a young undocumented woman with her child, who was a U.S. citizen. It was a victory for the Faith of Elvira! Marta Davillos, who had brought her deportation order and her two sons to Familia Latina Unida ten years ago and had struggled successfully to stay in this country, brought her two sons to apply for their two-year deferment—the fruits of her struggle.

Deferred Action for Childhood Applicants (DACA) was slow in taking off across the nation. Of the 1.6 million potential applicants, less than one hundred thousand applied in the first thirty days. The now-massive, not-for-profit immigrant rights organizations did not respond well to the challenge of assisting young applicants. The reason was all too evident. Funding was not available for the effort. Lawyers were charging applicants from $1,500 to $3,000 for an application, putting it out of the reach of most immigrants. The failure to respond to the DACA challenge was basically due to the organizer industrial complex, the same complex of funded organizations that had compromised the fight for reform legislation and failed to join the struggle to get President Obama to provide executive relief.

Relying on the expertise of Representative Gutierrez's staff and his own meetings with Homeland Security to clarify the procedures, Familia Latina Unida began a drive to assist young Latinos to file their own applications and to recruit them to assist others to apply: each one teach one! The new recruits swelled the ranks of our youth organization, La FuerZa Juventud. The grassroots movement was growing in preparation for the struggle that would begin immediately after the November elections.

✿ 23

Election Day Watershed

E lection Day in November of 2012 produced in us a deep feeling of anxiety. We felt confident in the Obama campaign's analysis, which promised an Electoral College victory. We were encouraged by President Obama's pre-election statements in support of legalization, and even by candidate Romney's last minute turnabout on immigration reform. On the other hand, a lot was at stake. Romney's election would mean a step backwards. Many of the families in our church had pending cases. Romney's election would mean their lives would be torn apart. The thousands of young people we had helped apply for DACA (the two-year deferment and work permit) would find themselves at risk if Romney were elected.

Had we done the right thing? We had initiated several campaigns over the last fifteen years: the fight for comprehensive immigration reform legislation; the fight to focus on family unity; the mass mobilizations; and sanctuary resistance. Most significantly, we had taken on President Obama, forcing him to use his executive authority on behalf of the undocumented. The stark contrast between Romney's stated policy of self-deportation and his opposition to the DREAM Act, and Obama's executive action to make temporary deferments and work authorizations available to 1.6 million Dreamers gave us hope that Latino voters would turn out for the President. Would the concessions we had won be enough to turn out the Latino vote, to re-elect President Obama and stop the Republicans? We had also worked hard for fifteen years to define the immigration issue as a Latino issue. Using the ideal of family unity, we had tried to unite Latinos with papers, and those without papers, and we had attempted to join Catholics and Protestants, who usually voted Democratic, with Latino Evangelicals, who usually voted Republican.

The Obama campaign advertised on Spanish-language TV. Speaking in pretty good Spanish, the President talked about his decision to offer relief to the Dreamers and his commitment to comprehensive immigration reform. English-language attack ads from the President's campaign focused on misstatements of the Republicans against abortion, one suggesting that rapes that ended in pregnancy were part of God's plan. The strong pro-choice emphasis of the Obama campaign risked losing the Latino Evangelicals and also the Catholics, who were listening to homilies and sermons each Sunday by their priests.

As we gathered for service the Sunday before the election, we prayed, relied on our faith, and placed our confidence in God that becoming a witness to His justice would sustain the grassroots movement that could transform this nation. In two days, voters would decide the future of our families and their right to stay together, though they themselves could not vote. Those who had no papers and could not vote, however, would still be active on Election Day. They would get out the vote and circulate a *consulta* to begin mobilizing for a new expanded moratorium, no matter who the President would be.

By ten o'clock on Tuesday night, it was clear that President Obama had won re-election, and that the Latino vote had been strong and decisive in that victory. We shared the excitement of millions of people in the President's victory over Romney, the Wall Street moneychangers, and the Tea Party Republicans to whom Romney had tied himself. We were equally excited by the nation's recognition of the demographic dawning of a new day. A national minority voice, representing nearly 30% of the electorate—comprised of African Americans, Latinos and Asians—had determined the outcome of the election and signaled its important role in the future of this country. We breathed a sigh of relief, free of Romney's threat of forced self-deportation and filled with hope for a steady transition to a just nation.

After the election, we heard the commentators and the President's spokespersons talk about the critical contribution of the strongly unified Latino vote, and their recognition that it would continue to grow. Then we heard them, one after another, begin to talk about passing comprehensive immigration reform, pointing to the 65% of voters who told exit pollsters that they favored legalization of undocumented immigrants. The Democrats joyfully pronounced the demise of the Republican Party if it refused to pass immigration reform.

For a moment we took leave of our senses, but were quickly brought back by a couple of comments. One of the White House surrogates came on a cable news station warning sternly that we would have to "keep the left in line" as the President moved to make a new coalition with moderate Republicans in order to maintain control of "the center" of the country. We remembered that President Clinton had gone through this same process, and wondered if President Obama was headed for a similar legacy. The difference was that President Clinton had started from the very beginning of his Presidency with the premise of making a coalition to control the center. In pursuit of that center, he had passed laws that the Republicans had been unable to get through Congress under the Reagan and Bush I administrations. By twisting Democratic arms and offering deals to hesitant congressmen, he signed the NAFTA bill in December of 1993, Goals 2000 in March of 1994, and the Crime bill in September of 1994—all in the first congressional session of his first term. Even after the Gingrich revolution of 1994—the mid-term equivalent of the Tea Party take-over—President Clinton had been able to pass welfare reform in August of 1996, as well as immigration reform that same September, before running for re-election. The unmitigated disaster of this "center-seeking" legislation especially harmed minority communities: waves of unemployed Mexicans crossing the border just to survive NAFTA; teachers saddled with the teaching-to-the-test curriculum of Goals 2000, that hobbled their creativity and doomed the public schools; and Black and Latino youth incarcerated on a massive scale by a Crime Bill that shackled an entire generation as effectively as had once the bonds of slavery. Kasich's Welfare Reform bill had played an equally significant role in punishing Latinos, and all other poor people. But it was President Clinton's 1996 Immigration Act that we had been calling "the broken law" for the last fifteen years. It was directly responsible for millions of deportations, deaths in the desert, and broken families.

The Democratic leadership's effort to claim the center had caused Barack Obama to disassemble the broad-based coalition that had originally elected him to the Presidency in 2008. President Obama's move to the right, and toward the center—signified by his one million deportations—did not win over the votes of white America. His share of the white vote declined. Even his concerted appeal to women voters failed to keep candidate Romney from getting a majority of their votes. In fact, the demographic that re-elected him was amazingly similar to the one that had originally elected him. There was a slight decrease in the overall vote and in the percentage that turned out, except for the Latino vote, where the turnout percentage increased.

If candidate Obama had chosen to maintain the core coalition during his first two years, instead of turning his back on them, the country might have been spared the Tea Party Congress. Immigration reform might have been passed, and the infrastructure and jobs program that the country so desperately needed might have been put in place. The insurance-company-based Affordable Care Act might have been replaced with a single-payer system that focused on providing, not just paying for, health care. The new relations with Latin America—which President Obama had promised, and from which he then retreated—might have been begun, and the continent might have been mobilized to deal with the scourge of the drug trade and the injustice of free trade agreements. Seventy thousand deaths in Mexico that resulted from the failed U.S. enforced war on drugs might have been prevented.

More realistically, though, the Constitution does not grant the President of the United States an executive power to maintain his core coalition. It was the grassroots movement, springing from Elvira's faith, which had won the hearts of a great majority of the people. Our numbers and our unity were growing, and we had the true responsibility to take a leadership role in the forthcoming struggle. In the words of Dr. King, the check we had gotten after President Obama's first election had come back marked "insufficient funds." President Obama's re-election marked a watershed in the immigration struggle, because a unified Latino community showed the strength of its growing numbers. Now was the time to begin the fight again, to assemble the disparate forces of this rainbow coalition, and to work to collect on that bad check.

RUDOLFO LOZANO AND EMMA LOZANO
Rudy Lozano was assasinated in 1983 after forming the Black-Latino coalition with Danny Davis that led to the election of Mayor Harold Washington.

MAYOR HAROLD WASHINGTON WITH EMMA
The movement that elected Harold Washington in 1983 began in 1968 with the "Rainbow Coalition" and opened the way for the election of the first African American President.

JACOBITA ALONSO AND EMMA
*Jacobita led the walkout from the
Catholic church that resulted in the
formation of Adalberto United
Methodist Church. She remained a
leader of Sin Fronteras for over two
decades.*

FATHER MARCO, ELVIRA, AND ROBERTO LOPEZ (*standing, center, left to right*)
*Sin Fronteras Chief of Staff Roberto Lopez joined Elvira and Father Marco Cardenas in the
first Mega March. Father Marco and Emma Lozano partnered with radio personality Rafael
"Pistolero" Pulido to call for, then mobilize, the mega marches of 2005 and 2006.*

HUNGER STRIKE ON THE PLACITA
The hunger strike on the Placita in Pilsen for the IFCO workers led to the first march for executive action—and attracted a mysterious visitor.

SUPPORTERS OF ELVIRA IN SANCTUARY
The AAAN was one of the many groups that gathered in solidarity with Elvira in sanctuary: in addition to the leaders of MALDEF, LULAC, and other national Latino and labor organizations, over 7,000 people came to pray with Elvira.

EMMA, THEN-STATE SENATOR BARACK
OBAMA, ELVIRA, AND SAULITO
*In the State Capitol Building in Springfield,
Illinois*

ELVIRA AND SAULITO
*In sanctuary at Adalberto
United Methodist Church*

ELVIRA AND REV. COLEMAN
In Los Angeles at Father Richard's church, just before ICE agents surrounded their car and arrested her

ELVIRA IN MEXICO
Elvira continued the struggle in Mexico after she was deported. She organized demonstrations at the U.S. Embassy and also demonstrated on behalf of migrants from Central America forced to ride "La Bestia."

CONGRESSMAN LUIS V. GUTIERREZ
Even in the Chicago City Council and during his first term in Congress in 1993, Gutierrez defended the rights of the undocumented. He became a vocal and beloved advocate by leading the Congressional Hispanic Caucus on immigration issues and by speaking in hundreds of cities across the nation.

GUTIERREZ WITH FAMILIA LATINA UNIDA IN WASHINGTON, D.C.
Gutierrez opened the doors of Congressman and Senators so that the families could present their cases, bringing their children on difficult trips to Washington over twenty five times.

GUTIERREZ AND GABINO SANCHEZ
Gutierrez's fight for Gabino Sanchez in 2012 signaled to the Democrats that they must act before the Democratic Convention in North Carolina or face the consequences.

ROSALBA VALDEZ
Her song, "Obama, Obama, Don't Deport my Father," became the anthem of the movement.

EMMA LOZANO AND JOSÉ LÓPEZ
This rally for Latino Unity joined the Mexican and Puerto Rican communities in the historic action which redefined the immigration issue as a shared struggle for all Latinos.

MINISTER LOUIS FARRAKHAN
The Minister spoke at Lincoln United Methodist Church in preparation for the 2015 march for "Justice or Else" in Washington D.C. This march represented the merging of the movements against racial profiling, mass deportation, and mass incarceration.

LINCOLN UNITED
METHODIST CHURCH
*In the neighborhood of
Pilsen in Chicago*

THE LADY OF GUADALUPE
*In the shrine in the garden of
the church*

REV. EMMA LOZANO AND REV. WALTER COLEMAN
Preaching together at Lincoln United Methodist Church

TO EVERYTHING A SEASON
Carved stone in the garden shrine to the Virgin of Guadalupe at Lincoln United Methodist Church

COLUMBIA AND THE INDIAN PRINCESS, HONORING GEORGE WASHINGTON.
In 1855 or 1856, Constantino Brumidi created this fresco detail, which is in Capitol room H-144, Washington, D.C. Brumidi, who also painted the giant fresco "The Apotheosis of Washington" on the interior of the Capitol dome, here depicted the guiding spirits of the nation standing in honor beside a bust of its greatest general and first President. Representations of Columbia were quite common in the 18th and 19th centuries—most U.S. coinage had an image of Columbia, and the national anthem for over a century was "Hail, Columbia!" She was often shown as a Greek goddess immigrating to American shores and being introduced to the Indian Princess by one of the Founding Fathers.

NUESTRA SEÑORA DE LA GUADALIBERTAD, PATRONA DE LOS MIGRANTES. *(Next page)*
Marta Sanchez Soler created this embossed metal relief, based on a print by Neftali de Leon, in 2011. The title, in translation, is "Our Lady of Guadalibertad, Patroness of Migrants." According to tradition, the Virgin Mary appeared to an indigenous man named Juan Diego on December 9, 1531. The Virgin asked that a shrine in her name be built on the spot where she appeared, Tepeyac Hill, close to Mexico City. The appearance of the Virgin of Guadalupe to an indigenous man is one of the forces behind creating the Mexico that we know today: a blend of Spanish and native blood. Her dark skin and the fact that the story of her apparition was told in the indigenous language of Nahuatl and in Spanish are said to have helped convert the indigenous people of Mexico to Christianity at the time of the conquest. She represents a blend of Aztec and Spanish heritage. Her image has played an important role as a national symbol of Mexico, not only as a religious icon but also as a sign of cultural unity and identity. The day of the Virgen de Guadalupe became a national holiday in Mexico in 1859. Pope John Paul II canonized Juan Diego in 2002, making him the first indigenous American saint, and declared Our Lady of Guadalupe the patroness of the Americas. This image shows the Virgen in the garb and pose of the Statue of Liberty (or Libertad, another name for Columbia), demonstrating artistically the insight that the two guiding spirits of each nation may actually be one.

PART THREE
THE RESURRECTION
SPIRIT OF THE
GRASSROOTS

₩ 24
A Return to the Moratorium

A fter the election, the President and his surrogates talked about passing immigration reform legislation in the Republican-controlled
House. It would be a difficult task. Tea Party Republicans, and
Republican Congressmen facing re-election in two years in Tea Party districts, would oppose it. While the growing Latino vote had a powerful
influence on national and statewide elections, it would have little influence
in Congressional districts gerrymandered to limit or exclude a Latino presence. We had to find a way to ensure that any legislation that did pass would
legalize all of the eleven million undocumented immigrants. We also had to
stop the deportations while the Congress deliberated.

We had successfully moved the President to grant temporary legal
status and work permits to some of the undocumented. We would now
demand that, pending the passage of a just comprehensive immigration
reform bill, he should extend and expand the DACA deferments and work
permits to include their parents, the parents of U.S. citizen children, and agricultural workers. Since we had made our case to the American people, and
the President had the power to issue executive orders, why should we wait
while another million people were deported and hundreds of thousands of
families were destroyed?

There was another reason to demand that the President act before dragging us through a long legislative process in a deadlocked Congress. As long as the President continued with mass deportations, e-verifications, and enhanced border patrols that funneled migrants to the most dangerous crossings, why would the Republicans negotiate a bill for immigration reform? They would already be getting everything they wanted without it. On the other hand, if the President gave temporary legal status and work permits to the undocumented, as was done for the first Cuban refugees, then the Republicans would have a compelling reason to pass a bill to bring those workers under the law. At the same time, our people would be protected, and we would not have to accept whatever repressive, criminalizing bill they wanted to pass.

Familia Latina Unida circulated a *consulta* outside polling places on Election Day. The *consulta* asked people if we should demand that the President use his executive authority to extend and expand the DACA deferments and work permits to the parents of both Dreamers and U.S. citizen children. The *consulta* also asked if we should demand that participation in the Affordable Care Act be extended to the undocumented and legal permanent residents who were presently excluded. Finally, it asked if we should mobilize to make these demands on January 21st—the day of the inauguration and of the holiday commemorating Dr. Martin Luther King's birthday—in cities across the country. The thousands of young people who were stepping forward to claim their legal status in America—the fruits of the harvest of our struggle—became the grassroots movement organizing the *consulta*.

One morning in December 2012, ICE and FBI agents broke into the Chicago Pallet Company, demanding proof of citizenship from the workers. Thirty-four workers were arrested. Also in Chicago, ICE agents gathered up a dozen *jornaleros*. In Palatine, ICE agents raided a restaurant. One week later, we learned that four workers from the South Side of Chicago were on their way to install commercial racks. They stopped at an oasis on the interstate highway in Ohio. When they approached the cashier, she picked up a microphone and announced over the loudspeaker, "Mike, I got some for you!" ICE agents arrested the four and scheduled them for deportation. What was happening?

We organized a collective defense for the thirty-four Chicago Pallet Company workers. Congressman Gutierrez joined them at a press conference at our church to demand that ICE use its policy of prosecutorial discretion to close their cases. The reality of the deportations seemed to frame the issue for the Congressman. "In the last year, this administration has deported over 100,000 parents of U.S. citizen children," he said publicly. "This is unacceptable."

Privately, the Congressman told us that while discussions were opening with the Republicans and even with Vice Presidential candidate Paul Ryan, the Democrats were content to wait until the normal course of business brought comprehensive immigration reform before the Congress. A bill was expected to come out of the House in March or April, then go to the Senate, and from there to a House-Senate conference committee. Such a timetable would bring the final bill for a vote in July, right before the August break. "Everybody is talking about comprehensive immigration reform," the Congressman told us, "but no one is talking about the deportations. Unless we focus on the deportations, there will be no urgency to pass a bill and no pressure for inclusion of all of the eleven million undocumented immigrants." We began to argue, along with the congressman, that inclusion was our first priority, as opposed to a road to citizenship. The Republican congressmen were opposed to granting eventual citizenship to the undocumented because they perceived them as Democratic voters. For the same reason, the Democratic leadership seemed willing to sacrifice the legalization of millions of people in order to ensure that those who were legalized could vote for them. We began a campaign with our contacts around the country to make inclusion the priority and to dramatize this demand by fighting for a moratorium.

In some ways, we felt that we had returned to the beginning of the struggle. Every day, more people facing deportations came to us asking for help. Now that the election prohibition was over, ICE was running wild, increasing their numbers to justify their budget. We were training new people to fight the deportations, sitting with new families, discussing their alternatives, supporting their faith, and bringing them into the movement.

We joined with Pastor Jose Landaverde and the Our Lady of Guadalupe Anglican Mission to call together some of the grassroots organizations in the city for the march on Inauguration Day. The immigrant rights organizations reluctantly and half-heartedly joined us. We hit the streets and the churches with flyers and held a series of press conferences about the new families facing separation. We organized a commission, at Congressman Gutierrez's behest, to monitor Homeland Security's lack of use of the policy of prosecutorial discretion. ICE clearly had almost stopped applying this policy after the election. We arranged a meeting with top ICE officials in

Chicago for January 17th, four days before the date of the march. Our plan was to bring the Pallet workers and other families to a vigil outside of the ICE headquarters while Gutierrez and the commission went inside to meet with directors Lundgren and Moss.

On January 17th we gathered in front of the Chicago ICE headquarters with the Pallet Company workers and went inside to meet with ICE officials, who smiled and stonewalled our demand for statistics on prosecutorial discretion dismissals. They vociferously denied that the arrests at the Chicago Pallet Company were part of an immigration raid. Instead, they claimed the raid was part of an investigation into money laundering at the company. Confronted by the Congressman and a room full of elected officials and organizational representatives, they said they would turn over the cases for consideration of prosecutorial discretion as soon as the workers were cleared of participation in the money-laundering scheme.

It was clear that the Obama administration's enforcement of immigration laws would continue at an even faster pace, now that the election was over. Raids based on unrelated warrants were being used to pick up dozens of the undocumented as collateral arrests. ICE now employed a new method to meet its quotas for deportation, quotas that apparently were set at nearly 500,000 per year. We were more determined than ever to launch a new moratorium movement. In the next few days, more reports of arrests and deportations kept pouring in. At the same time, radio personality Piolin, picked up the call to march and spent three hours each morning publicizing it.

It was ten degrees on a gray, windy Monday in Chicago. The young people of the FuerZa had spent Saturday making 500 hand-held signs and banners. They came early to the church, as did a group of students from DeKalb, whom we had been working with. The families of our church joined the Pallet workers and their families. Among the church families were many still fighting their own battles to stay together. Many had played key roles in the struggle of the last fifteen years. Diego and Francisca Lino were present with their children. Their example had inspired the first Familias Unidas national tour in 2009. We had successfully fought Francisca's deportation for six years, but her fight continued. Alberto Segura, whose successful fight to stay had inspired the demand for prosecutorial discretion, came early with his wife and son and a picture of their daughter, who had died in Kuwait. Doris Aquirre, still fighting her own deportation and that of her ten-year-old son, came ready to march. The Pedrozas came with their son, who had been picked up at their home and had spent five weeks in detention in Dallas, Texas, before we got his case transferred back to Chicago. His arrest was part of a so-called gang member round up by ICE, although he had no actual affiliation with any gang. We were pursuing his case to challenge the police practice of marking undocumented young men for deportation during routine identification checks on street corners.

While we had received endorsements for the march from the immigrant rights organizations, they were absent. Several thousand people marched to Daley Plaza, where the giant outdoor TV screen showed President Obama's inauguration speech. The march was accompanied by a troop of drums and trumpets, part of a Guatemalan group that practiced at the church on Thursday nights. In front of the members of La FuerZa Juventad were young people we had met when they came to get help in applying for their DACA deferments.

We announced to the assembled marchers that, in Mexico City, Elvira Arellano was leading a parallel march to the United States embassy. Fr. Landaverde rephrased Dr. King's "Dream Speech," and Emma brilliantly explained the reason for the moratorium demand. The workers told their stories, and the children cried. We were confident that the moratorium movement of 2013 would grow to millions by June because it was the truth. We had seen the movement grow from a thousand to millions before.

In his Second Inaugural Address, President Obama focused on the "Declaration of Independence," the Civil War, and the "Emancipation Proclamation." He appealed for an acceptance of gay marriage and for recognition of climate change. And he did use the word "immigrant" twice. But he said nothing about providing legalization for the eleven million immigrants and their families. Nothing: nothing for the issue that had become the cornerstone of his re-election, nothing for the very reason he stood on that exact spot to take the oath of office. We shared our thoughts about the President's oversight in a statement, "The Moratorium Movement in 2013," which we circulated to our contacts around the country.

✹ 25

The Children's Campaign

n late January 2013, Congressman Gutierrez reported to us about a discussion held in the White House between the President and the Congressional Hispanic Caucus. We remembered how many times Obama had postponed these meetings as he ducked the immigration issue during his first term. He was not ducking the issue any more. The President told the Latino congressmen that he didn't want to wait another month for legislation. He promised to make immigration reform his top priority and scheduled a major speech for the following Tuesday in Nevada. President Obama was clearly responding to the pressure and understood that we wouldn't go away. Calling us on his way out of the White House, Gutierrez exclaimed, "We were right. He is responding to the pressure. Keep it up!"

We awoke Monday morning to the news that eight senators—four Republican and four Democratic—were introducing a comprehensive immigration reform bill in the U.S. Senate. The bill followed the general principles established by Gutierrez in 2006. A similar bi-partisan group was moving a bill in the House of Representatives, and the lawmakers had set a timetable to reach an agreement before the August recess. On Tuesday, the President made his major policy address calling for immigration reform, announcing the principles that the McCain-Kennedy Bill had established years before.

Although it was still not clear who would be allowed to legalize and who would be left behind, there was significant momentum. Senator Melendez from New Jersey summed up the political situation: "The majority of the American people want it; the Latino community expects it; the Democrats support it; and the Republicans need it." Ironically, Senator Durbin stated, "our priority is on family unity, on keeping families together." His refusal to renew his private bill for Elvira had resulted in her deportation. The movement that began with Elvira and the struggle to keep families together had finally come home to Washington, D.C.

No matter the positive news, we were still fighting deportations everyday, and evidently would be for the next year. We wanted a moratorium on deportations while they debated in Washington, and we were pushing to get the maximum number of the undocumented included in the process of legalization. The road to citizenship was a good objective, but not one for which we were willing to sacrifice the inclusion of millions of people.

We set about the task of assembling those who would support our position and developing a way to bring that position into public view. Surveying our contacts both in Chicago and around the nation, we found few allies among the immigrant rights organizations. Of the national groups, only the National Day Labor Organizing Network was committed to making the case for the moratorium and for inclusion. We began to contact the pastors; here we made more progress. The pastors were confronted with cases of deportation every week and knew the details of each case. They knew if a person threatened with deportation had had a previous deportation, or an expedited deportation from the time when they first had tried to cross at the border. They knew if the person had had multiple driving-without-a-license tickets, or a DUI, or an arrest that showed they had had a gang affiliation at one time. They were aware that it would be a battle to get millions of less-than-perfect applicants included in the new legislation.

There was, in fact, a devil in the details. It was the demon of self-righteousness. The same human arrogance and greed that had led the United States into becoming the leader of the free world and creating the military-industrial complex prohibited the nation and its leaders from taking responsibility for wrongs they had done. In this case, they refused to admit that there was any guilt clinging to them for the system of undocumented labor that this nation had long operated: its recruitment and welcoming of cheap, exploitable labor, and its policies in Latin America which had driven people to come north to work. From this unrepentant, self-righteous position, the nation's leaders—both Democratic and Republican—reserved the right to judge who was worthy of the prize of living and working and having the rights of a citizen. Like true hypocrites, they looked down on their oppressed and exploited brethren and called them "illegal aliens."

The only way to fight this demon was with truth and with the witness of its victims. We again decided to take a busload of undocumented mothers and fathers with their children to Washington, D.C. We would join a delegation being organized by NDLON. We contacted Congressman Gutierrez and asked for his help in making public the testimonies that the families would give.

As we prepared the delegation going to Washington, D.C., the Illinois Coalition for Immigrant Rights (ICIRR) organized a roundtable discussion with Senator Durbin. While thousands had marched on the coldest day of the year to request a meeting with the Senator, neither Fr. Landaverde nor Lozano, who had led the march, nor any of the families in danger of deportation, were invited. Having the discussion in front of the media, the funded organizations followed a script, avoiding the question of the ongoing deportations and the issue of who would be included in the legislation. It was Congressman Gutierrez, invited at the last minute, who raised the issues of deportation and inclusion. Senator Durbin and the coalition stuck to the script—a path to citizenship.

In Washington, D.C., the President said definitively that he would take no action to stop the ongoing deportations. At the same time, the House Republican leadership expressed its opposition to any road to citizenship, with the possible exception of the Dreamers. Our communications with grassroots groups across the country revealed that demand was growing precipitously for maximum inclusion in the legislation and an immediate moratorium. The Democratic leadership had joined with the established advocacy groups to suppress these demands. Our worst fear was that the Democrats would sacrifice legalization for the sake of citizenship, in the hope of blaming the Republicans in the mid-term elections.

Negotiations among the "secret eight" group of four Democrats and four Republicans in the House of Representatives confirmed our view that the Democrats were using the citizenship demand to kill the bill—and that inclusion was definitely a problem. Republicans in the group took a strong position against the fifteen-year road to citizenship advocated by the President. Three of the Democrats then broke off discussions. Gutierrez, however, continued one-on-one discussions and received a commitment to approve citizenship "indirectly" for most of the undocumented. They would agree for U.S. citizen husbands, brothers, sisters, and employers to petition for legalizing individual undocumented immigrants without the undocumented person having to leave the country. When Gutierrez reported on the positive outcome he had negotiated, a representative of the Democratic leadership chastised him for having one-on-one discussions. We felt hopeful that Gutierrez could find a meaningful compromise in the House if the grassroots movement could keep the pressure on the Democrats from below.

The dark fog of duplicity in the Democratic Party, dependency among the advocacy organizations, and obstructionism from the Republicans belied the bright media reports of the growing consensus for immigration reform. We traveled through the night with a busload of men, women and children facing deportation and separation to make our case in Washington, D.C. Over five hundred undocumented workers and their families gathered there to make the demand for "inclusion" and "a moratorium." Those who had been stopped the first time they had tried to enter the country came forward with the witness of their lives and their children and asked, "Will we be included in the new law?" Those who had been deported and had returned to their families gave the witness of their faithfulness to their families and asked, "Will we be included?" Those who had been faithful wives and mothers, but who had not themselves worked a full-time job, came forward with their witness and asked, "Will we be included?" Those with sons who had a record of gang involvement, even though the record was false, came forward with their witness and asked, "Will our sons be included?" Those who had records, like Gabino Sanchez, of convictions for driving without a license, or other minor convictions, came forward with their witness and asked, "Will we be included?"

These testimonies were very effective because the United States Senators at the center of the immigration debate seemed not to have considered these issues. Congressman Gutierrez took Gabino Sanchez with him to the floor of the Congress to hear the President's State of the Union speech, and the media reported it. The voices of the undocumented were heard when some of them were arrested at a Senate committee hearing for demanding a moratorium on deportations. We then arranged a meeting with Congressman Gutierrez for the whole national delegation. The meeting began with Rosalba Valdez, singing her song to President Obama, "Don't Take Away My Father." Before the assembled Washington press corps, Gutierrez elicited the testimonies of those who feared they would not be included in the legislation and those who faced immediate deportation. The Illinois delegation later met with Senator Durbin, and he responded with a statement to the press in favor of suspending deportations while the debate continued.

While we were returning to Chicago on the long overnight bus ride through the snowy mountains of Pennsylvania, President Obama leaked his own immigration plan, one that prioritized the road to citizenship but ignored the issue of inclusion. The President also issued a clear statement that he would not use his executive power to stop the deportations. Republicans charged that the President was bent on killing the legislation and then blaming the Republicans in order to carry the Latino vote in the mid-term elections. We feared they were correct.

Writing in her weekly column in *El Diario*, Elvira traced the history of the dehumanization of the undocumented. "First, after 9/11, we were terrorists like Bin Laden. Then we were criminals. Then we were bringing diseases like the plague into the U.S. Then we were stealing jobs from Americans. Finally, through the testimony of our children, through their tears," she wrote, "we became known as mothers and fathers, hard-working people trying to raise our children, the victims of the global economy and of racism." Then Elvira said, "One last label remains to be removed, that of pawns in a political game between Democrats and Republicans."

Back in Chicago, we opened discussions with many of the immigrant rights organizations on the demands for inclusion and for a moratorium. We also announced a march to occur on March 10th. Emma began re-enlivening the old National Alliance of Latino Leaders around the country to build up the movement from below, from the grassroots.

The first grassroots movement of the Latino Evangelical churches, responding to the families in their congregations, had spread outward to parent white Evangelical mega-churches, upward through new Latino associations that followed the marching tune set by the veteran pastors of AMEN, and finally to a coalition of liberal and conservative white Evangelical power pastors. The latter coalition had surfaced with its support for immigration reform even before the 2012 election. Now the mostly conservative white Evangelical churches—so important to the right wing of the Republican Party—stepped forward again. They urged the Republican members of the House to support immigration reform and promised to give them political cover in their conservative districts.

Unlike the small Latino churches where the movement had started, the white Evangelical leaders were not really committed to protecting the undocumented or clear about how to do it. Like the D.C. advocacy organizations, they were concerned with a policy victory—not a victory for the people. We decided to go back to the pastors from whom the grassroots movement had begun in the first place. Within a month, support for the moratorium had worked its way to the top of the Evangelical pyramid. Jim Wallis, chief executive of Sojourners, called on the President to stop the deportations.

While some of the national immigrant rights coalitions were moving in the direction of inclusion and moratorium, we clearly had not moved the

White House or those organizations closest to the administration. One Washington policy activist suggested we were tone deaf to what was going on in the beltway. Basically, they were saying that it was necessary to sacrifice another 500,000 people to get immigration reform passed. Meanwhile, statistics showed that the Obama administration had deported over 200,000 parents of U.S. citizen children since 2010. Statistics also showed that the majority of those deported had violated no other laws than the broken immigration law of 1996. Univision anchor María Elena Salinas confronted the President directly, asking him to explain if there was anything other than political motivation for the continuing deportations. White House policy director, Cecilia Muñoz, responded to critics of the continuing deportations by saying, "It was necessary to get Republican support for comprehensive immigration reform." In other words, the deportations were being carried out for purely political reasons.

We argued that Republican opposition was focused on border security and that they had largely accepted the legalization of the eleven million undocumented immigrants. Deportations were not necessary to get an agreement on immigration reform. We believed that the Democratic leadership had another motivation. Many in the movement doubted the President's will to actually get reform passed, suggesting that the Democrats would instead like to use the issue again in the mid-term elections to get a Democratic majority in the Congress. The President reverted to his pre-election position that he didn't have the authority to suspend deportations or to extend the deferments, now granted to the Dreamers, to their parents. While most of the groups persisted in the practice of sending delegations to lobby members of Congress, something I now knew as a congressional staff member was almost useless, Elvira came up with her own plan of action. In her column in *El Diario*, she explained "Saulito's Plan" for a letter campaign by the children of undocumented immigrants and gave a powerful indictment of the inaction in Congress.

In church on Sunday, March 3rd, we reflected on the Gospel of Luke, in which Jesus attacked the sin of status seeking. The selfish drive to make oneself the most important affects all of us. On a larger scale, our struggle was with the denial of status to the undocumented. Jesus instructed his disciples against the evil of status, saying, "He is greatest who serves all." Directly following that instruction, Jesus called the little children to him, telling the disciples that they must become like these children to enter the kingdom of heaven. Elvira's plan of action would confront the hypocrisy of status with those who had the least status, the children. During Lent we were holding rosaries every Wednesday night at the church. The next Wednesday, at a prayer meeting, we gathered over one hundred children and young people who had at least one undocumented parent. While their parents prayed, the children and young people wrote letters to the President and read them to the press.

We began organizing the children's campaign on the following Sunday, the anniversary in Chicago of the first mega-march. Three thousand men, women, young Dreamers with their DACA deferments, and hundreds of children marched the same three miles from Union Park to the Federal Building that Emma had chosen for the march of half a million in 2006. "We have come a long way since then," we told the media. "Now we have to pressure the Congress and the President for inclusion of all undocumented immigrants in the new law, and a moratorium while they debate. We will pressure them with the letters of the children on both sides of the border."

On the evening of the march, we held a memorial for President Hugo Chavez at Adalberto United Methodist Church. Gathered at the memorial with the Venezuelan Counsel General, below the picture of Elvira in sanctuary, were two generations of the initiative we had undertaken for Puerto Rican and Mexican unity. Dr. José López recalled the development of the unity that made immigration "a Latino issue." Lopez pointed to that unity as an expression of the Bolivarian vision, which Chavez had done so much to move forward: a unified Latin America, made powerful by a unified Latino community in the United States, growing in solidarity with the poor of the South.

Emma had secured the support of grassroots organizations in fifteen states. On March 11th, they held joint press conferences announcing the children's campaign and launching the *Coordinadora 13*. Elvira began to organize collecting the children's letters in Mexico and Central America.

Congressman Gutierrez was focused on the legislative process in the House and, to some extent, in the Senate. At a public meeting in Chicago, Senator Durbin professed that any agreement the Gang of Eight agreed to in the Senate would have to have the approval of the Republicans in the House, as mediated by Senator Rubio, and the Congressional Hispanic Caucus, in the person of Gutierrez. Gutierrez rolled up his sleeves and worked tirelessly, leveraging the position of influence he had won by staunchly leading the immigration reform movement for the previous three years. Working with a group of eight in the House, Gutierrez began one-to-one work with

Republicans and key Democrats. He met with Vice Presidential candidate Paul Ryan and publicly praised Ryan for his openness on the issue, reminding reporters that Ryan had been a co-sponsor of one of Gutierrez's earlier immigration bills. When it looked like the Democrats would walk out of the negotiations in the House over the issue of the path to citizenship, Gutierrez went one-on-one with the Republican members and reached an agreement—over the objections of the Democratic leadership—for various indirect pathways to citizenship. Negotiations reconvened.

Gutierrez then went back on the road, taking trips to Florida, Texas, and California. He skillfully put himself and key members of Congress in front of large Latino crowds to move them to take stronger positions. Although Minority Leader Pelosi ducked out of a San Francisco meeting, the strength of Gutierrez's support was not lost on her. She commented the next week that, judging from the response of the crowd, she would lose the next election to Gutierrez if he chose to run against her in her own district.

We determined that the *Coordinadora* would have to focus grassroots pressure on specific points where it could be most effective. Our first objective was to make it clear to the Democratic leadership that if immigration legislation were sabotaged in order to get an advantage in the midterm elections, the President would face a massive movement demanding a moratorium. We hoped to convince the leadership that the pressure on the President would wipe out any gains Democrats might hope to make by blaming the Republicans for legislative failure.

We had done as much as we could to convince the established advocacy organizations that the "path to citizenship" was just a bargaining chip and that the prize was inclusion of all undocumented immigrants in some form of legalization. While negotiations in the House of Representatives were proceeding toward this goal, we were unable to get the advocates to focus their protests. They continued to raise general demands for comprehensive immigration reform, which would include a path to citizenship. We decided that it would be more effective for us to move independently with the grassroots organizations that Emma had called together in the *Coordinadora 13* than with the advocacy groups.

Our first action after the March 10th announcement of the Children's March was a Stations of the Cross protest at the ICE headquarters in Chicago. We had staged this action to close down ICE headquarters every Good Friday for several years. The procession circled the well-secured building at Clark and Congress, and featured U.S. citizen children and Dreamers with undocumented parents. Even blocking the doors in an act of civil disobedience did not provoke ICE to make their customary arrests this year. Instructions must have come down from the top. Our objective was simple: keep the issue of the deportations in the news while the Senate and House committees formulated a new and politically viable version of comprehensive immigration reform.

While the policy debate was going on, the reality of the struggle against injustice was again brought home to us. We met a Guatemalan named Pedro. Pedro worked at a good job in Guatemala. His brother-in-law came to visit, and they went out to lunch in the market. Pedro noticed that his brother-in-law had a tattoo of initials on his arm. "What are those initials?" Pedro asked. "They are my wife's initials," his brother-in-law responded. Unfortunately, they were also the initials of a drug cartel that was a rival of the MARAs, which dominated their town in Guatemala. Some of the MARAs came up to them and noticed the initials. Pedro was hit on the head with a lead pipe and woke up in the hospital to find that his brother-in-law had been killed—over an innocent tattoo of his wife's initials. The police questioned Pedro about the incident, and word spread that he was cooperating. A contract was put out on his life. Pedro left his wife and two children and headed for Mexico, only to find that the MARAs ran that town in Mexico as well. His aunt was told that he would have to leave by six o'clock that night or be killed. Pedro then headed for the United States border, where other family members promised to protect him and provide him with work to support his family back in Guatemala.

Pedro crossed the river with a *coyote*, but one of the women in the group fell behind and was drowning. The *coyote* ordered the group to go on, leaving her behind. Pedro went back for her, saved her, and then found himself surrounded by the border patrol. He spent six months in detention while his relatives in Denver filed a petition for political asylum and raised the two thousand dollars for bail. Although they paid the bail in Denver, ICE let Pedro out in Chicago without a dime in his pocket and only the clothes on his back, not knowing anybody. He walked out of ICE custody into the midst of the Stations of the Cross protest.

Pedro brought us a new ministry. Every week four or five detainees from Guatemala or the Dominican Republic were released in the same way. We would talk to them, put them in communication with family members in other cities, give them food and clothes, and listen to their stories. They were all fleeing from the violence. The reason for crossing the border had changed. Instead of immigrants coming to the United States due to harsh economic realities, they now came for physical survival in the face of death threats. While we met some Mexicans released in such strange fashion, for the most part they were simply turned back at the border. Central Americans, however, endured long stays in detention while relatives raised bail. We decided to stay focused on the legislation, which could provide security for millions, but we began to realize that the immigration issue had just become more complicated and would continue with us. The drug trade, motivated by the U.S. market, had created a wave of violence that now destabilized both American continents. As Elvira pointed out to us, the market for the drugs was in the United States, which was also the source of the guns.

Our second action after the demonstration at ICE headquarters was a march to President Obama's house in Hyde Park. Two hundred of the children and the Dreamers marched from Operation PUSH to the President's home. Rosalba Valdez sang her now-famous song to Obama, and the children and Dreamers told their stories to a dozen cameras while the Secret Service stood guard.

Keeping pressure on President Obama for the 1,400 daily deportations was controversial. The coalition of unions and advocacy organizations that were pressuring the Congress for immigration reform opposed it. It was an old battle for us. Now that the Republicans had been brought to change their minds on immigration reform by the Latino vote, our main problem remained the Democratic leadership, who would have liked a deadlocked Congress and blame heaped on Republicans by the Latino community in the upcoming midterm elections.

On April 10th, SEIU and the advocacy organizations planned a major demonstration in Washington, D.C. We lobbied with organizations around the country to keep the pressure on stopping the deportations and on increasing the number of the undocumented who would be included in legalization. Make the Road New York, which brought busloads of people from New York City, began the day with their own action in front of Homeland Security, protesting the deportations, before they joined the well-orchestrated rally at the Capitol. Speaker after speaker called for comprehensive immigration reform, challenging Republicans in the House and Senate. While the tightly controlled speakers kept to their talking points, Gutierrez maintained our key position. After introducing the members of Congress who came with him to the rally, he began criticizing the "1,400 deportations every day and hundreds of U.S. citizen children who are losing their mom or dad every day." Congressmen Gutierrez spoke in quiet defiance of the union leadership, who had told him to forget about the deportations and focus on the Republicans and the pending legislation.

The verdict from those who came to the march was clear. Gutierrez received over 300,000 positive hits on his Facebook page in the next 24 hours. The people wanted the deportations to stop. They wanted to be allowed to work legally and to stay with their families. As Gutierrez would explain to us the following week in Chicago, the issue was not how long it would take for people to become citizens but who, and how many, would be able to find the protection of legalization.

Gutierrez's Congressional office conducted a drive to make DACA applications available to eligible young people. Giovany Gomez directed the Congressman's Cicero office, which was dedicated to helping such applicants. After training a crew of volunteers, Giovany returned to Centro Sin Fronteras and our church to continue the campaign. Each Sunday after church, Gomez and his volunteers conducted "help sessions" and then followed up by arranging individual appointments to help the young people complete their applications. These young people, who came to us in increasing numbers, were different from the elite college students who had led the DREAM Act movement and had been willing to denounce their own parents to win their citizenship. They ranged in age from high school students to young workers with U.S. citizen children. Generally, they came to their appointments with their parents and family members. They showed the signs of living in the shadows for most of their young lives and exhibited the hope that something would now really change for them. Their parents came to support them, proud that their own long and difficult struggle had led to this opportunity for the children they had raised.

By April of 2013, seven months into the campaign drive, we had a list of over 2500 young people we had helped to apply. Many had come to us after dealing with unscrupulous attorneys who had tried to charge them as much as $5,000 to help fill out a simple, four-page application. We charged them no fees, but did ask them to join in the struggle to legalize their families.

On April 2nd we invited them to join us for Congressman Gutierrez's "Fight for Your Future Conference. " We established task forces to organize around issues of employment, education, health care, violence prevention, and empowerment. Many joined the Youth Health Service Corps that we had established in order to provide preventive screening and access to primary health care for undocumented immigrants, who were and would remain excluded from national health insurance, even in the new immigration law being written in Congress. We also formed a task force on "Conscientization," an educational effort that would allow these young people who had grown up in the United States to learn about their own roots in Latin America. Whatever lay in the future for the fast growing Latino community in the United States, we felt this group of over one-and-a-half million young people would be critical.

Gutierrez addressed the youth congress and gave a clear picture of the legislation that was developing. In introducing him, Emma read from Elvira's most recent statement: "This law will not be an Emancipation Proclamation that freed the slaves and promised forty acres and a mule. Nor will it be the Civil Rights Act that guaranteed Constitutional support for the full citizenship of African Americans." The Congressman explained the realities. The new law would provide millions of people the possibility to achieve provisional legal status, to have work permits, to stay together, and perhaps—for those who had been deported—to return to their families. Budget constraints on the legislation would prevent the newly legalized from receiving any federal benefits, including health insurance, for the estimated fifteen years it would take to become citizens.

In truth, the Congressman was fighting both Democrats and Republicans. The Democrats wanted a path to citizenship, even if it meant excluding millions from legalization. The Republicans wanted to walk the line between reopening access to the Latino vote and the rabid racism of their Tea Party base. To make the two come together, Gutierrez tried catching flies with honey instead of vinegar. On April 15th, Emma received a call from the Congressman: "I need your help in a meeting we are having here in Chicago with Congressman Ryan, the former Vice Presidential candidate. I want you to get Sergeant Nunez and some of the families together to give Ryan gifts for what I am trying to get him committed to in the legislation."

If balancing the disparate forces involved in the issue of immigration reform had been difficult for Gutierrez, it had been equally challenging for Lozano. She had defended the congressman from critics on the left while moving constantly to heighten the contradictions with ICE, the White House, and the Republican-controlled Congress. What made it possible for these two leaders to continue their relationship of trust was a common commitment to undocumented immigrants and what they themselves said they wanted. Right now, they wanted the law to be passed, and Ryan's support was critical in the House.

Congressman Ryan had agreed to appear with Gutierrez in Chicago in support of comprehensive immigration reform. Luis wanted the families to make Ryan feel that he could become popular in the Latino community if he took a strong stand for the proposed legislation. Gutierrez had successfully employed this tactic before. Even though the congressman had traveled across the country opposing President Obama's policies, he had also proclaimed how much he wanted to campaign for Obama in the Latino community—if only he would stop the deportations. When President Obama had responded, Gutierrez did in fact campaign across the nation for him. Now he was promising to reopen the Latino vote to the Republicans if they would join in passing immigration reform. Needless to say, the White House and the Democratic leadership were furious. On the other hand, it was a move that Lozano and the grassroots movement supported.

As we prepared for the meeting, lightning struck again. Just as the events of 9/11 had torpedoed immigration reform for years, the bombing of the Boston Marathon by two Russian Muslim students threatened to stop our momentum. Elvira's yearlong witness in sanctuary had turned back the hysteria of the fall of the twin towers: "I am not a terrorist. I am not a criminal. I am a worker and a mom." But it had taken time. We needed Ryan's affirmation now, more than ever.

Gutierrez had worked hard to establish his relationship with Congressman Ryan, and he worked hard to set up the events in Chicago. They appeared together at Erie House. Our objective was to make the former Vice Presidential candidate feel welcome. In spite of having campaigned on the strongly anti-immigrant slogan of self-deportation, Ryan had, in fact, cosponsored Gutierrez's immigration bill in 2006. We opened the meeting with the color guard from the Marine Academy for Math and Science and the pledge of allegiance. Emma Lozano introduced several families who testified about the anguish of being separated and their children gave Ryan gifts: pictures of their families and a small statue of the Virgin of Guadalupe.

Then Emma introduced Sergeant Hector Nunez, his wife Rosa, and their two U.S. citizen children. Emma explained that Hector had returned from active duty in Kuwait and had taken his wife, who was undocumented, to the consulate in Juarez to complete the application for her adjustment of status. At the interview they were told that she could not return to the United States for ten years. Under orders to deploy again to Afghanistan, his commanding officer had given him time to deal with his wife's situation. Seven months later, we met him and worked with Congressman Gutierrez to bring her back through a one-year humanitarian visa, a visa that would expire in a few weeks. Nunez stood upright in his uniform. He spoke clearly and told Congressman Ryan, "I will be able to focus in my next deployment tomorrow because I know you will be in Congress protecting my wife and family." Then he pinned one of his several medals on the congressman's coat. Applause filled the hall for several minutes.

Gutierrez spoke again of the 1,400 deportations a day, of the values of family life, and of the integrity of undocumented immigrants. Then he quickly outlined the bi-partisan agreement he was forging with the group of eight in the House. He went on to praise Ryan for his humanity and his principles. When Representative Ryan spoke, he talked about "a nation of immigrants" and outlined his commitment to passing immigration reform. Ryan's characterization of the United States as the greatest country in the world ignored the realities of racism and exploitation that had forced so many families to come here in the first place and had then subjected them to humiliation and intimidation. That day, it didn't matter to us. What did matter was the leading conservative voice in the Republican Party publicly endorsing a bill that would stop the deportations and bring millions out of the shadows. We surrounded Congressman Ryan and Congressman Gutierrez, both Catholics, with a dozen Catholic priests for a final blessing, and the meeting was over.

The next morning, the Chicago Sun Times ran a picture of the two congressmen over the title "The Odd Couple." CNN began its newscast with the question, "Will the Boston terrorist attack set back immigration reform?" The news anchor answered, "The leading voice in the Republican House says NO. In fact, Ryan says the terrorist attack is even more reason why we must pass immigration reform."

Ryan's public support was critical, but it revealed the contradiction we were faced with. We had worked hard to define the immigration issue as a Latino issue. The almost universal support among Latinos for legalization of undocumented immigrants, and especially the community's opposition to the separation of Latino families, was responsible for Congressman Ryan's turnaround. As part of the Republican leadership, and the party's Vice Presidential candidate, he knew that the Republicans had to find a way back into the Latino community on the issue of immigration reform if they hoped to win national elections. Representative Ryan justified his support for immigration reform based on his belief that immigrants were seeking the American dream. As a Latino issue, the nation would have to take responsibility for U.S. policies that had starved Latinos from Mexico and Central America, forced them to seek employment in the north, and then exploited them ruthlessly as cheap labor. While redefining the issue of undocumented immigrants as a Latino issue had provided the political basis for legislation that would stop the deportations, the debate in Congress ignored the realities facing the Latino community and treated the problem as an unreal abstraction—as an "immigrant issue." At the Erie House meeting, Congressman Ryan said, "America is an idea, the place where individuals can achieve individual success, and that idea attracts people from nations who don't embody this great idea, lesser nations." We had no choice but to work with this view of America to win protection for our families. No matter what else they said, the national politicians were finally agreeing with Gutierrez that deportation of 1,400 people yesterday, today, and tomorrow must stop. The separation of families and the forced abandonment of children must stop.

On Sunday, April 28th, Emma traveled to meet Elvira and Saulito at the border in Nuevo Laredo and bring their collection of letters to San Antonio, where Gutierrez and the Congressman John Carter, a Republican, were meeting. We had been informed that the issue of returning those who had been deported was a sticking point in the negotiations. Our plan was to join the witness of U.S. citizen children who had been forced into deportation with their mother or father, with the witness of U.S. citizen children and Dreamers who had been left behind when their mom or dad was deported.

For us there was a powerful spiritual component to the trip. The pattern of the year—of kingdom announcement, betrayal, crucifixion and resurrection—was playing out again. Now, in the final months before passage of the law we had so long struggled for, Elvira and Saulito would rise again, reaching across the border into the heart of the nation that had deported them. This time the fear and hatred that had been unleashed by desperate men committing terrorist acts would be met, and defeated.

Emma Lozano recounted the trip in a letter to one of our allies in San Antonio, Jaime Martinez, one of the great veterans of the struggle.

Dear Brother Jaime Martinez,

On behalf of Familia Latina Unida and La FuerZa Juventud, the Children's Campaign would like to express our gratitude for the reception and for organizing the events both in San Antonio and Laredo, Texas. We are so blessed to know you; although you are in recovery, you still held three events back-to-

back. Each one was well attended and meaningful, and the message was clear: stop the deportations, and include even those who were deported.

Day One— The trip was successful in every sense of the word. We arrived on Sunday, April 28, 2013, and were met by our guardian angel, Jaime Rios, who never left our side and took care of everything, including our food and accommodations. He picked us up at the airport and drove us directly to the border. Ana Munoz, our dreamer, couldn't join us for the border press conference, and Ana, Jaime's wonderful wife, got a hotel room for her where she could be safe and wait for us to return.

At the border between Laredo, Texas, and Nuevo Laredo, Tamaulipas, Mexico, Isidro Garza had organized an amazing press conference with a welcoming committee that included the mayor of Laredo, Raul Salinas, labor, community and religious leaders, and families hurt by a broken immigration system that criminalized them. A banquet was set for us on a single picnic table. The site will remain engraved on my heart and soul forever. The Rio Grande current was racing because of the earlier storm. Isidro, the mayor, leaders, and separated families were on the Texas side. On the other side in Mexico stood Elvira and Saulito Arellano and about fifty others, many U.S. children like Saulito, who lived with their parents in Mexico. The Rio Grande was all that separated us. The same river that had taken so many lives, but also where so many made it across to the so-called land of opportunity.

I watched Isidro as he introduced the speakers and I thought of him, and of you, brother Jaime, and myself, who were once the children of the migrants. I thought of Jaime Rios, who took such loving care of us, and how this successful businessman was once a migrant who came at age fourteen and slept at the cemetery until he could find work, was deported twice, and now employs over 100 workers. I wondered if they were reminded how so many suffer for broken immigration laws and NAFTA that have caused so much suffering and taken so many lives. Or, if they could feel the spirits and dreams of those who had lost their lives trying to get to their family on the other side. We were so close to the families on the other side, only about 150 feet of river and land separating us. And they heard every word we said. They cheered when the mayor spoke and called for the end of the deportations and reunification of families. One by one they welcomed and supported the causa. Isidro then called me to speak. He said that I was the one who had called for this event. It was really Elvira and Saulito who came up with this idea. My job was to bring the children who wrote and collected letters to President Obama and the Congress from other children and Dreamers who were threatened with separation because of the raids and deportations. They came to tell their stories and to unite with Saulito, who had been busy collecting letters from U.S. kids, and Dreamers who had been deported with their parents and wanted to come home. I mentioned the fact that 1400 people are deported every day and that it will continue unless we can convince them to stop the deportations until the new law is implemented, and that we want those people who were deported to be included in the new legislation.

Ana Munoz, age 15, a Dreamer and recent recipient of Deferred Action, said, "I was so grateful and happy to get my papers under President Obama's executive order, but soon my dream turned into a nightmare when my dad was one of 34 workers arrested at the Chicago Pallet Company. He had to pay thousands of dollars to get out of jail; he lost his job. This is not fair; I want him to have his papers too. I want my mom to have her papers so we can stay together as a family. If they take them, what am I supposed to do? I'm too young to take care of my little brothers. We will have to go to Mexico or go into foster care. We want to stay here together as a family. We want President Obama to stop the raids and deportations and give them their papers."

Then I introduced Britzy Lino. I explained how her mom was married to Diego, a U.S. Citizen, and together they had four U.S. citizen children. Diego had adopted her two children from a previous marriage, and now they were legal residents. Sixteen years ago Francisca tried to cross the border and was stopped and was expedited. Diego Lino sponsored his wife, Francisca, and when they went for their appointment, she was handcuffed and incarcerated for 21 days while Britzy's premature twin sisters were in the hospital. Diego was working full-time with twins in the hospital while little Britzy was just a baby and her brother was also at home. Diego became stressed and suffered a heart attack. Diego's mother stepped in to take care of the children. Frances has no criminal record and is in deportation proceedings. Britzy, fighting tears said, "I love my mom. We need my mom, and they won't take her away from me because you will help me keep my mom. And if they do take her, I'm going with her; I won't let her go alone. Please help me keep my mom. I want Obama to stop deporting our moms and dads." Ana held her, and they cried together. Like you said, Jaime, when a child cries, we all cry.

Jaime Rios requested that Rosalba Valdez sing the song that she had composed for President Obama. Isidro held the microphone for her. I didn't have the words, but I thanked Isidro for what he did for us. You know him, Jaime. He's a man of God and did not take the credit and gave all the glory to God and said he was just an instrument. I was moved to tears. I thanked Jaime Rios over and over *again because he took care of us for three days. He said he was following your instructions. You are his hero. He loved Rosalba's song and was always humming and singing the words, and again I was moved to tears.*

Then we went to the bridge, and we met Elvira and Saulito and other families that have similar stories. Jaime Rios introduced me to a mother, Laura Ojeda, and her 8-year-old son. They traveled three hours on a bus to see us to tell their story. She was stopped in Texas for a faulty taillight and deported. It has been two years. She works almost seven days a week just to keep her cell phone on to stay in contact with their family in Texas.

There on the bridge Saulito and the children told their stories, and they united their letters. Britzy, and Saulito have been in this struggle since they were four years old when armed agents arrested their moms. Rosalba, standing next to Ana, sang, "Obama, Obama ten piedad de mi padre, Prometistes la reforma, empiece ya la reforma para volver confiar en ti." *Giovany, who was there to record the event for his documentary, quickly gave me his camera to record while he, being the musician he is, pulled out his guitar and began singing backup for Rosie. Ana, Britzy, and an 8-year-old little boy we just met cried. When they cry, we all cry. Saulito, now much taller than his mother, Elvira, didn't shed tears but looked away in the distance as if to say, How long must we fight? Meanwhile his mom hugged the children.*

We were invited to a reception organized by Francisco Chavira from the Universidad Del Norte de Tamaulipas. Laura Ojeda and her son said goodbye. As much as they would have liked to stay, they had a three-hour ride and school and work tomorrow. She left me with a file saying, "I hope that Congressman Gutierrez can help us; he has helped so many." *I prayed and sent them with a blessing and watched them as they walked away, her arm around his little shoulders as he hung his head.*

At the University we were received with music and applause. It was a beautiful event. We were served dinner and given recognition for participating in the Encuentro de Lideres Migrantes, organized by Francisco Chavira and the students. Dora Hidalgo, a strong Christian woman and a leader in Laredo, Texas, was there with others who make it their business to bring needed clothes, medicine and food to those in need in Mexico. They came to support Elvira and the children's campaign. It was getting late, and we had to get back to Ana. We had been texting to tell her what was going on and that we were finally on our way. When we got to the border to cross, we were asked for all of our documents.

Giovany didn't have a passport but had everything else. Evidently it was not enough, and they took him from us and handcuffed him and held him until his fingerprints cleared. He returned to us three hours later, tired, serious, and quiet. Britzy asked, "What happened and what did they do to you, Gio?" It wasn't until the next day that he said he was handcuffed between an older woman and a man, for hours. I apologized because when he had asked if he needed a passport, I had said he didn't and U.S. identifications were enough. He said, "It's OK. I needed this." I understood. Those of us who are legal sympathize but really don't know what it's like. Giovany, a U.S. citizen had a little taste of what it is like. I'm sure this will make him even more dedicated to the work of getting the word and message out to the people. So many of our people are indifferent because they have their papers. They could care less about the suffering of others.

Jaime Rios and Ana took us to a La Quinta hotel where they had reserved three rooms. Oh my God, were we tired, sweaty, and bitten by fire ants. We couldn't wait to get inside. Jaime still asked, "Sra. Emma le ofrece algo?" Everything was done for us; all we needed to do was go to sleep and prepare for day two with you, brother Jaime Martinez.

Day Two Press Conference – Monday, April 29th— *Jaime Rios came for us early. We met in the lobby of La Quinta hotel for breakfast. We went over the letters and the testimony by the children. Saulito was a little anxious and said he felt nervous. I assured him he couldn't make a mistake. He just needed to speak from the heart. Jaime Rios took us to the press conference with you at the Cesar Chavez Center. When we arrived, we were met by brothers who appeared to be Brown Berets, who made sure we knew where to park and escorted us in. We were overwhelmed by the history in the Center, pictures of Cesar Chavez and you, when you were all so young and in different struggles for workers rights, for the campesinos, for Latino immigrants, and winning many victories. We loved the shrine of Sí Se Puede, resisting oppression, and mostly that la lucha sigue.*

You so eloquently opened the meeting with a history of our struggle and broke it down for everyone. "We marched together in D.C. with the Coordinadora 96, and millions were legalized, and now we fight to stop the 1400 deportations each day that divide children from their parents, and for comprehensive immigration reform that keeps families together. When the children cry, we all cry." Each of the children spoke of their situation. A Dreamer, who already had received his worker's permit and even his driver's license, told of having Homeland Security come to his home and when they couldn't take him, they took his father, who is still incarcerated and awaiting deportation. Saulito spoke of his plan of collecting letters from both sides of the border, and eventually going to D.C. to deliver them to President Obama and the Congress in the hopes that his mother, Elvira, and children like himself could be included in the upcoming leg-islation so they could come home. Britzy again spoke of her mother's deportation and asked everyone to help her keep her mom here. Ana again spoke of the raid in Chicago that placed her father in deportation. Separate and individual interviews with the children followed, and then off to lunch.

Lunch— If the day wasn't amazing enough, we were taken to the Mi Tierra Restaurant and a large table with distinguished guests and leaders. Who shows up—none other than the famous, Johnnie Canales, who always is there when you call for him to speak and support the families in need.

We returned to the Cesar Chavez Center for the public forum with Congressman Doggett and Congressman Gutierrez. The center was filled, every seat taken and only standing room was left. The hall was filled with leaders and members of the community, demanding answers regarding the upcoming immi-gration reform bill. Some were present who also had a deportation order or family member incarcerated. Jaime, you started on time as usual, and introduced leaders in the room, explained the situation, and then introduced the elected officials start-ing with Congressman Doggett. He also spoke eloquently of his support and how closely he is working with our own Illinois Congressman, Luis Gutierrez. They had met with Republican representatives that morning to get unity and understand-ing. Gutierrez was once again on a national tour to bring colleagues from both sides of the aisle to agree on including the maximum number of people in the new legislation.

Congressman Gutierrez was introduced and explained the dynamic. He was extremely optimistic and hopeful, but the fact that he was on a tour around the country meant that he needed to work very hard to get consensus in order to get the best possible law passed to keep the most families together. Gutierrez explained that he met with those most affected, the undocumented. When asked what they wanted, he said just to stay here and work and stay with their families without the threat of deportation, and to have the right to organize in the work-place. When questioned regarding citizenship, because all the preliminary discussions seemed to make citizenship a long way off, he made it very clear that, of course, he wanted citizenship for all, but his priority is to get the majority in a safe place where they can receive their worker's permit, their social security num-ber, and their driver's license. He explained how he had seen the pain and the destruction of families and how people had to live in the shadows. Although it won't be anywhere near perfect and the struggle will continue, they will have the right to stay with their families, work and travel. Congressman Gutierrez explained that this is a negotiation, and he reminded everyone that before the Presidential elections the Republican Party was talking about self-deportation, and now it is in favor of legalization: "We have come a long way, and I will fight to get the best possible bill to include the greatest number of people."

Then before the Congressman left to catch his plane to his next public forum in Brownsville, you asked him to listen to a special presentation. Your daughter was amazing and brought the focus back to what was still occurring even though the debates were going on for legalization. The young Dreamer of San Antonio spoke and said agents came for him but because he was a DACA recipient and had his documents, they took his dad. These collateral arrests happen every day, where agents are looking for someone and if they can't find them, they take whoever is there to meet their quotas. Saulito spoke of kids like him, and while he was speaking, Ana, Britzy, and Rosie displayed the letters of all the children like him from both sides of the border. I told all about Britzy and Ana, and this was nothing new for Congressman Gutierrez since he knows them personally. They are why he is here in Texas and on his way to another meeting, to fight for them. Although he has heard it all, he always tears up. He moved to put his arm around Britzy, and she laid her face on his chest to sob. He promised to do all he can to personally help her keep her mom. Congressman Gutierrez said, "This is what it's all about, folks, keeping these families together." He looks at her in her eyes and tells her something, and Britzy tries to smile. He moves towards the door to leave, and the media and others are surrounding him. You said it: when the children cry, we all cry.

Brother Jaime, this event was extremely historic and necessary. Please accept my deep appreciation, and please thank your comrades in the struggle, Isidro Garza, his team of leaders, and Jaime Rios, his wife, and Gabriel Velasquez, his brother and all of the amazing musicians that showed us such love and respect. Thank you all for your generosity and making this trip a success. Thank you for the amazing fundraiser at Jaime Rios's restaurant. Truly, you are blessed with an amazing wife, a true fighter, and awesome friends that follow your example and live to serve others so that we can all live as God wants, in respect, harmony and dignity.

Brother Jaime, I have good news. Britzy's mother was not deported Thursday, May 6th. She was instead given an extension until September, which gives us all time to make sure she, Elvira, and many who have unjustly been deported can be included in the new legislation. We should know something soon, but we won't wait. We will, like you and like Congressman Gutierrez, not wait, but instead keep raising our voices so that we can get everyone protected in the new *law. The Congress will be in session on June 5th when, if God is willing, we will raise the money necessary to get our kids to march to the White House and take the children's campaign to the Congress.*

> *Siempre Adelante:*
> *Pastora Emma Lozano*

Saul traveled back to Chicago with Emma, Rosalba Valdez and the other children. On Wednesday, several hundred members of Familia Latina Unida and the FuerZa Juventud joined five thousand marchers for the annual May Day rally. Anna and Saulito spoke to the crowd gathered at the end of the march in front of the Federal Building, calling for an immediate end to the deportations and full inclusion of all the families in the new legislation. Saul's picture had been on the front page of the newspaper that morning, a returning hero!

When Senator Durbin offered his hand and an embrace on the platform, Saul turned his back to him. He could not forget that Durbin had turned his back on Saulito and his mother years before when he refused to renew their private bill, resulting ultimately in Elvira's arrest and deportation. Saul's powerful presentation at the rally revealed that this young man was growing up to be a powerful speaker and a leader of his generation. His shunning of Durbin reminded us that this generation would not forget what this country had done to their families.

On Thursday, we went with Britzy's mother to the immigration office, and we were informed that she had been granted a stay of deportation. Francisca would be here again for Mother's Day, her fight against deportation now in its eighth year, as we all waited for the passage of a new law. Emma began preparations to bring the witness of the children from Mexico and from around the U.S. to Washington, D.C., on June 4th.

Gutierrez had worked for months with the group of eight in the House of Representatives, the bi-partisan group charged with developing a compromise bill. With determination like that of a long distance runner pushing himself towards the final kick, he relied on the strategy that had produced President Obama's executive orders at the end of his first term. The congressman organized joint appearances with Republican and Democratic Congressmen, including those in the Gang of Eight, in front of large Latino audiences. He would put his arm around the congressmen and praise them for working for families, for fairness, and demand that the crowd cheer them for their courage. His strategy was working. On Thursday, May 17th, the congressmen emerged from their meeting and announced to the press that they had reached agreement and would begin immediately to put it into legislative language.

Meanwhile, the parallel group in the Senate—the Gang of Eight—had finished its work: the Border Security, Economic Opportunity, and Immigration Modernization Act of 2013. Senator Schumer and his colleagues presented the bill to the Senate Judiciary committee, and passed it after fighting off a series of amendments that would have destroyed it. Yet the forward movement would prove short-lived. The White House called a quiet meeting with the House Democratic leadership, including Congressman Becerra, who was part of the group of eight in the House. Becerra came out of that meeting saying, "I don't think we have a deal." The Democratic leadership had given orders to stall the bill in the House. The plan was to shut down the House compromise bill until the Senate bill passed the full Senate, then try to stuff the latter bill down the throats of the Republican-controlled House. The House would of course reject it, setting the stage for the Democrats to increase their Latino support in the November elections.

It was not a winning strategy for undocumented immigrants. The Speaker of the House loudly proclaimed that the House would never consider the Senate Bill—that it was "dead on arrival." The White House and the Democratic leadership were looking at the next election. They could claim they had passed a bill in the Democratic-controlled Senate, but that the Republicans in the House had refused to even consider it. By this subterfuge, they hoped to capitalize on the anger in the Latino communities and gain control of the House in the midterm elections.

President Obama made it clear he would not suspend the deportations or decrease the rate of "e-verify" raids on factories, which put thousands out of work. Another million deportations would take place, and hundreds of thousands of families would be torn apart. Obama's strategy of deportations and workplace enforcement was aimed at lowering the unemployment rate, the most important political statistic of the time. When an undocumented worker was laid off, a job opened up for someone on the unemployment rolls to fill, but the undocumented worker could not himself apply for unemployment. By putting the blame for the failure of immigration reform on the Republicans, he could improve his unemployment statistics and still maintain the Latino supermajority that had given him a second term. Becerra became the Malinche to the President's Cortez, bargaining for a powerful leadership position should the Democrats regain their majority in the House.

Since Gutierrez had gotten the Republicans to agree to a path to citizenship, the Democratic leadership had to find another way to scuttle the House bi-partisan bill. Congressman Becerra continued to take the point position in opposing the House compromise by leaking misrepresentations of the bill to the press every other day. Becerra and the White House combined in an attempt to get the District of Columbia advocacy organizations to condemn the House bill and to condemn Gutierrez for having given too much away in the negotiations. They went so far as to draft a public letter, but word of the draft leaked to Gutierrez. He spent hours explaining the true facts of the House bill and exposing Becerra's lies and the White House strategy.

Tension between Becerra and Gutierrez rose, but Gutierrez seemed to be winning the argument. Work on putting the House immigration bill into legislative language continued. As we planned the trip to Washington, D.C., to begin the Children's Campaign, we formed a new objective. We saw the need to strike a decisive blow to shake the Democrats loose from their cynical strategy. We began a grassroots campaign to "pass the House bill and let the process go forward." For those of our moratorium movement allies still refusing to support any legislation, we developed an either/or position: "Either" the President implements an immediate moratorium on all deportations and e-verify operations, "or" the Democrats join in passing the compromise bill through the House to let the process go forward. We supplemented our argument with facts about the House bill, facts that showed the House bill was actually superior to the Senate bill on the issue of family reunification. We aimed the campaign at members of the Congressional Hispanic Caucus, the one voice in the District of Columbia that, after last November's Latino turnout, could stop the political games being played by the Democratic leadership and the Obama White House.

Elvira produced her weekly column for *El Diario* in New York, and we blitzed the internet with it. We needed an action to bring our position into public view. Emma and the children would have to find a way to make the case in the District of Columbia and get enough press to make it effective. In truth, we were exhausted and broke. We raised money for the trip by going to restaurants and bars over the Memorial Day weekend, playing songs and asking for donations. Still, it was Pentecost, and the Spirit rose at our

Sunday service. We began to get that feeling again, the feeling of being called, of being led.

On reflection, the decision to organize the *Coordinadora 13* and the Children's Campaign didn't make much sense for our organization. We had made a decision to cut financial ties with the Illinois Coalition for Immigrant Rights. We could not in good conscience, and without hypocrisy, criticize the dependence of the funded organizations across the nation if we shared in that funding. Our organizational plan called for building a base of support from among the many successful Mexican businesses in the community, a plan that would take hard work and time. The decision to launch the Children's Campaign disrupted that plan and threatened our survival. Coming after the elections in November 2012, comprehensive immigration reform seemed almost a sure thing. Was it really even necessary for us to continue to mobilize?

In spite of these considerations, Emma took on the campaign. Something or someone, perhaps the actual spirit of the movement for justice, was calling her to undertake another campaign. The organization and the church felt her deep commitment and followed. Elvira sent her agreement from Mexico.

We could not have known what would happen on that Wednesday, June 5th, when we planned to be in Washington. Led by Speaker Pelosi and Congressman Becerra, the Democratic staff for the Gang of Eight negotiations had come up with a proposal that opposed some of the health care provisions in the House bill. These were not serious provisions. In fact, the President had given away the right to health care for undocumented immigrants in the Affordable Care Act two years before. His health care proposal had ruled out participation of undocumented immigrants as well as legal permanent residents of less than five years. The Republicans wanted a stipulation that those granted legalization would have to take responsibility for their own health care bills, even though they could receive none of the government subsidies of the Affordable Care Act for five years. The Democratic proposals to the group of eight in the House did not present any substantial change to this stipulation, but they were enough to break the carefully worked out agreements of the previous months.

The headline story on NBC that morning was "Immigration Deal Dead in the House." We arrived in D.C. in an old school bus donated by Pilsen Wellness with fifteen children and young people whose parents had been deported. Other young people and their supporters came from Texas,

Florida, New York, South Carolina and California. Elvira sent Saul, accompanied by Pepe Jaques, along with five other children who had been forced to leave family and friends to go to Mexico with their mothers when they were deported. We had had discussions with most of the organizations around the nation, and the Children's Campaign was as much an effort to get them to break with the White House as it was to influence the Congress. Although these well-funded organizations were tied to the White House, they feared that voices like Lozano and Arellano could discredit them in the Latino community. We were encouraged that our allies in the demand for a moratorium also seemed willing to join the fight for a bipartisan bill in the House of Representatives.

Emma gathered the children in a large room that Gutierrez had reserved in the Rayburn House office building. Cameras and reporters lined the walls. The children were exhausted from the trip, having slept on the floor at CASA Maryland the night before. We needed to get focused. Emma and I began with a prayer: "Jesus called for the disciples to step aside and let the little children come to him. Then he told them they must become like these little children if they would enter the Kingdom of Heaven. Today, we ask the children to take on the responsibility that adults have abandoned, the responsibility to fight to keep together what You have joined together, to keep their families together. Lord, give them courage in their hearts." Then the children began their testimonies. They described the arrests of their parents, their own abandonment, the destruction of the lives they had known, the hardships and dangers they faced as they tried to continue their lives in broken families in the United States or in Mexico. Several of the Latino congressmen responded with heartfelt commitments to work to revive the legislation in the House.

When Gutierrez got up to speak before the children, he was deeply moved. Tears rolled down his face, and he was unable to speak for several tense minutes. He explained that the compromise legislation included provisions that he didn't like and provisions that the Republicans didn't like. He said, "The bottom line is that the bill they were developing would stop the 1,400 deportations that happen every day and would allow the return of parents that had been deported." The children responded with their own tears. He was speaking directly to their lives, their pain and their hopes. Several came forward and embraced him. Gutierrez then went on to call on President Obama to suspend the deportations of those who qualified for legalization under the proposed Senate bill. The meeting ended with Rosalba Valdez leading the children in her song, calling on Obama to return her father to her. The congressman's speech—as well as his tears—played on Spanish-language TV all over the nation that night. The President had to understand that if the Democratic leadership sabotaged the legislative process, the heat would fall on the Democrats going into the midterm elections.

Given the headlines of the day, we wondered if the Children's Campaign was enough. That evening, as the children prepared to make their way home, the group of eight in the House met one more time. Congressman Labrador announced he was leaving the group. But the other three Republicans agreed to continue on. I was sitting in the food court of Union Station with our group when the congressman called to tell me the news: "Labrador has left the group, but the good news is that we will continue. Thank the children for me. Thank Emma."

Labrador's defection meant that the legislation the group proposed would not enjoy his protection from Tea Party opposition. It was a loss, but Gutierrez argued in his public statement that they could still count on Labrador's support for the agreements he had negotiated, including the right of return for deported parents of U.S. citizen children and Dreamers. Significantly, the children's action had moved the advocacy organizations. We spent the next day in phone conversations with leaders around the country and began to formulate agreements on two points: 1) They would mount a campaign to support a compromise bi-partisan bill in the House and 2) They would join in a movement to get President Obama to suspend deportations. The President, Minority Leader Pelosi and other Democratic leaders would hopefully learn that the failure of an immigration bill would unleash a unified Latino movement against Democratic candidates in the midterm elections.

Emma returned to Chicago with Saulito and the other children and then boarded a plane with him to Miami, where he taped an appearance on Univision's main Sunday morning news show, "Al Punto." On Univision's highly watched Sunday show, Saulito, now fourteen years old, outlined the Children's Campaign and called for a March on Washington on August 15th. I was almost seventy and nearly crippled. Emma was nearly sixty and six months the other side of three heart attacks. Our main organizers were new to the struggle and mostly undocumented. We had less than four hundred dollars in all of our accounts and a mountain of debts. What kept us in the fight? What had inspired Emma to organize the Children's Campaign? What forces brought the children to Washington, D.C., on the day that the legislation in the House had fallen apart? We had no crystal ball—only the willingness to move on faith, "the faith of Elvira." That Sunday on television, Saul explained to the nation, "we are four million U.S. citizen children and two million Dreamers, six million young people who are, with our families, nearly twenty million, a nation within a nation. We will not give up." I believed with all my heart that God would not give up on them.

🔥 26

Fighting the Suppression of the Movement

Let perseverance finish its work so that you may be mature and complete, not lacking anything. If any of you lacks wisdom, you should ask God, who gives generously to all without finding fault, and it will be given to you. But when you ask, you must believe and not doubt, because the one who doubts is like a wave of the sea, blown and tossed by the wind.

— The Letter from James 1:4-6

Gutierrez defined our goals clearly: "The legislative process to reach immigration reform will take time, because first we have to make the presentation of the project, then the negotiations between Republicans and Democrats, then the voting. I think that while these negotiations are going on, first and foremost we need to put the brakes on the deportations, and the only way to do that is to create a sanctuary and put your arms around the immigrants and say 'you are in a safe place,' then grant them their work permits and ensure that that permit doesn't just allow them to work, but also to travel, and that it extends to the wife and the children; and furthermore, if they deported your wife or husband, now that you are legal, return them so they can be with their children, with their family."

"For me that is first: stop the deportations of the 1400 people a day, 400,000 a year. Every day 250 children are left behind without their mom or dad in this country." †

By June 27, 2013, the Senate finally passed a bill that would partially meet that objective. A ridiculous increase in border security had been attached to the bill to get a super majority in the Senate. We wanted some improvements in terms of unifying families and returning those who had been deported. We also knew that we needed a House bi-partisan bill because the Republican-controlled House would never even consider the

---

† Congressman Luis Gutierrez, campaigning for immigration reform in Houston, Texas. March 11, 2013.

Senate bill. Even as the bill passed in the Senate, House Speaker John Boehner reaffirmed that the House had no intention of considering the Senate bill. The House would have to develop its own bi-partisan bill or, alternatively, pass a series of piecemeal bills aimed mostly at increasing enforcement.

Some Republicans were beyond our reach. Others had been won over to the family unity position, or recognized the power of the unified Latino vote in their districts. We needed to encourage them. We also had to keep the Democrats and the White House from killing a bi-partisan House bill to gain political advantage. We would try to stimulate a movement to pass a bipartisan bill in the House, and we would keep the pressure on the Democratic leadership so that they would know that if the bill failed, they would pay the price at the voting booth. Such was our plan.

As of July 1st, however, in spite of a virtual one-man national campaign of optimism by Congressman Gutierrez, prospects for legalization in 2013 did not look good. The White House was manipulating the issue to create an electoral advantage for 2014, intending to blame the defeat of immigration reform on the Republican-controlled House. The bi-partisan bill in the House, yet to be introduced, was falling apart. Stalled by orders from the White House until the Senate bill passed, it was now under attacked by right wing Republicans. They attempted to load unacceptable provisions onto the bill, provisions that would make it impossible to get Democratic support. The stage was set to mobilize union and advocacy organizations in a partisan attack against the Republican Party aimed, not at immigration reform, but at the 2014 elections.

Elvira and Saulito had decided that he would return for the summer to help the struggle. Anticipating his arrival, Emma planned a march and press conference for July 4th. She chose the site of the 2005 grand march in Chicago in the Back of the Yards. That first march, stimulated by Spanish-language radio and Pistolero, laid the foundation for Chicago to take the lead in putting millions of people on the street on 2006. The march this year would end at an open market, The Swaporama, where the previous weekend ICE had conducted raids that enraged the community. The Children's March would be led by U.S. citizen children with undocumented parents, and it would feature Saulito Arellano.

The Children's Campaign had aimed to raise the issue of the right of return. One month after Emma and Elvira had organized their reunion of separated families at the border, one group of national Dreamers followed suit, getting permission for a small group of Dreamers to cross the border to be reunited with their deported family members and then returning to a press conference on the United States side. Three months later, three Dreamers crossed the border and attempted to bring six more of their friends back across the border. They were stopped and arrested. In spite of fairly good publicity, the Obama administration refused to release them. The Dream Nine remained in jail in Laredo. We noted that the response from the community was tepid, and the intransigence of the Obama administration quite strong. Two months later, the nine were released into the United States on asylum petitions. They claimed it was too dangerous for them to remain in Mexico. The results were typical of the individualistic actions of the well-funded Dreamer groups—they managed to negotiate their own individual solutions.

Congress would reconvene in September, but would be tied up in a highly partisan budget battle. Republicans were threatening to shut down the government in an effort to defund the Affordable Care Act. At best, the House would return to the issue of immigration reform in October. The national advocacy organizations gathered in Washington, D.C., to plan a mobilization strategy. They met with various unions at the AFL-CIO headquarters in Washington. Agreement was quickly reached to stage a symbolic national action in the District of Columbia on September 13th and then to mobilize in cities across the country on October 5th, and again in D.C. on October 8th.

Although the "Convening" in Washington invited Gutierrez to speak to them, it seemed to us they turned a deaf ear to the congressman's plea that they must avoid aligning themselves with either party. The White House strategy was working. The unions and the immigrant rights organizations were preparing for a month of confrontation with local Republican congressmen in their districts during the August recess. The September 13th demonstration was basically a partisan attack on the Republican Congress. Some fifty of the organization leaders staged a symbolic civil disobedience action the day after the convening to "stimulate the movement"—but the tactic failed.

After an intense schedule of events around the country, wooing Republican congressmen and continuing his effort to finalize the bi-partisan House bill, Gutierrez planned to take a two-week vacation beginning on August 10th. The congressman's sweeping popularity in the Latino community was now being recognized in the English-language media. The Washington Post ran a feature article noting his "rock star" status and praising his effort to develop a non-partisan approach to immigration reform. Yet he was pretty much alone in this effort, except for our grassroots operations. The organized advocacy groups had fallen in line with the White House strategy to attempt to set up the Republican Congress as the reason for the failure of immigration reform, in anticipation of the 2014 midterm election.

In our church, we were finishing eight weeks of Kingdom Time—a season guided especially by the words of scripture in the letter from James. James defined perseverance in the face of adversity as the way we would be perfected for the coming of the Harvest. This scripture fit our situation well as we fought a dozen deportation cases—and found ourselves ensnared in the White House political trap.

A few months earlier we had worked on an initiative with Chicago Latino pastors and the Latino members of the city council to introduce a resolution calling on President Obama to declare a moratorium on deportations. Emma had also led a second group of Latino pastors on a trip to Washington, D.C., to meet with both Republican and Democratic members of the Congress. These two efforts helped to establish a good collective understanding of the complicated political dynamic that the Democratic leadership had set in motion. Since the pastors were more independent of the White House than either the advocacy organizations or the unions, we decided to try a new approach. The problem with mobilizing behind a bi-partisan bill in the House was that there *was* no bi-partisan bill, at least in public. The group of seven had fallen apart as the Republican members withdrew. We formulated ten "principles" that reflected the agreements that Gutierrez had negotiated. Our proposal was for pastors across the country to get at least forty Republican Congressman to agree to the principles before the bill was made public in late September. At the same time, we would try to get churches in 100 cities to make a commitment to open their churches as sanctuaries if neither the Congress nor the President acted to stop the deportations, either by passing reform legislation or by executive action.

Emma and I chaired the meeting on August 8th that included both of the Latino Pastor groups we had been working with. Gutierrez addressed the meeting and made a strong argument for the "pastoral approach," as opposed to the partisan hypocrisy offered by the White House and the leadership of the Democratic Party. Gutierrez, a Catholic, had developed a deeper understanding of the Evangelical movement along with a somewhat humorous rapport with the Evangelical pastors. He explained in clear terms that the Democrats had been willing to give up a lot to get a one-size-fits-all thirteen-year road to citizenship in the Senate bill. Undocumented immigrants would be unable to redeem their social security contributions but would be required to continue to make them. The border security would be doubled. Deported family members would not be able to return if they had been deported before December of 2012—that is, the great majority. Worst of all, the Democrats had made the thirteen-year path to citizenship a red line that could not be crossed, guaranteeing the failure of reform legislation formulated in the House. The pastors agreed to the "principles campaign," as well as to making a commitment to open their churches as sanctuaries to send a message to President Obama. Our challenge was now to make the dual campaign go national.

We spent the eight weeks of the summer in prayer and study, fighting individual cases, completing DACA applications, and training the student leaders of the Youth Health Service Corps. We had faith that we would find a way to legalize in 2013 and then begin the offensive for health care for the twenty million that would still be excluded from the Affordable Care Act. The Youth Health Service Corps' "5 plus 1 to get 20" program was designed to build a base to launch that struggle. We seemed to be leaning very heavily on our faith to keep going. In fact, we felt as if the White House was locking us into a purely partisan battle for the sole purpose of creating an issue in the next election.

The White House reacted angrily to the demand for the President to use his executive authority to suspend deportations and offer the deferments he gave to the Dreamers to their parents and the parents of U.S. citizen children. White House staff called the advocacy organizations, basically threatening them. At the same time, Homeland Security was pursuing the tactic we had seen in Chicago with the Chicago Pallet Company and Pilsen Wellness. A Homeland Security audit of a car wash company in Phoenix resulted in the firing of some fifty undocumented workers. A few weeks later, the company evidently rehired a few of the workers in other locations. Homeland Security then staged a raid and moved to prosecute the workers on charges that would result in prison terms. Not the infamous Sheriff Arpaio, but the President of the United States was putting simple car wash workers in prison. The federal policy was still being carried out vigorously and viciously.

August marked the fiftieth anniversary of the March on Washington. The African American communities across the nation reacted strongly to the acquittal in the Travon Martin case, as well as the Supreme Court decision that gutted the Voting Rights Act. The August 28th "I Have a Dream" commemoration seemed almost out of place, rolling us back to the sixties in a weak attempt to hold on to gains that had been won fifty years ago.

The 1963 March on Washington reflected the divisions in the movements of the 1960s—the Civil Rights movement and the Black Liberation movement. While the media had defined the division as one between Dr. King and Malcolm X—based on King's call for non-violence and Malcolm's assertion of the right to self-defense—a more fundamental discussion involved "civil rights" and "human rights." This distinction had particular relevance for us in the immigrant rights struggle. In effect, Malcolm had sought to internationalize the struggle of African Americans. He called on Black people in the United States to redefine themselves, not as a minority in this country, but as a people of color, part of the majority in the world as a whole. Malcolm characterized the U.S. as an oppressor nation and took up the cause of anti-colonial struggles and movements of national liberation both in Africa and Latin America. Dr. King confined the Civil Rights movement to the demand that African Americans be given the rights promised in the U.S. Constitution. A super-patriotic force was unleashed to keep Dr. King from endorsing Malcolm's internationalist position. But by 1968, Dr. King formed the Poor Peoples Campaign and publicly opposed the Vietnam War. So too, today, a similar force has effectively drowned out our efforts to indict this nation for its role in the forced migration of Latinos from their native lands and their exploitation by both private employers and the government.

Rev. Al Sharpton orchestrated the commemorative march in August of 2013. Sharpton had emerged at the beginning of the Obama administration as his principal apologist in the Black community. While Rev. Jesse Jackson and other leaders of the Civil Rights movement found themselves ostracized and isolated, Sharpton and his National Action Network were elevated. Sharpton was given a nightly show on MSNBC; the cable network now devoted its corporate and media resources to organizing a march that drew some 50,000 people. The theme of the march was greatly influenced by the grassroots response to the murder of Travon Martin. The Obama administration had worked diligently to position itself on the side of this movement against criminalizing young African Americans. Attorney General Holder had issued an order curbing the mandated minimum sentences responsible for the mass imprisonment of young African American and Latino males for minor drug possession offenses.

The Supreme Court decision gutting the Voting Rights Act was the second theme of the march. The unions added on the demand for an increased minimum wage that President Obama had articulated in his Second Inaugural Address. Gay rights advocates, the only group that had actually won real concessions from Obama, also joined the march, so that it became a dramatic image of the progressive Democratic Party agenda. While Rev. Jackson gently called on the administration to shift its "agenda for the middle class" back to Johnson's war on poverty, and many progressive leaders called for a jobs program, there was no public protest to dramatize the President's failure to address the crisis in the African American community. Black unemployment was at its worst level since World War II, the prisons were filled with young Black men, segregated Black schools were failing to graduate half of their students, and the drug economy dominated Black neighborhoods.

Gutierrez, who did not speak at the march, issued a statement that for the first time in years indicted the nation for its implementation of a system of undocumented labor. He called on the nation to take "shared responsibility" for what it had done, echoing Dr. King's effort to indict the nation and call for redeeming action. His statement pinpointed the problem in our movement. Until this time not a word had been spoken in the Congress or at the White House to explain the policies, such as NAFTA, which had forced the migration to the north, or the vicious exploitation of a work force which had no rights under the law to amass prosperity in the United States. Instead, the debate had presupposed that the most vulnerable and the least culpable for the system of undocumented labor—that is, the Latino immigrants themselves—were its only cause and the ones to blame. Without an indictment of the nation's role—an indictment such as Dr. King had made, a call for justice to "roll down like waters and righteousness like a mighty stream"—was reduced to a plea for the "greatest country in the world" to allow immigrants to participate in the American Dream.

The Dreamers, who had been raised in the United States, certainly deserved citizenship. The narrow context of civil rights, however, offered a difficult road and little hope since these rights belonged exclusively to U.S. citizens. We had made our case based on the civil rights of the U.S. citizen children and spouses—that their rights to life, liberty, and the pursuit of happiness, embodied in the Latino family—were being violated by the deportations. Gutierrez, like Dr. King, attempted to bend the civil rights struggle towards the movement for justice and human rights. The rest of the eleven million immigrants were here primarily to keep their families together, to work, and, in many cases, to send money back home. Some wanted citizenship, but most just wanted to be able to work legally and live without the constant fear of deportation. They had a human right to these things because the United States had destroyed the economies of their countries, forced them to migrate to find a job, opened its borders, and exploited their cheap labor. The families that were formed here and the children who were born here should be given legal protection and treated with dignity. Significantly, almost the entire Latino community embraced undocumented immigrants and made its will clear at the polls. The movement for justice and the human rights of immigrants, however, was based on "Elvira's faith," the faith of a people who felt God gave them a destiny in this country. It was to that faith, and a new resurrection of the grassroots movement for justice, that we now turned. To that end, we developed a plan of action and began discussions with pastors and pastoral associations around the country.

Elvira wrote a series of columns explaining our position. They were published in the New York Spanish-language Daily, *El Diario*, and we distributed them widely on the internet. We began a series of meetings with every pastor we could find. We could not help but remark on Chicago's central location and how it brought together so many different political and religious streams. Not only were we in the heartland of both Gutierrez and Obama, but key pastors from every tradition in the Latino Evangelical movement that had taken a stand nationally on immigration reform were here, all within a few blocks of each other. These pastors had a long history of relationships to the Chicago grassroots movement and the Mexican/Puerto Rican "Latino unity" that Emma Lozano and José López began forging fifteen years ago. They had been key participants in the two successful Familias Unidas national campaign tours, and we were confident that they would be the key to the way we hoped to overcome the partisan paralysis that perpetuated the terror of 1400 deportations each day.

At the beginning of September, in a sign that seemed to parallel our inward journey through scripture, President Obama issued a new order to Homeland Security warning agents to avoid arresting parents with children and putting the highest priority on parents with children to receive prosecutorial discretion. At the same time, Homeland Security approved asylum requests from the nine Dreamers who had been arrested at the border. In our church, we won green cards in family separation cases we had been fighting for nine and four years, respectively. These developments gave us confidence that continued agitation around the demand for executive action to stop the deportations would bear fruit—even as we continued our plan to put a bi-partisan bill through the House. The following Sunday we continued our inward journey by reliving the exodus from Egypt. After the model of Moses, we felt called to put our staff into the waters and ask God to divide the Red Sea, Democrats on one side and Republicans on the other, so that the people of God could walk through.

Our first task for the fall was to organize Chicago pastors to implement our "October plan." We turned to Pastor Freddy Santiago, whose church had hosted the kick-off of the first Familias Unidas tour. Santiago had organized LEAP, the Latino Empowerment Association of Pastors. He agreed with our position and scheduled it for discussion at the next LEAP meeting. In preparation for the meeting, we approached two smaller associations of Latino pastors, many of whose members were also members of LEAP. At the meeting the pastors agreed to the plan, and LEAP made a commitment to meet each week in order to coordinate the Chicago action. Many of the pastors still found the demand for sanctuary to be problematic, and we decided to have a series of one-on-one meetings to build the necessary unity for the action.

There were three principal national organizations of Latino pastors that we needed to reach. We would work through Pastor Santiago to reach Esperanza; Pastor Choco to reach the National Hispanic Leadership Conference; and our old ally in New Jersey to bring CONLAMIC on board. We also reached out to key Catholic priests and asked them to become involved, although we realized that the Catholic hierarchy would not be with us.

We began a series of Saturday forums to involve the DACA applicants and the high school students. The first forum was spirited, but small, as were the meetings with the pastors. We had a long way to go and only a brief time to create the necessary momentum in Chicago, which we would then have to project nationally. We again turned to Pistolero to try to engage the radio DJs.

The Washington, D.C., meeting of the coalition of the labor unions and immigrant rights organizations was set for Friday, September 13th. We knew that a majority of the groups had signed on to the Democratic Party's Campaign for Citizenship and opposed making a demand on the President for executive action. We worked with Elvira on a column for *El Diario* to explain our position, and circulated the column to some fifty anticipated participants the day before the Friday meeting.

A well-controlled meeting of unions and advocacy organizations met to coordinate the October 5th actions. The organizers—a small group from the Center for Community Change and SEIU in California—carefully skimmed over a rising call for consideration of "Plan B." Plan B referred to a call to organize to get President Obama to use his executive authority to stop the deportations. The organizers' intent to hold demonstrations in cities throughout the nation meant that keeping the "Plan B" faction as part of the coalition was important in order to keep continuing pressure on the Republicans to consider the Democratic immigration reform bill. However, certain elements of the coalition held a rising skepticism about the value of continuing to push for a legislative solution. One labor leader opposing that position said, "We are winning. Can't you see we are winning? Look at how our support has grown." It was hard for those of us living with the families to see the victory. Yes, we had made progress in winning support in the nation. Yet how could you call two million deportations since our votes elected—and then re-elected—President Obama a victory? Was it a victory for those two million people and their families, and their children? It might have been a "political victory" for the President and the Democrats— but it was unending suffering and hardship for the people. The meeting ended with commitments for actions in over 100 cities—and a promise to reconvene to consider Plan B if no legislation passed in October. Of course, that promised meeting never occurred.

Coming home again to Chicago, we turned to the church for inspiration. We preached on the scripture in chapter 12 of Revelations, recalling the description of the Lady crossing the desert, pursued by a dragon of hate. The dragon chased the Lady with her child up to heaven, where he was defeated, mortally wounded, by the cloud of witnesses formed from those who had boldly testified truth to power. The dragon was thrown down to earth and continued to chase the Lady—who was given sanctuary by the very earth itself. That cloud of witnesses offered its power to the believers who would step forward at this time—who would claim the victory already won in heaven! We would assemble the testimony of those who would speak truth to both the Democrats and the Republicans, and we would assemble those who would offer sanctuary to the mothers and their children who are being chased by the dragon of hate and racism.

There were indeed one hundred and thirty demonstrations around the nation on October 5th—but many of them turned up no more than a dozen people. The largest action, in Los Angeles, had less than two thousand people.

These paltry crowds were a far cry from the millions that had once marched together in 2006! The clearly partisan character of the "Campaign for Citizenship," which was aimed at the Republicans in Congress, and the campaign's failure to confront the deportations, did not stir the Latino community into action. The style of the well-funded advocacy organizations—which aimed at producing "grass tops" instead of "grassroots"—served only to suppress the movement. The advocacy groups and the labor leaders seemed to want a press conference with a carefully crafted, political message, not a mobilization of the people.

In Chicago, we combined our mobilization of the Latino pastors with a small rally put on by the Chicago immigrant rights organization. As I looked out at the crowd gathered in Union Park, I saw union members singing with the faith bands and their singers. Shortly after the morning rally—which featured speeches by the pastors and by various politicians and advocate organization leaders—the immigrant rights organization took some 90 people to the suburbs to knock on doors and ask people to call their Republican Congressmen. Their position was clear—and narrow: Tell Congressman Roskam to demand a vote on the Democratic bill. No matter that, for a Republican, it was a political impossibility. The local press covered this small group, who proclaimed that "only the Republicans are responsible for the deportations."

The national Spanish-language press, on the other hand, followed the pastors and three thousand families and young people on a march downtown to the Federal Building. They demanded that the deportations stop: "By Act of Congress if possible; by Authority of the President, if necessary." We used the faith-based mobilization to build a breakaway coalition that called for a "March to Stop the Deportations" the following week. That march drew nearly ten thousand people. It was clear what the people wanted. They wanted some immediate relief from the campaign of terror that the President was still directing at them—while he pointed his finger at the Republicans.

On October 12th, with the government shut down over a budget battle stirred by Republican opposition to the Affordable Care Act, Democratic congressmen turned out to address a crowd of over 25,000 people—drawn to the National Mall in D.C. by the presence of the movement's most popular band, Los Tigres del Norte. Our friends in CASA Maryland had done an admirable job in mobilizing, joining with union officials and Democratic Party leaders to put on a well-funded event that cost nearly two million dollars. Union members we talked to had been paid to come from as far as New York and Philadelphia. Local residents came because of the band and the hope of a large demonstration against the deportations. Instead, what they heard from the well-controlled stage were partisan attacks railing against the Republican Party. After the rally, the crowd marched to the Capitol where one hundred and twenty-five activists and nine members of Congress participated in a well-organized, pre-planned act of civil disobedience. When some in the crowd chanted, "Obama, Obama, stop the deportations," they were quickly drowned out by staff members of the unions and the advocacy organizations, who responded with a chant aimed at Speaker John Boehner. We felt good that so many Democratic congressmen, including Gutierrez, were willing to get arrested to bring attention to the cause. Unfortunately, the strategy was clearly politically motivated—and it gave us little hope of breaking the paralysis in Congress or of forcing the President to take action.

Even the civil disobedience felt wrong. Actions of nonviolent direct action have historically demonstrated the rights of the people who were being disrespected. African American students sat at lunch counters to demonstrate their right to equal treatment. Rosa Parks sat down in the front of the bus to protest the racist segregation law. Mothers threw themselves in front of a bus to stop it from driving people to deportation. Elvira stayed in a church for a year so that she could be with her son, raise him, and guide him. The "civil disobedience" staged by public officials, in coordination with local police, to sit down in the park and subject themselves to a pre-arranged arrest just didn't measure up. It was a press conference!

Our friends at CASA Maryland who had done the organizing work were clearly disappointed at the turnout—even with all the money that had been spent. Their conclusion was the same as ours: the partisan objectives of the Democratic Party had suppressed the popular grassroots movement, the movement which alone had the power to bring Congress or the President to stop the deportations. Emma had been arrested along with the congressmen for her part in the sit-in. The congresspersons were immediately released and made their statements to the press. As we waited for Emma and the rest of the 125 to be released, we marveled at how many young, white staff members had been arrested. They clearly made up the majority of the protesters, but didn't seem to energize the base.

President Obama and the Democrats had taken control of the movement through the funded organizations and turned it into a partisan political force. The movement had been suppressed. We were left looking for a way to voice our demand to stop the deportations by December 1st.

Increasingly in this long struggle, we had turned to our faith—and to prayer and scripture—to find our way. Our church was our workshop. "Assembly time" is the eighth and final season of the cycle of the year in our spiritual calendar. We gather the seeds of the harvest, the Word of the world in each human soul, to plant in the soil of faith for the following year. We review the year and try to learn the lessons that we have been taught through the struggle for justice and the striving for truth. Every Sunday, we found new families and new young people at the service. Young people would come to the service and stay to fill out their applications for the "dreamer" deferments that we had won from President Obama before the last election. Some families came with new deportation cases. Some came to check up on ongoing cases. Now, in this Assembly time, we added a new initiative.

In an effort to silence the demand for executive action, Homeland Security had issued a new "Parent Protection order." The order mostly provided for protecting the rights of parents being detained so that they could attend hearings involving their children. Hidden away in the order was a single paragraph that required ICE agents to receive proof that the parents had U.S. citizen or legal permanent resident children—and to dismiss their cases using prosecutorial discretion. The original prosecutorial discretion order we had wrangled from the Obama administration during his first term had included parents with U.S. citizen children, but placed it at a low priority. Even that order, fought for so long, had born little fruit; ultimately it applied to less than 6% of those arrested. Parents had continued to be deported. The new order won letters of support from the D.C. immigrant rights groups, but was otherwise ignored by Homeland Security as well as the advocacy organizations.

As our response, we devised a "Parent Protection ID." Undocumented parents would come to the church with copies of their children's birth certificates or legal permanent resident status. We would make them an identification card with images of their documentation and a quotation from the new order. In the first month, two people were stopped, showed their IDs, and were released! We put our phone number on the IDs so that they could call if the policy were not being followed. The parents came during the week, but mostly they came on Sunday for church and stayed to get their Protection IDs.

As we gathered the seeds of Assembly time, something new rose up. We found ourselves in the midst of a marriage renewal movement in our church. The pressures on a marriage—on the whole family—from the broken immigration law are intense. You live not knowing if your spouse will come home, not knowing if the life you have built—the house you live in, the future you are building for your children—will all be taken away in a minute. Many of our families were already enduring the painful life of separation. When a man or a woman is deported and returns to Mexico or Central America, there is desperation. The temptation of infidelity is strong. A man who is no longer able to support his family may be reduced to receiving small checks from his working wife in America in order to eat. He may find solace with another woman. Sometimes a child is born. If he returns, the situation becomes very complicated.

These pressures come on top of the challenges that every marriage faces in this highly individualist and materialistic culture. We began several marriage counseling sessions every week. The word spread. In order to get the husbands to participate, we organized a "Father's Resolution," a commitment that the men made to be faithful in marriage and responsible as fathers. One Sunday, over fifty men came to the front of the congregation and signed on to the Resolution.

After that, Olivia and Alberto Segura organized two daylong Saturday marriage retreats. Alberto, with Olivia at his side, had fought his own deportation for several years. Their daughter had been killed in military service in Kuwait. The loss put Alberto, who had supported her decision to join the army despite Olivia's objection, in a state of depression. He started using cocaine, was arrested, and did time. His deportation case, of course, became much more difficult. Olivia took his case everywhere and finally got it closed. They fought to put their marriage back together, and became the leaders in the marriage renewal movement in the church.

The Youth Health Service Corps and its fight for health care for the undocumented had spread to five high schools and nine elementary schools over the previous year. Leaders of these young people met at the church each Saturday, helping Dreamers fill out their DACA applications and helping parents put together their Protection IDs.

The message on the last Sunday of Assembly time was "Gathering the Seeds of the Next Generation." That week, a young brother who had worked on and off with us, "Curly," was shot and killed in front of his house. The week spent in mourning and the funeral service brought the community together. His death stirred in us a determination to fight the criminal-ization of these young men who chose one or another of the only options available to them—to end up bleeding out on a cement sidewalk or to waste away in prison. The church had to become strong internally. The grassroots movement had to be built on truth and the love of our families. We knew from our history that if we were strong and united that the Latino commu-nity would rally around us. We needed to deepen our faith, our unity, and our commitment.

27

Toward a New Form of Organizing

O ur long struggle brought home to us a fundamental principle of democracy: When you have the votes, you have to act quickly, forcefully, and in unity. Locally in Illinois, we experienced the great harm that was done to the undocumented with regard to driver's licenses in 2003. Nationally, we continued to face the consequences that united pressure was not brought to bear on President Obama to pass immigration reform in his first 100 days, as he had promised. Why was unity not present when we had the votes? The answer is that leading elements of the coalition had agendas and priorities that differed from the people they claimed to represent. Most often, this conflict of interest involved funding for their organizations. Other times, it resulted from the character of their leadership. This latter problem confronted us with immigration reform legislation during President Obama's first 100 days.

The leading and best-funded national coalition included representatives of the White House in its decision-making group. They were told to "lay off" the President during the first 100 days—the only period, it turned out, when he had the ability to pass a decent bill.

These experiences convinced us that we had to work in concert with the faith-based organizations—and with the churches, directly—to maintain an effective and principled struggle and build a grassroots movement. While we prepared for 2014, the White House convinced most of the national immigrant advocacy organizations and unions to join the Campaign for Citizenship, which aimed exclusively at attacking the Republicans in Congress. With one hand, the Democratic leadership promised millions of dollars in federal and private philanthropic funding to these organizations for their support. With the other—our experience showed—they fostered conflict in the House and sabotaged an already difficult bi-partisan process. By now it had become clear to us that the leadership had long ago chosen the option to increase deportations as a way to open up low-wage jobs for the unemployed. After six years of struggle and protest, we had to confront the reality that the stepped-up deportations represented a policy decision, not a consequence of giving immigration reform a low priority.

Time and again we had worked with the Democrats, only to be disappointed at the lack of real progress in the legislation itself. The bill in the Democratic Senate, for example, left many of the undocumented unprotected and greatly increased the militarization of the border—while making the thirteen-year path to citizenship a "deal breaker" with the Republican-controlled House. Yet the "true lobby" for immigration reform—the now demonstrable reality of millions of Latino voters—was able to get to those Republicans who wanted the Latino vote. Republicans, who were committed to gaining control of the Senate and the White House, were willing to struggle with their Tea Party members to finally pass a bill through the House. We concluded that we needed to keep pressure on the White House as well as the Republican-controlled Congress. The President must be brought to understand that we would hold him responsible for the failure to pass legislation and bring the issue right to his doorstep. Speaker Boehner was not deporting 1100 people a day—but the President was!

We were certainly not alone in pushing the demand for the President to act unilaterally. Congressman Gutierrez, while continuing the fight in Congress, had called out the President publicly, saying it was his moral responsibility to offer deferments and work permits to the parents of Dreamers and the parents of U.S. citizen children. Perhaps the strongest national effort came from the National Day Labor Organizing Network. They had been on the front lines of the battle in Arizona, and they took the lead nationally in demanding Presidential action.

We were not alone, but the great majority of the national organizations were against us. In November, an NDLON leader confronted one of the national coalition organizers and asked, "We can understand a division of labor in our struggle, but why do you condemn our actions when we go after the White House?" Surprising those present with his blatant honesty, he answered, "We need to keep access to the White House to get funding." This same organizer had been the one who negotiated away the chance to secure driver's licenses for the undocumented immigrants in Illinois.

We were left with the overwhelming priority of defending 1100 people a day from deportation and separation from their families. We had learned one very important lesson through all these years: An organization must keep its promises, even if it stands alone. We had to act. We had said that if no legislation were passed by December 1st, we would initiate a sanctuary movement again. November 30th was Emma's sixtieth birthday, and 2013 was the seventh anniversary of Elvira entering sanctuary. We organized a celebration at the Adalberto United Methodist Church in Humboldt Park to celebrate both women—and to call for a renewal of the sanctuary movement, the "Sanctuary 13 Challenge."

The meeting itself celebrated both the Mexican/Puerto Rican coalition that Emma Lozano and José López had begun, and the broad Latino faith unity we had first established in Humboldt Park—both of which had spread across the nation and provided a foundation for the Latino unity that was now in place. Rosie Valdez sang her now-famous song, asking President Obama to stop the deportation of her father, but Rosalba—no longer a child—showed signs of becoming a strong and committed young woman. Dr. Lopez gave a sweeping description of the unity that had been achieved— a unity sought by Latin American leaders but realized by Latinos in the north. Emma, celebrating her sixtieth birthday, recalled her brother Rudy, Elvira, and the struggle we had gone through. She carried our message to bring the fight right to the President and "Stop the Deportations!" The church was full—as it had always been when Elvira was in sanctuary—but now a host of young faces were mixed in with a few of the original families.

I began a water-only fast that night. I was determined to continue fasting until 1,000 churches had joined our call to become sanctuary churches. The next day we began meeting with pastors in Chicago, and proceeded to connect electronically with pastors throughout the nation. This campaign would occupy the month of December.

Although the advocacy group was never reconvened to implement Plan B—the demand for the President to issue executive orders—things had nevertheless begun to move around the nation. An Asian student interrupted the President during a speech and demanded executive action. The President responded, "I don't have the power to stop the deportations" and pointed back to the Republicans. On Thanksgiving, the President visited with a group of leaders who were on a hunger strike to demand that Speaker Boehner pass the Democratic bill that had already passed the Senate. A former SEIU leader led the hunger strikers, the same leader who had responded to our call for sanctuary by asking us "to hold off" challenging the President. Visiting with them, the President repeated his claim that there was nothing he could do without Congress and again framed the issue in terms of the Republicans refusing his demand for a thirteen-year path to citizenship. The battle prior to the last election that we had waged and won would evidently have to be waged and won again, this time for the families.

We were encouraged by various reports that discredited the President's attempt to wash his hands of the deportations. In fact, now that the 2013 Congressional session was ending with no action taken, the desperation of those facing deportation was increasingly moving the local grassroots organizations to join with our demand. We were encouraged to find that many of the Dreamer groups were pressing the President to expand their deferments to their parents and to the parents of U.S. citizen children. The effort to use the Dreamers as a wedge against comprehensive immigration reform seemed to have backfired. The struggle that La FuerZa Juventud had undertaken four years ago was paying off in the heightened consciousness of the youth organizations springing up around the nation.

Gutierrez organized a press conference in front of the White House with over a dozen congressmen, all of whom signed a letter urging the President—by executive order—to extend the deferments that he had given the Dreamers to their parents, to the parents of U.S. citizen children, and to all who held a productive job in this country. Univision ran several stories covering Congressman Gutierrez and others who were pursuing this demand. Their reports cited Constitutional experts who affirmed the President's authority to do what the members of Congress were asking him to do.

Luis called to tell me that his position was clear: "We have to put pressure on both the White House and the Democrats as well as the Republicans or nothing will get done. We need more pressure on the President." We redoubled our efforts to establish a national network of sanctuary churches. Our approach to the churches was not only to encourage them to send a letter to the President, but to become active in defending people against orders of deportation. We gave them the examples of our Parent Protection ID and our initiative to help Dreamers use their DACA applications to fight orders for deportation. We sought to establish this more committed group of churches in order to have a network that would persevere in the demand on the President when the expected counter-pressure came from the White House. Indeed, the White House had already spent political capital in dissuading members of Congress from joining Gutierrez, and White House staffers and paid consultants continued to lobby the advocacy organizations to "lay off the President."

By now I was in the eleventh day of my water-only fast and beginning to feel it.

The political wheels were turning slowly, responding to our only true lobby, the unified Latino vote. After the government shutdown, which had cost the Republican Party severely, Gutierrez's dark horse in the Republican Party—Vice Presidential candidate Paul Ryan—had negotiated a budget deal that passed the House of Representatives with overwhelming support. Ryan was clearing the way to pass immigration reform and take away the barrier between Republicans and the Latino vote. Pressure on the President had won a significant concession: he would accept the "piecemeal" approach to immigration reform presented by the House. He was giving up on the effort to build support in the House for the un-passable Senate bill, which included the thirteen-year path to citizenship. We hoped for broader legalization in the House bill and a path to citizenship based on the normal means of family adjustment of status.

The prospects for passing an immigration reform bill, as we looked towards early 2014, were not great, but even a weak House bill would be something we could improve on in time. What stood in our way was the Democratic Party leadership. They still wanted to go into the next election blaming the Republicans for the failure to pass an immigration reform bill. They also wanted to clear the path for unemployed workers to take the low wage jobs of undocumented immigrants by deporting 1,400 people every day.

Influenced by the promises of funding from the White House, the majority of the advocacy organizations continued to attack the Republicans in Congress. Our task was to balance this pressure by heightening the campaign on the President to use his executive power and stop the reign of terror on our families. Senator Dick Durbin was as close to the heart of the Democratic leadership as we could reach. His DREAM Act initiative had been aimed at splitting the immigration reform movement and turning young people against their parents. He had helped orchestrate Barack Obama's campaign for the Presidency and continued to advise him. We were given the opportunity to speak right after him at an immigration forum on Saturday morning, December 14th. At times such as these, there are hard decisions for community leaders to make. Should we confront Durbin with the truth, or should we go gently in the hope of persuading him? Would speaking the truth alienate him and bring more attacks on us? On the Thursday before the speech, we got a call from the South African Embassy asking us to speak at a memorial for Nelson Mandela to be held at Operation PUSH. We took this offer as a sign that it was Mandela's example we should follow. We needed to speak truth to power, as he did, and forget the politics. I did the best that I could.

We call the first season of our church's spiritual year Preparation time. We prepare in ourselves the soil of faith in which the seeds of last year's Harvest can be planted. It is the season which the church universal calls Advent, and in which we remember the births of John the Baptist and of Jesus. We make a commitment to accept the intervention and working of the Lord in our lives in the coming year and the experience of being born into the Kingdom of God yet again. We leave behind hopelessness and bitterness and disappointment and look toward the future, while retaining the seeds, the lessons we have learned from what came before. The Virgin of Guadalupe stands at the center of this season.

We could not help but reflect on the last twenty years since Emma had led us into the movement for justice and the rights of undocumented immigrants, renewing the struggle her brother had begun twenty years yet again before that. We were still fighting deportations case-by-case and family-by-family. We were still working to change a broken immigration law in Congress. The daily procession of deportations, though, had grown larger, and President Barack Obama had attained the dubious distinction of having deported two million people. Yet something was different. The fastest growing and, now, the largest ethnic group in the United States was realizing its newfound unity—and power.

The movement had restored the dignity of a whole people and had made them part of a force that was now respected. Those who once had lived in the shadows of shame and exclusion seemed to have met the dark Virgin herself and been struck to their heart by her words, "Juan Diego, my dignified son!" The spirit that inspired Gandhi to devote his non-violent movement to overcoming the hatred and loathing directed at the Untouchables, the lowest caste of Hinduism; that prompted Dr. King to oppose the racial prejudice embodied in the Jim Crow laws of Southern segregationists; that led Nelson Mandela to take up the fight against apartheid in South Africa; that spirit of Peace and Brotherhood that the Founding Fathers called Columbia and pictured as an Indian princess is perhaps none other than the source of inspiration behind the effort to overcome the deep prejudice that named undocumented immigrants "illegal aliens."

In the course of this long struggle, we encountered people throughout the nation who could not be bought and who could not be intimidated. They were people who were willing to sacrifice for a cause greater than themselves.

They were activists in the community, in the unions, and in their churches. When the organizations and leaders who were "officially" recognized—and funded—to represent the undocumented conceded defeat, these grassroots soldiers persisted against "reasonableness" and continued to struggle. The organizations they built often lacked structure and professionalism, and always lacked adequate resources. Yet these grassroots organizations and faithful churches—from Houston, Texas, to Providence, Rhode Island, to Charleston, South Carolina, to San Jose, California—managed to continue the struggle when others turned to their own self-preservation.

One of the pastors involved in our struggle explained the two different approaches in terms of a distinction between "liberalism" and "liberation." The liberal organization retains its ties to the institutions of oppression while advocating for the oppressed. When its own interests are threatened, it concedes defeat. In the struggle for liberation, the person seeks first to free himself or herself, and then to work for the freedom of the oppressed.

A new generation has grown up in the struggle, one that learned to reject the temptations of assimilation and to hold fast to its heritage and traditions. A new form of popular organization was born in the diaspora nation, one that would free itself of dependency. Perhaps the most significant harvest of this movement for justice will be the development of a new form of people's organization, independent of the political parties and the web of not-for-profit organizations that have been funded in order to control the very people who have a right and an obligation to struggle. This new form must also be free of the arrogance of a leftist ideology that suggests, "We know better than the people what is good for them." This new organizational form will come from communities tempered and steeled by their faith. What this grassroots movement will reveal is that the families—who struggled to simply stay together, work hard and raise their children in the ways of the Lord—hold within themselves the strategy and the prophetic determination to defend their cause. Those who claim to represent them would do well to listen to their voices—the voices of a people with a destiny written in the heavens.

28

Breaking Through From Below

I n the final days of 2013, the Tea Party ran aground upon their own tactics. In a vain effort to defund Obamacare, they shut down the government for weeks by refusing to pass a continuing budget resolution. The polls showed support for the Republican-controlled Congress drop into the single digits. Thus Speaker Boehner and the Republican leadership gained some leverage in their effort to wrest back control of their party from its most conservative minority. A terrible rollout of the health care enrollment process, beset with technical failures, gave the Republicans hope that they could capture the Senate in the next election.

In an effort to overcome the shutdown, the pragmatic Congressman Ryan went one-on-one with the budget negotiator from the Senate and worked out a behind-the-scenes deal that no one was happy with. It cut important programs for the poor and impoverished, as well as military appropriations, but continued deficit spending. With the passage of the budget deal at the end of the year, Speaker Boehner—and more importantly, from our point of view, Representative Ryan—were back in control of the Republican Party. Unlike the Tea Party Congressmen, who seemed content to satisfy voters in their gerrymandered white districts, the party leaders needed to recover at least a percentage of the Latino vote to regain national power.

The stage was set for the President's State of the Union message and for the Republican House Caucus retreat, at which they would outline their principles for reform. We gathered two hundred members of our families—including Dreamers and U.S. citizen children—at our church in Pilsen to listen to President Obama's speech. We called the press and prepared a statement, knowing from advance leaks that the President would say little or nothing about immigration reform. It was worse than we thought. In a two-hour speech, the President spent less than thirty seconds on immigration reform. Vowing to use his executive powers on everything else in the face of a paralyzed Congress, he simply said that he hoped the Congress would pass immigration reform because it would be "good for the economy."

Most of those gathered in the church were young, part of a generation that had only joined the struggle a year or two ago. We tried to point out the ironies to them. We told them that three weeks before President Obama's first inauguration, we had brought a study to the White House that showed legalization would be a powerful stimulus to the economy—a job creator. At first the White House aides had been enthusiastic, even setting a date for the joint release of the study. As the study wound its way up to the Oval Office, however, the idea of a joint release of the study was killed. The Obama administration decided to follow a policy of deportation to relieve unemployment, not a policy of immigration reform and legalization. His statement now—that legalization would be good for the economy—seemed about five years late. Following nearly two million deportations, his callousness now appeared as heartless cruelty. Giving only thirty seconds to immigration reform was spending one second for every sixty thousand people he had deported, one second for every six thousand families he had destroyed and separated, one second for every ten thousand children he had left without a father or a mother.

The advocacy groups in Washington were generally silent about the speech. Some said that they would push the Republicans to meet the President's challenge to pass reform. It was not so easy for us. Doris Aguirre was in the audience of our church, still facing an order of deportation. ICE had ordered her deported to Colombia, and one of her children to another Latin American country where he had been born during her journey north. They would leave behind her U.S. citizen husband and another U.S. citizen child. Beside Doris sat another family facing deportation, and beside them another family.

Rosalba Valdez, who at ten years of age had composed the song demanding that President Obama return her father, read a statement in English in response to the President's State of the Union Address. A Dreamer whose father also faced deportation read the same statement in Spanish.

Speaker Boehner and Congressman Ryan had clearly regained control of the House Republicans. They had let the Tea Party members embarrass themselves by shutting down the government. Now they were calling the shots. The Republicans emerged from their retreat with a set of principles for reform. They agreed to a broad program of legalization, and to a path to citizenship only available to the Dreamers. It was essentially the same program that Gutierrez had negotiated with the group of eight in the spring of 2012, the agreement that the Democratic leadership had ordered Congressman Becerra to scuttle.

No amount of lobbying could have been responsible for the Republican turnaround. The unity of the Latino vote and the power of the Latino Evangelical churches produced the change. This time, President Obama signaled that he would agree to the Republican approach, giving up on the special thirteen-year road to citizenship he had once demanded as a condition. The advocacy groups were slow to catch on and continued to demand the citizenship condition that had been passed in the Senate.

Two weeks later, Speaker Boehner declared that his party was taking immigration reform off the table in the House of Representatives. Some still held out hope for passing a bill, and Gutierrez remained optimistic in his public statements. The Republicans then launched another attack on President Obama. They said they could not vote for immigration reform because they could not trust him to enforce whatever law they passed. We were facing the prospect of another year of legislative failure and another 400,000 deportations by the President.

We decided to return to the demand that the President use his executive authority to extend the deferments that he gave the Dreamers to their parents and to the parents of U.S. citizen children. If the Republicans felt the President was going to act, it might drive them to move legislation, fearing that what had begun when the President opened up deferments for the Dreamers before the 2012 election would now result in the consolidation of the Latino vote in the Democratic column. If the Republicans did not act— and the President did—we would be in a position to negotiate a better bill without being under the gun of 1100 deportations a day.

Moving the advocacy organizations away from their partisan attacks on the Republican Party and out from under the thumb of the White House would prove a difficult challenge. The coalition we had formed with the single national organization willing to take on the President—the National Day Labor Organizing Network—was beset on all sides. Congressman Becerra, acting at the behest of the Democratic leadership, locked down the Congressional Hispanic Caucus. The National Council of La Raza and FIRM refused to make any demands on the President. In an apparent effort to protect itself, the White House reached out to former United Farmworker leader and California SEIU leader Eliseo Medina, and convinced him to lead a Fast for Families. It would take place for twenty days on the Washington Mall— focused solely on the Republicans. He would then travel with a caravan and crisscross the country, attacking the Republicans and shielding the President from criticism for his deportation policy.

By March, the organizational veil protecting the President's deportation policy began to loosen, and then it fell to the floor. We campaigned directly against the D.C. coalitions, claiming that they had offered to protect the President in return for funding. A boycott of a major fundraising dinner for the National Council of La Raza was threatened. Minority Leader Pelosi felt the heat and called on the President to use his authority to stop the deportations. Gutierrez kept up his attacks as he traveled around the country, aiming both at intransigent Republicans and at the immorality of the President's deportation policy. NDLON issued a call for national actions on April 5th, although they miscalculated the actual date on which the Obama administration would reach the two million-person deportation mark. Gradually, the advocacy organizations signed on.

In mid-March, Senator Durbin held a public "leadership report" meeting with the Illinois Coalition. The Senator invited Congressman Gutierrez to join him, and the congressman added Emma Lozano to the list of organizational leaders. I attended as a member of his staff. Senator Durbin struck hard at the Republicans, but also reported that he had asked the new head of Homeland Security to find ways to slow down the deportations. The Senator then defended the President's policy, citing Republican statements that they could not pass immigration reform because they did not trust the President to enforce the law. Lozano countered with an impassioned demand to stop the ongoing destruction of families. Surprisingly, her demand drew sustained applause from the fifty advocate leaders around the table. Durbin had been challenged in front of the press at his own meeting. One week later, he called on the President to take executive action and was joined by Senators Melendez and Reid.

It felt like a house of cards was collapsing. From the floor of the House, Gutierrez called Obama the "deporter-in-chief." Janet Murguía, president and CEO of the National Council of La Raza, used the same term in calling for executive action. All the major Dreamer organizations persisted in their demand on the President. The rest of the D.C. coalitions joined the call through a series of press conferences.

We met with Gutierrez and got agreement for a march and rally on March 27th. He agreed to be arrested along with 300 others as part of a civil disobedience action. We went to work organizing the Latino pastors, the community organizations, and the high school students. Gutierrez reported to us: "I am winning the argument with the Democratic leadership. They listen and they agree, but then they do nothing. We need a spark."

🌿 29
Elvira's Return

I
n the years after her arrest in California and deportation to Mexico, Elvira Arellano never rested from the struggle that she had been thrust into. She began working with people on the border, establishing Casa Elvira for those waiting to cross the border and for those who were deported and then dumped into the dangerous border towns. Whenever Familia Latina Unida mobilized in the States, time and time again she mobilized parallel demonstrations in front of the U.S. embassy. Gradually, the global challenges facing migrants came within the scope of her attention. She was called to speak at conferences in a dozen different countries.

She began to focus on the plight of Central American migrants traveling up from Honduras, El Salvador, and Guatemala into Mexico. Many of these migrants were deportees, trying to make the thousand-mile trek back to their families in the United States. They were attacked by criminal organizations and sometimes by corrupt government police as they rode on top of the train they called "*La Bestia.*" At each 100-mile juncture another group went after the migrants—demanding money, threatening, often beating or even killing those who refused or who had nothing to give.

A network of human rights activists formed "sanctuaries" for the migrants along this route; some very courageous priests and activists raised a public outcry against the abuse, extortion and murder the migrants were subjected to. Many of these leaders were driven from the country by the threats of the criminal organizations and by attempts on their life. Elvira, too, lived with these threats, as she became increasingly well known for her defense of the migrants. Once she was cornered and shot at. We received a call from her in Mexico. I think she believed it would be her last call—but she survived.

The assaults and extortion were not limited to Central American migrants. In fact, every person who had been deported from the United States became an immediate target. The criminal groups realized that the deportees still had friends and families in the United States who could raise money to pay the extortion demands. We came to understand that thousands of deportees and their children were subject to kidnapping and extortion. "Sequester" became a common word in Mexico, as well as among family members still living in the United States. Our church alone had four families with a kidnapped family member in Mexico.

Living in danger and poverty, the deported family members were easy prey not only for the large cartels, but for smaller crews as well. They were also targets for organizations in the immigration movement looking to make a name for themselves in their constant search for funding. NIA was a splinter sect from one of the Dreamer groups that had begun in Chicago as "undocumented and unafraid." They were a small, cult-like group headed by an Iranian immigrant who was able to escape deportation because he was gay and could not be returned to Iran because of their anti-gay policy. NIA became increasingly isolated from the rest of the movement, but they came up with an interesting tactic. They brought several Dreamers to the Mexican border and demanded to be admitted. When they were denied entry, the group demanded that members of the Congressional Hispanic Caucus "find a way" to get them out of detention and admitted to the United States. At one point they staged a sit-in in Congressman Gutierrez's offices in the capital claiming he was "not doing enough" for the Dreamers held in detention. In fact, the Congressman had intervened in their cases, but he had counseled their families that the tactic of the poorly thought out "challenge at the border" would actually hurt their chances for legalization.

NIA next sent its organizers to different towns in Mexico to recruit parents with U.S. citizen or Dreamer children to join a group of 150 attempting to cross into the United States. NIA raised their hopes of being reunited with their families in the United States but did little to prepare them to make their cases when they reached the border. Five of these families were from Maravatío and had participated in the grassroots movement there under Elvira's leadership, and Elvira agreed to join them on their journey to the border in Tijuana.

The situation she found in Tijuana was disheartening. The families had no money. No lawyers were present, and no preparations had been made for what would happen when they presented themselves at the border. The families were kept isolated and told they would have to bring their children, but without papers, even if they were U.S. citizens. Days went by, and the families began to lose hope and become desperate. The attempted crossings failed to draw much media attention, and it seemed as if the organizers were avoiding contact with Latino media. They preferred to report their actions via Facebook. In an effort to keep the families' spirits up, Elvira agreed to present herself and Saul with them at the border.

When she called us to explain her decision, we set up a conference call with attorney Chris Bergin. Chris explained that she could face prison—anywhere from six months to ten years—for attempting to enter the country, since she had a twenty-year ban against her re-entry. Fear of prison had never intimidated Elvira before, and it did not do so this time. Actually, she felt she would just be turned back at the border, but she hoped it would bring media attention to the families she accompanied. Elvira sent for Saulito to cross with her. She now had another family member as well, her four-month-old baby, Emiliano, still nursing at her breast.

Emma flew to San Diego and then crossed the border to meet with her. Elvira left the compound where the families were being kept by NIA, and she and Emma developed a strategy. As Saul's legal guardian, Emma would immediately demand Saul's release. Because Elvira was still nursing the baby, they were sure she would not be separated from Emiliano. Emma returned to San Diego, where she began talking to the media. NIA continued to operate in a secretive manner, working independently of the many groups in California that were offering to support the families, especially since Elvira was joining them in the crossing.

At the border, Elvira, her baby, and Saul presented themselves, along with over forty of the families, and were taken into custody. It was March 18th. She requested humanitarian parole because of the danger and threats she had received in Mexico. By this time her crossing had become a major media event in California. Emma held a series of press conferences, and the next day presented herself to take custody of Saulito. Elvira and Emiliano remained in custody.

Although Congressman Gutierrez had formally broken relations with NIA, he made a series of calls on Elvira's behalf. We had little hope that she would be released into the United States. Late one evening, Emma called to say she had been notified by one of the guards holding Elvira in custody: "Don't go anywhere. Elvira is going to be released to you." Emma was excited. I just didn't believe it. While Elvira was being held at the border, both Univision and Telemundo contacted us to do background stories on Elvira at the church where she had stayed in sanctuary. When Emma relayed the message that she had received to Jacobita Alonso, Jacobita contacted Univision, and the national news on Univision led with the story that Elvira was to be released into the United States.

We still did not believe it, at least I didn't. Emma continued a steady stream of TV and radio interviews with Saul, suggesting at one point that perhaps ICE was playing a cruel joke, playing with Saul's emotions. One day later Emma was informed that Elvira was being transferred from her detention facility to ICE headquarters for a review of her claim for humanitarian parole. ICE officers crowded around the agent who had been sent to interview her. Several of the officers made derogatory remarks, suggesting that she had stolen the baby she was nursing at her breast. The interviewer silenced the other officers and continued with a brief set of questions. He clearly was acting on orders. Elvira explained that she was a human rights activist who had been threatened with death by several of the cartels.

Then came the unexpected. Emma was called by an ICE official and told to come immediately to pick up Elvira. She was being paroled for six months into the United States to pursue her legal options. She was free to travel and to go immediately to her residence in the United States, Adalberto United Methodist Church, where she had spent a year in sanctuary.

What had happened? One week later, we learned that Univision's top political reporter, Jorge Ramos, had been interviewing the President when ICE took Elvira into detention. Ramos asked the President if he knew that "ICE was holding Elvira Arellano in detention at the border." The history of his relationship with Elvira must have crossed the President's mind. The pressure on him to introduce a private bill for her and the charge that he had failed to do so, which probably cost him the California primary when running against Hillary Clinton, may have given him pause. He was also well aware of the symbol she had become in the nation and especially in the Latino community. We do not know what action the President took, but we know that orders came down from Washington, D.C., to ICE in San Diego right after Ramos's interview with Barack Obama: parole Elvira Arellano into the United States.

Elvira was back! She was free to travel and to speak and to organize. She led the newscasts on Spanish television and appeared in over fifty interviews on radio and television over the next eight days. Everywhere she went—even on the street—she got standing ovations, and throngs of people wanting to have their picture taken with her.

Elvira came back swinging, demanding that the President extend deferments to the families and provide the same parole he gave to her to other deported parents facing extortion and threats in Mexico and Central America. In Chicago, she threw herself into organizing the rally and civil disobedience action we had planned with Gutierrez for March 27th. Gutier-rez had told us we "needed a spark" to build pressure on the President. The Virgin of Guadalupe had provided us with Elvira's return!

At the time Elvira was attempting to cross the border, Gutierrez initi-ated a moderate resolution for consideration by the Congressional Hispanic Caucus, calling on the President to use his prosecutorial discretion to stop deporting those who would have qualified for legalization under the bill passed by the United States Senate. Under pressure from NDLON and other groups, the resolution was strengthened to demand that the President extend deferments to the parents of the Dreamers and the parents of five million U.S. citizen children. The vote in the caucus was scheduled for a Thursday night.

At two o'clock on Thursday afternoon, March 13th, Gutierrez, Becerra, and the Chairman of the Hispanic Caucus—Ruben Hinojosa of Texas—were called to an urgent meeting with the President in the White House. According to Luis, the President seemed to listen to their account of the sep-aration of families as if for the first time. He promised that if the Republicans did not take action in the House before the summer break, he would take "bold action." He ordered his new Secretary of Homeland Security, Jeh Johnson, to conduct a review of his alternatives. He empowered Gutierrez to meet with Homeland Security, to oversee the review, and to discuss the options with them. Then he asked the congressmen to hold off the vote on the caucus resolution and see if the Republicans would act.

The President had a strong hold on the Hispanic Caucus through Con-gressman Becerra, who also served as the chair of the Democratic Caucus in the House. Anticipating that the Hispanic Caucus would fold, Gutierrez took a new tack. "I believe the President is sincere and is prepared to take bold executive action," he announced. "Therefore, I am giving the Republi-cans a warning, a lifeline. Either take legislative action in the next thirty-eight working days of Congress or the President will."

Minority Leader Pelosi and the Democrats in the House produced a motion to call up their version of the Senate bill in the House and began gathering signatures from House members. While all the Democrats signed onto the discharge petition, not a single Republican joined. Gutier-rez explained to us that this was just more of the same political posturing we had already seen. He remained optimistic that either the Republicans would act or the President would be forced to act in July. Given the new situation with the President, Luis's chief of staff informed me that it might be inappropriate for the congressman to appear and be arrested at our march and rally in Chicago. I wrote a long email to Luis suggesting that we needed to keep the pressure on the President. We continued to build for the march and rally, boosted by Elvira's presence in the media. We had planned for the event to include Gutierrez in order to emphasize the demand for extension of the deferments. Without Gutierrez, the action would have much less significance. Three days before the march, I received a text from Luis that said simply, "O.K. I'm coming."

Gutierrez and Elvira led the march and gave dozens of media interviews, clearly stating our demand on the President. Gutierrez continued to warn the Republicans to act or be preempted by the President. We were joined by fifty Methodist pastors, led by our new Bishop, Sally Dyck, and a strong contingent of Latino pastors, led by Pastor Freddy Santiago. The pastors joined Familia Latina Unida members in blocking the doors to ICE headquarters and in being arrested for this symbolic act of civil disobedience. The picture of Gutierrez and Arellano standing together, marching together, lifted spirits around the nation and certainly lifted our spirits. As Easter approached, we began preparing for the May 1st marches and responded to requests from all around the country for Elvira to speak. We also developed a plan for a Texas initiative on Mother's Day, May 10, 2014.

While Gutierrez persisted in his challenge to the Republicans, our task was to ensure that the President would actually carry through on his promise to take bold action if the Republicans did not act. Those groups under the influence of the White House firmly opposed the demand on the President for executive action and continued their political attacks on the Republicans in preparation for the midterm elections. We set out to revive full participation in the grassroots movement and to strengthen the resolve of the Congressional Hispanic Caucus. The caucus would have to hold firm and thus needed a strong demonstration of support from large numbers of the Latino community.

Emma began a series of calls to the most stalwart of our leadership around the country, beginning with Pablo Alvarado, the president of NDLON. NDLON had established a commission of the undocumented to speak for the 11 million others and had posted a continuous 24-hour night-and-day sit-in of families and Dreamers in front of the White House. Elvira planned to join them in their protest, then to go to the frontlines of the struggle in Arizona. Elvira plunged into the work of organizing, took up residence in her church, enrolled Saul in the Puerto Rican high school across the street, and began preparation of her case for political asylum. Although personally very critical of the tactics used by NIA—the isolation and abuse of the families—she sought simply to ignore the group, rather than publicly criticize it. Familia Latina Unida quietly took on the defense of those families from Maravatío who were still held in detention, and received assistance from the congressman's office.

NIA, however, had other ideas. The group advertised a "national tour" to build the defense of those still held in detention and proclaimed that Elvira would be leading the tour. When she informed them that she would not accompany them, they unleashed phone calls, texts, and emails by the hundreds. Finally, she agreed to go with them to one event in Detroit. Strangely, they sent a cab to pick her up before dawn. The cab took her to a van a few blocks away, and they took off for Detroit. Three hours into the trip, the driver—a key organizer in NIA—offered her a Mexican candy. She ate the candy and in twenty minutes began to lose control of her body as well as her thoughts. She could hear the driver and his companion discussing what they would do with her. She felt they were discussing a kidnapping of some kind. She grew almost hysterical, unable to breathe, and they decided to take her to an emergency room in Kalamazoo, Michigan. In the emergency room she called Emma and said, "Señora Emma, save me. I'm dying."

We jumped into a car with Roberto driving—the same Roberto who had been driving when she was arrested in California. When we arrived at the emergency room three hours later, Elvira was laying on a bed with an intravenous tube in her arm, barely able to speak. The female companion from NIA was still sitting with her in the room and told us that Elvira had become sick before she ate the candy. The attending physician then informed us that tests had shown an extremely high dose of toxic chemicals in Elvira's system. She had been poisoned. After more contradictory explanations, the female companion and the driver disappeared from the hospital. It took 24 hours to get the chemicals out of her system and to pump the poisoned milk from her breasts. Emma and Beti drove her back to Chicago, where she began five days of slow but steady recovery.

The incident of poisoning ended any relations we might have had with NIA, though we persisted in the defense of the families that had been thrust without preparation or defense into such a horrible situation. We still are not clear what the intentions of this small cult-like organization really were. Did they intend to kidnap her, or discredit her? An event in Detroit had indeed been arranged, but they moved it to a different location and drew less than twenty people, suggesting the group never intended to organize a real defense campaign. Whatever their motivations, if their intent was to break her spirit, they failed. Within a week, Elvira Arellano was at full strength.

We did research, however, and learned more about this renegade group. Its leader had been a strong Republican supporter only a few years before. NIA organizers were walking around with rolls of fifties and hundreds in their pockets, driving rental cars, and staying in the best hotels. In February of 2014, the organization's leadership had promised that they would take actions during the coming summer that would destroy the immigration movement. We found credible evidence that the organization had been paid to go through Honduras spreading the false rumor that separated family members could just present themselves at the Mexican-United States border and be given legal status. We would see the fruit of their underhanded work in the coming summer, with a resulting surge of Honduran children who would present themselves at the border. The right of separated family members—many of who had U.S. citizen children—to return to the United States was an important issue. We would have to find a way to do it right, to organize for their return without endangering thousands of people with false information.

Gustavo came to our church, like many others, having heard that we fought hard and effectively against deportations. He told us about his situation. His wife had been deported and had been living in Mexico with their U.S. citizen son for almost seven years. During that time he had worked as a bilingual teacher, sending them money each month. He made frequent trips to Mexico, when he could afford to, and his wife had given birth to a daughter who was now five years old. He had acted quickly to make her a U.S. citizen.

Gustavo became a committed member of our church and never missed a Sunday. Frequently during congregational prayers, he asked for prayers for his wife and children. He was one among many. Seven years is a long time to be separated, especially for a couple so young and deeply in love. During prayers one Sunday, Gustavo explained that his wife had been threatened with harm if he did not pay monthly extortion demands.

Gustavo was now one of five members of our church with family members in Mexico or Guatemala who had been deported and were now facing extortion demands. We spoke privately with Gustavo to counsel him, but his story came out each week during prayers. He traveled to Mexico to move his family out of the neighborhood, and his wife kept his children out of school. The criminal organization found them again. On one trip to Mexico, Gustavo witnessed the daylight murder of a neighbor who had refused to pay extortion demands because the family had been unable to keep up the payments. He prayed for help.

Elvira's re-entry into the country had given hope to many that their loved ones could also re-enter. For our part, we wanted to make a high pro-file example in order to continue our campaign for the second demand—the demand that those who had been deported and were now facing extortion should be given emergency parole back into the country. When we began this campaign a year ago in Laredo, with the reading of the children's letters at the border, our goal had been to include the return of deportees in the immigration reform legislation. Now, we hoped to convince the President to include them in his executive orders.

We began preparations for the trip to Laredo. It was early May. Our friend Pepe Jaques had made contact with Gustavo's wife, Marlene. She and the children went to stay with Pepe in safety as we began a series of press conferences to explain her situation and the plan for her to present herself at the border for parole. We wanted to show people the careful preparation required to make these re-entries successful, in contrast to the blitz attempt by NIA that had resulted in disaster for so many people. Pepe arranged for Marlene to make an official denunciation of the extortion attempts against her and the children.

We went first to San Antonio, where we held two days of press events with our allies from the League of United Latin American Citizens. Members of LULAC had helped us the year before when we began the Children's Campaign. Now they organized the press events and a march to City Council, where Gustavo entered testimony of his situation into the official record. While he testified, the San Antonio group renewed its effort to have the city declared a "sanctuary city." The mayor of San Antonio, Julián Castro, had been holding off on passing their resolution, angering the community. A few weeks later, Castro was invited by President Obama to be the new Secretary of Housing and Urban Development. We could not help but view the appointment as a reward for staving off the sanctuary movement in San Antonio. A month before, the President had held a showing in the White House of the new movie about Cesar Chavez, and had appointed one of Cesar's children to a post in the White House. The President seemed to be cultivating a visible Hispanic presence in his administration. By challenging the mayor of San Antonio, we were at the same time challenging the President's deportation policy, and the

White House had to take notice. Through events such as these, we felt ourselves to be part of a direct dialogue between the grassroots movement and the President of the United States.

After two days in San Antonio, we went to Laredo. Julie Contreras from LULAC had gone ahead to meet with border officials and to let them know what we were going to do. She led them on a walk-through, having them march across the bridge with her. On Saturday—Mother's Day in Mexico—we gathered in a small park that lies next to the Rio Grande, nestled under the bridge that crosses the river known as "the two Marias." As we had done a year earlier, Pepe and a crowd gathered in a park on the Mexican side of the river. This time Marlene and her children were on the Mexican side; Gustavo was on the U.S. side, along with us, the mayor of Laredo, and a large group of pastors, priests, and local community leaders. Loud speakers allowed us to pray and speak together across the river, interrupted every fifteen minutes or so by the loud noise of the border patrol boat.

Gustavo, a quiet and intelligent man, came alive at the rally by the river. Calling across the river to his wife and children, he cried out for justice as tears fell from his eyes. Many of us shed tears with him in the blazing hot Texas sun. Then, from both sides of the border, the delegations made their way to the center of the bridge. At the midpoint, Marlene was taken into custody. Her daughter broke down in hysterics, watching her mother being taken away by men with guns. We returned with the press to a nearby hotel and waited with our attorney, John Antia. Gradually, the little girl stopped crying. We were prepared for several days of waiting. Three hours later, our attorney received a call from the ICE agent: "I am going to release her to you in one hour. You can pick her up as long as you don't bring the media." Marlene was granted a one-year humanitarian parole.

As in San Antonio, Jaime Martinez and the group of long-time activists in Laredo seemed like an extension of our church in Chicago. We shared common prayers and a common faith. They were one of the groups around the country who had a long history of grassroots struggle. Like the movement leaders in Arizona, these activists knew how to organize effectively around immigration issues. While the national movement, dominated by well-funded immigrant rights organizations, was divided and controlled by various political forces, these "struggle families" were a constant source of hope and a wellspring of effective action.

The Garza family was central to the grassroots movement in Laredo. Timoteo Garza had been a member of the state legislature when Republicans forced through a remap of the state that dramatically diluted the representation of African Americans and Latinos. With other Democratic legislators, Timoteo had traveled to Oklahoma to prevent a quorum in the legislature from approving the remap. The governor called him on his cell phone: "You have sixty seconds to agree to come back. If not, you and your family will pay." Within months, Timoteo, his father, and his mother were framed on corruption charges, tried, and sent to jail. After two hard years in the federal penitentiaries, they won their case on appeal and returned to their leadership role in the Texas Latino community.

The members of the Garza family were strong Christians before their imprisonment, but their time behind bars became a test, a genuine trial of their convictions. Their ordeal and their faith set an example for the community, and made it possible for the grassroots movement to deepen. Hundreds and thousands of individuals and families took heart, and their faith and perseverance further ennobled the movement for justice for undocumented immigrants. Yet even for these veterans, the quick parole of this young mother and her children seemed to be a miracle, more an answer to prayer than to political action.

The next Sunday in church in Chicago, the congregation celebrated the reunion of Gustavo's family after seven long years. We watched the children light the candles and heard Gustavo and his wife read the Scriptures. If the nation was paralyzed over the immigration issue and much of the movement was discouraged, hope was still strong in our church.

Our fast-growing youth movement organized a continuing "Promise Watch" on successive "Moral Mondays" in front of ICE headquarters in Chicago. Elvira's clear, powerful statements strengthened their increasing numbers and enthusiastic spirit. Their goal was to dramatize the need to stop the parade of families fighting deportation, and encourage the President to take executive action by the July 4th deadline. Gutierrez took the floor each week in the House of Representatives to count down the days until July 4th. The ongoing battle within the advocacy organizations continued apace. Some pressed for executive action, while others pressured the Republican Party and tried to mobilize the Latino vote for Democrats in November. The tide seemed to be turning away from the paralysis of the political parties; a shift seemed to be in the air.

The President turned to the D.C. organizations for cover. A coalition of advocacy organizations and religious groups came together to ask the President to hold off on executive action to give the Republican Congress a chance to act. A press conference, well orchestrated by the White House, received broad coverage. The President seized the opportunity to suspend Homeland Security's survey of possible executive actions.

While the President may have felt a lessening of pressure in D.C., widespread expressions of anger arose throughout the country, and local actions against the deportations increased dramatically. We continued with Moral Monday protests at ICE headquarters. Two hundred cadets from the Marine Math and Science Academy, a military public high school in Chicago, gathered around one of their own, whose father had been deported nine years before: "I am committed to join the marines and serve this country. Why does this country refuse to let my father live with me?" The cadets marched in military formation for over an hour.

The weekly Promise Watch mobilizations were mainly made up now of young people, members of La FuerZa Juventud. During the decade-long struggle of Familia Latina Unida, the children of the original families had grown up. Some were Dreamers and had received their deferments through our efforts. Others were finishing high school. Saul Arellano, who had been barely four years old when Elvira was first arrested, turned fifteen and entered high school as a sophomore upon his mother's return. We needed this new generation to carry us through the next phase of the struggle. We were not disappointed.

The Affordable Care Act had coldly excluded undocumented immigrants. Familia Latina Unida and its youth organization, La FuerZa Juventud, had moved to establish the Youth Health Service Corps in five high schools and a dozen elementary schools. The "five plus one to get twenty" campaign equipped the students to get their families and neighbors screened for the five chronic diseases that were the main cause of lower life expectancy in the Latino community—twenty years fewer than that in the nearby, affluent community of Hyde Park. In June we held a "graduation" for the youth who had completed their certification, honoring their work in saving lives.

Some of the students came from the Marine Math and Science Academy, the same who had protested at ICE headquarters. This school had led the fight for the DREAM Act and for the right of Dreamers to enter the military. The leadership and discipline of the military school carried over and influenced students from the other high schools. One by one they marched to the front to receive their recognition medals as their families applauded. Much more than parental pride prompted this applause for the accomplishments of their sons and daughters. These young people had discovered previously undetected cases of heart disease, cancer and diabetes in their own families, and their neighbors and had gotten them treatment. The nation may have turned its back on health care for undocumented immigrants—but their children were fighting for it, and winning.

As the three hundred youth corps members presented themselves, they shouted out in unison: "The Youth are not the Problem. The Youth are the Solution!" The candidate for Lieutenant Governor, Paul Vallas—along with Emma and Elvira—then addressed the graduating youth corp. Yet it was the sharp, clear speeches of the young men and women themselves that moved those assembled. They were Mexican, Puerto Rican, African American, citizens and undocumented; disciplined and committed; fighting for health care and legalization; survivors of the attacks of the immigration system and of the criminalization of the gangs by the criminal justice system; survivors of the efforts to get them to turn their backs on their families and their people; ready to do whatever was necessary—humble but strong, respectful, and united.

The graduation lifted our spirits, which soared even higher when one hundred young people signed up full time for the summer campaign for health care and legalization. The true test of a grassroots movement is its ability to sustain itself, to outlast the opposition. What we were learning is that the power to sustain a movement over two decades depends on the strength of the generation that is coming of age within it. We were ready for the summer of struggle.

⚘ 30
The Spirit of Truth and the Border Crisis

T he Bible tells the story of the disciples coming out of hiding after the crucifixion of Jesus Christ. On the day of Pentecost the Spirit of Truth, the Holy Spirit, gave the disciples courage. They proclaimed that the priests and landowners conspired with the Romans to murder an innocent man, Jesus of Nazareth, and that the Lord had raised Him from the dead to convict the hypocrites. Pentecost is always a powerful spiritual season for our ministry. During the season of Pentecost in 2006, Familia Latina Unida organized a march of 80,000 people in Chicago to bring forward the demand for executive action after Congress failed to pass immigration reform. Pentecost always provided us with courage and spiritual strength to come back from discouragement, defeat, and betrayal to take the truth of our cause to the people, as the disciples did centuries before.

On Father's Day, one week into the season of Pentecost, we again made the long journey to Laredo, Texas, to reunite a mother and her child with her husband who had been deported. Working with our allies in Laredo, we followed the same pattern we had followed on Mother's Day and, miraculously, we were again successful. We returned to Chicago to bring the reunited family to the Moral Monday protest in front of ICE headquarters. The reunified family brought a new spirit to our Promise Watch protests over the next two weeks, and soon we found ourselves at the last Monday before the July 4th deadline.

We felt we were in a spiritual battle, especially after the betrayal of the D.C. establishment coalition that had called on President Obama to delay executive action. Elvira's return and the two successful reunifications at the border gave us a surprising confidence. In the season of Pentecost and in the spirit of the Advocate of Truth, we encouraged Congressman Gutierrez to stay the course and to hold President to the July 4th deadline for executive action. We knew the White House was bringing strong pressure on the congressman to back down. We also knew that the dynamic of the previous months had put him in a critical position to influence how the Latino community would view the President. Emma and I recalled the first time we had met Luis over a quarter of a century ago. He had been working as a cab driver and had sought our support for an improbable run for ward committeeman against then-Congressman Dan Rostenkowski. The Harold Washington movement had later swept him into the city council to give Chicago's first African American Mayor the decisive 26th vote in the city council. In 1997, Emma had brought thousands of post cards to the congressman and persuaded him to introduce the first comprehensive legislation to legalize the undocumented. Now, after two national Familias Unidas tours, and working with his caucus to pressure the President to take executive action, he had become the national champion of immigration reform. History and powerful spiritual forces had combined to put him in this position. We hoped these forces were more powerful than the political pressures to keep him silent. We sent him a message to that effect, with a summary of our understanding of the present situation and a detailed timetable that expressed our view of how to proceed.

Luis responded by text that he was in agreement. On Wednesday, June 25th, he pulled the trigger, delivering a powerful speech on the House floor that declared the legislative effort dead and insisted that it was now time for the President to act. We did not expect the President to act until August, but felt it was imperative to build "the moral mountain" on which the President could stand and take actions that would allow millions to live with security and dignity, and would help to reunify those families already torn apart by deportations.†

Within an hour of the speech, we forwarded the YouTube link to several thousand of our strongest allies so that they could watch the speech themselves. We also urged them to begin to take action. We were in for a pleasant surprise! We learned that the President and his advisors had already discussed the threat of a summer of protests against the deportations. Within days, the President held a press conference. He explained that the Republican Speaker of the House had informed him that the Republicans would take no further action on immigration reform. He stated that he had given instructions to Secretary of Homeland Security Jeh Johnson and Attorney General Eric Holder to formulate all the options available to him within the

---

† The message—written by myself, Emma, and Elvira—appears in Appendix E. The penultimate speech that Congressmen Gutierrez gave in the House follows in Appendix F.

law so that he could move on immigration reform. He stated unequivocally that he intended to implement those options by the end of summer.

The objective Familia Latina Unida had initiated in 2006—that the road to immigration reform led through executive action at the White House—now seemed within reach. The exact character and extent of the executive action was the crucial question that now remained. We revised the summer campaign of confrontation and initiated a call for a voter registration campaign aimed at "DACA PARA TODOS" for undocumented immigrants and "EMERGENCY PAROLE" for the reunification of families already separated by deportation. The Congressional Hispanic Caucus adopted our position and said that they would meet again with the President to push for these demands. While the President assured the Caucus that he would take executive action, he added, "I won't probably go as far as you would like."

In our church we read the letter from James, in which he counseled that we should "take joy in trials and temptations" because "perseverance would perfect us." As if to encourage us to develop this virtue, a new crisis arose at the border of Mexico and the United States. The exodus of women and children fleeing the poverty and violence of Honduras, Guatemala, and El Salvador, which had engaged Elvira Arellano for five years in Mexico, suddenly became a crisis. The headlines of newspapers and cable news stations focused on thousands of children from those countries appearing at the border. Republican hearts hardened, demanding that the children be immediately sent back to their countries. Moreover, they blamed Obama's policy of offering deferments to the Dreamers for encouraging children to seek refuge in the United States. The dark irony of this accusation, knowing as we did about the work of the NIA organizers, was not lost on us. The press reported the presence of over 40,000 unaccompanied children at the border in the Rio Grande valley. Right wing militia on the border regrouped after a period of relative quiet. When buses transported the children to various detention centers from Texas to California, they were met by loud groups of white people calling for a halt to the Latino invasion.

The President, quickly joined by Gutierrez, called it a humanitarian crisis separate from the ongoing immigration issue and suggested that the Republican failure to pass comprehensive immigration reform was to blame. President Obama requested nearly four billion dollars from the Congress to beef up patrols, to expand detention and processing centers, and to add more administrative judges to hear their cases—as well as pay the costs to deport them to their home countries. The President stood by the law, and the advocacy groups supported his position. A 2008 law, passed almost unanimously through Congress and signed by President Bush, outlined a procedure for processing undocumented children at the border from countries other than Mexico. The children were supposed to be processed, then housed in the least oppressive conditions possible and placed with family members, whenever possible, pending their day in immigration court. Republicans argued that the 2008 law should be amended to allow immediate deportation of the children.

For five years we had heard Elvira's reports about the plight of migrants from Honduras, Guatemala and El Salvador. She had organized groups to ride on top of the trains with them to provide sanctuary, and had stood up to both cartel gangsters and corrupt Mexican police. Emma and I had traveled to Mexico City to meet with the mothers whose children had disappeared on the journey north, and to hear their testimonies of torture and murder. This issue, well known in Mexico, had been almost completely ignored in the United States. In our own church we had two Guatemalan families whose children had been kidnapped and held for ransom. Familia Latina Unida felt obligated to support the children. Moreover, the children were winning the compassionate response of almost the entire Latino community.

The resurgence of bigotry and racism threatened the President's commitment to executive action. It also posed a threat to our demand for an expansion of DACA, since the Republicans in Congress were targetting DACA as the cause for the children coming to the border. Both the continuing stream of children and the likely extended debate in Congress over the President's budget request, along with Republican calls to change the law requiring special treatment for the children, ensured that the issue would hold the headlines for the month of July.

The truth of why the children journeyed to the border went deeper than any of our political leaders or well-funded advocates were willing to talk about. It touched on a truth about the issue of undocumented immigrants that had been submerged during the last fifteen years of debate. The children were coming from three countries, and especially from Honduras. It was instructive that they were not coming from Nicaragua. We asked why and looked more closely at Honduras. Honduras had a democratically elected government, installed after a long history of military coups. The elected government of President Zelaya had sided with Venezuela and the association of Latin American giants in the south. The nation was beginning to benefit from generous contributions of oil from Venezuela and the fair trade agreements they had received from the emerging Latin American block. U.S. leaders looked on in alarm as Chavez's influence moved into Central America.

In 2009, a military coup arrested President Zelaya at four o'clock in the morning, took him to a U.S. military base, and then shipped him out of the country to Costa Rica. While President Obama condemned the coup—as did almost all the presidents of Latin America—the United States poured money into Honduras to support the military leaders with whom the U.S. military and the CIA had had a long relationship. Four years of brutal suppression of the popular movement that had elected Zelaya ensued, including military raids, arrests, imprisonments, and death squads. At the same time, the military enjoyed a comfortable relationship with the cartels, which grew in numbers, guns, and power. The cartels, in turn, made enormous profits from the sale of illegal drugs in the United States and received huge supplies of North American-made guns.

The resulting mix of poverty and violence drove desperate families to send their women and children on an exodus to the United States-Mexico border. They chose the United States because they had family members there. The years of mass deportations had contributed to the crisis. Surveys showed that 90% of the children at the border had family members in the United States, and 50% had a mother or father—or both—in the States. Family separation, owing to the deportations and the broken law that kept undocumented immigrants from bringing in their children, was the reason the children came to this country. The increase in violence and poverty dictated the timing.

The long history of U.S. military intervention, as well as economic intervention through free trade policies, had actually intensified during President Obama's terms in office. The effects of these policies on Honduras were replicated in Guatemala and El Salvador. Nicaragua, however, had held firm to its relationship with President Chavez and other Latin American nations. Once the poorest country in Central America, Nicaragua's improving economy and strengthened community institutions did not give rise to the conditions that caused the exodus from the other three Central American countries. Nicaragua became a haven for refugees, receiving them with dignity and generosity.

We had long argued that the migration of undocumented workers was a forced migration, owing to U.S. policies like NAFTA, which caused massive unemployment. In spite of our efforts, the general debate had continued to treat Mexican immigrants as typical 19th century European immigrants seeking the great American Dream. The children of Central America were actually bringing the truth of the immigration issue forward for all to see. Elvira established an aggressive, national speaking tour to explain the reasons and the realities of the children's exodus. She demanded that they be reunited with their families in the United States. At the same time, she blamed the deportations and argued that executive action was necessary to deal with the fundamental cause of the crisis.

Familia Latina Unida wanted to bring our position to the national Rainbow/PUSH convention, a national gathering of religious leaders in Chicago. We then hoped to begin an aggressive campaign within the League of United Latin American Citizens (LULAC), the nation's largest Latino organization. Our aim was to tie our demands to a voter registration drive aimed especially at young Latinos to help "strengthen the backbone of the President." The FuerZa Juventud stepped up its Moral Monday mobilizations in front of the ICE office in Chicago. We hoped that these weekly mobilizations would inspire similar demonstrations around the country in the critical months of July and August. The young people of the FuerZa Juventud also went door-to-door registering people to vote, and organized citizenship and DACA renewal workshops with great energy and dedication.

The House Democratic leader, Nancy Pelosi, called for a repeal of the 2008 law so that the unaccompanied children at the border could be immediately deported. The President seemed willing to take the same position. He called for the Republican Congress to give him four billion dollars to step up enforcement at the border and send the children back. He indicated he was willing to deal on the repeal of the law.

Grassroots groups throughout the country joined Familia Latina Unida in its Moral Monday demonstrations, calling for the children to be reunited with their families. Gutierrez strongly backed the President's original characterization of this situation as a humanitarian crisis. Demanding that Democrats stand up for the 2008 law, he won the support of the Congressional Hispanic Caucus. The tide began to turn, as Gutierrez angrily asked America how it could treat children as anything other than children. Sensing the sea change in the country, Congresswoman Pelosi—reversing her position—stood next to Gutierrez and even demanded that the Congress provide funds for legal representation for the children. Meanwhile, the Republicans in the House succumbed to their own internal divisions. In the dark of night right before summer recess, they passed a bill which attempted to repeal DACA for the Dreamers, repeal the 2008 law, and provide one billion dollars to the National Guard to shore up the border. They went home, knowing that their bill was dead in the Senate, and that the President would be left to deal with the crisis at the border by means of executive action.

Victorious, Gutierrez began calling for the advocacy groups to provide legal representation for the children. The vision of a two-year-old, maybe still in diapers, facing an immigration judge alone touched the conscience of many Americans. Homeland Security transported some thirty thousand children to different states, from which most were deported. Familia Latina Unida, led by Lozano and Arellano, went to court with a fourteen-year-old Honduran boy who had made the journey to the border in order to return to his family. He won a six-month continuance. The next week, we traveled to Waukegan, Illinois, where Hondurans occupied a small housing project. We found sixteen cases. As we had expected, the children who came from Honduras all had family in the United States. In some instances, the family members were undocumented and afraid, but in every case they claimed their children and embraced them after the long journey. The call for attorneys, however, produced few that were willing to take their cases.

In the summer of 2014, the world seemed to come unglued. The Israelis were bombing Gaza, killing hundreds with missiles, and then they launched an armed invasion, killing mostly women and children. The Palestinians fought back, launching missiles that mostly failed to get through the Iron Shield, the U.S.- funded anti-missile defense system. In Libya, the murder of Gaddafi left the country in chaos and tribal conflict. With their embassy destroyed, the United States was powerless to restore order. In Syria, the United States opposed the Iranian-allied government. While the United States blockaded the Shiite government, ISIS rose up suddenly— some estimates put their strength as high as 200,000—and invaded Iraq, seizing enough territory to establish a Caliphate state on both sides of the Syria/Iraq border—a haunting consequence of the Iraq war.

In the midst of these rising international crises, an 18-year-old African American young man walked down the street with his friend in a suburb of St. Louis. A white Ferguson police officer yelled to the boys to get out of the street. When they did not immediately respond, he pulled his car over and tried to grab young Mike Brown by his neck and pull him into the car. Mike Brown resisted, and the officer shot him. Brown turned and tried to walk away, wounded. The officer got out of his car and shot him four times in the back. When he turned around, raising his hands and saying, "Don't shoot," the officer put three more bullets into him, one in the middle of his forehead. Mike Brown fell dead.

Ferguson was about 70% African American, but the police force of fifty had only three African Americans. The town erupted. For eleven days, hundreds gathered in the streets, growing to thousands in the hot, Missouri nights. Police from Ferguson and the surrounding suburbs met them, dressed in riot gear and armed with automatic weapons and personnel carriers provided by Homeland Security. The national press focused its 24-hour cable coverage on Ferguson for ten days until Mike Brown was buried. National black leaders came from across the country. Demonstrations occurred in over eighty cities. The President expressed his sympathy for the family, and called for justice. The Attorney General of the United States came with one hundred FBI agents to conduct a parallel federal investigation.

The last Sunday in August, as we were beginning our service, Kaleed London walked into our church with five African American companions. I had not seen Kaleed in thirty years, since the battle in Cabrini Green leading up to the election of Harold Washington. What moved him to come to our service that Sunday? For us, it was a sign. It was time to call the Chicago coalition back together again. We began a series of meetings with African American organizations, leaders, and pastors. Our plan was to organize a Black Latino unity rally, "Freedom from Fear." The fear of mothers and fathers, that their African American or Latino sons would be killed by trigger-happy police, mirrored the fear of every undocumented person, that police would profile them while driving, arrest them, and have them deported, and the fear of children, that their parents would have disappeared before they came home from school. The date for the rally was September 18th. At the same time, we got assurances from the Obama administration that the President would indeed issue his executive orders in September, that the orders would be broad and generous, and that they would provide security for more than five million people. This nation's first African American President had sided with the young African American men of Ferguson, Missouri. If he proceeded to use his authority to provide legal status to millions of undocumented immigrants, his administration would have accomplished much. African Americans and Latinos in Chicago could again stand together in support of the President they had nurtured and then elected.

Congressman Gutierrez met with Mayor Rahm Emanuel and planned a meeting to gather the city's immigrant rights organizations in preparation for an executive order. The usual suspects gathered on the fifth floor of City Hall with Mayor Emanuel, who had been the main obstacle to comprehensive immigration reform as a Congressman and then as White House Chief of Staff. After losing badly in the Latino community in his first election and facing a tough re-election, he emphasized his newfound support for undocumented immigrants.

The mayor gave assurances that his sources in the White House had told him the executive orders would come soon and would be generous. The same advocacy groups who had refused to pressure Present Obama in his first 100 days now lined up to assist people in their applications for the promised deferments. You could almost see them counting the money. The former executive director of the Chicago immigrant rights coalition spoke at the meeting. He now directed a national empire of "integration services" for immigrants. I recalled that Gutierrez had once bought his support for our cause by getting him a three million dollar contract with the state to assist with citizenship applications. He had personally brought a White House consultant to national coalition meetings during President Obama's first 100 days to stifle pressure on the President, and now he reaped his reward. He explained the probable process facing five or six million people and emphasized the employment opportunities for the agencies. A Familia Latina Unida volunteer explained the model we had used to process DACA claims for the Dreamers—using the Dreamers themselves to assist others—a model that required no funding, but which had processed more successful applications than any agency in the city. Her words fell on deaf ears, like someone speaking an indigenous language at a meeting of Spanish Conquistadors after their conquest of the Aztecs.

Mayor Emanuel was the person in Chicago closest to the President, and his assurance that the executive order would come soon was encouraging. We left the meeting more confident that the executive order we had been demanding and fighting for since 2006 would finally arrive. Executive orders, however, would not change the broken law, and many of the abuses would continue. The fundamental structure of the military and economic domination of Latin America, which had led to the system of undocumented labor in the first place, would continue. Yet history had taught us that laws are changed only when human spiritual and social realities have changed first. The presence of millions of undocumented immigrants and their families living and working with legal security, and raising U.S. citizen children, would produce an important change in the character of the American people. Such a change would bode well for America's future.

⚘ 31

A 21ˢᵗ Century Emancipation Proclamation

B arack Obama had campaigned as an anti-war candidate, the first to win the Presidency in a century. Under his watch, a sectarian Muslim group had grown strong in Syria and spread into Iraq, picking up Baathists, whom the United States had purged from the military, and many of the Sunnis, who had been disenfranchised and persecuted by the Shiite government that the Bush administration had installed. As August came to an end, ISIS (also known as ISIL) executed a U.S. journalist and then a second one. The videos of these beheadings stirred the people of the U.S. more than the specter of this sectarian group's conquest of a swath of land in both Syria and Iraq. We realized that the hundreds of beheadings of Mexicans by the cartels, spread by video on social media across the Latino community, had had virtually no effect on the same people who now demanded revenge for the beheadings of two white men.

The President ordered bombings of ISIS in Iraq. When asked about his plan to deal with the terrorist threat, he made the mistake of saying, "We don't have a strategy yet." He plunged in the polls, just as the midterm elections drew near and control of the Senate was at stake. The President's plan was to develop a broad coalition among the Europeans and the oil-rich Sunni nations of the Middle East. He would continue to escalate the bombing, but stop short of sending troops into combat. ISIS had baited the United States, and the President had been forced to respond. His first step was to meet with NATO. On his way back from the NATO trip, he announced that he was delaying his executive order for the undocumented until after the election. In fact, he caved to the demands of Senatorial candidates running in Red states who feared the immigration issue could destroy their chances to win.

Latinos were angry. It was yet another broken promise, another betrayal. The Dreamers and some of the advocacy organizations held angry press conferences and conducted civil disobedience actions in front of the

White House. The leadership of the Congreso Latino organized a campaign to boycott the Democratic candidates for Senate who had pressured the President to delay his promised executive action. Elvira's weekly column in *El Diario* outlined the Familia Latina Unida position. The column circulated broadly on the internet. We urged Latinos to vote on November 4th to show their power. We demanded that the Congressional Hispanic Caucus meet with Homeland Security and press the agency to implement existing policies of prosecutorial discretion to slow the deportations. Familia Latina Unida then set a "Last Chance Final Day of Redemption" rally for November 27th. If the President did not act by that date, then we would march in the hundreds of thousands, and we would run an independent Latino candidate for the Presidency in 2016. Such a candidacy would deny the Democrats the White House, just as the Latino vote had delivered it to them in the last two elections. Moreover, we circulated petitions to draft Gutierrez to run as our candidate.

The plan excited organizers across the country. Gutierrez added to the enthusiasm by announcing his own date for the President's decision—November 27th, Thanksgiving Day. He pledged to travel around the country from now until then. The Congressional Hispanic Caucus spoke publicly about their anger and frustration with the President. President Obama responded that he still intended to act after the election, and that he was delaying in order to ensure that he could properly explain his executive actions to the general public.

We were haunted by the fact that our latest opponent in the fight for legalization was the first African American President. His response to the police murder in Ferguson showed a commitment to justice that moved us. It was powerful for the President of the United States to take the side of the oppressed. His reluctance to return to a full-scale war in Iraq reminded us that he was the first anti-war candidate to win the Presidency. Even so, he was committing the nation to war in the Middle East.

We began to feel that although his ambition had driven him to the Presidency and a series of compromises and betrayals, yet he was as much a prisoner of the nation's historical position as the world's policeman and the bastion of Uncle Sam's capitalism as were the undocumented, who had been forced to migrate and become pawns in the system of undocumented labor. President Obama's first statements about the relations of the United States with Latin America had been optimistic. He had called for a new era when relationships would be based on equality and mutual respect. He even shook hands with President Chavez when he attended his first summit of the Organization of American States. On the other hand, within a few months, his administration had resumed the Bush policy of intervention in Honduras and throughout Central America. Whatever the President's personal thoughts and beliefs, once he entered the White House, he became the leader of a nation already locked into commitments around the world.

Finally, we recalled the events surrounding Senator Obama and his respected Chicago pastor, Jeremiah Wright. He finally denounced his pastor and severed relations with him after a concerted right-wing campaign had attacked the pastor. We remembered Pastor Wright's initial statements. He supported Barack for the Presidency and called him a great man. He also said that if he were elected, he would have to immediately organize against him "as the leader of the empire."

In our approach to date, we had focused on the President himself, had felt ourselves to be in a direct dialog with him, gaining momentum from his promises and feeling betrayed by his retreats. Our new understanding led us to formulate our demand in a different way. Our attack focused on the Democratic Party. We called for the people to support President Obama's decision to use his executive authority and to oppose the Democratic Party leaders who wanted him to delay. Our threat to run an independent candidate for the White House was not aimed at President Obama, but at the Party itself. This new understanding made it easier to find unity with the African American community. They supported the President because of the racist attacks of the right wing of the Republican Party against him, even though they were well aware that the President had also not delivered on his promises to them.

Our new understanding came on the eve of the first Black Latino unity rally in Chicago. That rally joined Congressman Luis Gutierrez with Congressman Danny K. Davis, who had initiated the Black Latino unity movement with Rudy Lozano in 1982. It joined the issues of the police murder in Ferguson with the demand for executive action to stop the deportations by November 27th. We hoped to revive the coalition that had changed the city and had shaken the nation in 1983 with the election of Mayor Harold Washington. We planned to hold the unity rally at an historic church in Chicago, the First Baptist Congregational Church, which had served as a headquarters for Dr. King when he came to Chicago. The church sits across the street from Union Park, from which we had staged most of the immigration marches.

Dr. Leon Finney brought people from his church on the Southside, and a dozen African American youth groups showed up *en masse*. A small delegation came from the United Neighborhood Organization, but the majority of Latinos—about 400—came from La FuerZa Juventud in the high schools. Emma chaired the rally, as speakers talked about Ferguson and Chicago. The chant from the crowd was "Hands up – Don't Shoot; Hands Up – Don't Deport." With this new generation, the historical African American and Latino political tensions held no weight. They were a new generation, fighting together.

Congressman Davis spoke about the legacy of the old Harold Washington coalition. Joline Lozano read the proposed resolution that said in part, that if the President did not act by Thanksgiving, we would begin the campaign for an independent candidate for the Presidency in 2016. The resolution called for drafting Gutierrez to run. Then Gutierrez spoke. He carried the crowd to a new high as he went from the days of the Harold Washington coalition to the struggle against police murder and mass incarceration. He then reviewed the immigration struggle and stated his opinion that the President would keep his word this time. Then he made it clear that if he did not, the Democrats would have to be punished in 2016. He also announced that he would accept the draft.

Lozano and Arellano took another delegation to the border for the sake of three families seeking to win humanitarian paroles for their deported loved ones. The border trips had become a part of the church's mission, but we also sought to raise the issue of the return of deported parents with U.S. citizen children and make it part of the discussion for the proposed executive orders. After three days of protests and pressure in Laredo, the families returned to Chicago. The border patrol would take longer to give us a decision this time.

After the border trip, Lozano and Arellano went to Washington, D.C., along with a delegation from Chicago. There they met with Familia Latina Unida leaders from a dozen cities. Standing in front of the Democratic National Committee headquarters, they unveiled the campaign for running Gutierrez as an independent in 2016, if the President did not act by Thanksgiving. Feedback to Gutierrez's office and extensive media coverage convinced us that our message had gotten through: "No Executive Order Now—No White House in 2016!"

The Democratic Senatorial candidates who had asked Obama to delay executive action to help them win their elections continued to distance themselves, not only from the immigration issue, but also from the President. In some cases, they asked the President to come in for an evening fundraiser and then got him out of town before daybreak. Their effort to distance themselves from the President in Red states was a losing strategy. They did not communicate or align themselves with the relatively positive accomplishments of his administration and failed to mobilize the African American, Latino, and white youth base of the Democratic Party. They lost badly in the November elections, giving the Republicans control of the U.S. Senate and an expanded majority in the House of Representatives. The loss of the Senate race in Colorado was directly attributable to a lackluster Latino turnout and 38% of the Latino vote going to the Republican candidate. Democratic Party progressives blasted the candidates for not standing up for the President, the Affordable Care Act, and his commitment to executive action.

Lozano and Arellano returned to the District of Columbia to honor their commitment to the Dream moms, who were staging a hunger strike in front of the White House. The group of mothers with Dreamer kids had been active a year ago in the caravan led by Eliseo Medina. The caravan had deflected criticism of the administration's deportation policies and focused on the need to get the Republicans to vote for reform. The caravan had been part of the Democratic Party's effort to silence the movement for executive action. Time had changed the minds of the Dream mothers. When they went back to Medina for support for their hunger strike, they were told not do it. As the mothers recounted the conversation, they spoke of being "ordered not to carry out the hunger strike in front of the White House." They refused to listen, and they spent three weeks in the cold demanding executive action. Lozano, Arellano, and the national delegation that joined the mothers found Gutierrez and Congresswoman Lofgren already with the mothers, supporting the President's commitment to executive action.

The failure of his fellow Democratic candidates to stand by him during an all-out, bigoted, racist campaign against him by the Republican Party seemed to set the President free. The rumor mill began to churn: the President would issue the executive orders before the end of the year. Republicans countered with threats to shut down the government if he did. They promised to sue him, and some demanded impeachment. Republicans threats only seemed to make the President more determined. On Monday, November 17th, he scheduled an Oval Office address to the nation for the coming Thursday. He planned to outline his executive order to give deferments and work permits to an estimated five million undocumented parents of U.S. citizen children. When it finally came, the President's address was clear, decisive, and grounded in a powerful morality. It was the order that we had fought for since 2006.[†]

In practical terms, the President's executive order provided three-year deferments and work permits for the parents of U.S. citizen children or legal permanent resident children. The effect of this order went far beyond the four million individuals who could now come out of the shadows, since fully 17 million people had an undocumented person in their family. The order was clearly a pro-family action. It also covered exactly the five million U.S. citizen children and their undocumented parents that Familia Latina Unida had been formed to defend.

The President's action also removed the age limit on Dreamer deferments that would allow an estimated 400,000 more people to live in this country legally. Significantly, one of the ten executive orders signed by the President eliminated the hated Secure Communities Program. It was replaced with Priority Enforcement Program (PEP), which refocused the ICE partnership with local law enforcement on arresting those with criminal records.

In his comments on the executive orders, Congressman Gutierrez pointed to the division in the immigration movement between those organizations that had continued to push for legislative action and those groups that had demanded the immediate end to deportations. What he did not say was that the leadership of the Democratic Party had used its funding leverage so that the advocacy groups would be locked into the legislative track, even while Democrats deviously undermined a legislative solution and blamed the Republicans in hopes of keeping their popularity in the Latino community. The battle to force executive action had been carried out by those who received the least funding, those who were not on the White House invitation list. The issue that remained unaddressed was the return of those parents with U.S. citizen children who had been unjustly deported. Familia Latina Unida had documented the inconsistencies of the policies at the border; we were taking our case, through Gutierrez, to the head of Homeland Security.

The struggle was nowhere near over. It was improbable that the Republican House would pass an immigration reform law that the President could sign. The Republican Party apparently believed that tougher voting restrictions would provide them with a chance to take the White House. The hard

---

† The text of the President's announcement of the executive order appears in Appendix G.

right wing of the Republican Party might not even care about the White House, as they seemed more focused on an attempt to bring new life to a white supremacist movement. If the Republican-controlled Congress did not take up the challenge of passing immigration reform, the likelihood of reestablishing a Democratic majority in both Houses and a Democratic President in 2016 was much greater. A unified Latino community would vote even more strongly against the Republicans. It was likely that the division between the President and the Republican Party would widen. The President had chosen to take his stand with the undocumented and—in spite of his earlier betrayals—that stand promised to be a great part of the legacy of his Presidency. "The stone the builders had thrown away" had indeed become the cornerstone of Obama's Presidency.

The roots of the immigration problem can be found in the relationship of the United States to Mexico and the countries of Latin America. Yet the grassroots movement for justice was already having an effect on this relationship. In building a unified movement for executive action, the grassroots had given the President a base for other executive actions. He followed with actions on the environment and the federal minimum wage but, most significantly, in opening diplomatic relations with Cuba. The grassroots movement of Latinos made it possible for the President to respond to the unanimous Latin American demand for an end to the fifty-year embargo against Cuba. What had changed was the development of a united Latino community with the potential to advocate for their home countries. Familia Latina Unida/Sin Fronteras would now be able to turn more of their attention to these issues, and to bring the true history of these various peoples and governments to a new generation.

The Latino community had questioned and challenged the first African American President for six long years, only returning to support him in 2012 after he gave relief to the Dreamers. When President Barack Obama finally reversed himself on Thanksgiving Day in 2014 and took broad and generous executive action, the Latino community instantly embraced him. In truth, the Latino community had always wanted to support this first African American President. Now they could, and whole-heartedly. The broad Latino support for an African American President, himself under attack in an overtly racist manner, produced a new basis for a Black Latino unity. A quarter century earlier, the coalition that had elected Harold Washington had been betrayed in the middle of the night in Chicago when Daley forces moved to take over city hall after the Mayor's death. That coalition was now back on track.

As hundreds gathered in our church to hear the President's message, the media focused on Elvira. There she was, still faithful despite betrayal and deportation, standing humbly but defiantly with her U.S. citizen son, for whom she had fought so that they could stay together. She was the stone the builders had thrown away, who became the cornerstone of Obama's Presidency and the resurrection of a grassroots movement that possessed the potential power to transform the Americas. As the Civil Rights Movement had done for South Africa, so could this movement take on the greater mission to inspire grassroots movements in Latin America and bring justice to the homelands of so many.

❧ 32
The Political Reset

Twenty-nine states with Republican governors filed suit in an obscure federal court in Texas to block the new executive orders. The right wing judge issued an injunction stalling the application process for several months while the Department of Justice appealed. The strength of Latino unity, however, had reset the table of U.S. politics, and the line of demarcation drawn by the President's executive orders. The candidates for the Presidency in 2016 would have to sit on one side of the table or the other.

Familia Latina Unida determined to continue its defense of undocumented immigrants while waiting for the executive orders to clear the courts. Congressman Gutierrez began an aggressive campaign to assist potential applicants in gathering the documents they would need to apply. The Congressman crisscrossed the country with these "preparation rallies" in what amounted to yet another Familias Unidas tour. This time, however, Democratic congressmen in dozens of states joined him.

In Chicago, the mayoral elections provided an opportunity for the renewal of the Harold Washington coalition. The Chicago Teachers Union had led a four-year fight against Mayor Rahm Emanuel, the President's former Chief of Staff. The union planned to challenge the mayor by running their president, Karen Lewis. When Lewis became ill, the union looked to Cook County Commissioner Jesus "Chuy" Garcia. Garcia had been Rudy Lozano's number two man when Rudy was assassinated in 1983. Garcia had continued with Rudy's 22nd ward independent political organization and was elected alderman in Washington's midterm effort to gain control of the city council. He had gone on to serve as a state senator and then as a county commissioner. Garcia had worked hard to maintain the Black Latino coalition that Lozano had begun in 1982. Garcia did not ultimately win, though he forced Emanuel into a runoff election that garnered national attention.

While there were echoes of the Washington coalition of 1983, we noticed a significant difference. Rudy Lozano had been a leader in two movements: the movement of the disenfranchised undocumented immigrants, and the movement of independent, grassroots political power. While Emma Lozano had carried on the first, joined by Elvira, Garcia had focused on the second. In redefining the immigration struggle as a Latino issue, Emma's movement had fused together these two movements and created an explosion of unity in the Latino community. The mayoral campaign lacked this dynamic, although it inspired great pride among Latinos across the city.

Some leaders in the campaign feared they would lose voters if they attacked Rahm for what he did in Washington when he blocked immigration reform and when he urged stronger enforcement that led to two million deportations. Others were afraid they would lose police votes if they went after the racial profiling and brutality of the Chicago Police Department. Struggling inside Chuy's campaign, Emma said, "I am sure that there are voters who wanted to hear Chuy say he would add one thousand police—but, brothers and sisters, the entire African American community, across the nation, is standing up in outrage at police murder of young black men! And this week we have this beautiful Dominican brother who courageously stood his ground and videoed the murder of a Black man by a racist, killer cop in Charleston, South Carolina; a Dominican brother who went on national TV to say that the undocumented in north Charleston faced these same racist police every day. *There* is the Black-Latino coalition we are looking for! Not in the call to hire a thousand more cops!"

It was a good campaign, but the two issues of the disenfranchised—the deportations and police racial profiling, brutality and murder—were ignored for fear of losing the votes of those who had papers and those who had good city jobs. We have learned *that when* those with and those without papers *stand together, that when* those who are safe and those who walk the streets at risk *stand together*, in that **unity** there is *the power of the Kingdom*, the power of *justice*, the power of *faith*. That is the movement we must commit ourselves to continue to build, the movement that begins with the disenfranchised, with the excluded. That is a movement *we know how to build* if we open our eyes and see that it already exists in the hearts of the people. Garcia's campaign became the product of the progressive wing of the Democratic Party. Its failure to mobilize voter turnout in the Latino and African American communities was an early warning sign that an energized Republican party could retake the White House, with disastrous consequences for undocumented immigrants.

In the season of Harvest in our churches, we celebrate the separation of "the good wheat from the weeds." Current events helped to dramatize this metaphor's meaning. In June 2015, Donald Trump began his campaign for the Republican nomination by promising to deport all eleven million undocumented immigrants, including the Dreamers. He went further by saying he would challenge the Fourteenth Amendment and seek to deport five million U.S. citizen children born in this country to undocumented parents. Then he would build a wall at the border and make the Mexican government pay for it. He said, "Mexico is sending us its drug dealers, criminals, and rapists." The rest of the Republican candidates followed his lead as Trump gathered larger and larger crowds and led all candidates in the polls. On the other hand, Hillary Clinton made her first policy statement on immigration and promised to continue Obama's executive orders, and extend them to the parents of the Dreamers. She even committed to bringing deported parents of U.S. citizen children or Dreamers back from Mexico. The other Democratic candidates followed her lead. One went further, to commit to extending the Affordable Care Act to undocumented immigrants.

The first Latin American Pope made an awesome seven day visit to the United States, speaking to the U.S. Congress in Washington, D.C., addressing the United Nations in New York, and finishing his visit in Philadelphia by celebrating a mass with tens of thousands. The Pope captivated the media. He defended the immigrants, with and without papers, and stood up for the incarcerated by visiting a prison in Philadelphia. The Pope countered the Democratic focus on "the middle class" with the Christian demand to focus on "the least of these, the poor, the disabled, the immigrant."

Familia Latina Unida responded to the separations of the Harvest with its own campaigns. We sent a busload of mostly young high school students to Minister Louis Farrakhan's "Justice or Else" March on Washington on October 10th. In preparation, we brought the Minister to a kickoff rally at our church in Pilsen to formally announce the march's commitment to Black Latino Unity and the joint demands to stop mass deportation and mass incarceration. On the 20th anniversary of the Million Man March in the nation's capital, Farrakhan and the Nation of Islam mobilized over one million people on the National Mall—some said two million attended! Emma Lozano and Elvira Arellano spoke at the massive D.C. mobilization shortly before Farrakhan, and the Latino youth we had brought found themselves welcomed everywhere by young African Americas. For Familia Latina Unida, it was a culmination of a twenty-year campaign to join the African American Freedom Movement with the Latino Justice Movement.

The FuerZa Juventud, with some 1,500 high school students enrolled in the Youth Health Service Corps, began the mobilization of the high school students and the Dreamers we had assisted with their DACA applicants in a drive for maximum Latino voter power. We argued that although they were ineligible to vote, they constituted a committed army to get eligible voters to register and turn out in the upcoming Presidential election. They would call on the Latino community to elect the Democratic nominee and reject the racism of the Republican Party, and then prepare to mobilize to "bend whoever was elected towards justice."

Deportations had dropped to 40% of what they had been the previous year. Still, every week, people facing deportations or seeking the return of their loved ones came to our church. ICE had increasingly moved to audits of companies, forcing them into e-verification of their workers. Workers were told to bring invalid social security numbers or be fired. In some cases, ICE followed up with arrests at the worker's home. We took on their cases, fighting for discretion for the workers to block their deportations and pressuring the companies to keep them on with ITIN numbers.

Emma Lozano and Julie Contreras made several trips to the border in attempts to bring back those who had been deported. Sometimes they were successful in bringing public attention to the cases and preparing strong legal arguments for humanitarian parole. The decisions were very subjective, depending on which border control officer had the case. In an effort to keep the injustice of the immigration system in the public eye, Emma began organizing for the return of deported veterans.

The Harvest Season in our churches brought with it the formal installation of Emma Lozano as our senior pastor. In truth, Emma had always led the church we founded, and the congregation called her and Jacobita Alonso their "Pastores Sin Papeles." Now Reverend Lozano would take her place among the clergy of the United Methodist Church—and among the growing unity of Latino/a pastors across the country. At her installation we recommitted to our vision of organizing seven churches on the model of Adalberto United Methodist Church, centers of faith and annual renewal in the struggle of a people without borders.†

---

† Emma's sermon delivered on this occasion can be found in Appendix H.

✷ 33

Spiritual Renewal Through the Eight Seasons of Faith

T he President began his ascension at the Democratic Convention
of 2004 with his keynote address: "There is not a liberal America
and a conservative America—there is the United States of America." His vision of a united nation did not conform to reality and,
emboldened by the movement's demand for executive action, he reluctantly
abandoned his original vision. He undertook a bold set of Presidential
actions, both in domestic and foreign policy. His executive orders would
provide deferments and work permits to some five million undocumented
parents with U.S. citizen children, along with the one million "Dreamers."
He pardoned hundreds of federal prisoners to dramatize the injustice that
had brought about mass incarceration. It was a resurrection of the force that
had brought about the election of the first African American President, the
force born in the struggle in Chicago.

There remained one last hurdle for the President's executive orders on
immigration: the Supreme Court. The blocking suit brought by the Texas governor had survived lower courts, and the Obama administration had made
final appeal to the highest court in the land. In January, the court agreed to
hear the case in June of 2016. We would have to wait while the Presidential
primary campaigns roared around us, and while the line of demarcation—the
line which the immigration movement had drawn between the two parties—
brought forth ever-sharper antagonisms in the nation.

Over the last two decades, Familia Latina Unida had adopted the discipline of our faith. Each year the Scriptures led us through eight seasons of
faith and struggle. Each year, we were called to begin the journey again, and
to renew both our faith and our struggle. During the first season, which we
called the Time of Preparation, we immersed ourselves in the appearance
of the Virgin of Guadalupe, the Gospel account of Joseph and Mary and the
birth of Jesus. In a struggle that seeks to maintain itself over decades, it is
natural for many to become tired or to be diverted. To continue we need to

make a commitment to *"begin again,"* to let God *make us new each year.* We called on each individual to renew his or her commitment, each family to share in forgiveness so that love could be reborn. We let the Scriptures illuminate the challenge our movement faced, and we prayed together. Our study revealed both a great warning and great promise in the year to come.

The warning manifested in the wave of racist hate in the Republican Presidential campaigns. Republicans controlled 60% of the nation's governorships and both houses of Congress. The danger came not only from the anti-immigrant statements and policies advocated by Republican candidates, but from the enthusiasm of the large crowds across the country for destroying the lives of Latino families. The crowds had the mark of cheering, celebrating lynch mobs. They were not indifferent to the suffering. They *rejoiced* in the suffering.

The promise came from two sources. Perhaps most important was the resurgence of a movement of young people, a next generation of struggle. The second part of the promise was the commitment of all three Democratic Party candidates to support and extend the Obama executive orders. If we could mobilize to defeat the Republican nominee, then we could mobilize to bend the President we elected towards justice with a new generation in the lead of the struggle.

The true promise, however, lay in what was revealed by our faith. God had his hand on a people from the south, whom He had planted here for the transformation of this nation, and had made them to be fruitful and to multiply. We had received so many signs—so many families defended, so many reunited, and Elvira's return—against all odds. The "signs" would continue and be seen in the testimony and faces and the tears of the united families in our church each Sunday. It was time to make this true promise visible. We agreed to put our full energies towards building the foundations of a new movement of Latino unity, one that would spring from what we had built over the last two decades.

Both the warning and the promise of 2016 came quickly and forced us into action. Trump took credit for it, but it was Obama's Department of Homeland Security that put it into action. Fearful of growing numbers of Central Americans appearing at the border, Homeland Security initiated a door-to-door sweep of Central Americans who had received orders of deportation. The truth was that most of these were children who had had little or no representation in immigration court. The reality also was that when ICE agents were set loose on the community, they picked up anyone without papers. The dramatic reduction in deportations over the last year had lulled people into a false sense of security. Univision and Telemundo reported a new sense of panic in the community.

We responded to the new fear of deportation by intensifying our "discretion defense" initiative. Workshops provided undocumented persons with a picture ID and documentation that they qualified for discretion under Homeland Security guidelines. We also assisted those who came so that they could take speedy advantage of the President's executive order, if the Supreme Court approved it. At the workshops, Elvira organized Mexican citizens to participate in elections in Mexico and reminded participants that they were *Un Pueblo Sin Fronteras*, a people without borders. The workshops also recruited Familia Latina Unida members and began marshaling an army of undocumented and legal permanent resident volunteers to register and get out the vote of those in the community who could vote.

Emma took these "Family Defense" workshops on the road, going first to Las Vegas, Nevada, and then to South Carolina on the eve of the Democratic primaries in those states. In both places, Familia Latina Unida chapters were established. The national network of Latino faith communities and grassroots youth and family defense organizations, established first after Elvira's deportation and then accelerated through Gutierrez's two Familias Unidas tours, was once more taking shape in preparation for the 2016 elections. In Las Vegas, Emma helped to force the issue of the deported veterans in the Democratic Presidential debates. Three thousand legal permanent residents who had served honorably in the armed services in Vietnam, Iraq, and Afghanistan had returned to a life of unemployment and PTSD, many introduced to drug use while serving in the military. Arrested for drug-related charges, their legal permanent resident status was revoked, and they were deported. Most of them struggled to survive in border towns in Mexico, trying to stay in communication with family members and their children in the United States. Both Democratic Party Presidential candidates supported their cause in the Las Vegas debate.

After Las Vegas, Emma Lozano and Julie Contreras responded to a call to go to rural Alabama. ICE had visited a group of migrants at a small Latino company that collected pine needles for sale. Alabama had just voted strongly for Donald Trump, and a few encounters while Emma was there exposed a police force ready to do Trump's work. She brought them through the workshops, preparing them for a "discretion defense," and found four that were eligible for DACA. While they worked as migrants, most had families and U.S. citizen children. A favorable Supreme Court ruling, now due in June, would bring them out of the shadows. They formed a chapter of Familia Latina Unida and extended our network into Alabama for the first time.

It was time to put to the test our theory that undocumented immigrants could be a significant force in registering and getting out the vote of those who could vote. Chicago was allowing same-day registration on Election Day for the first time, but it was a virtual secret. We met with Gutierrez and invited him to hold a press conference with us in front of the Board of Elections. We gathered the witnesses, Honduran refugees, undocumented families facing deportation, and young Latinos who were able to vote for the first time. Joined by other Latino elected officials, Emma brought forth the witnesses, including Elvira, one at a time, culminating with the Congressman. After the press conference, the Congressman took a naturalized citizen and three first time young voters into the Board of Elections to register to vote. The "Latinos Alive" campaign had been announced!

The Youth Health Service Corps had established a 10-10-10 program to reach into the community and to provide preventive health care. Now we began to use it for voter registration. At the Phoenix Military High School, Youth Coordinator Miriam Perez and I addressed the entire student body and set up "a competition" with other high schools for voter registration.

As Election Day for the Republican Presidential primary approached, the Trump campaign announced its intention to hold one of his well-publicized mass rallies at the UIC Pavilion in Chicago. Trump was going to bring his racist campaign into the heart of Chicago and was going to the university with the largest Latino student body in the Midwest—to the very site of the mass rallies that had launched the victory of the Harold Washington mayoral campaign. Trump was almost halfway to the number of delegates necessary to clinch the nomination. Key to his rise in the Republican primaries had been weekly rallies that gathered as many as twenty thousand followers. Trump called them "love fests." He actually repeated the phrase often, that "They love me!" A few protesters had made their way into some of the rallies and had been mauled by Trump supporters. Trump had egged them on, calling on his supporters to rough them up, promising to pay the legal fees of any who got arrested. The mass rallies fed the impression that Trump was leading what he frequently called "a movement."

The evening before the rally, Emma and Gutierrez held a press conference putting out the call for Latinos and people of conscience to show up to "send Trump a message." Over ten thousand gathered outside the Pavilion, and over four thousand protestors went inside. Almost immediately, conflict broke out between the protesters and the Trump supporters, whites who had come in from the suburbs. Thousands shouted slogans, cheered, pushed, and shoved. Within an hour, a Trump campaign spokesman came out to say, "The rally has been canceled." The protesters began shouting and then jumping up and down in victory. Several fights broke out. Gradually, police emptied out the Pavilion. The Trump supporters were moved by police to a protected area and gradually disappeared. The protesters stayed in the streets.

National media ran with Trump's reaction for three days. Trump claimed that "thugs" had denied him his first amendment right to free speech. Even Republican candidates joined in, saying that Trump had incited the violence by his previous treatment of protesters. The "Love Fests" were exposed as "Hate Fests." Trump claimed it was "an organized attack." In truth, young and old in the community had been listening to Trump's insults and his promises to deport twelve million people for six months. While many protesters supported Bernie Sanders, it was not a political mobilization and was not organized by the Democrats, with the exception of Congressman Gutierrez, who had called for it. It was, in fact, an expression of the two mass movements that were forcing the nation to decide where it stood: the movements against mass deportation and mass incarceration. Trump came into their neighborhood, but he could not speak.

While Sanders and Clinton battled, the Republican primaries eclipsed the Democratic primaries—both in the media and in voter turnout. All the Republican candidates continued the party's vicious, racist attack on President Barack Obama in order to rally a racial mobilization. Trump and Cruz added their slander of the undocumented, and their promise to deport millions, and to build a wall to separate families permanently. The flamboyant, reality show-style debates drew massive attention. The result: Republican primary turnout tripled that of the Democratic primary. With Clinton likely to become the Democratic nominee, there would likely be a fall off of the Sanders voters in the general election. Facing the most popular upsurge in the Republican Party in decades, a Democratic victory would depend on a massive African American and Latino turnout in the general elections.

We reflected on our experience of the last ten years. We had won the active support of the Latino Evangelicals for immigration reform and then for the executive orders. It had been a complicated struggle, working with the established, well-funded national pastoral associations and mobilizing local congregations in the two Familias Unidas tours. The enormous growth in the Latino congregations over that decade had given them a voice with the established white Evangelical pastors, their congregations, and the established political formations. They had begun to bend towards "a path to legalization" for undocumented immigrants. When the 2016 primaries began, all that changed. The white Evangelicals thronged to Trump, and then shared their votes with Cruz. Latino Evangelicals became deathly silent. We reflected that many of the Latino pastors owed their beginnings to white Evangelical leaders; they had initially subsidized many of the Latino churches. While Trump and Cruz could not hope to take much of the Latino vote because of their stand on immigration and deportations, the Latino Evangelical vote could be depressed.

More importantly, we felt that the Latino Evangelicals could again stand up to the all-out mobilization of white Evangelicals, who now made up the largest single voting bloc for the Republicans. We decided to launch a national campaign to "Wake-up the Latino Evangelicals." What lay before us was a spiritual struggle for the Christian soul, a spiritual struggle that might well determine the outcome of the Presidential election and the fate of millions of Latino families.

Our message in church was based on two Scriptures from the Gospel of Luke. First, Jesus explained that he came to bring, not peace, but division. Then he told the parable of the Ten Minas. As so many times before, our church served as a workshop for the way we should carry out the struggle. On Sunday morning, our congregation gathered at Lincoln United Methodist Church in Pilsen. Almost every single person, every single family, was affected by the deportations. We had reunited some, but usually on a temporary basis. A father and son, or a mother and daughter, often read the Scriptures, in English, followed by a reading in Spanish. Each of those family readers was facing separation. One of the little girls that helped with the collection had walked across the bridge in Texas with her mother, crying as she watched the officers take her mother into custody, and then waited with us for the ruling the border patrol would make. She came each Sunday, joyfully reunited with both mother and father. The "Good News" proclamation was read each week by a ten-year-old, her voice ringing out with the faith that God is with us all. Each day she waited for the return of her father from deportation.

Our message to the congregation was that their struggle, their painful witness, had inspired a movement which divided the nation between a party that now embraced them, and a party that was committed to deporting eleven million undocumented immigrants and one million Dreamers, and to stripping citizenship from five million children of undocumented parents. Their witness, along with thousands of others, had brought about the division, a separation like that prefigured in the tale of the wheat and the tares. The Parable of the Ten Minas told of a King who gave one of his subjects ten minas, another five minas, and a third one mina. Then he went away. When the King returned, the one the King had given ten minas invested the money and multiplied it, as had the one given five. The subject given one mina, however, had buried his mina in the ground, afraid that he might lose it before the King returned. The King ordered the one he had given ten minas to be given control of ten cities, the one he had given five minas control of five cities. Then he ordered that the mina given the third subject be taken away and given to the one he had given ten. Jesus explained, "To those who have much, more will be given."

Our message to the families and the young activists who had brought us to this time of national decision was that they had been given many gifts. They knew in their hearts that God had planted a people here in this nation and made them "to be fruitful and multiply." The challenge was to use what they had been given to continue the struggle, to defeat Trump, and to win justice for millions. The Scripture warned that if we "buried our gifts in the ground," we would lose them. The Scripture challenged us to use what we had been given for the salvation of God's people! We felt a strong spirit growing in our congregation. The question before us was winning the *Spiritual Struggle* among Latino Christians, a battle we would have to win if we were to successfully confront the false Christianity of the thousands of white Evangelicals supporting Trump. We were ready to take our case to the Latino Pastors. We would ask them once again to host a national "Familias Unidas" campaign.

It would not be difficult to organize Latino Christians, both Evangelical and Catholic, against the Republicans. It would be more difficult to organize turnout for a Democrat. The "Kingdom Movement" had to assert its independence and then make a tactical decision. We had to deal with the necessity to vote for either Clinton or for Sanders. The Clinton-Sanders competition was reflected in Chicago in the division between Luis Gutierrez and Chuy Garcia. Gutierrez had been our most powerful weapon against the deportations across the nation. He alone among Democrats had taken on President Obama. We had a long history with the Congressman, with his uncompromising support for the independence of Puerto Rico and the cause of the Puerto Rican political prisoners. The unity of Mexicans and Puerto Ricans had been the key to making immigration a Latino issue. Gutierrez's long and faithful campaign on behalf of undocumented immigrants had led him to endorse Rahm Emanuel and then Hillary Clinton in order to consolidate support for the undocumented, and for the President's executive orders, in the Democratic Party. This endorsement put him at odds with Garcia, who now became a national surrogate for Bernie Sanders.

Familia Latina Unida formally took no position between Sanders and Clinton. Lozano explained publicly that the role of the organization was to ensure unity in the Latino community behind the eventual winner. I had served on the staff of Gutierrez for ten years. Emma was his main ally in the Mexican community. Gutierrez had helped in literally hundreds of individual immigration cases. On the other hand, we had supported Chuy in the mayoral race. We could feel the membership turning towards Sanders. On the Sunday before the Illinois primary, I "gave my vote" to the congregation and asked how I should cast it. The congregation overwhelmingly chose "Bernie."

Leading up to the Midwestern primaries in Michigan, Ohio, and Illinois, Clinton received an overwhelming majority among African Americans and Latinos. She was the wife of a former Democratic President and well known in her own right. Sanders was an obscure Vermont congressman with little national profile. There was something else, a phenomenon once described by W.E.B. Dubois as the "General Strike" on the part of slaves during the Civil War. Dubois documented the amazing consensus decision of the slaves to go on strike on the plantations two years into the Civil War. Prohibited from traveling, and with no means of communication, the majority of the slave population yet acted within a few weeks of each other. Dubois described how they waited, watching to see if Lincoln really would stand with them, and if he could win. The same could be said of the African American and Latino communities in the choice between Clinton and Sanders.

In fact, Sanders represented the historic tradition of the white left from which he came. He took a "class position," arguing on the issue of economic disparities and "income inequality" between the super rich and the middle class. While supportive of equality issues, including a clear opposition to mass deportation and mass incarceration, the lead issue for him was the attack on Wall Street. Older African American leadership, represented in the Congressional Black Caucus, distrusted the implicit racism in this position. On the other hand, the Clintons supported the principal mass incarceration legislation in the 1990s. The Clintons were responsible for NAFTA, the trade agreement that not only cost hundreds of thousands of U.S. jobs but destroyed the lives of five million agricultural workers in Mexico—including Elvira's family! Finally, Clinton was known to have supported the coup in Honduras, which overthrew the elected progressive President and unleashed a repression that drove thousands of Hondurans to make the long journey north to the U.S. Our community not only knew these issues; they were personal.

Neither Clinton nor Sanders had taken strong positions in the fight for immigration reform and for the President's executive orders until the battle was already won in the Democratic Party. They both, however, now fully supported the executive orders, and both pledged to extend protections to millions of others. In Chicago, the Sanders campaign linked Clinton to Mayor Emanuel, who ultimately endorsed her. Sentiment began to shift towards Sanders, but Clinton won a narrow victory in the Illinois primary.

🔥 34
The Signs of the Times

The final chapter in our struggle for the executive order that would provide security for the undocumented families of U.S. citizen children began with Easter. It would end during the time of Pentecost. The Supreme Court held hearings for a few hours in April. Their decision would come down in June.

The electoral results in both Presidential primaries also became clear. Clinton locked up the Democratic nomination. In spite of his more progressive platform, Sanders carried no more than 40% of the non-white vote in most of the primaries. Raising as much as forty million dollars a month through his online network, Sanders vowed to continue his campaign to the convention and to take his campaign positions to the Democratic Party platform committee. Clinton maintained her position in favor of the executive orders and her promise to extend them to cover millions of other families. Meanwhile, Donald Trump had locked down the Republican nomination. He won majority margins with fiscal conservatives, Evangelical conservatives, and millions of blue-collar white workers. The one thing that united the different factions of the Republican Party was his opposition to the first African American President, and his appeal to the fear that America was becoming a country with a non-white majority.

W.E.B. Dubois said that the most important issue in the United States was the color line. The scholar Nathan Newman modified his statement by saying that "the color line was now drawn at the southern border." Trump had used his promise to build a wall at the border and to deport all undocumented immigrants to become the champion of white fear and reaction. Many in the Republican Party leadership reversed themselves and rallied around Trump. Trump, however, did not make it easy for them. A flurry of lawsuits had been brought against his "Trump University," alleging that it was a fraudulent scheme to drain money from those seeking "the secret to Donald Trump's success." When a federal judge in California released the documents in the case, Trump faced a problem. He was being accused of defrauding the very middle class whites that were the base of his campaign.

Like white politicians have done for over 100 years, Trump played the race card. He stated that the judge in this case should recuse himself because he was "a Mexican," and therefore biased against Donald Trump, who was campaigning on "Building the wall." Criticized for attacking a federal judge for his ethnic heritage, Trump doubled down, repeating the charge over and over for two weeks. Although successfully taking the focus off his fraudulent university, his comments forced Paul Ryan—now Speaker of the House—to repudiate his statement as "textbook racism." Nevertheless, Speaker Ryan and other Republican leadership continued to endorse Trump as the elected Republican nominee, racism and all.

Obama's executive orders polarized the nation as once Lincoln's "Emancipation Proclamation" had done. Hillary Clinton seemed to see what was coming more clearly than Sanders. She campaigned primarily on breaking down racial barriers and set herself up as the opposition to Trump's blatantly racial mobilization. We had come a long way since Pepe Jaques Medina called us to Washington, D.C., in 1996, a long way since Elvira determined to fight her deportation in 2002. The fifty days that followed Easter this year, and the remembrance of the crucifixion of Jesus on the cross, did indeed mark a resurrection of the movement. At least half the country was with us now, and half the nation was against us. It remained to be seen which "half" would prevail in November. Although the undocumented were the defining issue in the Presidential election, they had no vote themselves. With the most to lose, the undocumented could only wait and watch while the Supreme Court deliberated, and the nation's citizens prepared to elect the next President. Nevertheless, our faith called us into action.

Year in and year out, for twenty years, we had celebrated the season of Pentecost. It was the season in Scripture in which the Holy Spirit came on the disciples and gave them the courage to come out of hiding, risk arrest and resume the movement that Jesus had left them. The Spirit, which had propelled us into action each year, demanded that we continue, that we not just sit and wait on the Supreme Court decision. We looked for signs—the small victories that came to those who struggled, the signs that had given us courage to continue the struggle for two decades. We were not disappointed.

Elvira re-emerged on this side of the border again with her new baby, Emiliano. Emiliano's father was a Honduran whom she had met in the movement to defend Central American refugees traveling north through Mexico. Unwilling to wait years for a visa, Armando presented himself at the border and asked for humanitarian parole as Elvira had done the year before.

Armando was held in detention for sixty days, awaiting the decision, while we exercised all the legal and political pressure we could muster. Suddenly, he was released. Elvira's faith had once given her courage to refuse to be separated from her son. Now she was here, still living above the little church on Division Street, with a completed family. Was this a sign that the Spirit of our movement would move the Supreme Court in our favor, and then the Presidential election, or was it a sign that the Spirit would be with us as we continued the struggle?

Pentecost, the season of the Spirit, revealed the different aspects of ministry to which we were called. Our church had never really engaged in the debate over gay marriage that had deeply divided the national, as well as the international United Methodist Church. We held a memorial for a young gay man who had committed suicide because his brother had brought his death to us. His picture remained in the church. During Pentecost, a married lesbian couple joined our church and asked to pursue their ministry for LGBT youth in the church. They were welcomed, and each week they reported on the progress of their work.

Just as the immigration ministry of the church had grown, not from an ideology, but from the people in struggle who came to us, so our ministry to the LGBT community developed from those whom the Spirit brought to us. The congregation welcomed the ministry without controversy, with love and solidarity. The ministry prepared us for the mass murder of forty-nine people at a Latino LGBT celebration in Orlando. Donald Trump's angry response to these murders was an attack on immigrants. The 9/11 terrorist attacks in 2001 had unleashed the deportations against the Latino community. Trump's statement let us know that the mobilization against our families was still strong, ready to pounce on us if Trump won the upcoming election.

We had been fighting to bring the family of Señor Funes to the United States from Guatemala. He had come to our church the year before, and we listened to his prayers and felt his tears. His son had been kidnapped by a cartel. When his release was won, his son agreed to testify against the kidnappers in court. The whole family was threatened and forced into hiding. We listened and watched his heart break as he described for us in church how his fourteen-year-old daughter was tortured and raped. We determined that we needed to bring thirteen of the extended family to safety from the cartels. The first problem was to bring them to Mexico. U.S. pressure had forced the Mexican government to virtually close their southern border. While Mexicans could pass easily to Guatemala, Guatemalans had to apply for visas that were almost impossible to get. We had worked through our congressional representatives and through the Guatemalan consulate to no avail. We turned to Pepe Jaques and Marta, and their Mesoamerican Organization.

While we waited, Emma Lozano and Julie Contreras took a busload of Honduran children to Washington, D.C. There they joined with Gutierrez and several other members of Congress at a press conference to protest the administration's stepped-up deportation of Central Americans. They learned that, through Cuban intervention, the thirteen Guatemalans had received their visas and were on their way to Mexico. Within a week, they presented themselves at the U.S. border, and within a few more days, they mounted the bus from Laredo to Chicago for a reunion with a father and mother who had not seen their children in twelve years. They were safe amid prayers of thanksgiving in our church! Was this a sign—that we would not only win the executive order, but also win changes in the nation's opposition to refugees from the south who had family members in the U.S.—or was it a sign only that God would be with us as we continued the struggle?

Emma focused on "Project Ashley," our effort to bring back veterans who had been deported and to prevent more from being deported. Over three thousand legal permanent residents who had served honorably in the nation's wars had been deported after conviction on criminal charges related to the drug epidemic. We also fought against the deportation of the family members of veterans and focused on the Segura family in our church, whose daughter Ashley had been killed in Kuwait. We had brought the Valenzuela brothers, both Vietnam veterans now facing deportation, to Chicago. Through their testimony we got resolutions passed in the city council, county board, and state senate in support of the three thousand veterans. Emma then set out with the Valenzuela brothers and Segura family to testify in Washington, D.C.

We had one case, however, that was closer to our church. Miguel Perez was finishing a long sentence for selling drugs in Chicago. He was due to be released in September. A legal permanent resident who had served with distinction in Afghanistan, Miguel was called up to immigration court for a hearing on June 14th. ICE intended to deport him directly from prison on the day of his release. We could not help but remember Pentecost in 2006, when we won a reprieve from deportation for the IFCO workers. It had seemed like a miracle then. As we listened on Sunday to Miguel's father praying, we prayed for another miracle. Emma went to see Miguel in prison the next day. We held a press conference on Tuesday morning and then went to court.

Not only was Miguel Perez a veteran with a confirmed diagnosis of PTSD—one of thousands of veterans who fell into drugs on their return from the war—but he had joined the army when he was eighteen at a time when he was actually eligible to apply for citizenship. The army should have facilitated that application while he was in the service, but they did not. Attorney Chris Bergin argued the case in court, as he had argued hundreds of cases for us over twenty years. We waited. We wanted to win for Miguel. We also wanted a sign that we would prevail in the Supreme Court on the executive orders. The judge refused to issue the order of deportation.

While we waited on the Supreme Court, we stepped up our work with the Youth Health Service Corps. Now over one thousand five hundred strong in the high schools, with nearly two hundred medical and nursing student volunteers, we held six health fairs in June. We also made a last effort to register eligible high school seniors to vote, and certified over one hundred of them as deputy registrars. No matter what the decision in the Supreme Court, we were committed to begin mobilizations in July. We hoped to spur mass mobilizations around the nation in late August to energize the electorate in November. We believed these young people were the spark that would bring the fire.

During Pentecost in 2006, the Spirit had moved us to organize a march of 100,000 to demand executive action to stop the deportations, the first time that demand had been made by the movement. Now, ten years later, we waited. We waited on the Spirit that had led us for over three decades.

❦ 35

The Supreme Court Non-decision

hange moves slowly, painfully, but steadily through the history of the Americas. Even so, each year, like the farmers, we move through the seasons. As the season of Pentecost turned into the season of Kingdom Time in our church, as spring turned into summer, we waited for the Supreme Court to rule on President Obama's executive action. On Thursday, June 23rd, our wait ended. The Scripture for the coming Sunday came from the Letter from James, and it should have prepared us for what was to come.

> *Consider it pure joy, my brothers and sisters, whenever you face trials of many kinds, because you know that the testing of your faith produces perseverance. Let perseverance finish its work so that you may be mature and complete, not lacking anything.*
> —James 1:2-4

The Supreme Court, crippled by the failure of the Senate to even consider President Obama's nominee to fill its one vacancy, announced that they were caught in a four-four tie, and therefore had failed to come to a decision. The court's one-sentence "non-decision" left the Texas lower court order in place and continued the nation's paralysis on immigration reform. It also pinned the fate of millions of families to the outcome of the November national elections. While it would be difficult to win a Democratic majority in the House of Representatives, and therefore to pass comprehensive immigration reform, Democratic victories for the White House and the U.S. Senate would allow a President Clinton to appoint a tie-breaking ninth judge to the Supreme Court. *The Supreme Court non-decision set no precedent and would permit the next President to bring the case again to the court.*

The current non-decision did not affect other executive orders, *including DACA*, which gave legal status to dreamers, and *the revision of enforcement priorities*, which set aside deportation of individuals and families with no criminal records if they had children living in this country. It does not seem fair that these families must move an entire nation, just so that they can work hard and raise their children in the ways of the Lord. It seems, however, that that is what they have been asked to do.

Emma Lozano's statement to the press that day was painful, but resolute:

> For twenty years our families have struggled for a basic human right to exist as families in this nation. Through Elvira Arellano's yearlong sanctuary, and marches of millions, and testimonies, and sit-ins, and rallies across the nation, and legal challenges, we fought for and finally won the full support of one of the two major political parties. The racist opposition to this basic human right for mainly Latino families has stiffened and continues to paralyze both the Congress and the Supreme Court. It is ironic and unfair to families that the November elections, which will determine their future, will not allow them to vote. We are confident, however, that millions of our Latino brothers and sisters will turn out as never before. This nation is in a political civil war. The stakes are high. Demagogic politicians are using millions of families to mobilize the fear and hate of those who would 'Make America White Again.' We continue to rely on our faith to grow stronger in the face of adversity, for adversity gives birth to persistence and 'persistence will perfect us, making us complete, mature, and not lacking in anything.' We will persist because of the love of our families, and we will overcome.

Elvira's faith, which touched the hearts of millions, challenged President Obama to issue a 21st century Emancipation Proclamation. As we were reminded on the anniversary of Juneteenth, the previous Sunday, the slaves did not achieve freedom until after the Civil War was won. Our civil war would come in November.

✹ 35
Make America "White Again"?

Pundits and journalists and politicians will continue to analyze Trump's successful campaign. The popular vote, which Clinton won by over three million votes, confirmed that the majority of U.S. citizens oppose the policies of mass deportation and the separation of families. At last the Democratic Party had placed itself firmly in our camp on the issue of immigration.

A full out attack on Latinos and Muslims mobilized the racialist movement to elect Trump. The new President was quick to fulfill the expectations of these almost entirely white sections of the electorate. Trump, in fact, only prevailed because of the Electoral College and its use of the winner-takes-all method of counting the electoral votes of individual states. The votes of the states reflected the historic pattern of segregation as well as the barrage of voter suppression laws passed in those states. Shock waves hit an over-confident Democratic Party, which simply did not believe that U.S. citizens—no matter how racially motivated—would vote for a morally discredited individual like Donald Trump. Control of the Congress also remained with the Republican Party and its commitment to mass deportation and mass incarceration.

For the Latino community, for the Dreamers, and for the millions of families with at least one undocumented family member, the Trump victory represented a real and immediate danger. An undocumented mother in Seattle went into sanctuary in a church. Media attention focused on Elvira again, and Telemundo broadcast Elvira's phone conversation from her Chicago church with this brave mother. The issues they discussed were familiar as were both the sadness and the courage that they displayed. It seemed as if we were starting all over again—*but there were real differences.*

On the one hand, President Trump issued a series of executive orders upon taking office. The new President did away with the enforcement priorities we had won from President Obama. He insisted they were going after "criminals" and "bad hombres," the first two days of raids captured over six hundred people across the nation, half of whom had no criminal convictions. At least eight million people were identified as eligible for arrest and deportation. Even DACA, the deferments given to the Dreamers, came under attack since, in the first wave of raids, a dreamer in Seattle, Washington, was arrested and detained.

On the other hand, truly massive support for the undocumented arose in "the resistance" to a wide range of Trump policies. One of the largest mobilizations in U.S. history came to life the day after the President's inauguration. Tens of thousands marched and protested against the deportations. Organizations and churches everywhere began to train "defenders" and establish emergency mobilization networks. When Elvira had first been arrested in the wake of the terrorist attack on 9/11, the undocumented were virtually alone. The terrorist action had created a suspicious nation that quickly focused on Latinos. As Elvira had said, "They couldn't find Osama Bin Ladin but they found me—because I wasn't hiding." Now, the majority of U.S. citizens showed their opposition to the deportations at the polls and demonstrated that opposition in the streets.

The problem for the grassroots movement was to find ways to defend against individual deportations as well as to mobilize in the streets and to push back against Trump's policies. True, Trump's base of support represented less than forty percent of U.S. citizens—but the government was in Trump's control and he was committed to utilizing that power "to the max." The central focus of Trump's mass deportation campaign focused on enlisting local police to check papers and refer the undocumented to immigration authorities. During Elvira's sanctuary, Familia Latina Unida had gotten a "sanctuary city" ordinance passed in the Chicago city council. Cook County Commissioner Jesus Garcia had followed up with similar legislation at the county level. City after city with large Latino populations had joined Chicago's example by declaring themselves "sanctuary cities." Although the specific laws differed from city to city, these sanctuary cities prevented local police from carrying out Trump's strategy to arrest and deport millions of people. Trump responded by threatening to cut federal funding to sanctuary cities.

The movement grew as universities and even elementary schools declared themselves as sanctuary schools, and nearly eight hundred churches designated themselves as sanctuary churches. President Trump seemed undeterred by the resistance. He attempted to implement a "Muslim ban," which would deny citizens from eight majority Muslim nations any entrance to the United States. This ban set off massive demonstrations at airports where 100,000 individuals with approved visas and even legal permanent resident green cards were being turned back. Legal actions by state attorney generals got the federal courts to halt enforcement of the ban by arguing that excluding people based on their religion was a violation of the U.S. Constitution. The Supreme Court has since allowed parts of the ban to proceed until it rules on the entirety of the executive order.

President Trump's often-repeated campaign promise to "build a wall on the border with Mexico and make Mexico pay for it" stirred massive protests in Mexico. The protests forced an unpopular Mexican President to refuse to pay for any wall. President Trump responded with bombastic threats that fell just short of declaring war on Mexico. Just as the massive demonstrations of resistance to Trump's policies gave courage to the undocumented, so too did Mexico's support.

The raids, however, made President Trump's intent clear. He had the power, and he intended to use it immediately in a campaign of mass deportation. Not only were his cabinet appointments right wing billionaires, but the President also made a well-known white nationalist his principal White House advisor. The KKK was in the White House, and the Republican Congress was under its control.

For people of faith, Trump's election was a modern day crucifixion of the movement for justice for people of color. In our church, we struggled with discouragement and fear and depression, but gained insight into how the disciples and the followers of Jesus must have struggled after his public torture and execution. Our church was filled with people who were now immediately vulnerable to arrest and deportation. We followed the seasons of faith and struggle, from the appearance of the Virgin of Guadalupe and the births of John the Baptist and Jesus, through to the teaching and acts of Jesus as he recruited and trained his disciples, in an attempt to renew the spirit of a demoralized people. We engaged in a step-by-step effort to strengthen our spiritual understanding and abilities, and to take concrete actions to stop the deportation of longtime church members as well as new ones. A CNN reporter commented that all the different aspects of the immigration battle were to be found in the life stories of our members.

Twelve members of a Guatemalan family, refugees from cartel violence, were now again in jeopardy. We also formed a new church community of Central Americans in Waukegan, Illinois. Each week, young people came to sign up or renew their applications for DACA, making use of the program for as long as it continued. We had assisted in filing over three thousand applications, and each week we tried to answer the questions and allay the fears of those who applied. The Lino family, the Aquirre family, and others like them, whose deportations had been prevented by private bills or legal motions, were required to "check in" with ICE every six months. A well pub-licized arrest and deportation after one such check-in in Arizona raised the real possibility that these families would be arrested at their next check-in. We continued the fight for Miguel Perez, Jr., the "green card veteran" under order of deportation, by going to court and by holding meetings with sena-tors and representatives of Congress in Washington, D.C. Elvira was back with us—but her effort to remain faced a new Trump appointee at the head of the Department of Homeland Security.

Our youth organization, La FuerZa Juventud, began weekly "Moral Monday" protests at ICE headquarters in Chicago. We began training hun-dreds of Defenders who could prepare people to fight deportation and Mobilizers who could turn people out when emergencies arose. All three ini-tiatives grew closer to the Black Lives Matter movement in Chicago. President Trump's pressure to unleash local police had increased the tension on the street in both communities.

As President Trump and the Republicans moved to eliminate Obama's Affordable Care Act, the FuerZa intensified its activity with the Youth Health Service Corps, working with medical students to screen the unin-sured for prevention and early detection of chronic diseases, as well as organizing to open access for the uninsured to the city's clinics and hospi-tals. The undocumented had never been covered by ObamaCare. This volunteer "survival program" developed by the Youth Health Service Corps provided a model that could serve those who would lose coverage under the Republican plan to give a tax break to the rich.

Elvira's son, Saul, turned eighteen and emerged in the leadership of the youth organization. Attending the Pedro Albizu Campos High School in Humboldt Park, he helped develop further the unity of the Mexican and the Puerto Rican communities for the next generation. Puerto Ricans, facing the most severe economic crisis on the island in decades, found that the U.S. Congress had imposed a financial control board, which then instituted severe cuts in services. A massive protest movement, however, had forced President Obama in the waning days of his administration to finally pardon Oscar Lopez Rivera. His release reenergized the Puerto Rican independence movement, a fitting complement to the electric rise of Lopez Obredor and the "Morena" movement in Mexico against a very unpopular president, which gave promise of the most militant resistance to U.S. domination in years. Hundreds of our members joined Morena and welcomed Lopez Obrador to Chicago.

———————————

The struggle of Familia Latina Unida to establish a *Unified Latino Resistance* faced the challenges of all genuine grassroots social movements: the ability to meet setbacks creatively and persistently and the ability to pass on the leadership to a new generation. Facing those challenges would guide our day-to-day work.

Trump's drastic shift of resources to the military, to Homeland Security, and to immigration enforcement, and the militarization of local police, represented an effort to build political support for an authoritarian, white nationalist government. Scripture teaches that "His ways are not our ways." The ups and downs, the hopes and disappointments of the struggle, create a deepening consciousness among the people facing oppression of what is truly important in life and of the destiny that the wretched of the earth have in bringing justice to the social organism. As Emma Lozano, Elvira Arellano, and the new generation of leadership of Familia Latina Unida/Sin Fronteras face a new decade of struggle at the grassroots, they rely on a history of struggle in which a powerful faith has emerged: "the faith of Elvira," *ever renewing*, just as fall becomes winter, and winter becomes spring, and summer brings yet another harvest—and each harvest brings another planting of the seeds of justice.

REFLECTIONS ON THE MOVEMENT

"¡BORICUA Y MEXICANO, LUCHANDO MANO A MANO!": THE PUERTO RICAN STORY WITHIN FAMILIA LATINA UNIDA

By Dr. José E. López, Executive Director of the
Juan Antonio Corretjer Puerto Rican Cultural Center

AS THIS IMPORTANT BOOK REVEALS, THE STORY OF Familia Latina Unida is composed of a multitude of stories. Many of these stories, if not for documentation in text and memory, could easily disappear with the passage of time. Among these stories, or rather interwoven with many of them, is the story of Puerto Rican involvement in the struggle for immigrant rights and amnesty. Within the history of this broader movement, the solidarity expressed in word and deed by Puerto Rican activists, leaders, and elected officials has often been ignored and marginalized. The inclusion of this chapter, as well as the many traces found throughout this volume, not only attests to the active presence of Puerto Ricans, but also reflects the longstanding and intimate relationship between two organizations and their leadership: Pueblo Sin Fronteras (PSF) and the Juan Antonio Corretjer Puerto Rican Cultural Center (PRCC).

The PRCC was founded in 1973 as an experiment in radical practices of community- building and anti-colonial politics within Chicago's Puerto Rican community. As a parallel institution, it has developed numerous programs and initiatives addressing community needs such as education, health, culture, teen pregnancy, AIDS/HIV, and youth engagement. The PRCC is built on a philosophy of self-determination, a methodology of self-actualization and critical thought, and an ethics of self-reliance. PRCC activists have played an active and influential role in the Puerto Rican independence movement and each of the defining struggles concerning Puerto Rican human rights, such as the international campaigns to free two generations of Puerto Rican political prisoners and the movement to end the military occupation of the Puerto Rican island of Vieques. Alongside these efforts, the PRCC has also dedicated itself to cultivating lasting bonds with other oppressed communities and peoples. Through these ties, the PRCC has engaged consistently in acts of solidarity, such as support for Palestinian liberation, Hawaiian independence, and the self-determination of the Black community. As this chapter will recount, the PRCC has elaborated a close relationship with our Mexican and Latin American brothers and sisters, and has witnessed us work alongside them to defend the human rights and dignity of undocumented peoples.

Historical Origins

Our journey could begin in the 19th century, in the heat of Latin American independence struggles, with figures like Antonio Valero de Bernabé, a Puerto Rican who fought for Mexico's liberation and later served as Brigadier General in Simon Bolivar's army. No doubt, this revolutionary activity could be followed into the early 20th century, through the travels of Puerto Rican nationalist leader, Dr. Pedro Albizu Campos, and the refuge Mexico's President Cardenas gave to revolutionaries throughout the Americas. To these political currents, we could add cultural and economic ties among Latin American countries and peoples, which came long before the concept of globalization was abuzz. Yet for present purposes, a more direct starting point is Chicago, the birthplace of Familia Latina Unida.

Throughout the 20th century, Mexicans and Puerto Ricans migrated to Chicago, a fact that transformed the city into a unique social laboratory for the study of the formation of "Latino" identities and political projects. Distinct from New York and Los Angeles, where a single Latino group once predominated, Chicago has experienced the cohabitation, intermingling, and collaboration of the country's two largest Latino populations, as well as the presence of other Latin American migrant communities. The recent diversification of Latino groups in New York, Los Angeles, and other major urban centers only further increases political and intellectual interest in "Latino Chicago."

Mexican and Puerto Rican migrants came into contact beginning in the 1940s, when Puerto Rican contract laborers joined an established and growing Mexican population. In her pioneering comparative research of Puerto Rican acculturation, anthropologist Elena Padilla (1947), then a graduate student at the University of Chicago, provides invaluable insight into the experiences of early Puerto Rican migrant workers. Typically working side-by-side, Puerto Ricans often settled in Mexican neighborhoods. As Padilla notes, "Puerto Ricans contacted many Mexican *braceros* with whom they developed certain kinds of social relationships that in some occasions manifest themselves as conflictual, whereas on other occasions they were cliquish in nature" (p.86). These social interactions led to intimate relations and the formation of "Mexi-Rican" families, as well as social enterprises and political coalitions. In his influential book, *Latino Ethnic Consciousness*, sociologist Felix Padilla (1985) describes the emergence of pan ethnic "Latino" politics among liberal and progressive Mexican and Puerto Rican community leaders in the decades following the Civil Rights era. Within the same period, particularly the 1970s, as Pulido (2006) has documented in the West Coast, radical and militant Puerto Rican and Mexican movements (along with other movements) also engaged in projects of collaboration and acts of solidarity. Within these two left-of-center developments, relationships began to develop between the leadership of the Puerto Rican Cultural Center and the Lozano family, which later founded Pueblo Sin Fronteras. In this period, one of the major, if not defining, struggles waged by Mexican and Puerto Rican activists was fought at the local universities. Our peoples were systematically being excluded from entering the university and given little to no support if we managed to enter. Out of these fights, spearheaded by student groups, we forced administrations to open admissions programs like Proyecto Pa'Lante at Northeastern Illinois University and the Latin American Recruitment and Education Services (L.A.R.E.S.) at the University of Illinois at Chicago. Puerto Rican and Mexican students and community leaders further fought for Latino and Latin American Studies programs, Latino cultural centers, and the hiring of Latino and Latina faculty. Today, we continue to fight for the maintenance and expansion of these programs and initiatives. But collaboration was not limited to the university, but developed also in our communities in struggles over education, employment, housing, and health care.

Building a Latino Agenda

In the first decade of the new century, the PRCC and PSF began to work aggressively to articulate a progressive "Latino Agenda," which could unify the various Latino communities. It is out of this effort that the concept of Familia Latina Unida was developed and articulated. Initially, two distinct social movements were joined together: the struggle for amnesty for the un-documented, and the struggle to end U.S military training on the Puerto Rican island of Vieques.

During that period, Puerto Rico and its Diaspora in the U.S. were em-broiled in an intense struggle to rid the U.S. military from the island of Vieques. On April 19, 1999, Puerto Ricans rose to their feet in disgust over the death of a young Puerto Rican killed by an accidental bombing. This tragedy, coupled with nearly 60 years of resistance to U.S. militarism on the island, led to an international peace movement calling for peace for Vieques. Within months, the struggle became one of the largest movements in Puerto Rican history, successfully uniting a cross-section of Puerto Rican civil soci-ety, which is often divided by political ideology, class, and race. Several anti-US military marches in Puerto Rico attracted between 100,000 to 200,000 participants. In addition to demonstrations, over 1,000 Puerto Ricans and al-lies committed acts of civil disobedience on Vieques. For its part, activists from PRCC and its sister organization, the National Boricua Human Rights Network (NBHRN), organized a protest in Washington, D.C., where 79 in-dividuals were arrested in an act of civil disobedience in front of the White House. Among those arrested were several members of Pueblo Sin Fron-teras.

On May Day 2000, PSF and PRCC organized the first major demon-stration of the "Latino Agenda." On the major thoroughfare of Ashland Av-enue, individuals numbering in the hundreds stood hand-in-hand for much of the length of the city. Following this event, leaders began planning a na-tional mobilization to the country's capitol. It was scheduled to take place on September 25, 2001, but was cancelled after the 9/11 tragedy. After some time of reflection and analysis, the PSF and PRCC began organizing events and actions to advance their agenda. This activity included several local and national lobbying efforts and community forums. In 2004, at the Democratic National Convention, PRCC, NBHRN, and PSF activists distributed thou-sands of leaflets calling for a "Latino Agenda." In addition to amnesty and Vieques, the leaflet also demanded the release of Puerto Rican political prisoners, an end to deportations, and the demilitarization of the U.S./Mexico border, among other issues.

During this period, the PRCC established Café Teatro Batey Urbano, a Puerto Rican/Latin@ youth space for creative expression and community building. The youth organizers and participants of Batey Urbano, which included Puerto Ricans, Mexicans, and other Latinos and persons of color, hosted poetry and hip-hop events aimed to stimulate greater unity within the Latino population. With support from the PRCC and Batey Urbano, PSF opened a sister organization, El Zócalo Urbano, which provided an important outlet for Mexican youth for a number of years. Going beyond merely supporting each other's events, Batey and Zócalo jointly participated in the World Festival of Youth and Students held in Venezuela in 2005. After months of fundraising over thirty thousand dollars, they sponsored thirty-three youth to participate in the World Festival for Youth and Students. In preparation for the trip, these youth developed and circulated a pledge calling for Latino unity on several issues related to the Puerto Rican, Mexican, and broader Latino experience. Thousands of pledges were collected and given as a symbolic gesture to several Venezuelan elected officials, including the then-mayor of Caracas.

Familia Latina Unida emerged out of these efforts and the growing frustration with the separation of families. For its part, PRCC activists worked aggressively to increase Puerto Rican consciousness about the plight of the undocumented. Concretely, it made public challenges to other Puerto Rican organizations and leaders to support comprehensive immigration reform. This effort was carried out both locally and nationally. For instance, in 2004, the PRCC hosted a national conference in New York City titled, "Building Puerto Rican Unity to Ensure a Latino Agenda." Though some leaders initially resisted, the PRCC was instrumental in bringing several influential Puerto Rican elected officials and community leaders closer to the movement. Locally, with PSF and other immigrant organizations, PRCC organized a busload to participate in the precursor to the "mega-marches" of 2006. In 2005, we joined thousands upon thousands in Little Village, the city's largest Mexican barrio, to protest against the attacks on the undocumented.

On March 10, 2006, in Chicago, over 100,000 individuals took to the streets in dramatic opposition to the draconian Congressional bill, Sensenbrenner H.R. 4437. This bill sought to make undocumented legal status and support for undocumented persons a felony. Within this diverse and historic march was a youthful contingent of the PRCC. The size and vitality of the march breathed new life and energy into the movement. Just months later, the PRCC organized a feeder march from Humboldt Park to the massive May Day demonstration, which attracted over 500,000 people from all over the region. Feeder-marches would leave from the Northwest side for the next several years.

Elvira Arellano's decision to seek sanctuary at Adalberto Methodist Church opened up greater space for the PRCC and the Puerto Rican community to participate in the movement. Adalberto Methodist Church is located on a section of Division Street popularly known as "Paseo Boricua." This half-mile long cultural and economic corridor is encased by two massive steel Puerto Rican flags—the largest monuments to a flag on the planet. For Chicago's Puerto Ricans, Division Street and these flags are heart of the city's Puerto Rican community. In fact, this street and Humboldt Park, the neighborhood in which it is nestled, are popularly viewed as synonymous with Puerto Ricans. For some, Arellano's choice of a Puerto Rican barrio was peculiar and even unsettling. Why a church in this area? The close relationship between PSF and PRCC, which Arellano experienced as a leader of Familia Latina Unida, surely played a key part.

As Arellano's decision became public, PRCC activists welcomed her to the community and stationed individuals in the storefront of the church with a Puerto Rican flag in hand. Taking two to three hour shifts, over thirty people stood outside of the newly established sanctuary. This action was undertaken to send a strong message of support for Arellano. Overall, the community was very supportive of Arellano, but whenever contrary voices emerged the PRCC reiterated the importance of Puerto Ricans mobilizing their voices in solidarity. Months later, during the 29th Puerto Rican People's Parade, held on Division Street, the PRCC named Arellano an honorary parade marshal. From within the church, Arellano waved a small Puerto Rican flag as a contingent including her son, Saulito, Roberto Maldonado, a local Puerto Rican official, and a number of Mexican and Puerto Rican activists walked down Division Street. As the parade proceeded, and thousands watched alongside, the chant "¡Boricua y Mexicano, Luchando Mano a Mano!" erupted.

In the years since, Puerto Ricans activists and elected officials have not ceased their support or participation in the pro-immigrant rights movement, and the broader effort to establish a progressive "Latino Agenda." The PRCC, in particular, has continued to make the plight of the undocumented an issue of top priority. From helping to organize community forums, such as one held in May 2013, with Congressman Gutiérrez and Emma Lozano at Roberto Clemente High School, to participation in immigrant freedom rides, lobbying trips to Springfield and Washington, D.C., recent demonstrations, press conferences, and vigils, the PRCC has further deepened its relationship to Centro Sin Fronteras and manifested its solidarity with undocumented peoples and its Latin American brothers and sisters.

Concluding Remarks

The chant that serves as the title of this article, I contend, is truly emblematic of the future being forged inside the U.S. among Latinos. It invokes the Bolivarian ideal of a united América, which departs radically from the commercialized and sanitized pan-Latino construction and instead points to an organic vision about the future of the United States and the future of this hemisphere. Without a doubt, José Martí's daring perspective, accentuated in his essay, "Nuestra América," in which he discusses the Americano continent, began—in very real ways—on the streets of Chicago. What happened in Chicago was that, unlike Los Angeles, New York, and Miami, here, Mexicans, Puerto Ricans, Cubans, and Central Americans existed in the 1960s in pretty equal numbers—no group dominated outright. That demographic reality created something unique and different, and that was a Latino consciousness that was not about losing or giving up our respective national identities—as Mexicans, Puerto Ricans, Cubans, Dominicans, or Ecuadorians—but rather it was about articulating, step by step, a unified political agenda.

Now forty or fifty years later, we are celebrating the fruits of this unique encounter of Latin Americans in this Midwest metropolis. In the 2012 election, no one can underestimate the political weight of the Latino vote—no one can ignore the fact that the Latino vote was decisive in the re-election of President Barak Obama, or that since, immigration reform has become a mainstream issue.

If we peer closer at this past Presidential election, we will notice that Puerto Ricans played an important part in the Latino electorate. If you take Central Florida today, the majority of the Latinos who voted for Obama were Puerto Ricans. If you look at Pennsylvania, Puerto Ricans composed the majority of the Latinos that voted for the President. Lastly, if you take Ohio—realizing that Obama could have never won the state without the Latino vote—the majority of the Latino votes, again, were Puerto Rican.

One theme that ran through these states and the Puerto Rican communities within them was the theme of immigration reform. But we could ask, why was immigration such an important theme for this community of automatic U.S. citizens?

One answer, which I believe is rarely acknowledged, is the work that has been done in Chicago and other local contexts to transform immigration into a Latino issue, an issue that Puerto Ricans could rally around and actively support. The long and arduous work carried out in Chicago, of which I am proud to be a part, has spread across the country, perhaps most effectively by Congressman Luis Gutierrez, a Puerto Rican who has become the strongest Latino voice for immigration reform.

We are surely living in historic times, full of challenges and reactions. However, the possibilities are plentiful, and the responsibility to act never greater. One of the ideas that we have been discussing within the PRCC and with our comrades at PSF is the concept of the "Citizenship of the Americas." We reject the idea that the United States can continue to treat the rest of the Americas as its backyard, imposing military and economic policies like "free trade" on our homelands. I am encouraged by the rejection of neoliberal economic policies throughout many parts of the hemisphere. But I am also encouraged by our growing presence in the United States. The struggle for immigration reform, we cannot forget, is but one part of a much larger fight. As we continue to demand an end to the separation of families, the demilitarization of borders, and an end to the exploitation and exclusion of undocumented immigrants, we must hold on to the fact that, as the journalist Juan Gonzalez so rightly put it, our presence in this country is a "harvest of empire." It is time to demand and organize our communities, here and abroad, for a citizenship of the Americas, which allows for the free movement of people with dignity. In this vein, I recall the words of the late sociologist Frank Bonilla (1993): "Puerto Ricans and other Latinos/Latinas in the United States will not become passive tools of U.S. policy nor willing, uncritical agents of home governments eager to capitalize on their presence in the metropolis. It may yet be that in the long run, [we] will help change the Americas—by changing the United States from inside."

References

BONILLA, F. 1993. Migrants, Citizenship, and Social Pacts. In: MELÉNDEZ, E. & MELÉNDEZ, E. (eds.) Colonial Dilemma: Critical Perspectives on Contemporary Puerto Rico. Boston: South End Press.

PADILLA, E. 1947. Puerto Rican Immigrants in New York and Chicago: A Study in Comparative Assimilation. Master's thesis, University of Chicago.

PADILLA, F. M. 1985. Latino Ethnic Consciousness, Norte Dame, University of Notre Dame.

PULIDO, L. 2006. Black, brown, yellow, and left: radical activism in Southern California, Los Angeles, University of California Press.

A Very Short History of Maravatío

By John Womack
Introductory remarks by Walter Coleman

E
VEN IN THE RELATIVE SECURITY OF HER HOME IN MARAVATÍO, ELVIRA
*was confronted daily with the reality of separated families. Nearly every
home had family members working in the north, driven to find work by
the same forces that had driven her north years before. Stricter border controls
meant that some children had not seen their fathers or mothers for years. Wives
remembered their husbands only through distant memories—and remittances
they received though the mail. Small houses everywhere were always under construction as people waited for checks from the north to add on needed rooms.*

*Maravatío is, in many respects, a suburb of the United States. If the Latino
ghettos in the United States can be compared to the townships in South Africa,
then Maravatío could be seen as one of the homelands, with a dependent economy and family members kept from seeing their loved ones for years by apartheid.*

*Dr. John Womack, as a noted historian, was also well qualified to con-
tribute to this book because he has been an active advisor to Familia Latina
Unida since its beginning and has supported the struggle in many ways. We have
included our brother John Womack's insightful history of Maravatío for what
we think are important reasons.*

*History lives in the hearts and in the faith of its people and "the faith of
Elvira" brought the history of her pueblo north with her. We find in this history
the devastation of her family's way of life by the combination of U.S. policy and
Mexican governmental corruption. We also find the roots of a faith that developed and persevered from its indigenous roots, its resistance to European
occupation, its militant refusal to concede to the corruption of political parties,
and its ability to bind together families in which so many members were forced to
migrate north to find work. Familia Latina Unida grew like an oak tree, with its
roots in the history of this pueblo.*

*The tragedy of Mexico's development as a nation, under the shadow of its
imperial and arrogant neighbor to the north, is that the great civic coherence of
the parish was separated and isolated from its governing parties, leaving them
disconnected from the faith and accountability and energy of the people.*

THE LERMA RIVER RISES IN THE GREAT MOUNTAINS NORTHWEST OF
Mexico City and winds slowly west 300 miles down to a big freshwater lake
(Mexico's biggest), from which its waters flow northwest another 250 miles
down into the Pacific. It is Mexico's second-biggest river. Since the 16th century, its upper watershed, the Lerma Basin, the Bajío, has been the main
source of grain for 200 to 300 miles around. Historically, the river tends to
divide Mexico's western regions into north and south. North of its watershed, along mountains and high plateaus, the country runs to the U.S.
border, geographically and culturally. Farther south, over mountains and valleys, it breaks into geographic and cultural complications, many more
changes from place to place, all the way into Guatemala.

Not far down from the Lerma's sources, worn by a little tributary from
the south, is the Maravatío Valley. It is high, nearly 7,000 feet, but temperate,
wet in the summer, dry in the winter, around 36 inches of rain a year, tem-
peratures from sixty degrees to eighty-five degrees Fahrenheit. There is still
silver in the mountains upriver, up east. The forests are pine, oak, poplar, ash,
willow, cypress, firs, and juniper. This is the Monarch butterfly's homeland.
In the valley, the soil is rich.

The people living there when the Spanish arrived in the 1520s were
mostly Otomí- and Mazahua-speaking serfs. The men were also border
guards, with forts to defend. Their Purépecha-speaking lords paid dues to
their king, based some 80 miles west; collected dues from the Otomí and
Mazahua; and forced their local military service, to block nomadic raids from
the north and invasion from the east by the Mexica, or Aztecs. There was no
court or temple or market in the Maravatío valley, which, when the Spanish
came, bore a Purépecha name, "precious place." It was all little communities
and neighborhoods, farming abundant patches of corn, beans, squash, tomatoes, chiles, and amaranth.

Like Spanish expeditions of conquest elsewhere, the first Spanish expe-
dition into Purépecha country claimed it politically for the king of Spain and
religiously for the Roman Catholic Church. And, as elsewhere, the first material claims on the conquered people (Purépecha, Otomí, Mazahua, and
others) were for tribute, local products, the material sign of subjection and
loyalty; the tribute the conquered used to pay their old king, they now owed
to their new king. Registered in "Indian" pueblos—"villages" legally under
royal protection for their tribute—conquered communities for decades
actually delivered their dues to local agents of private lords to whom the king

had given royal trusts. The new Indian pueblo of communities in the Mara-vatío Valley at first paid its tribute to a local agent for a private lawyer in Mexico City, then to his successor. But by the 1550s, it was paying its dues (by then monetized in gold) to a royal district commissioner.

Right behind the military expeditions and the tribute-collectors came the first missionaries, Franciscans. They established several houses in the old Purépecha kingdom, managed the first mass conversions of local people to Catholicism, and first taught them the catechism. Already in the 1530s, they had a chapel in the Maravatío Valley, dedicated to St. John the Baptist. In 1536, the authorities in Spain and Rome created a fourth bishopric in the vast world they now called New Spain, one for the old Purépecha kingdom and all the unknown north—the diocese of Michoacán. The new bishop founded its cathedral and seminary in the heart of Purépecha country, and by the 1550s had organized the diocese into several parishes, among them San Juan Maravatío.

By then, Spanish landlords had also brought their cattle and pigs into the valley. This might not have mattered much to the local economy, if there had not been much demand for hides, beef, pork, or lard—none of which Indians much wanted. But in 1558, Spaniards discovered a big silver lode, and gold, up in the mountains just east and quickly opened mines there, drafting Indians and buying African slaves for workers. The mining boom, the demand for hides—and the need to feed the mining camp, men, and mules—made cattle ranching, pig farming, and commercial agriculture in the Maravatío Valley boom. As the landlords hoped, their animals thrived. But they did much damage to Indian agriculture. The mining business con-solidated, which brought regular freight traffic through the valley, mulatto muleteers and their long strings, steady demand for grain and pasture.

Under Spanish pressure, the elders of the pueblo of Maravatío in 1581 agreed to move their main community farther down the valley, to where it stayed for (at least) the next 430 years. The lands it left were better than the lands it received farther down, but the new place was rich enough. Spaniards soon moved into the community, illegally, but freely. The pueblo's other communities and neighborhoods moved down nearby. In the 1590s, the main community, becoming a regular little village, started building its first parish church, San Juan Bautista. The other communities and neighbor-hoods took other patron saints; for example, a few miles southwest of Maravatío village, a Mazahua neighborhood took St. Michael the Archangel, to become San Miguel Curahuango.

In the 1640s, another mining boom not far away, up in the mountains to the southeast, increased ranching and commercial agriculture in the valley, and increased the traffic through it. Maravatío became a district crossroads— east-west, north-south. Private estates took form: a few small haciendas, maybe 10 square miles, farmed by local Indian tenants and sharecroppers, producing for the landlords' sales to the mining camps. As the Indians of Maravatío increasingly dealt with the Spanish there and farmed for them, as they dealt too with the mulatto mule drivers, they became less clannish, less Indian, more *mestizo*, not so much a question of genes as of culture, language, behavior, values. In a census of the district in 1681, the pueblo of Maravatío counted 102 Indians (adults, men and women); *mestizos* there probably numbered some 50. By then San Miguel was a pueblo too, but not so busy. It counted 94 Indians, probably only 20 *mestizos*.

Yet another mining boom began in the 1730s, back up near the original lode in the mountains to the east. Bigger than before, its silver paid for a "golden age" up there and the expansion of ranching and commercial agriculture in all the valleys around, including Maravatío. A couple of small haciendas grew bigger, maybe 20 square miles; more small haciendas appeared, and many tenants bought land, turning into proprietary farmers. This development cost Maravatío's pueblos and other communities most of their common lands; most Indians now had to work on the haciendas and farms to make a living, which made more mestizos. By 1800, a landed capitalist oligarchy dominated the valley, with proprietary farmers taking its power for granted over the general population of some 15,000. The village of Maravatío was a prosperous place then, maybe 1,000 people, probably two-thirds of them *mestizos*. And in justification of the established order there, the diocese—no more Franciscans—managed its Catholicism, so that in support of the local order the parish priest decided what was right and wrong.

After 1805, because of great wars in Europe—critically, because of Napoleon's invasion of Spain in 1808—the Spanish empire began to collapse. In 1810, a terrific rebellion exploded in New Spain, in the Lerma Basin. Its leader, a diocesan priest, Father Miguel Hidalgo, brought an army of maybe 50,000 (more throngs than army) through Maravatío on the way toward Mexico City. Maravatío contributed nothing, except a house for Hidalgo to spend the night. Nor did it respond to his call soon after for "Americans" (native-born in Spain's empire in the Americas) to seize the government of New Spain in the Spanish king's name and defend its "independence" against the French. Meanwhile people from villages over the mountains to the south, where Franciscan influence had endured and Indian communities remained stronger, sent men and material to the rebel cause.

After Hidalgo's campaign failed in the next few months, some surviving rebels tried to organize a "national" government at a town only 30 miles over the mountains south of Maravatío. San Juan Maravatío did not contribute anything to the "national" cause either. Nor did it offer the town any help when royal troops went there, drove out the rebels, and burned the town down. Nor did it even hint at helping a new, much more organized and effective rebellion for national independence, led by another diocesan priest, Father José María Morelos—a serious threat to royal forces west, south, and east of Mexico City, from 1812 to 1815. But for local order, the town did support a bishops-backed royal commanders' coup in 1821, as well as their declaration of national independence, constitution of "the Mexican Empire," and coronation of a royal general born and raised in the Michoacán cathedral city—incidentally also a Maravatío landlord—as Mexico's emperor.

The emperor did not last long. In 1824, Mexico was reconstituted as a republic. But it then went through more than fifty years of deep conflicts, in the course of which the United States took by conquest over half its territory, all its northern provinces. The conflicts were over a question of geopolitical economy: how to keep as much national territory as possible together and independent, and get its wealth developed. The question turned on Mexico's 300-year-old chartered corporations—first and above all the Catholic Church, its immense properties and privileges—not to mention scores of guilds in every major business, profession, and trade, all these defended by the newest corps, the Army, in order to protect its pre-republican privileges. Radically, the question was whether to preserve this inherited regime or to abolish corporate privileges. And there were intercontinental consequences. For parties convinced that national integrity and economic development required corporate institutions and economic policy, it was first essential to preserve the Church's privileges, because of its wealth and nationally extensive powers of local, parochial convocation, discipline, and proscription. Such a commitment, to a state-protected Church—therefore also to the military establishment—indicated European Catholic alliances, principally France. For parties convinced that national integrity and economic development required freedom—in politics, finance, business, and careers—it was essential to abolish simultaneously both the Church's and the Army's privileges, which indicated (a geopolitical tragedy) a U.S. alliance. The conflicts between these parties continued, eventually in civil wars of Conservatives versus Liberals, until the U.S. Civil War ended in the victory of the Union over the Confederate States in 1865. Though Mexico's propertied classes and local, popular culture remained very Catholic, largely conservative, the republic's government would henceforth be Liberal.

Through all these struggles the Maravatío Valley's Church-blessed capitalist oligarchy and yeomanry were faithfully, almost uniformly Conservative. The one remarkable exception was an adopted son of the owner of the biggest hacienda in the valley. And Maravatío's Catholic businessmen could not stand him. Melchor Ocampo—lawyer, European traveler, scientist, linguist, Liberal—served as governor of Michoacán in 1846-47 because of the national political collapse over the U.S. invasion, not because Liberals were suddenly popular in Michoacán. He could raise a National Guard battalion in the state because the Church and Conservatives opposed the invasion as much as Liberal patriots did (or more). It was because of the Maravatío parish priest urging defense of the fatherland that the valley sent volunteers, who fought and died in the war.

Governor of Michoacán again because of national politics in 1852-53, Ocampo applied his Liberal principles to cut parochial fees for the sacraments, which outraged the bishop and the priests. He also eased his Liberalism to protect the state's Indian communities from a recent law mandating the sale of their remaining communal properties, which outraged landlords and farmers. A clerical/business rebellion, starting in Maravatío, forced his resignation. When, in a new national Liberal-Conservative crisis, the Conservative president passed through the village, Maravatío erected a floral arch and dedicated a *Te Deum* to him, for which he decreed the place now a town. National Conservative divisions allowed Liberal revolutionaries to take Mexico City and write a new constitution in 1857, abolishing all corporate privileges; in the new government, Ocampo served as minister of internal security and foreign relations. Conservatives rallied, and Mexico's worst civil war yet commenced—not only regular military battles, but Conservative and Liberal towns and villages fighting each other, neighbors attacking each other. Maravatío was a violently loyal Conservative town. After dire Liberal concessions to the United States, once-Liberal forces won a major battle over Conservatives. Ocampo resigned in 1861 and retired to his *hacienda* in the valley. A few months later, Conservative guerrillas kidnapped him on behalf of a Conservative general, who had him shot. During the French occupation of Mexico (1863-1867) and Maximilian's Empire, the same general commanded Mexican imperial forces in Michoacán. While he faced fierce Liberal republican resistance from towns over the mountains to the south, he met firm collaborators in Maravatío, happy to have a republican turncoat in charge there.

After the war, under Liberal republican rule, the Catholic landlords and farmers of Maravatío backed riots and rebellions opposing enforcement of Liberal laws that separated Church and State. And they won, not in law, but in practice, so that the valley remained a Catholic clerical stronghold. But they nevertheless resolutely took Liberalism's many new economic opportunities. Village after village lost its commons to federal sales, where the local gentry and yeomen bought disentailed Church and community land to expand their operations. In 1883, a year before the first railroad opened north between Mexico City and the U.S. border, a line opened west from Mexico City through Maravatío to a junction for a second main line that was building north to the border. The valley's agricultural products could sell much more widely, and farming boomed. As private enterprise determined production, the valley's few remaining Indian communities lost almost all their productive commons. Yet another mining boom started up east in the 1890s—gold and silver, more business for Maravatío. By 1900, the valley featured three or four haciendas around twenty square miles each, some fifteen or more half that size, and some 500 farms averaging 100 acres; as a U.S. American visitor saw it, "hundreds of square miles of well-cultivated valley land" and "grazing grounds for many herds of horses and cattle." The only commons left were cemeteries. Most people, including the Indians—still Indian, though without commons—worked as tenant farmers, sharecroppers, or small farmers, or for wages on railroad track crews, or up east in mining and logging.

The political conflicts of 1910 that exploded into the Mexican Revolution did not involve the Maravatío Valley. In free elections in 1911, the propertied classes there went for a new National Catholic Party. When politics turned into civil war, again, in 1913, they took cover as before under the best protection available for their religion and their business. The people without property kept working. In 1911-12 they may have heard of the Liberating Army's national program to take land for villages, though in 1915 they certainly did hear of the Constitutionalist Army's decree of agrarian reform; yet the valley yielded no armed popular action for any side in the war. At the Revolutionary Constitutional Congress held in 1916-17 by the war's winning faction, Maravatío district had a representative, but he was from a northern border state, appointed by the winning faction's headquarters. Had the powers of Maravatío elected its representative, he would have opposed two intensely significant articles of the new Constitution: one mandating federal grants in trust of lands specifically expropriated for "agrarian communities," local commons for them, *ejidos*; the other barring any religious role or language in official affairs, denying legal status to all religious "groups," and severely restricting all private religious functions.

During the Revolutionary wars, cracks opened in the valley's power structure. A few men without property followed others from the Bajío north to the United States, to work the harvests, to the railroads, or to Chicago's steel mills and packing plants—all in full swing because of World War I. Several miles northwest of town, in 1915, a village petitioned Constitutionalist Army offices for land. In 1916, another village in that direction followed suit. Neither got anything. In 1917, under the new Constitution, a third village, just east of town, petitioned the new state agrarian commission for a grant. In 1919, San Miguel Curahuango likewise asked for its *ejido*. In 1921, even some landless Maravatío town laborers filed a petition, and San Miguel repeated its request. In 1922, thanks to an ex-seminarian-turned-socialist in the governor's seat, the third village actually received a grant: 2,300 acres for some 200 families. San Miguel got a provisional grant. But thanks to landlords, farmers, and the bishop, the governor was soon gone. Priests organized Catholic mothers, youth, rural missions, and farmworker unions; landlords armed their tenants, who forcefully reclaimed *ejidos* (e.g., San Miguel's) as theirs by custom to rent and farm, and no more grants happened for another five years.

A new civil war exploded in Mexico in 1926, fought mostly in the Bajío, including the Maravatío Valley, and ending only in armed truces in 1929. The radical question was Christus Rex, Christ the King, and whether the Catholic Church could ignore—indeed had to defy—the new Mexican Constitution's anti-clerical article. Was there a higher power in Mexico than the Mexican federal government? (If so, foreign oil companies also wanted to know, for besides Christ, maybe their property rights were beyond earthly jurisdiction too.) With Pius XI's approval, the bishops tested the government. Catholic lay organizations provoked it, bearing arms in acts of civil disobedience. The government used the army in response. Over months, scores died, among them priests and chaplains. A formally declared national Catholic laity rebellion started in 1927. It was serious, and extended across much of Western Mexico. But worse, as in the Conservative-Liberal wars of the 1850s, was the mounting local violence: towns and villages angling for land, *agraristas*, therefore politically loyal, anti-clerical; and towns and villages against redistribution of land and loyal to the Church, *Cristeros*, fighting each other. In the Bajío most people of all classes were fervent *Cristeros*. Beyond the bishops and their priests, they were "God's Army." Perceiving it as Holier than the Church, many came to believe that it, too, might betray their Lord Jesus Christ. So the Maravatío Valley was *Cristero*, as now-devout farmers led faithful tenants, sharecroppers, and hired hands to rout Satan's *agraristas* from their district. By 1929, all told, nationally, some 75,000 people had died: 15,000 soldiers, 30,000 *agraristas*, 30,000 *Cristeros*.

At war, depending on the perspective, some did betray their faith, or compromised it, or saw the light. To divide Maravatío's powers, in 1927 the governor approved the landless laborer's pending petition for an *ejido* there: 1,700 acres for 135 families, and the families took the land. A month later, he approved San Miguel Curahuango's second try: 2,500 acres for 250 families, and they took it. Meanwhile more local men bailed out of the violence and went off to the United States to work. But the Cristero War confirmed the valley's deepest popular tradition: Government is evil, higher authorities of any kind may lie; trust only in the Word of the Lord.

The armed truces of 1929 held, for the most part. But within a year, some Bajío country *Cristeros* (despite the bishops) started another rebellion. *Cristero* guerrillas fought off and on for almost a decade. *Cristeros* in Bajío cities and towns, more educated and calculating, tried to form a secret brotherhood in the region to press respectable (Catholic) public opinion on the government. Briefly connecting with the guerrillas, then disconnected from them, the brotherhood soon fell apart. Reoriented in 1934, connected now with the Jesuits and some rich Mexican conservatives, these militants then planned a clandestine national organization to re-Catholicize Mexican civil society—not by violence, or by setting the Church against the State, but by force of (Catholic) civil demonstrations, moral example, and moral reason— so that ultimately a reborn Catholic society would redeem the nation. This effort failed too; its civic religiosity could not match the new Mexican (and Michoácano) president's commitment to a popular front in national politics; his alliance with a radically new, nationally comprehensive labor movement; and his eventual establishment of more than 10,000 *ejidos*. But they did not quit, and their next try succeeded. In 1937, they started a national, public organization for the positive promotion of social Catholicism (*Rerum Novarum et seq.*) against the Godless Communist Left, whom they thought then ran Mexico. This was the Unión Nacional Sinarquista, Sinarquismo, driving a Catholic people's programmatic civil struggle for a Catholic "Father-

land, Justice, and Liberty." It quickly grew into the biggest mass organization—without official subsidy—ever yet in Mexico, people of all classes,
mostly in rural districts, 230,000 active members by 1940. Of these, 60,000
were in Michoacán. Encouraged by federal policies of "national unity" during World War II, the UNS more than doubled its membership by the war's
end, maybe 600,000 by 1945, 100,000 of them in Michoacán. The state's
northeastern Sinarquista base was Maravatío.

After the war, as Mexico's national political machine readjusted to the
right for the Cold War, Sinarquismo broke down as a national force. But its
cadres remained strong in the Bajío's civil society. When the hoof-and-
mouth plague began ravaging the Mexican countryside in 1947, and official
teams of Mexican and U.S. veterinarians—often with military protection—
went slaughtering suspected animals (a million of them that year), it
devastated thousands of small farms and *ejidos*, terrified rural families, and
provoked bloody showdowns. The critical turn happened in the Maravatío
Valley, just twelve miles up south from Maravatío town, when *agraristas* in
defense of their cattle killed a vet, an Army officer, and six soldiers. It was
then that local Bajío Sinarquistas, standing by private farmers and *agraristas*,
convinced the Mexican government to slow down the slaughter, to only
quarantine suspected cases, and to pay compensation for animals lost.

The Sinarquista movement left two major legacies. One (well known)
was a fund of terrific social, cultural, and political assets for the far right in
Mexico, put to much use on the right all during the Cold War and to date.
The other legacy (barely known) was a fund of the social, cultural, and moral
influence vivid in advocacy for the Bajío's rural poor in 1947. This influence
was not only regional. Because it came from the Bajío, which since the first
railroads had been Mexico's most prolific source of internal and external
migrant labor, it spread far and wide, increasingly unrecognized even by the
people who carried it, but nevertheless unusual and strong—a kind of intu-
itive Catholic anarcho-syndicalism. Post-war it spread. As Bajío migrants took
it to work in Mexico's new agribusinesses east, west, and north, and in the
new factories around Mexico City, a new rebellious streak in Mexico's now
officially-controlled labor movement. And it reached far beyond the border
north, as by the mid-1950s, tens of thousands of once-Sinarquistas were
among the 150,000 *braceros* a year going from the Bajío to work in the United
States. It made for extraordinary moral courage, fortitude, and devotion to
righteousness against all odds.

By the late 1950s, big Mexican business anticipated its profits from Mexico's post-war structure of markets would soon decline. In 1958, the Mexican government accordingly reformed its economic policies to open more profitable opportunities. For the Bajío, the main result was a 20-year run of heavily subsidized big agro-tech business. Already, agribusiness had learned from the Green Revolution in wheat ("Lerma Rojo"), which took strong doses of pesticide, fertilizer, and water—i.e., fat contracts for DuPont and Worthington. It now shifted the region quickly into production of sorghum and alfalfa, which took loads of chemical additives and aquifer-fed irrigation, all for the new food industry: sorghum to feed the chickens and pigs, alfalfa to feed the cattle for meat and dairy products for Mexico City's (and Guadalajara's) new middle class. It was fully modern agro-industry, established for sure in the Bajío in 1975, when Anderson Clayton started its first big grinding mill there. Foreign giants, big Mexican companies, landlords, big farmers, and some luckily placed *ejidos* prospered. Most working people in agriculture suffered. Small farmers and *ejidatarios* generally persevered, though some cashed out and moved to town to start little businesses, or work for them; for example, in the shops making mats or chairs in Maravatío. Landless laborers, used to migrating, tried the new industrial fields, or the poultry plants and packing houses. If they were landless, young, and desperate, they headed to Mexico City, or north to the United States, no more *braceros*, now undocumented.

In 1982 this regime—state-subsidized, finally debt-fueled capitalism—crashed in bankruptcy. Huge foreign debts practically prevented any national economic recovery, except in autarky or by prodigious exporting. Given the debts were due very largely to U.S. banks, an attempt at autarky would have been revolutionary. Such powers as there were in Mexican business and politics then went *against* repudiation, *for* renegotiating the debt and exporting. The economic result was several years of severe stagflation, complicated by a surprising wave of international corruption, followed by a few years of mixed recovery, then catastrophe—U.S. banks in control of Mexican finances, massive immigration.

During the stagflation, in 1982-89, Bajío agriculture shifted again, from production for domestic sales to production for foreign sales. There were still vast fields of sorghum and alfalfa for Mexico's still-functional markets. But capital looking for profit led to new fields of fruit and vegetables, and new processing plants to ship clean, cool strawberries, tomatoes, asparagus, broccoli, and cauliflower to U.S. markets. These exports immediately raised complaints from U.S. growers and their Congressmen, and often drew bans by the U.S. Department of Agriculture or Commerce. Some exporters, including the new unions of *ejidos*, kept at it, and survived the continual harassment at the U.S. border. But many small farms failed, more *ejidatarios* quit, and many more of the landless found nobody in the region to hire them. Where there were jobs, real wages (from 1982) had fallen 30%. Bajío migration increased to Mexico City and other big Mexican cities. It increased much more to the United States, forming probably a third of the 3,000,000 undocumented Mexican immigrants (more from Michoacán than any other state), then passing yearly into U.S. labor markets. The new corruption came largely from the U.S.-backed counter-revolutions in Central America; U.S. protection of cocaine traffic from Colombia to the United States; and arms traffic from the United States to Central America. Both movements went via Mexico, mainly through its western states—e.g., Michoacán—facilitated by substantial U.S. bribes in dollars (in this period of incredible inflation and painful federal budgets) to Mexico's armed forces and federal police there.

During the mixed recovery, 1989-94, the Bajío did better than most other regions. The new government's privatization of state-owned companies did not involve electricity or water, where the Bajío's key subsidies were. The drastic reduction of inflation raised real wages there (from the pits of the '80s) almost 25%. On the government's industrial policy, old and new factories in the region resumed serious production, and assembly plants on the U.S. border, the *maquiladoras*, multiplied and boomed, paying wages higher than Michoacán's shops. Big and small farmers could get credit again. The constitutional reform of the agrarian system suited most Bajío *ejidatarios* fine; they had resented the system's bosses, and now began registering their *ejidos* for assignment of individual plot titles. New, targeted anti-poverty programs combined community organizing, construction of local infrastructure, and support for local co-ops. Migrant remittances were no longer for survival, but for investment in livestock, tractors, and children staying in school. Migrants themselves were bringing pickups and vans back to their hometowns. Most worrisome was NAFTA's threat to *ejidatarios*, who depended on selling corn at subsidized prices. Probably 40% of Michoacán's 300,000 *ejidatarios* could have been ruined unless the government protected them, until they could produce something competitive. Politically Michoacán was contentious again, not over religion, but over Mexico's presidency. The presidential succession of 1988 had broken the old ruling machine in two, which affected Michoacán worse than any other state, because the losing faction's chief was the state's most famous politician, and he opposed NAFTA. Compounded by the region's narco-corruption, the new political feuds were often bloody.

Even so, a new kind of hope had come to Maravatío. In 1990, for the first time, a schoolteacher became mayor there, elected by the leftist opposition. A federally backed local project for a Maravatío Valley strawberry-processing plant failed. But a similar project, involving the Maravatío Cattlemen's Association and its Union of Ejidos, for a co-op dairy, went successfully into production. A girl from San Miguel Curahuango finishing Maravatío high school—clear- minded, perceptive, thoughtful, hoping to be a secretary in town—believed that on a secretary's wages, she could support her invalid parents and live decently herself there.

Through the catastrophe, 1994-2000, speculative capital freely plundered Mexico, and inequality spiked higher than ever before in the country's history. The richest Mexican businessmen swindled the nation of its savings, and the biggest New York, London, and Madrid bankers bought practically sovereign powers of exploitation. Under their regime, NAFTA brought the world's food-industry giants into the Lerma Basin to glory in enormous production and processing of fruit and vegetables, for U.S. and European markets, meanwhile pumping Bajío aquifers dry and polluting the river and lakes. Starved of credit, the region's middle class folded (as it did elsewhere). Small farms went to weeds. *Ejidatarios* lost original NAFTA protections and scratched still lower for a living, or migrated. In 1997, real wages in Mexico were lower than they had been in 20 years. From the Bajío, so many men had already migrated north that now women were the majority of the migrants, to work in the *maquiladoras,* or cross the borderline into the broken-promised land. It was a strange export: extraordinary moral courage, fortitude, and devotion, for $30 a week as a secretary in Maravatío, $60 a week in an electronics plant in Reynosa, $5 an hour at a Laundromat in Yakima, $6.50 an hour cleaning airplane interiors at O'Hare....

An Interview with Congressman Luis V. Gutierrez

Interview questions from Rev. Coleman and answers of Congressman Gutierrez

I RECALL THAT AFTER A MEETING IN THE OVAL OFFICE, YOU RELATED THAT the President had reminded you, "We're both from Chicago...." In what ways do you think the movement in Chicago influenced the immigration dynamic, which finally resulted in a fairly sweeping executive order from President Barack Obama?

𝒜. Well, first of all—not to be arrogant, Chicago is the breeding ground, the laboratory, the first manifestation, the people with ideas, the place that germinates ideas across the country.

Chicago is a place of doers, of people who set examples. You know, we had to get Barack Obama to come to our immigration rally in Chicago. You know, he was a little annoyed when he was still a U.S. Senator. The first rally [March 10, 2006], he refused to come. The second one he said, "Yes Luis, I'll march." In fact he didn't really march, he just showed up at the end. I found that interesting, when later in the Presidential campaign he said he marched, when in fact he didn't quite march. So in the beginning he didn't quite grasp the significance of the immigration issue. If he hadn't been from Chicago, it might have been even more difficult to bring him to our point of view.

From my own perspective, because he and I were both from Chicago, I was the first and for a long time the only member of the Congressional Hispanic Caucus to endorse him. For a while I was all he had. So it became clear to me that he had a responsibility to keep his promise [on immigration reform]—first to the greater community, which is the most important aspect—but from a purely political perspective, to keep his personal promise to me. And all that happened because we were both from Chicago.

The lessons learned by Barack Obama were clearer because he came from Chicago, where the movement was so strong. They would not have been so clear if he were from a different place. Looking back, maybe he needed a stronger "smacking down" in Chicago when he voted for the fence. He didn't really understand the reaction when everybody got together. He just thought it was a "communication problem." It wasn't a communication problem; it was a policy problem. It was a problem of how you see the immigration issue.

So how did Chicago affect the process? All of these factors. And then the dynamic in the White House—Valerie Jarrett, Axelrod—all from Chicago.

Q. Contained in this volume is an analytical article by Dr. José López on the Puerto Rican role in Familia Latina Unida, going back to an historic unity march calling for the navy to get out of Vieques, and for an end to the deportations and separation of families. Do you recall that march and rally, to which you came fresh from jail in Puerto Rico? How do you see the role of Mexican-Puerto Rican unity in Chicago as it affected the almost unanimous Latino unity that developed later across the nation on the immigration issue?

A. Well look, across the Latino community there is an almost monolithic support for immigration reform, for stopping the deportations and separation of families. In terms of Puerto Ricans—I listen to them on the radio, or in a group discussion, a community discussion, on a panel, in favor of our position. Everywhere across the country I go, there is always a Puerto Rican with his flag making sure they are represented in this struggle. But there was a time that I was criticized by Puerto Ricans in Chicago for being only for Mexicans; why wasn't I more preoccupied with the Puerto Rican community.

If you look at the example that we gave from Chicago—it's not enough what we say, we have to show examples—we have to make it concrete. And let me tell you something, everywhere I went in the Mexican community I was asked by someone, "How's that little island doing? It's just terrible what they are doing to them." So it's not just immigration, although immigration is the greatest winner of unity, but if you associate things people will develop a broader agenda that can be derived from the unity of our community. But it has to start somewhere.

I can remember back in the eighties that the talk from U.S. citizens was about wetbacks—even among Mexican U.S. citizens—and no one really cared. Immigration wasn't that big an issue. We had just passed the 1986 immigration act and people were talking about IRCA money and signing people up. But if you weren't part of signing people up, you were nowhere on the radar screen. I do remember that we were the first- burgeoning of this unity. I recall going with Jesus Garcia from the Mexican community to the INS director's office to protest. That was kind of early when not many people across the country were engaged. And even before the immigration issue in Chicago, there were the citizenship campaigns. No one did citizenship like Chicago. If you look at citizenship applications across the country in the nineties, we out-did everyone else here.

Even today, when you look at DACA applications, Chicago outperformed other areas. There is a reason for that. We don't necessarily have the smartest Mexicans and Guatemalans—although they are pretty smart. But we have a team in Chicago, a healthy awareness and competition for justice, a competitiveness for justice. So people wake up in the morning and say, "What can I do today? I saw what my friend Fernando did, what can Maria do today?"

Q. Perhaps you recall a meeting with Emma and "Pistolero" in the fall of 2005 in which a plan for local city mass marches was formulated. After those marches materialized in 2006, the Sensenbrenner bill was defeated and a bill was passed in the Senate on which the House refused to act. Then in June of 2006, Familia Latina Unida organized a march to demand executive action to stop the deportations and separation of families at which both you and Mayor Daley spoke. You brought that demand for the first time to the Congressional Hispanic Caucus and began an "either/or" dynamic between the passage of legislation or executive action to stop the deportations. I wonder if you would comment on the development of that dynamic and its significance in the overall struggle?

A. Yes, it was the first time it was raised, and it subsequently led to where we are today with the executive action from the President. At that time we weren't sophisticated enough to understand how you got that done, necessarily. We just said, "Stop the deportations," but we didn't say, here's how you do it. Here is your formula. Here is how the government works to do it. Here are the precedents for it. We hadn't gotten there yet. We said, "This is evil, this is wrong, stop it." What we got in response was a fence bill and Barack Obama saying, I voted for the fence so that later on we could get more. I said, no, that is bad policy, Barack. We've got to get something today. The Republicans will always go to enforcement—they will always go back to that—and they will ask Democrats to join them and then we would not get anything.

But that march was the first time, and it continues to build from there, and the Familias Unidas grows, it morphs. It started with Bush, and then it had such power that in the 2008 campaign—unlike the 2004 campaign where we couldn't break through—immigration was everywhere. Hillary and Barack were debating about their commitment to the Latino community. Hillary said, I have Solis, the first Latina campaign manager, and Barack came back that he had the support of Luis Gutierrez, the champion of the immigration movement. So now it was front and center in their debates, in the LA debates, in the debate on Univision. Now everybody has to talk about it. It's everywhere, to the point where when Barack Obama spoke at NALEO he gave the best answer: "I am not going to come back here to say I support reform, I am going to come back here to sign the bill!" And there was the genesis of "the promise, of the promise of Barack Obama that no one has ever let him forget."

Q. Shortly after that march, Elvira Arellano began a yearlong sanctuary demanding the right of undocumented parents to stay with their U.S. citizen children. You made a decision to support her action and visit the church. Elvira's Faith and Resistance is a central theme of this volume. I wonder if you would comment on your opinion of that sanctuary and its effect on redefining the immigration issue as well as its effect on the role of churches across the nation in your two Familias Unidas tours?

𝒜. Yes, it had an effect. Again, it was about setting a bar and setting an example. It raised awareness. Now you have to come into our community, you have to go into a church to deport someone, and there are people here who are going to stand up and protect them. It is really about protecting.

I think, very, very important, just as it was for civil rights in the Black community, it was making the church very, very central to the movement, giving the church a central and key role, a role which we developed even further during the Familias tours.

Q. The first Familias Unidas tour ended with a commitment for prosecutorial discretion, and the second ended with a more significant implementation of that discretion in the deferments for early childhood arrivals. Could you favor us with some of your recollections of those two historic campaigns?

A. In the first tour in 2009, our premise was very, very simple. We all get together. The President had just been elected, and he promised us that he would move on immigration reform in the first year. Yet for some reason, we wanted to make sure he did it. We felt that somewhere during the campaign—and during the first 100 days—the issue had been dropped. We had an economic crisis and no one was talking about immigration. There was a healthy suspicion that we needed to do our work.

We began in Chicago. We went to St. Pius. And I remember that Rev. Coleman showed up and put his arm around me and said, the weather is bad, and the turn out is a little light. I told him, I don't care if the church is a third empty, I am going to make the same passionate plea to stop the separation of families. And then it was Biblical. You have two people saying, the weather is bad and we are going to go ahead anyway, and then the church filled up to overflowing!

We were giving an example to everybody because people were not convinced that this was the way to go. We were just saying that we could go to churches and get people to sign up. We heard the testimonies, and then we did our petitions. We took those petitions to the White House. I remember that our first stop outside of Chicago was Providence, Rhode Island. Without any national organization, without any national funding, sometimes with just you and me getting on an airplane and going from place to place. (Nancy Pelosi thought I was so blessed that you were my own personal priest that traveled around with me).

That campaign was the beginning. It led to the second half, where we said, we are going to go back again. We made another call for a second round of Familias Unidas. From Chicago, we had said we would go to all of these cities. From Chicago, we used Pastor Freddy Santiago and Pastor Choco. Each of them helped. Some places had more people than others. Some places had better testimonies than others, but everybody did something, and Congress people came forward. By the time we did the second tour, coming around the second time, people were used to it and ready for it. Organizations that had not worked with the Evangelicals or the faith-based community began to join in.

Then we came back to Chicago, and there were people who still didn't understand us, including the Cardinal. He said, "You can't come to the church, Luis, because you don't share our position on abortion." I told the Cardinal, "But this event is ecumenical;" and to his credit he said, "I'll call you back in five minutes." When he called back he said, "You are right, this is an Ecumenical event, not a Catholic event." He gave me different options. We chose to sit in the front pew and listen to him make a very strong statement. But you see, in Chicago, the Familias Unidas was like a magnifying glass for the movement.

Q. I recall your reflections one evening in Alabama after speaking at an NAACP rally on the significance of the Civil Rights movement for the Immigrant Rights movement, particularly in relation to taking on the leadership of the Democratic Party. You asked the question, "Did Rosa Parks consult the Democratic Party on the effects on their election strategy before she sat down on that bus in Montgomery—I don't think so!" How do you see the lessons of the Civil Rights legacy for the current movement, and can you recount some of the main points of the relationship with President Obama beginning with his first hundred days in office, his re-election action for the Dreamers, and the continuing of mass deportations and the Secure Communities program in his second term?

𝒜. There were differences. The difference is that I had to deal within the context of a party structure. Party structures are about gaining power and then maintaining power. Your values and your principles and your agenda that you utilize to gain power, many times, become secondary to whether or not you can keep power. So you will amend the agenda if you think it interferes with what it takes to keep power. Whereas in the Civil Rights movement, it was about values, about principles, and you are fighting for those. You might change strategies, you might change tactics, but you don't turn your back on the ultimate goal and say, "wait," because waiting is not an option in a Civil Rights movement.

But we learned a lot of wonderful things. For some of us in the Democratic Party, it was hard to get this done. A lot of Democrats showed up—Jan Shakowsky showed up. Congressman Keith Ellison from Minneapolis showed up. There were people that said, O.K., we'll stand with you. They understood the consequences, but they still showed up. And we did give importance to our values.

Look, here is how it was like the Civil Rights movement. I hate to personalize it, but it helps to make it clear. I have never been elected to a party leadership position. Not ever, and yet the Democratic Caucus and the Democratic Party was dictated to by what I said and how I interacted with a broader movement. They know I am not speaking for myself. They know I have a connection that is not the Democratic Party, that is not controlled by the Democratic Party—that is the immigrant community. To that extent we built something. Did it ever have a membership so that you got a card in the mail that said you were a member? No. We didn't have weekly meetings. But we created something, and to that extent it has always been very, very respectful. As many times as the leadership hasn't wanted to include me, they have. So today when people think about Luis Gutierrez and the Democratic Caucus, they think of this.

Now did we have to have political considerations? Were there some times I wanted to say things and I didn't say them? Yes. But in the end, the fact that the President of the United States took the action that he took was a response to the Familias Unidas movement.

Some of the Dreamers said, "It is about me and me first. I am special and I am important and I should go to the front of the line first, and all the rest of you, all the ten million of you, you are holding me back." But in the end, the Dreamers came into the fold too. That was a learning experience of a movement, not of a political party, but of a movement. And the greater movement, without any recrimination, said, "Yes, let's all be together, and"—check it out—the actual deferred action, even though they were the first, we were happy as a community. We said, "Good for them and good for us. It was a step in the right direction." In that sense it is like the Civil Rights movement because we understood that you don't get everything at once.

So we began to work. Unfortunately, many did not work to sign up the Dreamers. A lot of times in the movement, the protest part is hard to get people into, but then it becomes hard to get them to transition to actually doing the day-to-day work.

I still remember that, because of who we are in Chicago, and because we had always looked at both passing legislation and stopping the deportations, we were ready when we lost the House of Representatives and were weakened in the Senate. We were ready to move to the next phase. I remember that the dreamers did not come up with the demand for the deferred action. We did because we were prepared. We had been talking about it since that march in 2006. Then we hadn't thought it out, but by 2010, we had grown in sophistication and knowledge. A lot of the activists across the country thought our demand for deferred action was a bit extreme. I remember them saying, "That's a great idea but can we really get that? Does the President have that power?" You had to start this demand somewhere, and it started with us in Chicago.

Q. I believe you have spoken of two different viewpoints in the movement: those who persisted in the singular demand for a legislative solution and those who worked for an immediate end to the deportations and separation of families. Could you comment on that dichotomy and how it played out in terms of the politics of the Democratic Party Leadership and that Party's influence over various components of the immigrant rights coalition?

𝒜. For my colleagues on Capitol Hill, working on specific legislation is easier and being partisan is easier. It is within the comfort zone for a member of Congress to be partisan. Getting a bunch of Democrats to protest or voice their opposition to Republicans who are blocking immigration reform or are always proposing harsh enforcement, over time, that became easier. But getting Democrats to protest or voice their opposition to the deportation policies of their own Democratic leader, the President, that's a lot harder because the partisanship kicks in. Around the country and in Chicago, I think there were some people who felt more comfortable fighting for a bill or a legislative approach than fighting from a more morally-based perspective that deportations were breaking up families. There was probably more overlap than saying that there were two distinct camps, but occasionally one approach was easier to organize around than the other.

Q. Many of us in the movement have suggested that, like Harold Washington before you in Chicago, you showed a movement—which knew how to fight— how to win. In this light, you took a surprising stance in 2014, having previously led the pressure on the President, you suddenly, confidently, began committing the President to taking executive action if the Congress did not act (without exactly his consent), while reaching further into the Republican Party seeking unity than any other Democrat. Could you comment on how you developed that strategy and how it played out leading up to the "countdown" to July 4, 2014?

𝒜. Look, there was a real failure of the Democratic Party after the election of Barack Obama. There was a clear plan. They were going to work in a bipartisan manner, but where he was limited was in his understanding of how to obtain the vote to reach the goal. In his view, we are going to pass the bill in the Senate, we're going to get such support—that it is going to be so overwhelming, that the support from the grassroots will be so unanimous, that the House will have to pass it. So they never took into consideration, and never allowed us to develop, a plan that reflected that the Republicans had a majority in the House. The President ignored that the Republicans had a majority, and that this was the beast in 2006 we had been unable to slay. It wasn't as if we hadn't had advances before.

So I always looked at it to say, "This is a civil rights movement. This is a human rights movement"—but it needs a political consideration here, and the people in charge in the House are the Republicans, and I have to do the greatest good for the greatest number. These folks are not my enemy. My enemy is the deportations. My enemy is the separation of families. My enemy is the destructive immigration policy that this President continues to execute. That's the enemy. Anywhere I can find somebody who will stop this—there is a friend and an ally regardless of their political party. Let me tell you, I had to hold my tongue at what people would say. But I said that if I fight and condemn every ignorant statement that the other side makes, especially in conversations personally with me, I'd never get anywhere. I just have to say, "He doesn't understand so let me just work with him." My job was to get as many people together to get the best bill I could, so I never worried about Republican proposals that denied citizenship. Will they become citizens eventually? Of course they would.

We are in an even better position today. Because of the positions we took, we showed the nation that the Democratic Party was actually putting the people ahead of partisanship and party politics. Want to do it piecemeal? O.K. There was resistance, but many times when I said O.K., the rest of the movement said, "Do we really want to get into an argument here"—because I had a relationship, years of fighting, so that if I said that's all we can get, they accepted it. It's about the practicality of talking to people, what it is that the people need, and not putting yourself ahead of them.

Today I think that the Republicans just do not understand that if they developed something greater than the President's executive order, the people would move in their direction. What the President did was not immigration reform. What he did was alleviate the deportations. It was the second rung of our strategy, but it wasn't our ultimate goal. We had a lot of the characteristics of the Civil Rights movement. The movement had civil disobedience, the movement had marches, the movement had protests, the movement had taking over people's offices, and all that emerged.

I took a positive approach to the President during this last year because he said to me in March, "I am going to change this stuff, but I need more time;" and we started having conversations. I started saying that the President was going to take executive action, because if I continued to repeat it, it would become true—that we would be the ones filling in the sentences, that we would be the ones filling in the future. There was no contradiction between me saying he was going to do it and him delaying. It just meant we would have to protest some more.

I did know that he was going to do it, but one of the reasons I kept saying it was to make the 5 million a number—Look it was no coincidence that it came out to be five million! The White House said we are locked into this conversation that if it is less than five million it is not a victory. You create a demand that is meaningful. It was going to be ten years with American citizen children but then they said, "that won't get us to the five million," and so they dropped the requirement to five years residence.

Q. Some have compared the President's executive orders to the Emancipation Proclamation, in that they made the process of an eventual legislative solution irreversible. Do you agree with this assessment, and how do you see the future of the immigration issue in the United States?

𝒜. Look, it [the President's executive order] made stark the difference between Republicans and Democrats—between those who believed in immigrants and those who did not—and it made people have to step up. We have always said to the President, "You have to be our leader, you have to set the example and they will follow you, including the Republicans, regardless of what you see them doing today." They must eventually act to compete on the basis of the actions the President has taken vis-a-vis our community. And our community now can clearly judge who has their back and who doesn't— whereas before it was kind of muddled with "the deporter in chief," etc. But now 90% of Latinos support the President—that's irreversible!

But that's an outgrowth of our work. It didn't happen in a vacuum. That's the protests, that's the testimonies, that's the going to this church and that church, impacting the way people think and the way the media portrays the issue. It's about building consciousness in a community to the point where they say, Yes, I will take it. So none of this happened without our work. I just want to say this. In the end, it also demonstrates that individuals do matter. People do matter. You need many people in the collective, but individual people do matter. There were times when it was just me and you or Emma on the road, with the logistical support from my office. It was good that we did have a campaign fund, Gutierrez for Congress, because we never wanted to use the office expense account, although we could have legitimately. I still remember that we were driving in Indiana, and I remember telling Emma that you better hope that nothing happens to this car, because if we disappear I don't know who is going to go to the next church. At some point we had to say, "We're it, Let's keep it going."

Q. While the immigration issues have been formally debated in U.S. domestic policy terms, it is clear that the relationship between the U.S. and Latin America, especially with Mexico, Central America and the Caribbean, is at the root of these issues. For instance, many point to NAFTA as the engine leading to the crossing of 5 million Mexican undocumented workers in the 1990s. How do you think the unity that developed in the Latino community over the last decade and the energetic growth of the Latino community in the United States will—or could—affect these relationships—including the relationship with Puerto Rico?

𝒜. Moving forward, given what I believe will be more growth in economic activity with Mexico, and subsequent stabilization in Central America, we will have to invest in economic development. Look, a lot of times America thinks we are going to take a kind act of generosity with our neighbors south of the border—no! It is in our self-interest to act. If we reduced drug consumption in America by 25%, it would mean billions of dollars and thousands of lives. We can't do that if we are not cooperating, if we are not contributing to civil institutions that are strong in Mexico and Central America. The drug cartels impact what happens in the lives of millions of Americans every day, and the drug trafficking and the cost to our society.

Millions of Americans wake up everyday to the reality that they owe their jobs to what gets consumed by Mexican workers. Mexico is our second largest trading partner. If you really shut down our border to nothing, do you realize the damage it would do to the economy of the United States?

The Ecuadorians are electing people. The Dominicans are electing people. More and more those people are coming into the Untied States of America. The Mexican government has been at it for a long time. They have a policy of no interference, but they have probably the largest consular operation in the world in the United States. So there will be more and more influence on U.S. policies towards Latin America.

Q. Finally, we could not close this interview without asking you to comment on the unique relationship you have had with Emma Lozano, Elvira Arellano, and Familia Latina Unida—and to the Chicago-based coalition between Mexicans and Puerto Ricans that has not only supported self-determination in Puerto Rico, but the release of Oscar Lopez and the Puerto Rican political prisoners.

𝒜. I have to say that a very unique set of circumstances creates the person that I am today. Back when I was at Northeastern in the seventies, I still remember the Chicano student union, the African American students, the Puerto Rican student organization—we were all there. We didn't always get along, but we were talking to each other. We always had a conversation with one another.

And I think the commitment that Emma Lozano, that Familia Latina Unida, that the church has to this movement, has been a basis of my strength. A lot of people say it's tough taking on the President, but it's not tough walking into the White House if you know you have a committed cadre of people that are there, and that you are reflecting their views, and to the extent you are reflecting their views you are together and you are protected. So I always felt protected. The other thing is, it's always good to have company along the road. I don't know many people who do anything all by themselves, so God bless them, they are greater men and women than I am. I need the camaraderie, I need the support, I need the warmth and the strength that was derived from this relationship. Emma and the movement here drive me; it pushes me; I push it; we push each other. We are always together because we know none of us will turn our backs on our immigrant families.

In terms of the Puerto Rican community, show me another place in the United States of America where the national origin of Latinos is 75% or greater, and the Congressman does not reflect that percentage. Are you going to elect a Puerto Rican in L.A.? In the South Bronx, you are going to elect a Mexican American—really? But in the city of Chicago I don't hear it anymore. Nobody notices it anymore.

Do I notice a greater warmth of support from the Mexican community? Yes. You see, for Puerto Ricans, I am kind of like the baseball guy who did good, the teacher that won the apple award, the actor that won the Oscar, I made the community proud. When it comes to the greater community, I was a soldier, a fighter, protecting them from injustice. There will always be a great support on this basis. That is why in the Puerto Rican community, when it comes to those who understand Vieques, the prisoners, Oscar Lopez, there is more of a sense there because it is about justice, not just about pride. It is better than being the Puerto Rican CEO of a corporation because "this guy fights for justice for us." I understand that. But to this day, the greater community across the United States does not understand it.

So I'll end with this. I have learned so much over the last few years. I remember going to Pilsen with a reporter from WTTW as part of a program where they take you around Chicago to show "his Chicago." I remember the look of astonishment on her face when we walked into Nuevo Leon, and one table after another asked to take a picture, and asked the reporter to hold their phone cameras, relegating her to taking a picture between "us and our congressman." She didn't understand, because she never saw me in that light; she had no reason to understand why people had such an intimate relationship with me. I understand that—and that's Chicago, and that's special. I hope that other congressmen have this relationship. I doubt it very much.

APPENDICES

Appendix A

An Account of the First March

Interview with Father Marco Cardenas and Emma Lozano
August 2011

FATHER MARCO CARDENAS: I DON'T REMEMBER EXACTLY THE DATE, BUT I remember one evening I was watching the news and suddenly appears this lady by the name of Roxanna Pulido. She was inviting people to come forward and form a Minuteman group in Chicago. So it caught my attention and I listened very closely, and she started accusing the immigrants for all the failures and all the problems and she was pretty much—for me, as I was listening to her, I thought, this is a bunch of lies and this is totally untrue. I don't agree with her and I have to do something about it. All of her statements have no basis.

I took the phone and called Pistolero and he said, "I watched the news as well," and I said, "What are you going to do about it?" And he said, "Tomorrow I am going to make some comments on the radio," and I said, "Don't you think we should do something more about it?" He said, "What?" I said, "If they are forming the minutemen, then we have to be the voice of the voiceless."

He said, "What if you join with me tomorrow at 5 am on the program?" And I said, "Absolutely, I will come tomorrow." So the following day I went to the radio station. I thought it was going to be a matter of just a few minutes to comment on the statement the lady made, but then the calls started invading the station and I ended up being there until 11 o'clock. So pretty much it showed that people were tired of being in the shadows; that people were talking about their struggles, their contributions, so then, you know, I mentioned to him, I said to Pistolero, "Why don't we NOT just form a coalition or an organization. Let's march!" He said, "Father, do you think people will come out?" I said, "I think so. I think we have nothing to fear. So let's do it."

At the end of the program, we spent about five minutes talking about how to do that. Pistolero said, "What about you coming once a week to the program, and you and I will extend the invitation to march." We became a little nervous. What if we call for the march and nobody shows up? So we said, "Let's plan on doing something not really big initially and see what the response of the people is. Let's give ourselves a period of time, and we will sense the interest of the people in participating in this march."

Emma Lozano: Alexandro Dominguez called and said, "Emma, listen to the radio. Right now the Pistolero show is on with Padre Marco, and they are talking about a march." I called up Elvira and sent her to the place they were transmitting. Elvira— who is a very disciplined soldier—went right away.

We had done many marches before, but never with the aid of the radio. Our marches had never been more than 10,000 people and we knew that with the radio this was going to be huge. My heart was beating, and I could already hear the people's footsteps. Elvira went and made contact with Pistolero, and we offered to bring him the children of the families, the children whose parents were being deported. So Pistolero put them on the radio, and the children made some spots to go on the radio promoting the march.

Father Marco: Yes, I was asked to make some of those spots with Richard, and Saulito and Emma. Then Pistolero started transmitting from different stores around the community. Wherever Pistolero was transmitting the show, we would come with poster boards and markers, and people would make their own signs.

I told Pistolero, "I don't think we should first go downtown because this is going to make the people upset. Let's go south, somewhere on the South Side." When we were talking about it, I thought I should start inviting other priests, other pastors from different denominations. I remember I had the opportunity to be in front of the mic. I would address myself to the other pastors. I said, "It is our duty, a matter of justice, to come together. We are not asking for the impossible, and we need to do this."

The people would call and say, "We are with you but we don't know for sure if we will be able to participate." We started getting a little bit nervous, and Pistolero and I thought people might not be able to come out. So I started saying to myself, if a lot of us come out, there will be no way that Immigration will arrest all of us.

Emma: Pistolero was calling for the march and you, as a religious person, were telling them it was all right to come out, and reading some passages from the Bible.

Father Marco: Yes, I remember reading some passage about the Israelites in Egypt, about the Book of Exodus, talking about immigration movements in other countries. Every time in the following weeks I focused on "Don't be afraid." And every time Pistolero said, "Do you think one thousand will participate," I would say, "Oh no, twenty thousand!"

Then Pistolero asked me to call other pastors and deacons in the church. And so after the radio program, I would come back to my church and start calling other pastors. I was amazed by the responses and how many said, "We already know, and we are with you."

Then we got a call from someone who owned a big department store on

Ashland, who offered us the parking lot at the Swaporama. Pistolero announced that, "We are going to march on the South Side to the Swaporama, and we are going to march on the sidewalk. This person who owns the store will allow us to have our event in his parking lot."

And then someone else called and said, "I will pay for the sound system," and then another one called to donate something else. So I felt, pretty much, we are getting a lot of support, and I thought, let's call the clubs—the club Michoacán, the club Guerrero, etc. So I called to ascertain if they would participate. To my big surprise they said, "Father, no, we are not interested." I was amazed that the leaders of these clubs, not one of them wanted to participate. Neither did the official immigrant rights coalitions, the funded organizations.

It was interesting, though, that the big stores like Jimenez said they would pay for the water. And some guys who owned buses offered buses, and others said, we will pay for the buses.

I remember a senior citizen called, a white lady. She said, "I don't understand Spanish very well, but someone told me about the march." She said she would pay for three buses. Even though she was not Latina!

So then it was like a snowball. And then one morning, again I came to the radio station, and Jerry Ryan, the manager of that time, called me. I thought maybe he was upset, but he said, "Stop by my office." All kinds of ideas come through your mind. I didn't know what was going to happen. I was so grateful to God when he said, "Whatever you need you can count on us." He started telling me that his grandparents were immigrants from Ireland, and they had been parishioners at my church, St. Basil, in those days. "So whatever you need from us, you can count on us."

We started making recommendations: be quiet, don't throw garbage on the streets, don't be belligerent to the police, wear white, don't bring Mexican flags,and don't be afraid. We started to make an appeal to the patrons, to the bosses, to allow the workers to march. Then we got calls from them that they were supporting the march and would close that day.

And there was a slogan, "The Sleeping Giant Awakes!" We tried to invite several speakers and pretty much they all said no, but Emma got some people to appear on the program.

Emma: We had already planned to go to Washington, D.C., with the families and the children to visit different congressman and senators on the days before the march was scheduled. So we would be coming back the day before the march, and we thought the publicity about the families coming back from D.C. would help to mobilize for the march. So I went to Carlos to arrange for some of the old timers to MC the program. We were in charge of renting all the buses and getting the permits and the bathroom and the stage and the sound system. Responding to the radio, the people were donating, but they couldn't donate to the station, so they donated to us. And we produced the flyers and distributed them everywhere. Meanwhile, on the show, we also had both you and Rosalba Pena, who was an attorney, and that was important so that she could talk about the law and answer questions. Even though the recommendation was to use the sidewalks so we wouldn't interrupt the traffic, I said, "I hope that we have a good turnout!"

Another *locutor* on another station, called Chocolate, started to call for a march on another day to compete with Pistolero. So Elvira had a press conference calling for unity, and we organized a meeting with both of the *locutores* to get agreement on the date and the place. Chocolate promoted the march and came with a delegation—but this day was Pistolero's.

Pistolero contacted his friends in California and Washington, D.C., and all over the country, and he believed that they would call for something similar in their towns. But I believe they were all watching what would happen in Chicago. After the July march, Pistolero got Piolin on the radio and challenged Piolin to do the same thing in California. I remember Piolin was surprised that Pisto was on his radio show. And that's when all the other radio DJs began to say, "We have to do something."

Father Marco: When we started getting all these responses I started worrying about my order, the Claretians. Should I explain to them what is going on? On the other hand, they were aware and some of the Claretians came out to the march. They knew what was happening, never said anything, but were there to support me.

The day of the march we were amazed. I remember that there were more than a hundred thousand. We tried to walk on the sidewalks, but we had to take the whole street. The police were very civil, very friendly, but as we were marching more people joined us, so the march was getting bigger and bigger.

We had to go around the bridge on Ashland because they said the weight of the people would make the bridge fall down. The police closed the parking lot of the Swaporama because there were so many people.

I remember, then, that once we were there, all kinds of leaders showed up, and all of them wanted to get the microphone. Some of them didn't even want Rosalba to speak, and I never got the microphone. But that wasn't my intention. "Let's march. Let's not be afraid. We are planting a little seed. Let's just show immigration that we are here and we are not going anywhere."

I remember the following day I went back to the station to thank the people, and I said to Pistolero that this is just the beginning. That was when other leaders came up and began participating. Let's organize a second march.

Appendix B

Statement on Entering Sanctuary

Elvira Arellano
Adalberto United Methodist Church, Chicago, IL
August 15, 2006

TODAY, I WAS ORDERED BY THE DEPARTMENT OF HOMELAND SECURITY TO TURN myself in for deportation at 10 W. Jackson Street in Chicago, Illinois.

I believe that this order is selective, vindictive, retaliatory, and inhumane. One year ago, I was granted a stay of deportation while private bills on my behalf were pending in the Congress. Nothing has changed since that stay was granted. Homeland Security has the legal power—and I believe, the obligation—to extend this stay of deportation.

In the three years since I was first arrested in my home in front of my son, I have struggled day in and day out for all of the 12 million undocumented in this country, for the families and for the children, many of who like mine are U.S. citizens. I am not a criminal. I am not a terrorist. I am a mother and a worker.

I am also a person of faith and scripture. In the Book of Acts, Peter tells the authorities, I leave it to you to judge whether I should obey you or obey God. For my part, I cannot deny what I have seen and heard.

What I have seen and heard is the injustices of a broken law heaped upon our families. We were welcomed here to work and pay taxes. Now we are being tortured and our families broken to serve the interest of racist politicians.

President Bush has said he is in favor of legalization. He has said that Family Values do not stop at the Rio Grande. And yet President Bush is pursuing a relentless policy of raids, deportations, separation of families, and sanctions. This is hypocrisy.

I cannot submit to hypocrisy. My faith will not let me.

I have asked for and been granted sanctuary by my church. I am here and I will remain here for as long as necessary.

If Homeland Security chooses to send its agents on the Holy Ground to arrest me, then I will know that God wants me to be an example of the hatred and hypocrisy of the current policy of this government. I am at peace with my decision.

I have instructed my attorney to send a letter to Ms. Deborah Achem at Homeland Security informing her of my decision and my location. I have done this because I do not wish my friends and community to be subjected to raids and harassment. Nor do I want Homeland Security to use me as an excuse to arrest and deport others like me and to try to destroy their families and the lives of their children.

Let this press conference put it on the public record that Homeland Security knows where I am.

I ask President Bush to pray and to listen to God. I ask him to stop his administration from doing what it is doing to all of the families and all of the children.

Appendix C
Announcement on Leaving Sanctuary

Elvira Arellano
Adalberto United Methodist Church, Chicago, IL
August 15, 2007

Flanked by Jacqueline Jackson and about 100 religious and community leaders, Elvira made the following statement in both English and Spanish:

FOR THE LAST 15 DAYS, I HAVE FASTED AND PRAYED. I HAVE CONSULTED WITH spiritual leaders and with those who face the same situation I face. I have made my decision.

Today marks one year since I came here to sanctuary, to live in this church and raise my U.S. citizen son in peaceful witness against an unjust law. One year ago, many of us believed that the government of this nation had the will to fix the broken law, but that will also appears now to be broken.

Like many others, I came here to work. I came because of what NAFTA and other U.S. economic policies had done to my country, in which I could no longer find work.

I came here to work, America, and you welcomed my labor. Although I had to struggle very hard, you invited me to work hard, and I did. You invited me to pay taxes, and I did. You invited me to buy a home, and I did. You invited me to contribute my earnings to your economy, and I did.

As I did these things you welcomed me to do, I had a child, a son, who has rights as a U.S. citizen and who knows no other country but this country. I promised God that I would raise him in God's ways and that I would teach him that he had dignity and rights, and that he was a child of God, not a piece of garbage to be used and thrown away.

Then, America, you were struck by the terrorists. You were angry and afraid and filled with hatred. You could not find Bin Laden, but you found Elvira Arellano, because I was not hiding. You decided to change your rules to protect yourself and to drive out those you had invited in to serve your dinners, clean your houses, take care of your children, and cut your grass.

You say that I broke the law by crossing the border and working without proper papers. I did that. Yet that law was only something written on a piece of paper, and I was not a lawyer. I am a worker, and you offered me work. I am a consumer, and you accepted my hard won earnings. I am a taxpayer, and you took my taxes.

My son Saul and I are not alone. We are twenty million people, 12 million undocumented and our legal and U.S. citizen children, spouses, and extended families. We do not disappear because you change the rules. We have the lives we have built here, when you wanted us to be here.

Out of fear and hatred of an enemy you cannot find, you have set out to destroy our lives and our families. As you knocked on my door, you are knocking on thousands of doors, ripping mothers and fathers away from their terrified children. You have a list of 17 million social security No Match numbers, and you are following that list as if we were terrorists and criminals instead of workers with families. You are denying us work and the seniority and benefits we have earned, and you are taking the property we have saved for and bought.

We respect your high goal to be a nation of laws. We understand your fears. But where is the love and justice in your hearts? We supported a solution that would restore the rule of law and allow you to protect your borders. We accepted the fines and tests you wanted to impose on us. But this was not enough.

Bin Laden has won. He has turned you into a nation of hate and fear. Out of fear and hatred, you are destroying our lives and the communities and churches we are a part of. This is not the way God teaches us to live.

When I entered sanctuary, I promised God that I would stay here and raise my son in his country, no matter what the consequences. God has protected me for this long year, but I cannot sit by now and watch the lives of mothers and fathers like me, and children like Saul, be destroyed. I believe in my heart that the people of this nation do not, in their hearts, want to destroy our lives, our families, and our communities. I believe, however, that we must come forward in the witness of faith to bring a resolution to this crisis.

Therefore, I have made my decision. On September 12th, I will go to Washington D.C. I will go to pray and fast in front of the Congress. I will go with my Bible and my son, and I will read to him from the Holy Scriptures, as I do every day.

If this government would separate me from my son, let them do it in front of the men and women who have the responsibility to fix this broken law and uphold the principles of human dignity.

I will accept whatever God gives me to accept. But I ask my community, the families facing separation, to join me. I ask all people of conscience and good will to join me in eight hours of prayer, from 2 p.m. until 10 p.m. on the Washington Mall in front of Congress. Together in faith we will try to heal the will that is broken in Congress so that Congress can fix the broken law.

From now until September 12th, I will pray for my people, and I will pray for this nation. May God Bless and Have Mercy on us all.

Appendix D
The Campaign for American
Children and Families

La Causa de Familias Unidas
May 2011

CHILDREN UNDER SIEGE: THE CONSEQUENCES OF THE IRRESPONSIBILITY OF A NATION

We are talking about 5.1 million of our children:

Who are the 5.1 million children with unauthorized parents?

• 4 million or 80% are U.S. citizens
• 1.1 million are themselves unauthorized or legal permanent residents

What percentage of the U.S. population do they represent?

These represent 7% of all the children in the United States under 18.

• U.S. citizen children (the children of mixed status families) are younger, so that 90% of pre-school age children with unauthorized parents are U.S. citizens, whereas only 60% of children in high school with unauthorized parents are U.S. citizens.
• One out of every sixteen K-12 students is a child of unauthorized parents; 70% of these are U.S. citizens; 1 out of 50 are themselves unauthorized.

Is this population of children growing?

Yes. Although there has been a slight decline in the number of undocumented adults, the numbers of children of unauthorized parents is increasing steadily.

• The number of children has grown 42% faster than the population of unauthorized adults.
• The birth rate of these children is much greater than of the citizen families because:

  1) There are more two-person head-of-family households. Over 50% of the families of the 5.1 million children are two-person head-of-household families, and are married, while the average for U.S. citizen families is only 21%

  2) The average age of the families is younger than the median age of U.S. citizen families

  3) There is a higher fertility rate

What percentage of the population—and the potential workforce—will the 5.1 million represent in the future?

A growing percentage...

- The children of unauthorized parents now represent 7% of all children in the U.S. under 18. This percentage will continue to increase over the next five to ten years. As the aging U.S. workforce declines, children of the undocumented will make up as much as 10% of the U.S. workforce.
- The U.S. citizen Population is much older than the immigrant and mixed status population and is having fewer children—and therefore the children of unauthorized parents will represent an increasingly large percentage of the U.S. population and workforce.
- The U.S. will require more young workers and more well educated young workers than are being produced by U.S. citizen families to provide for an economy strong enough to support the increasing number of retirees in the global economy. (The average retirement age for the baby boomers began last month!)

Are these families and their children likely to leave the U.S. voluntarily?

No. In fact, while there has been an increase in the number of undocumented workers leaving the country voluntarily this year because of stricter enforcement and declining opportunities, families with U.S. citizen or dream act eligible children show no evidence of leaving voluntarily.

- In addition, most of these families are Mexican: about 75%, with easier access to return if deported.
- Over 100,000 U.S. citizen children saw one of their parents deported by official estimates in 2008. Anecdotal evidence shows that a great number of these, motivated by their responsibility and ties to family, returned or attempted to return illegally.

Is there evidence that women are crossing the border to have children born as U.S. citizen children?

No.

- 90% of children born to an unauthorized parent were born after the parent had been here 15 months or more. 50% were born of mothers who had been here 5 years or more.
- Instead, the high birthrate reflects the high percentage of marriage and the youthful age of the young workers who come to the United States to work without papers.

What is happening to the 5.1 million children?

These children are growing up with unequal access to education and health care and in poverty—although in strong families.

- 1 out of 3 live in poverty, higher than the national average of less than 1 in 5

- Studies show they have a slower rate of cognitive development because of lack of access to programs like Head Start, Day Care Centers, Program offerings both in the schools and in the communities because their parents can't qualify for them or don't have access to information about them.
- Children of unauthorized parents are twice as likely to lack health insurance as children of citizens or legal residents.

These children are growing up in high stress homes:
- Because of the constant threat of deportation of one or more parent
- Because of the necessity of hiding information and avoiding the risk of exposure of their parents
- Because of the long work hours, often below the minimum wage, of their parents.

Children are growing up in families where one parent has been deported
- Because they cannot afford to follow the deported parent who often is unable to find work in the country to which they are deported.
- Because the remaining parent seeks to maintain their children's right to continue their lives in the only community they have ever known, with the opportunities for a future that they have a right to.

What would happen to the 5.1 million if they returned with unauthorized family members to their native countries?
- Economic realities in Mexico, Central America, and the Caribbean mean that they would be raised in severe poverty with poor access to education and would return when they were of age, as early as 15 or 16, to claim their rights as U.S. citizens—unprepared to participate successfully in the U.S. economy—and become a part of a permanent underclass.
- Because many of the families have one parent that is a citizen or a legal permanent resident, the children would be separated from one parent or the other, because economic realities would require that the parent who can stay legally in the country stay and work to provide for them when the other parent is deported.

THERE IS NO FREEDOM WITHOUT RESPONSIBILITY!

Saying that this is a nation of laws does not free this nation from taking responsibility for its failure to observe these laws. The Reagan administration recognized that the nation itself had failed to comply with immigration law and sponsored the first amnesty, after implementing a moratorium on deportations. Following that partial remediation, the nation and its businesses actually offered employment to 12 million more undocumented workers, accepted their irretrievable contributions to social security, gave many of them tax numbers, and collected their taxes, while banks and unscrupulous mortgage companies sold them mortgages.

While it is true that millions of workers crossed the border without authorization and worked without authorization, it is also true that almost every component of this nation's economic system knowingly utilized their labor, and every citizen of the nation received the benefits of their labor and their financial contributions to the government. Meanwhile, neither Democratic nor Republican administrations moved to enforce the increasingly stringent laws against employers.

It should be said that the current enforcement-only policy leading to 1100 deportations every day punishes the most vulnerable of those who violated the laws of this nation. At the same time, those U.S. citizens who benefitted from the frequently cruel exploitation of the undocumented have pocketed their profits and have gotten off scot-free.

Because undocumented labor was not officially recognized for its part in the nation's economic system, the hard won protections for—and right to the dignity of—American workers were never applied to these 12 million undocumented workers. Principal among these rights is the right to form families and raise children.

As a consequence of the nation's irresponsibility and violation of its own laws, there are now 5.1 million children, 80% of whom are U.S. citizens, the rest children who know no other country but this one, who face discrimination, inequality, and perhaps the greatest violation of their human rights—the right to be raised in the covenant of a family.

Morally and spiritually, this nation must redeem itself for the wrongs it has committed and the consequences now visited on these 5.1 million young human beings. Economically, the nation's economy may well depend on preparing them for the roles they can and should be allowed to play in the future of this country.

The failure to accept responsibility for the consequences of unethical practices has plunged this nation and the world into the greatest economic collapse since the great depression. Our government has responded by rewarding the majority of those responsible with greater wealth. A nation that does not take responsibility for its actions is a nation doomed to failure.

The consequences of this nation's permissive exploitation of 12 million human beings, driven here not by the search for the American Dream, but because of what the American nightmare did to the economies of their own countries, are in front of our eyes. The consequences are 5.1 million children who are being denied equal opportunity and the fundamental security of family.

There is no freedom without responsibility. Dignity, and human rights, and a necessary role in this nation's future require that action be taken to stop the separation of families IMMEDIATELY by moratorium and then by reform of the law.

LET US REMEMBER, AS THESE CHILDREN GROW ANOTHER YEAR OLDER, THAT JUSTICE DELAYED IS JUSTICE DENIED!

The Call

We call to the attention of the President and the nation the cruel and unacceptable realities of family separation faced now by 5.1 million children. 80% of these children are U.S. citizens, and the remainder would have been eligible for the DREAM Act solution, which enjoyed the support of a majority of members of both the House and Senate.

In order to provide immediate interim relief to these American Families and Children now threatened with separation because of our current broken immigration laws, we hereby petition President Barack Obama to *immediately* use his executive powers to expand hardship eligibility for humanitarian parole in place, deferred action, or improved access to stateside waivers to these families

We further call to the attention of the President and the nation, that current enforcement programs that partner with local law enforcement authorities are detrimental to police-community relations and have failed in their design to target those with criminal convictions. We call on the President to immediately suspend the 287(g) and Secure Communities programs.

Appendix E

Message to Congressman Gutierrez

Walter Coleman, Emma Lozano, and Elvira Arellano
March 2014

LUIS, WE WANT TO EXPRESS OUR CONCERN AS TO THE NEXT STEPS. WE WERE geared up with allies across the country to demand executive action after July 4th. The delay has created confusion, and the talk of extension of demand for action to the lame duck session and beyond is devastatingly demoralizing.

In order to pressure **the President to act** there must be a declaration that the Republican controlled Congress **will not** act. That declaration appears to grow in conflict with a continual hopeful and optimistic perspective on the possibility of Republican action—although the sincere quest for that possibility has created *enormous credibility* in declaring that the time is over for such action.

From our perspective, we need to pull the trigger on the Republicans in July in order to unleash the demand on the president for executive action in August. Secondly, we need to generate a standard for the level of executive action: e.g., an extension of DACA, not just a limited prosecutorial discretion.

Following is our understanding of the unfolding of the current phase of the campaign for legalization: Are we sticking to the deadline? If so, what moves can we make to raise the standard on executive orders?

Timetable of this phase of the struggle

1. Following the mandate represented by Obama's reelection, a sincere effort is made to develop an immigration reform proposal in both the House and the Senate. Our perspective was to gain the greatest possible protection for the greatest number of people. We recognized the Republican control of the House and realized that there needed to be a Republican bill.

2. The collapse of the group of eight in the House, *provoked by Democratic leadership*, in effect spells the end of this process. On reflection Ryan, Bush, etc., were probably more interested in cleaning up their own image than in passing legislation.

3. The Senate passes a bill with a special road to citizenship and Democrats demand that the House accept it. This effectively further polarized the situation in the House, undermining those few Republicans sincere about putting forth a series of proposals.

4. The demand gained steam for executive action if the Congress fails to act.

5. We continue to pursue Republican participation in a reform proposal with little result in the polarized situation. However, frustration at the *sincere pursuit* very effectively heightened the justification for executive action.

6. The caucus resolution for executive action moves the President to commit to executive action if the congress doesn't act. A "July 4th" deadline is established in the public.

7. The President gets a delay by an appeal from established immigrant rights organizations.

8. The delay begins to take root and members of congress start talking about the lame duck session. Here we go again. The defeat of the majority leader by a know-nothing Tea Party candidate effectively seals the possibility for a meaningful Republican alternative. Whatever proposal produced by the Republican congress at this point—if any—will *not* provide security for the undocumented and will be stalemated in the complex process of unification with the Senate. Moreover, if the Republicans push through a totally unacceptable proposal—or bring a proposal to the floor and vote it down—then the President will be in the position of defying congressional action instead of acting on the inaction of the House on a bill passed by the Senate.

9. Our only real hope of temporary protection and forward motion is through executive action. In order to trigger executive action, there must be a credible assertion that the Republican Congress will not act or is incapable of action on reform at this time—because the Republican Party has allowed itself to be held captive to the Tea Party. If this does not come in July, there will not be a case for executive action, and this horror goes on. Obviously those most identified with a sincere effort to work with Republicans on their own terms—mostly you— have the *most credibility* in declaring the effort stalemated. *But when?* We are concerned that the President would rather let this issue fester for another two years.

Luis, we have the greatest respect for the commitment, genius and role you have played, both as a legislator and a movement leader. Moreover, we have noted the enormous respect you have generated in very broad and disparate sectors because of the sincerity with which you have pursued a legislative solution, exhausting all options, without regard to partisanship, with a commitment to protecting the lives of millions of people. One of the effects of this sincerity has been that few want to just flatly turn you down to your face. Barack and Johnson, who have a genuine commitment to civil rights for Black people, no matter what they say, do not have a real commitment to the undocumented and their families. They will use their positions to placate you and string all of us along. The Clintons want this issue alive for the next election. Those who continue to say that legislation is possible are doing so to pursue their own agendas, collect their fat salaries, and gather influence and privileges from the game of partisan politics.

The historical reality is that the Republican leadership enabled the control of Congress by truly racist parochial forces after the 2008 defeats—while the Democratic Party of Obama and the Clintons moved continually to the right. We are in a very weak position with few cards to play but—on this issue—have a way to move. We should take it.

Luis, we need to protect our people. The devastation of these deportations is deepening every day and, perhaps most importantly, *people are losing hope in their lives*. Your hard work has positioned you to pull the trigger on the Republican-controlled Congress—with plenty of recrimination to the Democrats for their failure to negotiate. We have never had a stronger position with Obama in terms of getting him to act.

In addition to your excellent leadership, many have worked tirelessly to secure for you this pivotal position in history. We feel very strongly that you should use the position you have now to declare legislation dead in the House and put our case for meaningful executive action before the President. It seems this would require outlining an energetic July campaign with speeches at the key national Latino organizational events and a corresponding grassroots drive.

We think this reflects the position of every *honest force* in our coalition.

—*Slim, Emma, Elvira*

Appendix F

"Craft an Immigration Policy"

Congressman Luis Gutierrez, in the House of Representatives
113th Congress, 2nd Session. June 15, 2014
Available on YouTube at https://www.youtube.com/watch?v=_O_oneQGHvc

MADAM SPEAKER, I CAME TO THE FLOOR ON APRIL 2 TO TELL MY REPUBLICAN colleagues that they had three months to craft an immigration policy before the July Fourth recess. At the time, there was still hope that sensible Republicans would see that their existence as a national party depended on getting the immigration issue resolved. I came back to this well almost every week to remind my Republican colleagues that time was running out. With the nation gripped by World Cup fever, let me give you a visual representation of my message for the last three months.

[YELLOW CARD] I gave Republicans a yellow card to put them on warning that they must act on immigration—and if they failed to act—they would be out of the game. Having met with the President in March, I knew he was prepared to give Republicans time to craft an immigration reform bill but if they failed to take action, I knew the President intended to use his pen and pad to save families at risk of being deported.

Let's review where we stand three months after I gave you that first warning.

A year ago this Friday marks the one-year anniversary of passage of the bi-partisan Senate immigration reform bill that passed with 68 votes in the Senate. We had our own group of eight in the House crafting a tough but fair immigration compromise, but politics slowed us down and the effort collapsed. Some leaders in the Republican Party—knowing that immigration reform is the only way to achieve border security and workplace verification like E-Verify, legal immigration to feed our economy, and compassion and justice for how we treat our immigrant neighbors and friends—some in the Republican Party kept trying, and I thank them.

On my side of the aisle we kept an open mind. When the Speaker said no to the Senate bill, I said, OK, let's find a way to craft a House bill. When Republicans said no to a conference, I said, we will find a way to make it work if that is what needs to be done.

Piecemeal bills they said, not a comprehensive bill—I said, we will work with you. No direct path to citizenship for most immigrants, well, we didn't like it, but we kept talking. No one tried harder than I did to keep the two parties talking about how to move forward on immigration.

There are Members of the House Republican Conference who need immigration reform politically, others who want it because it restores law and order, and others for reasons deeply grounded in their conservative philosophy. Still others in the Republican Conference are fighting for reform out of a sense of compassion and doing the right thing, as my friend Mr. Diaz-Balart from Florida has.

But months passed and Republicans turned their backs on their own members, turned their backs on the American people, turned their backs on the business community, on Latino and Asian voters, and on those trying to save the Republican Party from itself.

You know, Madam Speaker, I kept hoping the better angels in the Republican Party would tamp down the irrational and angry angels blocking reform the American people want and deserve.

And then the last straw. As violence, poverty, and gangs drive families out of Central America, I see Republican Members of Congress and their allies in talk radio and TV taking advantage of a humanitarian crisis to score cheap political points. In a few hours, the Judiciary Committee—which has done nothing to help move the Republican Party and the Congress forward on immigration—will hold a hearing on what it calls "Administration-made disaster at the U.S.-Mexico border."

I gave you the warning three-months ago and now I have no other choice. *[RED CARD]* You are done. You are done. Leave the field. Too many flagrant offenses and unfair attacks and too little action. You are out. Hit the showers. It's the red card for you.

First of all, your chance to play a role in how immigration and deportation policies are carried out this year is over. Having been given ample time and space to craft legislation, you failed, the President now has no other choice but to act within existing law to ensure that our deportation policies are humane, that due-process rights are protected, that detention conditions are as they should be, and most importantly—that the people we are deporting are detriments to our communities, not assets to our families, economy, and society.

And I think we all know that you are out when it comes to the White House. By taking no action—even after repeated warnings—you have decided it is up to the Democrats to pick Supreme Court Justices, conduct foreign policy, and carry out all of the functions of the Executive Branch for a generation, for the next thirty years. The Republican presidential nominee, whoever he or she may be, will enter the race with an Electoral College deficit they cannot make up.

Republicans in the House simply have no answer when it comes to immigration reform, and Republicans have failed America and failed themselves.

Madam Speaker, it is now time for the President to act.

Appendix G
Announcement of Immigration Executive Order

President Barack Obama
November 20, 2014
Available on YouTube at https://www.youtube.com/watch?v=wejt939QXko

THE PRESIDENT: My fellow Americans, tonight, I'd like to talk with you about immigration.

For more than 200 years, our tradition of welcoming immigrants from around the world has given us a tremendous advantage over other nations. It's kept us youthful, dynamic, and entrepreneurial. It has shaped our character as a people with limitless possibilities—people not trapped by our past, but able to remake ourselves as we choose.

But today, our immigration system is broken—and everybody knows it.

Families who enter our country the right way and play by the rules watch others flout the rules. Business owners who offer their workers good wages and benefits see the competition exploit the undocumented by paying them far less. All of us take offense to anyone who reaps the rewards of living in America without taking on the responsibilities of living in America. And undocumented immigrants who desperately want to embrace those responsibilities see little option but to remain in the shadows, or risk their families being torn apart.

It's been this way for decades. And for decades, we haven't done much about it. When I took office, I committed to fixing this broken immigration system. And I began by doing what I could to secure our borders. Today, we have more agents and technology deployed to secure our southern border than at any time in our history. And over the past six years, illegal border crossings have been cut by more than half. Although this summer, there was a brief spike in unaccompanied children being apprehended at our border, the number of such children is now actually lower than it's been in nearly two years. Overall, the number of people trying to cross our border illegally is at its lowest level since the 1970s. Those are the facts.

Meanwhile, I worked with Congress on a comprehensive fix, and last year, 68 Democrats, Republicans, and independents came together to pass a bipartisan bill in the Senate. It wasn't perfect. It was a compromise. But it reflected common sense. It would have doubled the number of border patrol agents while giving undocumented immigrants a pathway to citizenship if they paid a fine, started paying their taxes, and went to the back of the line. And independent experts said that it would help grow our economy and shrink our deficits.

Had the House of Representatives allowed that kind of bill a simple yes-or-no vote, it would have passed with support from both parties, and today it would be the law. But for a year and a half now, Republican leaders in the House have refused to allow that simple vote.

Now, I continue to believe that the best way to solve this problem is by working together to pass that kind of common sense law. But until that happens, there are actions I have the legal authority to take as President—the same kinds of actions taken by Democratic and Republican presidents before me—that will help make our immigration system more fair and more just.

Tonight, I am announcing those actions.

First, we'll build on our progress at the border with additional resources for our law enforcement personnel so that they can stem the flow of illegal crossings, and speed the return of those who do cross over.

Second, I'll make it easier and faster for high-skilled immigrants, graduates, and entrepreneurs to stay and contribute to our economy, as so many business leaders have proposed.

Third, we'll take steps to deal responsibly with the millions of undocumented immigrants who already live in our country.

I want to say more about this third issue, because it generates the most passion and controversy. Even as we are a nation of immigrants, we're also a nation of laws. Undocumented workers broke our immigration laws, and I believe that they must be held accountable—especially those who may be dangerous. That's why, over the past six years, deportations of criminals are up 80 percent. And that's why we're going to keep focusing enforcement resources on actual threats to our security. Felons, not families. Criminals, not children. Gang members, not a mom who's working hard to provide for her kids. We'll prioritize, just like law enforcement does every day.

But even as we focus on deporting criminals, the fact is, millions of immigrants in every state, of every race and nationality still live here illegally. And let's be honest—tracking down, rounding up, and deporting millions of people isn't realistic. Anyone who suggests otherwise isn't being straight with you. It's also not who we are as Americans. After all, most of these immigrants have been here a long time. They work hard, often in tough, low-paying jobs. They support their families. They worship at our churches. Many of their kids are American-born or spent most of their lives here, and their hopes, dreams, and patriotism are just like ours. As my predecessor, President Bush, once put it: They are a part of American life.

Now here's the thing: We expect people who live in this country to play by the rules. We expect that those who cut the line will not be unfairly rewarded. So we're going to offer the following deal: If you've been in America for more than five years; if you have children who are American citizens or legal residents; if you register, pass a criminal background check, and you're willing to pay your fair share of taxes—you'll be able to apply to stay in this country temporarily without fear of deportation. You can come out of the shadows and get right with the law. That's what this deal is.

Now, let's be clear about what it isn't. This deal does not apply to anyone who has come to this country recently. It does not apply to anyone who might come to America illegally in the future. It does not grant citizenship, or the right to stay here permanently, or offer the same benefits that citizens receive—only Congress can do that. All we're saying is we're not going to deport you.

I know some of the critics of this action call it amnesty. Well, it's not. Amnesty is the immigration system we have today—millions of people who live here without paying their taxes or playing by the rules while politicians use the issue to scare people and whip up votes at election time.

That's the real amnesty—leaving this broken system the way it is. Mass amnesty would be unfair. Mass deportation would be both impossible and contrary to our character. What I'm describing is accountability—a common-sense, middle-ground approach: If you meet the criteria, you can come out of the shadows and get right with the law. If you're a criminal, you'll be deported. If you plan to enter the U.S. illegally, your chances of getting caught and sent back just went up.

The actions I'm taking are not only lawful, they're the kinds of actions taken by every single Republican President and every single Democratic President for the past half century. And to those members of Congress who question my authority to make our immigration system work better, or question the wisdom of me acting where Congress has failed, I have one answer: Pass a bill.

I want to work with both parties to pass a more permanent legislative solution. And the day I sign that bill into law, the actions I take will no longer be necessary. Meanwhile, don't let a disagreement over a single issue be a deal breaker on every issue. That's not how our democracy works, and Congress certainly shouldn't shut down our government again just because we disagree on this. Americans are tired of gridlock. What our country needs from us right now is a common purpose—a higher purpose.

Most Americans support the types of reforms I talked about tonight. But I understand the disagreements held by many of you at home. Millions of us, myself included, go back generations in this country, with ancestors who put in the painstaking work to become citizens. So we don't like the notion that anyone might get a free pass to American citizenship.

I know some worry immigration will change the very fabric of who we are, or take our jobs, or stick it to middle-class families at a time when they already feel like they've gotten the raw deal for over a decade. I hear these concerns. But that's not what these steps would do. Our history and the facts show that immigrants are a net plus for our economy and our society. And I believe it's important that all of us have this debate without impugning each other's character.

Because for all the back and forth of Washington, we have to remember that this debate is about something bigger. It's about who we are as a country, and who we want to be for future generations.

Are we a nation that tolerates the hypocrisy of a system where workers who pick our fruit and make our beds never have a chance to get right with the law? Or are we a nation that gives them a chance to make amends, take responsibility, and give their kids a better future? Are we a nation that accepts the cruelty of ripping children from their parents' arms? Or are we a nation that values families, and works together to keep them together?

Are we a nation that educates the worlds best and brightest in our universities, only to send them home to create businesses in countries that compete against us? Or are we a nation that encourages them to stay and create jobs here, create businesses here, create industries right here in America?

That's what this debate is all about. We need more than politics as usual when it comes to immigration. We need reasoned, thoughtful, compassionate debate that focuses on our hopes, not our fears. I know the politics of this issue are tough. But let me tell you why I have come to feel so strongly about it.

Over the past few years, I have seen the determination of immigrant fathers who worked two or three jobs without taking a dime from the government, and at risk any moment of losing it all, just to build a better life for their kids. I've seen the heartbreak and anxiety of children whose mothers might be taken away from them just because they didn't have the right papers. I've seen the courage of students who, except for the circumstances of their birth, are as American as Malia or Sasha; students who bravely come out as undocumented in hopes they could make a difference in the country they love.

These people—our neighbors, our classmates, our friends—they did not come here in search of a free ride or an easy life. They came to work, and study, and serve in our military, and above all, contribute to America's success.

Tomorrow, I'll travel to Las Vegas and meet with some of these students, including a young woman named Astrid Silva. Astrid was brought to America when she was four years old. Her only possessions were a cross, her doll, and the frilly dress she had on. When she started school, she didn't speak any English. She caught up to other kids by reading newspapers and watching PBS, and she became a good student. Her father worked in landscaping. Her mom cleaned other people's homes. They wouldn't let Astrid apply to a technology magnet school, not because they didn't love her, but because they were afraid the paperwork would out her as an undocumented immigrant—so she applied behind their back and got in. Still, she mostly lived in the shadows—until her grandmother, who visited every year from Mexico, passed away, and she couldn't travel to the funeral without risk of being found out and deported. It was around that time she decided to begin advocating for herself and others like her, and today, Astrid Silva is a college student working on her third degree.

Are we a nation that kicks out a striving, hopeful immigrant like Astrid, or are we a nation that finds a way to welcome her in? Scripture tells us that we shall not oppress a stranger, for we know the heart of a stranger—we were strangers once, too.

My fellow Americans, we are and always will be a nation of immigrants. We were strangers once, too. And whether our forebears were strangers who crossed the Atlantic, or the Pacific, or the Rio Grande, we are here only because this country welcomed them in, and taught them that to be an American is about something more than what we look like, or what our last names are, or how we worship. What makes us Americans is our shared commitment to an ideal—that all of us are created equal, and all of us have the chance to make of our lives what we will.

That's the country our parents and grandparents and generations before them built for us. That's the tradition we must uphold. That's the legacy we must leave for those who are yet to come.

Thank you. God bless you. And God bless this country we love.

Appendix H

A Church of Resistance and Love

Rev. Emma Lozano
1st Sunday in the Harvest, August 23, 2015
Sermon on the Occasion of Her Installation as Senior Pastor of
  Lincoln United Methodist Church

LET ME BEGIN BY OFFERING MY THANKS TO BISHOP DYCK AND THE NORTHERN Illinois Conference, to our special guests—Commissioner Chuy Garcia, Alderman Danny Solis, Rep. Acevedo, Rev. Jeannette Wilson, and Rainbow PUSH, and Brother Antonio from the Nation of Islam—and most of all to my church. My message today is this: A church of resistance and love is a gift protected by the angel; it is our rock and our salvation!

We made a decision, together with Jacobita and Roberto and many others who are still with us here today, to put the church at the center of our struggle. Some questioned that decision, choosing instead not-for-profit organizations or political organizations to pursue justice for our Latino community.

We chose the church because of the faith of our people—because it is our faith that has sustained our struggle.

It was BY FAITH that undocumented parents came out of the shadows to vote and join local school councils to fight against overcrowded schools for the education of their children.

It was BY FAITH that we organized our young people against violence and defended them from police and mass incarceration.

It was BY FAITH that families facing separation joined together to form Familia Latina Unida and make Family Unity the theme of the movement against the deportations.

It was BY FAITH that we joined with Pistolero to call for the largest marches in U.S. history.

It was BY FAITH that Elvira Arellano chose—and our church provided—sanctuary with her U.S. citizen son, Saul

It was BY FAITH that we organized the first march for executive action—for a Latino Emancipation Proclamation!

It was BY FAITH that we joined with faith communities across the nation—Catholic, Protestant, Evangelical, and Pentecostal—to demand executive action.

It was BY FAITH that we went again and again to the border to reunite mothers and fathers with their spouses and their children.

It was BY FAITH that we joined the dreamers with sons and daughters of undocumented parents in direct action to stop the deportations, to win the executive orders and to organize a massive campaign to provide health care for those ineligible for insurance, and close the twenty-year death gap in our community.

And certainly today, it is BY FAITH that we will resist the Trump movement of hate that would deport eleven million people and one million dreamers and strip citizenship from five million children of undocumented parents!

I have been witness to the Faith that accomplished these things—but there is something else. It is no secret that I truly became active after my brother Rudy was assassinated. I know what his commitment was. I know that he was willing to give his life for our people.

Is not that commitment the true test of faith? Politics is about self-interest—but where is the self-interest in giving up your life? No, that commitment is made from faith. Jesus told the disciples before he was crucified that there is no greater love than to give up your life for your friends.

That is the faith I seek and pray that God will perfect in me.

Yet Faith is one thing, and church is often another. Faith without action, without deeds, is empty and, just as Jesus did, we experienced the hypocrisy of our churches. It wounded us, and it made us question the church. By the faith of women like Jacobita Alonso, we found ourselves forming a new community of faith in the midst of our struggle—and we chose the United Methodists.

In our two churches we are guided by the Word and by the Holy Spirit. Our prayers together sustain us. The Word guides us through eight seasons of renewal each year—just as the farmer prepares, plants, nurtures and harvests his crop each year. We are the corn, the crop of the Lord. And today we begin the seventh season, the season of the harvest. We are guided in this season by the Book of Revelations, the message of a prophet to communities of people living in a hostile nation, planted there by the Lord, surviving by faith.

Our text begins with the prophet's letters to seven churches, containing messages he has received from the resurrected Jesus.

There is conflict in each church, and the prophet points out their weaknesses and strengths. He calls on them to be victorious over the obstacles they face. He praises them for their resistance but points out that they must also have love, solidarity. Without this they are not only cut off from each other, but from communion with Jesus. In one letter he gives little criticism, but much hope. This is the poorest church, in which the people are illegal. They do not have the mark of the beast, citizenship, and therefore are not allowed to buy and sell. Yet there is an angel for every church.

Our churches began in resistance, in the oppression of the deportations and the shadows of fear. They began in resistance and—with much love. We see ourselves in the seven churches, to whom the prophet writes. We struggle for courage and we struggle for the love and humility that overcomes ego and desire and fear, that overcomes materialism and infidelity.

In the middle of the book of Revelations, in chapter 12, in the central section, we see the Lady with a Child, passing through the desert, pursued by a Dragon who seeks to devour her children. The woman and the child are taken up to heaven by the angels. The dragon follows but is defeated by the angels and by the Lamb. He is mortally wounded and thrown down to earth where he continues to pursue other children of the people of God.

We have lived this experience, and the meaning of the church as that Lady was revealed to us. We saw the Lady in the mothers that swam the river and crossed the desert. We saw the Lady and her child in Elvira and Saul in the church at Adalberto, pursued by the dragon of hate—protected by the angels.

In the final passage of this text, we are given a vision of the church when the Kingdom really lives in our lives—this Kingdom Church needs no walls. Not only does it not have lights, it does not even need the sun, because it shares the light of God. There is no death here, nor is there oppression. The believers are free to eat from the tree of life. They live by the river of life. The Lion lays down with the Lamb. Each year God perfects us to experience that vision of the church, the church that is the people of God, where the Kingdom of God lives among us, it lives in and among the hearts of the believers.

Each year we renew the process that brings us closer to this church: a church of resistance and love, a church in which a people give birth to and raise the next generation protected by the angels, a church in which the Kingdom can live. In our church we embrace the Grace.

We are a church that exists through the Grace of God:

We embrace the Grace of God, who plants a seed of faith and a vision of the Kingdom of God in every child—so that child will be able to know they are a child of God and know they have a home of holiness in the Kingdom of God, know that their lives matter, and that none of them are illegal in God's eyes.

We embrace the Grace of God, who offers forgiveness in response to confession and atonement, and who opens the door of reconciliation to the Kingdom of God.

We embrace the Grace of God, who gives us the strength to walk in the footsteps of Jesus on the sanctifying road to perfection in His Kingdom, alive on earth, planted and growing in the hearts of the believers.

Let me outline the vision of our ministry:

We begin with the reality of an American apartheid, aimed at delaying the emerging new majority, in which over 30 million people are disenfranchised through the realities of mass deportation and mass incarceration.

We stand on our churches as a foundation to organize the councils of Familia Latina Unida and the chapters of the FuerZa Juventud in high schools, colleges, and neighborhoods throughout our community, fighting for dignity and fighting for the lives of our people.

We stand on our churches to call together assemblies—organized to validate the one person, one vote denied in this nation but certified by Heaven—and to act together.

Each council of Familia Latina Unida is a seed planted in the faith of the people. In the next few years, we see seven churches surrounding this church, giving strength and foundation to the councils and the assemblies. In addition to our two churches we have already begun to plant a third church in Hermosa on the North Side.

Finally, we have formed the Elvira Arellano/Emma Lozano Leadership Institute to insure that we deepen the faith and skills of our leaders and that we share our vision with other churches.

That is the work of this ministry—but there is more that God is calling us to do. In the second section of Revelations, the prophet leads us through the faith realization of the original exodus. The exodus came as God responded to the cries of the people—cries that we are hearing now: "Black and Brown Lives Matter" and "No Human Being is Illegal." These are the cries of the people today. We cry out and march because of the seed that God has planted in each of us, the knowledge that we are children of God created in His image. We will march together on October 10, 2015. We will march with assurance because we know God has given us a destiny to transform this nation.

In the Scripture, after the courageous emergence of the church, the Lady with her child, God answers those cries, by defeating the false prophet, the Donald Trump, who acts on behalf of the dragon of hate who once pursued the Lady. Our ministry grows in confidence every day that two peoples—one planted in this country from the east through slavery and the other forced to migrate here from communities of the south whose roots are in the indigenous of this continent—that these two peoples are the emerging majority in this nation and have as their destiny the transformation of this country.

Our faith calls us to humbly atone as we courageously resist and prepares us for the hatred that rises against us today through the arrogance and hate now sweeping across the nation. We are blessed by God to be fruitful and multiply, while those who bear the mark of the dragon of hate fade in their numbers before our eyes. The sound and fury of the movement of hate signifies nothing but a vain effort to delay what our faith and our numbers and our unity will deliver through the promise of God.

And so today I accept this appointment. One of my first commitments is to help certify the many spiritual leaders in our congregation so that they can lead the seven churches we are organizing. My commitment is to help you to organize your Familia Latina Unida Faith Councils. My commitment is to continue to make the way ready for the next generation of leaders in faith and in resistance, and to support them in their ministry of service and resistance. I am not alone. I am surrounded by so many who are filled with the Holy Spirit. I am truly blessed.

We live in difficult times, but we have learned to live BY FAITH, and we have been blessed with a community of great love. We are not afraid of the darkness, because we know the light is coming in the morning. We do not fear the crucifixion, because we have seen the resurrection. God is with us. God has always been with us. And today we commit ourselves that we will always be with God

And let the congregation say Amen!

ABOUT THE AUTHOR

 REV. WALTER COLEMAN SPENT FIFTY YEARS IN the struggle in Chicago—from the anti-war and Civil Rights movements of the 1960s, to the Rainbow coalition organized by the Black Panther Party, to the historic election of Mayor Harold Washington. He served as Pastor of Adalberto United Methodist Church during Elvira's time in sanctuary and worked as an aide to Congressman Luis Gutierrez for ten years. He is married to the current pastor of Lincoln United Methodist Church, Rev. Emma Lozano, who continues to lead the ministry for the undocumented. He holds a Masters of Divinity degree from Garrett Evangelical Theological Seminary. He previously wrote *Fair Share: The Struggle for the Rights of the People*, an account of the movement that led to the election of Mayor Harold Washington in Chicago.

CPSIA information can be obtained
at www.ICGtesting.com
Printed in the USA
FSHW010112051120
75457FS

9 780980 119053